Praise for INDIVISIBLE

"Everywhere I go, Christians have a sense of urgency concerning reclaiming the prophetic voice of the Church in the culture. INDIVISIBLE gives us a framework for understanding and advancing God's agenda in our lifetime. As an African-American leader, I applaud the sensitivity and clarity with which James Robison and Jay Richards have addressed 'biblical justice' issues. Their heart for the poor and the least among us is clear, and their biblical solutions are revolutionary. It's time for the true 'rainbow coalition' to come forth. This coalition is indivisible as it relates to believing God's covenant. It is indivisible as it relates to unity in the body of Christ. Finally, it's indivisible as it relates to walking our talk in the communities in which we live. As you peruse the pages of this excellent work, may you receive the inspiration to become an agent of His will in your own life, in your family, in your church, and in our nation."

—Bishop Harry R. Jackson, Jr., Senior Pastor, Hope Christian Church, Beltsville, Maryland; President, High Impact Leadership Coalition; Presiding Bishop, International Communion of Evangelical Churches

"A powerful, well-informed, persuasive argument that the 'social' and 'economic' issues ultimately will stand or fall together. James Robison and Jay Richards provide a fascinating analysis of all the major political issues today and show that conservative policies are both beneficial for the nation and consistent with Christian moral teachings."

—Wayne Grudem, PhD, Research Professor, Theology and Biblical Studies, Phoenix Seminary, Phoenix, Arizona

"In a era when Washington's reach continues to exceed its grasp, INDIVISIBLE defines the right role of government, explains why social and fiscal conservatives should embrace both the morality of markets and the efficiency of the markets—and why doing so requires no simple act of faith."   —Arthur Brooks, President, American Enterprise Institute

"James Robison and Jay Richards have presented to every believer and concerned citizen the issues that must be placed on the table of reason and as focal points for prayer. This is a must-read, and if these truths are embraced, both the church and nation will experience much-needed restoration."

—Dr. Tony Evans, President, The Urban Alternative;
Senior Pastor, Oak Cliff Bible
Fellowship, Dallas, Texas

"Rather than accept the common view that faith and politics are ever to be divided, James Robison and Jay Richards appeal convincingly to indivisible principles to show not only that our moral beliefs are compatible with a free market, but also that—now more than ever—religious believers and the advocates of economic freedom must work together to help get our country back on course."

—Matthew Spalding, Vice President of American Studies,
The Heritage Foundation; Author, *We Still
Hold These Truths: Rediscovering Our
Principles, Reclaiming Our Future*

"James Robison and Jay Richards have given America a tremendous gift. INDIVISIBLE is a stunning synthesis and super-clear explanation of the most important issues facing us today, full of wisdom and grace and truth. It should give all who read it real hope that God has not forsaken this nation and that there is indeed a way forward. I pray that book groups will study this book and use it to become part of the solution, so that America might again fulfill God's call upon her, to be a beacon of hope and freedom for the world."

—Eric Metaxas, *New York Times* best-selling author
of *Bonhoeffer: Pastor, Martyr, Prophet, Spy* and
*Amazing Grace: William Wilberforce and
the Heroic Campaign to End Slavery*

"We cannot have a strong national defense without a strong economy. We cannot have a strong economy without a healthy culture and vibrant, intact families. These assertions are demonstrable; a blizzard of research proves them. In their moving new book, INDIVISIBLE, James Robison and Jay Richards make a compelling case that Christians must continue working—with grace, humility, diligence, and determination—to advance the sanctity of life, the dignity of marriage and the traditional family, and the centrality of religious liberty to our nation."

—Tony Perkins, President, Family Research Council

"This is no grocery store romance novel. But it is full of love and truth— the twin sources of every great romance. So…'read and heed'…and step up to an active role in restoring America to her glorious roots—'with liberty and justice for all.'"

—Stu Weber, Pastor and Author

"It is relatively easy to observe that our society is fast reaching a climactic moment. How to discern a wise, credible, effective, and prudent course of action to avoid disaster is not so easy to come across. Jay Richards and James Robison make an important contribution in pointing the way to avoid the worst effects of a coming cultural and economic tsunami."

—Rev. Robert A. Sirico, President, Acton Institute

"Finally, someone has provided the road map for how America gets through the difficulties we are currently experiencing. With their book INDIVISIBLE, James Robison and Jay Richards review American history in great depth, as a prelude to outlining the process for recapturing American Exceptionalism. This book is a critical read for every concerned American and a blueprint for the Christian church. I am encouraged by the unity of effort between these two men of different theologies who put aside their differences in order to help save the nation. Great job, guys!"

—LTG(R) Jerry Boykin, Former Deputy Undersecretary of Defense for Intelligence; Founding Member of the US Army's Delta Force

"A personal relationship with the Lord should affect every area of life, including the political. Politics can be confusing for many—even more so for Christians—as we struggle to make faith and political actions work together in a healthy way. INDIVISIBLE delivers concise, godly truth that will cut through the noise and help you develop a biblical perspective on political responsibilities."

—Robert Morris, Senior Pastor, Gateway
Church, Southlake, Texas

"James Robison and Jay Richards remind us that good stewardship of freedom's blessings means recognizing that the moral and economic foundations of American liberty are indeed indivisible."

—Jennifer Marshall, Director, Domestic Policy Studies,
The Heritage Foundation

"Biblical clarity is a great gift today in the midst of our country's complex set of moral and social issues. In this book, Jay Richards and James Robison have given that gift to serious Christians who want to follow and serve Jesus Christ in America with wisdom, courage, and compassion."

—Dr. E. Andrew McQuitty, Pastor,
Irving Bible Church, Irving, Texas

"James Robison and Jay Richards inspire us to find the necessary common ground to address our serious challenges. It is not a question of right vs. left; it is right vs. wrong. INDIVISIBLE provides the understanding that concerned people of faith need to help correct our nation's perilous course."

—Dr. Jim Garlow, Pastor, Skyline Church, San Diego; Chairman,
Renewing American Leadership, Washington, DC

"WOW! James Robison and Jay Richards's book, INDIVISIBLE, makes a courageous stand for the foundation of America. This is a recipe for restoring our culture."

—Dave Stone, Senior Minister, Southeast Christian
Church, Louisville, Kentucky

"For years I was a bystander concerning national issues. I felt it wasn't necessary for me to get involved, especially since my husband is on the front lines. The Lord has shown me how important it is to know the issues so I can pray and stand up for what is right. INDIVISIBLE will equip you with what you need to know so you can present, discuss, and defend your beliefs effectively in these trying times. You, too, can make a difference!"

—Betty Robison, Cohost, "LIFE Today"
Television, Fort Worth, Texas

"People are destroyed for lack of knowledge. Knowledge is damaged if not destroyed when it is detached from reality. INDIVISIBLE contains knowledge, reality, and life. For the classroom, living room, board room, and war room, James Robison and Jay Richards have addressed issues that must be faced."

—Jim Hylton, Pastor, Skyline Fellowship, Fort Worth,
Texas; Author, *The Supernatural Skyline*

INDIVISIBLE

RESTORING FAITH, FAMILY, AND FREEDOM BEFORE IT'S TOO LATE

JAMES ROBISON

and

JAY W. RICHARDS

Faith
Words

New York · Boston · Nashville

The Catholic Edition of the Revised Standard Version of the Bible, copyright 1965, 1966 by the Division of Christian Education of the National Council of the Churches of Christ in the United States of America. Used by permission. All rights reserved.

FaithWords
Hachette Book Group
237 Park Avenue
New York, NY 10017

www.faithwords.com

Printed in the United States of America

RRD-C

First Edition: February 2012

10 9 8 7 6 5 4

FaithWords is a division of Hachette Book Group, Inc.
The FaithWords name and logo are trademarks of Hachette Book Group, Inc.

The Hachette Speakers Bureau provides a wide range of authors for speaking events. To find out more, go to www.hachettespeakersbureau.com or call (866) 376-6591.

The publisher is not responsible for websites (or their content) that are not owned by the publisher.

Library of Congress Cataloging-in-Publication Data
Robison, James, 1943–
Indivisible : restoring faith, family, and freedom before it's too late /
James Robison and Jay W. Richards. — ed.
    p. cm.
ISBN 978-1-4555-0312-4
1. Christianity and politics—United States.   2. Christian conservatism—United
States.   3. Christianity and culture—United States.
I. Richards, Jay Wesley, 1967–   II. Title.
BR115.P7R716 2012
261.70973—dc23
2011047667

To Betty and Ginny

CONTENTS

ACKNOWLEDGMENTS

We could not have written this book, which covers a smorgasbord of subjects, without the help and support of many friends. We're especially grateful to Jonathan Witt, who read the entire manuscript under a tight deadline and made many valuable suggestions. Thanks also to John West, Greg Forster, and Guillermo Gonzalez for reviewing portions of the manuscript and providing guidance on some tricky technical issues.

Thanks to Adrienne Ingrum, Jana Burson, and Father Joseph Fessio for valuable editorial advice.

Thanks to Ruth Triplett for reading and editing several chapters, and to Ben Hastings for chasing down many sources and obscure references. Thanks to Lance Anderson and Geoff and Tami Biehn for providing information that found its way into the book.

We would like to thank Bruce Chapman, Steve Buri, and Steve Meyer at Discovery Institute for their support of this project, and Jennifer Marshall and J. D. Foster at the Heritage Foundation, who initially provided one of us (Jay) with the impetus to pursue some of the issues in this book.

Coauthoring a book when the two authors live fifteen hundred miles apart is not easy, so we're grateful to Carol Stertzer and Victoria Beckham, who mediated and coordinated our schedules, drafts, and communications.

In addition, we want to thank all the religious and media leaders who attended two very important Summit meetings in 2010 and 2011. They inspired and encouraged us. Many of the concerns they shared with us helped the content of this book.[1]

Finally, we must thank our lovely and patient wives, Betty and Ginny, who supported us with prayers and encouragement from the day we first talked about this project, until its completion.

Though we could not have pulled off this project without the help of others, we are responsible for any glitches or errors that remain.

Where Were You When Freedom Died?

Now is our chance to choose the right side. God is holding back to give us that chance. It won't last forever. We must take it or leave it.

—C. S. LEWIS

"If there must be trouble," said American revolutionary Thomas Paine, "let it be in my day, that my child may have peace." Americans in every era have shared Paine's sentiment. They might have suffered through a Civil War, an economic depression, or a World War, but they hoped that the next generation would be better off than their own. We, too, live in a time of trouble. If we want our children to live in peace, we must make hard choices.

Our freedom, our way of life, and our future are in peril, and not just from hostile enemies abroad. During the twentieth century, we stood against the aggression of Nazi Germany and the communist Soviet Union. Now we contend with militant Islamists who see the United States as the Great Satan. But they will never defeat us without help from a more dangerous enemy within: *corrosive ideas and the destructive policies they inspire.* "If destruction be our lot," Abraham Lincoln observed, "we must ourselves be its author and finisher."

Prominent intellectuals and their equally prominent fellow travelers in the media teach that every value and every culture are equally valid, that there's nothing exceptional about the American Experiment, that the right to life and the sanctity of marriage are just "social constructs" we are free to "deconstruct" and abandon, that the idea of God might be a helpful coping device for some but has no place in public life, that free enterprise causes poverty and destroys the environment, and that the solution to these and virtually every other problem you can think of is an ever more powerful state.

These ideas have a practical impact.

Government spends pathologically and incurs runaway debt. A Supreme Court with unchecked power discovers new laws and principles in the Constitution, including ones that contradict the plain meaning of the text and the stated intentions of the Founders. In effectively denying the *inalienable* human rights the American Experiment is based on, the Supreme Court opines, "At the heart of liberty is the right to define one's own concept of existence, of meaning, of the universe, and of the mystery of human life."[1]

As government has waxed, our liberties have waned. The loss is often just a petty inconvenience: a new form to fill out, a new permit or regulation, a new tax. Once in a while, though, the loss is dramatic enough to get our attention. In 2010, the federal government expanded its reach into health care—one-sixth of our economy. Even this power grab, staggering as it is, is incremental. The new system is a kludge of private insurance and public regulations rather than full-blown socialism like the British have, and we won't see the most dramatic changes until after the next presidential election. It can't be sustained, though, so it sets in motion a series of events that will lead, inevitably, to socialized, government-rationed health care. Unless we dismantle this monstrosity, our private medical decisions will come under the authority of government bureaucrats. Once the Feds have jurisdiction over your liver and kidneys, the American ideal of limited government will surely be an empty phrase.

Many Christians and other people of faith support these programs not because they want to grow government but because they want to help the poor and needy. That's laudable. Social justice, however, should not mean government leveling. Dr. Tony Evans has noted that the phrase "social justice" "is often used as a catch phrase for illegitimate forms of government that promote the redistribution of wealth as well as the collectivistic expansion of civil government."[2] Such expansion doesn't solve problems. Instead, it creates generational cycles of poverty and pathology in communities that were once poor but socially healthy and upwardly mobile. If we want to help the poor rather than just feel bad for them, then we need to learn how poverty is eradicated and wealth is created.

As freedom retreats and government grows, our basic human institutions—the Church, marriage, and family—are battered by forces in the media and culture. People of faith are marginalized and squeezed out of the public square. Divorce and cohabitation rates continue to rise so fast that families with a married father and mother could soon be the exception rather than the rule.[3] And we could soon reach the day when defending conjugal marriage between a man and a woman will be denounced as bigotry and hatred, and compared with the truly unjust treatment of minorities.

Still, most Americans have decent lives. Even in a time of high unemployment, most of us have our basic needs met, with some left over for extras. Law-abiding citizens don't fear being abducted by secret police in the middle of the night. Man has eradicated diseases that killed millions of people just a few decades ago. Americans live twice as long on average as our ancestors did a few hundred years ago. Ordinary people enjoy more food, technology, leisure, and entertainment choices than the greatest kings and queens in history. Advances in technology happen so fast that our computers and cell phones are obsolete before we figure out how to use them. Tech guru Ray Kurzweil notes that "your average cell phone is about a millionth the size of, a millionth the price of and a thousand times more powerful than the computer he had at MIT 40 years ago."[4]

Other bright spots: Violent crime is down in our major cities (after reaching a peak in the 1970s). Abortion rates have declined every year since 1990,[5] and more Americans than ever claim to be pro-life. Though polls show that support for traditional marriage is shrinking, thirty-one states have had votes on marriage-related issues, and traditional marriage has won every time. (In New York, same-sex marriage was legalized by the legislature and the governor, not a public referendum.)

Despite these encouraging signs, you don't need the gift of prophecy to see the long-term trends. We're like tourists on a sunny beach. We've heard news of an earthquake on the seafloor, hundreds of miles away, but everything still looks normal. People are sipping iced tea or mai tais with little umbrellas, enjoying the warm sand and the sun overhead. Many think, "We've never had it so good." And yet, when we look closely, we notice that the beach is growing wider as the tide recedes toward the horizon.

If trends continue, a tsunami will come. If government doesn't cut spending, the debt alone will drown us. We will become so buried in trillions of dollars of debt that the government will have to print huge amounts of money or default. Either way, we'll witness an economic catastrophe that no living American has ever experienced and few can imagine. Imagine a dollar that buys just 1 percent, or one-tenth of 1 percent, of what it buys today, and you'll have some idea of what's in store if we don't get off the beach and onto much higher ground.

The dwindling American family makes the debt crisis even more serious. Americans have fewer and fewer children. With lower birthrates,[6] our population is getting top-heavy—with far too few workers to support far too many retirees. If this continues, Social Security and Medicare entitlements alone will bankrupt us. Most advanced societies, including the United Kingdom, Italy, Spain, and Japan, are in the same, if not a worse, dilemma.

This litany of doom and gloom hasn't made the two of us pessimists. The heart of God is to forgive and to restore. As Jesus wept over the fate of Jerusalem, which killed the prophets and stoned those sent by God, He said, "How often would I have gathered your children together as a hen gathers her brood under her wings, and you would not!" (Luke 13:34). He knew of the coming desolation when not a stone would be left upon the other. And yet the only thing that prevented Jerusalem from coming under His protection was that it refused to do so. Even in the face of disaster, God offers us renewal and restoration, if only we will come to Him.

God is not finished with us as a country. Decline is not inevitable. But if we're going to escape decline, we have to make a hard turn—and fast.

Will our grandchildren enjoy the freedom and prosperity we enjoy, or will they ask us, "Where were you when freedom died?" The choices we make in the next few years—in our personal lives, families, churches, and politics—will determine the answer.

PART I

FIRST THINGS

CHAPTER 1

Principles, Policies, and Prayer

There is not a square inch in the whole domain of our human existence over which Christ, who is Sovereign over all, does not cry: "Mine!"

—ABRAHAM KUYPER

In this book we add our voices to those Christians who are calling on believers to pray for a historic outpouring of God's Spirit on His Church. Without that, there's no hope. But we shouldn't just pray or get riled up for a few months, endorse the right policies, and elect politicians who claim to support them. To see our culture restored, Christians must do a lot more. We must understand the sources of the ideas that ail us as well as their alternatives. We must learn to connect and apply these alternatives and think clearly about them. We must argue persuasively in the public square; apply our convictions consistently in our personal lives; build lasting alliances among Christians, other believers, and friends of freedom who share some but not all of our views; and act strategically to influence the people and institutions that shape culture over the long term. First, though, we need to clear out the weeds and fog in our thinking that have kept us from succeeding in the past, and clear a path to understanding and progress in restoring our culture.

Principles, Not Partisanship

A popular bumper sticker says, GOD IS NOT A REPUBLICAN...OR A DEMOCRAT. The statement is certainly true. God isn't a member of any political party. Hope doesn't ride on the back of an elephant or a donkey. The Bible and Christian theology don't provide a detailed blueprint for public policy. No biblical text tells us if we should prefer an income tax or a sales tax, a direct election or an electoral college, a president or a prime minister. Faithful and well-meaning Christians disagree about politics and will do so until the Lord returns in all His glory.

Still, conflicting ideas about politics and economics can't *all* be right. Some policies contradict basic Christian principles—even if Christians support them. Some Christians in previous centuries tried to justify chattel slavery from Scripture, but they were wrong to do so. Today, some Christians think there is a right to abortion that the law should protect. Their view flies in the face of the moral truth, almost two thousand years of Christian teaching, and the Founders' firm conviction of the right to life, liberty, and the pursuit of happiness. Life comes first.

Other policies have a good purpose and are based on a sound moral principle, but don't work because they aren't well thought out. You might believe that since we should care for the poor (a principle), Congress should raise the minimum wage to $100 an hour (a policy) and then everyone will be rich (a purpose). But the policy won't work the way you believe it will. It will create massive unemployment.

In general, a good public policy will apply a true principle in the right way. That means that if we want to help people, if we want policies that allow people to thrive, then we need to know not just moral truth but economic truth as well.

A Coalition of Faith, Family, and Freedom

We wish every American would read this book; but there are three groups we really want to reach. If all three will come together as allies, with God's help, we can restore the culture, stabilize the economy, and secure our freedom.

Think Well, Don't Just Mean Well

First, we've spent many hours talking with and hearing from people of faith, including some good-hearted and intelligent people who disagree with us. The contact has sharpened our thinking. We know believers who think their faith requires them to support certain progressive or liberal policies. For instance, many believe free enterprise or capitalism is all about greed and keeping down the poor. Many also are opposed to the use of military force.

We understand these views. One of us (Jay) once shared them. In college, I thought the "free market" economy was based on greed and exploited the poor, so Christians shouldn't support it. I also thought that Christ's command to turn the other cheek was impossible to square with military service. I concluded that Christians should be pacifists.

I slowly came to realize that my views on these subjects were a motley mix of good intentions, bad economics, and a misreading of the Bible and the Christian tradition. I'm now convinced that a free economy is the best way to alleviate poverty and create wealth, and that sometimes we should take up arms *because* we value human life. We'll explain why in later chapters.

Freedom Is Indivisible

We also have interacted with Americans who prize limited government and free markets, but aren't so keen on what they call social conservatism. Some libertarians and businesspeople fall into this camp. They are pro-choice on abortion, don't have a problem with same-sex

"marriage," and aren't interested in religion. One so-called fiscal conservative, reflecting on Republican losses after the 2008 elections, wrote
in a blog forum, "Social conservatives need to understand that their
positions on abortion, gay marriage, and creationism are radioactive to
many who would otherwise vote Republican. They need to understand
that moderates, libertarians, small government conservatives, national
security conservatives generally share their values on the issues of lower
taxes, reducing government spending, strong defense, gun control, but
that the social conservatives' positions on abortion, gay rights, etc., are
seen as government intrusion on personal liberty based on a particular
religious belief system."[1]

All who support limited government and free markets, however,
have a stake in defending religious freedom, life, and marriage, even
if they aren't religious. We make that argument throughout the book,
connecting the dots among the causes of economic freedom, life, marriage, and religious liberty. Wisconsin Congressman Paul Ryan recently
made the connection this way:

> A "libertarian" who wants limited government should embrace
> the means to his freedom: thriving mediating institutions
> that create the moral preconditions for economic markets and
> choice. A "social issues" conservative with a zeal for righteous-
> ness should insist on a free market economy to supply the mate-
> rial needs for families, schools, and churches that inspire moral
> and spiritual life. In a nutshell, the notion of separating the
> social from the economic issues is a false choice. They stem from
> the same root.[2]

Not to Stand Is to Stand

The third group we encounter and want to reach are those who see politics as useless and corrupt, a distraction from putting in a good day's
work, paying the bills, loving their families, and perhaps serving their

local church or synagogue. For such people, Washington, DC, is best ignored. Does it really matter whom we vote for or what policies we support? Yes, it does matter. Politics isn't everything, and certainly we should tend our own proverbial gardens. But in today's world, having no political effect is not an option. As Dietrich Bonhoeffer said, "Not to stand is to stand. Not to speak is to speak." The question is, "Will you stand idly by while our culture collapses, or join those who seek to restore it?"

What Was Right About the Religious Right?

The success and failures of the so-called religious right, which burst onto the scene about thirty years ago, provide some key lessons in that regard. One of us (James) was there at its inception.

Critics often depict the religious right as a bunch of Christians trying to "impose their morality" on everybody else. The truth was, in the 1970s, we felt the secular forces of culture crowding us out of the public square and pushing *us* to conform. The threat of the Soviet Union had gotten worse after America's loss of confidence in Vietnam. Inflation was spiraling upward. We struggled with moral decay—the sexual revolution was destroying marriage; divorce and illegitimacy rates were skyrocketing. The Supreme Court had prohibited voluntary school prayer and overturned state laws against abortion, eroding respect for innocent human life. The moral fabric of our country seemed to be tearing apart.

Evangelicals had been active in politics and social reform for more than two centuries. The failure of Prohibition, however, had led many to conclude that politics was a worldly distraction. In 1965, Rev. Jerry Falwell said, "Believing the Bible as I do, I would find it impossible to stop preaching the pure saving gospel of Jesus Christ and begin doing anything else—including the fighting of communism, or participating in the civil rights reform....Preachers are not called to be politicians, but to be soul winners."[3] That was the prevailing attitude: The Lord will return soon and take us to live with Him in heaven, so we should focus on evangelism. As Dwight L. Moody once said, "You don't polish the brass on a sinking ship."

By 1980, many of us, including Falwell, saw that we had made a mistake. While millions of Americans were minding their own business, going to work and church, and raising their children, a poisonous ideology had seeped into our schools, courts, government, media, and even churches. We realized that the gospel isn't just about evangelism; it's about being salt and light and leaven throughout the whole culture. God came to reconcile not just our souls but everything to Himself (Colossians 1:20).

I (James) had been an evangelist for my entire adult life, but began to feel called to mobilize other Christians to shape the political direction of our country. I was inspired during a private prayer meeting called by evangelist Billy Graham and Campus Crusade founder Bill Bright. Both Billy and Bill said they were convinced that the Soviet threat, unless successfully opposed, would bring an end to freedom as we had known it. We agreed that our nation needed strong principled leadership to avoid this tragedy. So in the summer of 1980, I, along with other Christian leaders, helped organize the National Affairs Briefing in Dallas, Texas. The event brought together more than fifteen thousand pastors, leaders, and members of evangelical churches.

At my invitation, then-Governor Ronald Reagan spoke to the group. He opened with a statement that I had suggested to him privately. "This is a nonpartisan gathering," he said, "and I know you can't endorse me, but I endorse you." It not only cemented his ties to many evangelical Christians and the religious right, but became one of his most famous quotes.

The 1980 briefing drew national headlines and helped catapult Reagan to the lead in the presidential race. National polls indicated that the gathering and subsequent support among Evangelicals gave Reagan the momentum to win the election. Looking back on the event in light of Reagan's role in helping defeat the Soviet Union and end the Cold War, it seems providential.

Critics said the religious right wanted to impose a theocracy, which was absurd. But I did think the name for the movement, the Moral Majority, struck the wrong chord. It sounded as if we were claiming to be the moral compass for everyone else. Instead, what people often saw in the media were anger and big egos. I struggled with anger myself and, eventually, felt called to go in another direction, although I continued to pray with and counsel political leaders. While I shared the goals of the religious right, I worried about the dangers of Christians being viewed as a wing of one political party.

God led me to spend my time inspiring compassionate expressions of God's love. For years now I have focused my attention on the ministry I founded, called LIFE Outreach International. We spread the good news to TV audiences around the world and share the love of Christ with hundreds of thousands of destitute people in the poverty-ridden developing world. With the help of faithful viewers, God has used us to save the lives of millions, drill thousands of water wells for poor villages, care for orphans, rescue children from sex trafficking, and encourage more loving and effective social programs.

I will never waver in these efforts. In recent years, however, I've started to sense, again, the need to address the direction of our nation and government.

Before Jay and I met, he had been making the case that Christians should embrace free enterprise while also urging free marketers to embrace the causes of life, marriage, and religion. He was convinced, as I was, that the defenders of faith, family, and freedom had to work together. Through a providential turn of events, the two of us connected. It's unusual for an Evangelical and a Catholic to come together on a project like this, but we hope to provide an example of unity. We haven't compromised the theological convictions on which we differ, but built on the deep principles that all Christians share.

We do so with an acute awareness of what has been done and how far we have to go. Christian activism since 1980 has helped the country become more pro-life and has slowed the forces that seek to dismantle marriage and secularize society; but we're still losing the culture. Christians talk a lot about the Church transforming culture, but too often, a hostile culture transforms the Church. If the culture is stampeding toward a cliff, it's not enough for us to walk more slowly in the same direction while muttering an occasional warning. We must stop, turn around, and march the other way.

"That They May Be One..."

Aside from muddled thinking, though, why has Christian activism failed to turn the culture?

A severe problem is our lack of unity. On the night He was betrayed, Jesus prayed that His disciples might be one, as He and the Father are one. For a thousand years, the Body of Christ was unified. In 1054, however, tensions between East and West led to a tragic split that has never fully healed.

Then, in 1517, Martin Luther, responding to widespread corruption, sparked the Protestant Reformation in the West—though he didn't intend to create a split. Since then, Protestants and Catholics have spilled time, energy, and blood fighting each other—to say nothing of how Christians have often treated Jews. There are now some 42,000 denominations worldwide and still counting.[4] We seem to be better at splitting than at working together. But we know that the Lord wants us to discover the unity He prayed for. Surely we can agree on the need to address serious moral and social issues by standing together.

With Christians divided, secularists have pushed believers farther and farther to the margins and turned millions of Americans against free enterprise. What our grandparents treated as common sense—the right to life, the dignity of marriage—are now treated as bigotry. The moral consensus that sustained our country has ceased to exist.

Ironically, the progress of secularism has brought believers together. Though the media often portrayed the religious right as an evangelical and "fundamentalist" concern, it was always ecumenical—including not just Evangelicals but Catholics, Eastern Orthodox Christians, Jews, and Mormons.[5]

People of faith have come together in recent years over issues such as abortion and marriage. Praying outside Planned Parenthood offices, orthodox Catholics have found they have more in common with faithful Lutherans than with liberal Catholics who think like secularists. While campaigning for a state referendum on marriage, Southern Baptists have joined forces with Pentecostals, whom they used to avoid. At crisis pregnancy centers, staunch Calvinists have learned they have a lot more in common with evangelical Methodists than they do with liberal Presbyterians. It's sad that it's taken aggressive secularism, abortion on demand, and a frontal attack on marriage for Christians to discover that we have much in common.

Baptist theologian Timothy George has called this phenomenon an "ecumenism of the trenches." It's a unity based on certain policies and born of the strategy that the enemy of my enemy is my friend. If we're only held together by shared policy opinions and a common opponent, however, then our alliance will look like a weak marriage of convenience.

Believers need to go beyond defensive alliances on public policy and strive for a deeper and more lasting unity. Sure, we have important doctrinal disagreements. Yet *we share core beliefs and moral principles and we worship the same God*. (There's only one.) If believers stand on these, we can partly fulfill Jesus's prayer for our unity, even though we're still divided by institutions and doctrines.

The two of us are convinced that the Holy Spirit is drawing together *all* of those in the Judeo-Christian tradition despite our differences. In that spirit, over the last two years, we have met with Protestant, Catholic, Orthodox, and Jewish leaders. We've listened to their concerns and tried to write this book to resonate with all Christians and, wherever possible, with Jews and other people of faith as well.

Our goal is highest common denominator ecumenism, which is different from the ecumenical movement of the last century. That movement was centered in the National Council of Churches (NCC) in the United States and the World Council of Churches (WCC) internationally. Despite a hopeful beginning, these organizations ended up as outlets for left-wing political activists in mainline denominations, who were reliably wrong on every major issue. In the 1980s, these bodies denounced Israel and the United States but provided support for the Soviet Union and leftist movements in Latin America.[6] Thankfully, these groups have lost most of their influence. Even the media seem to know that they speak only for themselves and not for Christians in general.

The NCC and WCC were right to strive for unity. Their error was to ground that unity in partisan politics rather than in the Living God, His eternal principles, and fundamental truths about his creation, such as in economics. We must avoid their mistake. Still, Jesus would never have prayed for His followers to be one with Him and perfected in unity if it were impossible or unimportant. Oneness is not sameness. In fact, diversity grounded in unity can be an asset.

Paul also challenged the church at Ephesus to make "every effort to preserve the unity of the Spirit in a bond of peace" (Ephesians 4:3). Unity is a sign of the kingdom of God; in our division we have reduced God's kingdom to a future reward rather than a living, present reality. It's no surprise we have not shaped our culture as we should.

Let's Try Sanctity

The second problem is a lack of holiness. While the religious right drew conservative Christians into the rough-and-tumble of politics, it didn't arise from a deeper moral and spiritual renewal in the Church. On many statistical measures, professing Christians are hard to distinguish from the general population. We're concerned about the moral decay of our culture, but have not done much to reverse the moral decay in the Church. We talk about transforming culture; we should spend more energy on transforming Christians. That can come only through the cross—through suffering.

To restore faith, family, and freedom in America, we need God's Spirit to transform our individual lives. Our public engagement should be accompanied by tangible, Spirit-filled growth in holiness and humility that others will see. If we were to pray hard for a real outpouring of the Spirit and zealously pursue lives of prayer and heroic virtue, surely we would have a more lasting impact on our culture.

The profound movements of renewal in Western history—from the Christianization of the Roman world to the Reformation, the Counter-Reformation, the American Revolution, and the British and American abolition of slavery—coincided with spiritual renewal. The American Revolution grew out of the First Great Awakening. The abolition of the slave trade in the United States grew out of the Second Great Awakening.

The British statesman William Wilberforce linked public witness and personal holiness with two life causes: the abolition of slavery and the "reformation of manners" (that is, moral behavior). Those weren't unrelated interests. Wilberforce understood the link between policy and personal conduct, and used his position as a political elite for good. Whether you are in a position to influence millions, like Wilberforce, or just two people, you can make a difference.

Political discussions should never become an excuse for avoiding the question "What should I do?" If you're concerned about world poverty, the first question should be, "What should I do about it?" Compassion doesn't mean feeling sad because someone somewhere is in need. It means "to suffer alongside."

If you're worried that families are falling apart, you can't just focus on divorce law, welfare programs, and Internet porn, but should also think about how you treat your spouse and children.

If you're panicked that the national debt is spiraling out of control, then look at your own finances, and reflect on how you view the costly entitlements that the government has promised you.

Linking public witness to personal holiness means someone is bound to ask: Who are *you* to call Christians to a change of mind and spirit? Our exhortations convict us as we write them! The pursuit of holiness is a challenge for us. We're reminded of a story by the great British author G. K. Chesterton. About a century ago, the *London Times* asked him and some other writers to submit essays on the topic "What's wrong with the world?" Chesterton's essay was brief. "Dear Sirs," he wrote, "I am." The Russian author Aleksandr Solzhenitsyn said, "The line dividing good and evil cuts through the heart of every human being."

We point to the ideal, even though we fail. Strong character is often shaped in the crucible of failure. Some of the greatest leaders in history missed the mark at one point in their lives; but they did not try to move the standard. The standard moved them. They repented and became stronger as a result.

The standard of holiness, though lofty, is not otherworldly. God calls each of us to a holy life overflowing with His Spirit. Kingdom life isn't just reserved for the distant future. It's living in His presence in the present.

Saint Catherine of Siena said, "If you are what you should be, you will set the whole world on fire." Our world needs a multitude of torches aflame with the Spirit of God. Jesus said believers are to be salt and light. Salt preserves what it touches. Light reveals the dangers we must avoid, as well as the path to safety. Let us pray that we can, by our public witness and our personal holiness, preserve the good in our culture, expose the bad, and give guidance to those who are headed for disaster.

CHAPTER 2

What Is Freedom?

The truth shall make you free.

—John 8:32

Americans value freedom, but many have a hard time defining it. For instance, if you ask a teenager who keeps breaking her curfew what freedom means, she'll probably say something like, "Not having to obey the rules" or "Getting to choose whatever you want." If she thinks of a dictionary definition, she might say it is *getting to choose between alternatives*. If she can choose whatever she wants from the dinner buffet, she's free. If she's forced to start with a salad and not to go back for seconds on dessert, she's not free. But if freedom means everyone does whatever he wants, then the meaner or stronger person will soon prevail, and force everybody else to do what *he* wants. That's oppression, not freedom.

The problem here is a bad definition. Freedom does include choice, of course, but even the staunchest libertarian will say a free society allows people to do what they want to do as long as they don't harm anyone else. Your freedom to fling your fist ends just short of your neighbor's nose.

This view of freedom is still not complete, however, since it suggests that freedom and law are at odds, when in fact, the right law gives us more freedom.

Ordered Liberty

The American Founders had a much broader idea in mind, called ordered liberty. In her great hymn "America the Beautiful," Katherine Lee Bates says, "Confirm thy soul in self-control/Thy liberty in law." When the Founders defended liberty, *that* is what they meant. Freedom is the power to do what you don't want to do, and not to do what you want to do.

This thicker view of freedom is what distinguished the American from the French Revolution. A few of the Founders, such as Thomas Jefferson, saw the French Revolution of 1789 as continuing in the spirit of the American Revolution. John Adams, however, worried that the French experiment would end in grief. Adams was right. While the French revolutionaries toasted to liberty, fraternity, and equality, they cut off the roots of those ideals. They were vehemently anti-Christian. At one point they even dressed up a woman as the goddess "Reason" and placed her on the high altar at the Cathedral of Notre Dame in Paris. Their view of liberty had more to do with freedom from restraint than with the ordered liberty championed by American patriots. So it's no surprise that the French Revolution quickly descended into terror. The French Revolutionaries started by beheading priests, royalty, and aristocrats, and ended by killing each other. Order was only restored by the military dictatorship of Napoleon Bonaparte in 1799.

In 1823, John Adams, writing to his fellow Founder Benjamin Rush, described the French Revolution as producing "all the calamities and desolations to the human race."[1] The American Revolution had a quite different ending because it was based on a better view of liberty.

Unfortunately, even ardent defenders of freedom can talk as if freedom is just getting to do what you want to do, as if freedom and rules were on opposite sides. This is a mistake. Imagine a young girl, Mary, who has never had a violin lesson. Mary can pick up a violin and grind out some sounds. No one forces her to pull the bow across any particular string, so she's "free" to play as she wants, and to drive her parents crazy in the process. But is she free to make beautiful music? Is she free to play Mozart in the New York Philharmonic? Is she free to get a full scholarship to the Juilliard School or even to entertain friends and family in the backyard? No, of course not. She can't express either her own or the violin's potential, because she hasn't submitted to years of disciplined practice. She hasn't gotten the rules for excellent violin playing into her mind, her fingers, and her bones. Only then will she be truly free to play the violin. Only then will she enjoy *freedom for excellence*.[2]

Freedom for Excellence

So, rather than limiting our freedom, the right rules allow us to enjoy a much richer freedom. They are the rules that allow us to become what we're supposed to become—to do what we're designed to do.

A while back, I (Jay) was driving my wife and daughters to church. I decided to use the long drive over the bridge from Seattle to Mercer Island (where we go to church) to get a lesson in. "Girls, what do you think eyes are for?" "For seeing," they said. "And what about ears?" They replied, "For hearing." "And what about a heart?" "For pumping blood." "And feet?" "For walking." I did this for a few minutes, until I had exhausted my knowledge of anatomy. Then I asked, "Okay, now I want you to think really hard. What are *you* for?" The inside of the car became as silent as the grave. They thought it was a trick question and wouldn't venture a guess. I told them to think about it.

After church, on the way home, our younger daughter, Ellie, said, "Daddy, I'm still thinking about that question, but I'm really stumped." With their interest piqued, I finally told them, "Well, if you look at the very beginning of the Catholic Catechism, it says that our purpose is to seek, know, and love God. And the very first question of the Westminster Confession, 'What is the chief end of man?' says, 'To glorify God and enjoy him forever.' So we're supposed to love, seek, know, glorify, and enjoy God forever. That's what we're for." Both girls were glad to get an answer, though I had the feeling we would need to go through the lesson a few dozen more times before it really sank in.

A free society allows us to love, seek, and enjoy God. It frees us to fulfill our other God-given purposes as free beings made in the image of God—to love our families and fellow human beings and exercise the virtues required to do that. It lets us be fruitful and multiply, and exercise our dominion as God's stewards over His creation.

Jesus said that the greatest commandment is to love God, and the second is like it, to love our neighbor as ourselves. Love that is coerced is not love. To fully obey Christ's commandments, then, we must be free.

CHAPTER 3

The Law Is Written on the Heart, Stone, and Parchment

The very idea of freedom presupposes some objective moral law which overarches rulers and ruled alike. Unless we return to the crude and nursery-like belief in objective values, we perish.

—C. S. Lewis

We enjoy a greater freedom when our society is based on the rules that allow us to become what we are meant to become. But not everyone knows that his chief end is to love and glorify God and, therefore, to love others. Many reject the idea of Godly purpose; but because everyone has some grasp of universal moral truth, a free society is possible even among those who have different beliefs.

The Laws of Nature and Nature's God

The Founders, following Christian tradition, referred to these unchanging moral truths as the *natural law*. That's why Thomas Jefferson appealed to the "laws of nature and nature's God" in the Declaration of Independence. He was talking about moral principles that everyone knows, or ought to know. In the words of one philosopher, the natural law is "what we can't not know."[1] It's natural because it's built into the structure of things and fits our created nature. The natural law is like the instruction manual for how we're supposed to live.

Natural law stands above even the law of the land. As Rev. Samuel West told the Massachusetts legislature in 1776, in a sermon encouraging the American Revolution, "The most perfect freedom consists in obeying the dictates of right reason, and submitting to natural law."[2]

We all know that it's wrong to murder. We know that parents should care for their children and husbands should care for their wives. Our moral knowledge is reinforced by "witnesses" such as our conscience, the design of the world and our bodies, and the natural consequences of our actions. We discover that the world is set up a certain way. We see that children generally prosper best with a mother and a father, that the male body fits with the female body, that sex outside of marriage causes problems, that gluttony leads to obesity, and promiscuity to venereal disease.[3] In these and thousands of other ways, we learn the basic contours of the natural law. At some point, through these *witnesses*, we come to know certain moral truths, just as we know—once we've been taught—that two plus two equals four. We know these moral truths as well, if not better, than any truth of history or science.

Natural Law and Divine Law

The Bible teaches that the natural law exists in so many words. In the first chapter of Romans, Paul says that we can clearly see enough of God's "eternal power and divine nature" from the creation so that we are "without excuse" when we violate God's laws.[4] Later in the same letter, Paul says, "When Gentiles who have not the law [given to the Jews through Moses] do by nature what the law requires, they are a law to themselves, even though they do not have the law. They show that what the law requires is written on their hearts, while their conscience also bears witness and their conflicting thoughts accuse or perhaps excuse them on that day when, according to my gospel, God judges the secrets of men by Christ Jesus" (Romans 2:14–16). If Gentiles knew nothing of the natural law, God would be unfair to hold them accountable. Since they know enough of that law even if they don't have the Ten Commandments written on tablets, they are accountable for their sins.[5]

But if we already know the natural law, why did God bother revealing the Ten Commandments to Moses on Mount Sinai? Why give us Scripture? Paul answers these questions, too. Earlier in Romans, he says that although human beings "knew God they did not honor him as God or give thanks to him, but they became futile in their thinking and their senseless minds were darkened. Claiming to be wise, they became fools and exchanged the glory of the immortal God for images resembling mortal man or birds or animals or reptiles" (Romans 1:21–23). In other words, the creation transmits the truth loudly and clearly, but we, in our rebellion against God, aren't tuned to the right frequency. The heavens declare the glory of God always and everywhere (as Psalm 19 says), but sin blinds us to it, so we see only stars and empty space when we look at the night sky.

As a consequence of sin, Paul says, we do things that are "unnatural"—men lie with men, women with women. Our sin causes us to wage war against our bodies. We devise clever ways to deny what we know of the natural law. For example, rather than defending murder by name, human beings often try to define certain groups of people out of membership in the human race. Nazis tried to pretend Jews were subhuman, some whites once did the same thing with blacks, and it's now popular to refer to unborn babies as nonpersons. Notice that few defenders of legal abortion say murder is okay. They say that abortion isn't murder, but rather "reproductive rights" or a "choice." These word games betray their half-remembered sense of the natural law.

We see examples of this guilty knowledge every day. A second-grade boy pretends not to know that it's unfair for him to take more than his allotted share of cookies. First he'll deny what he's done, and then he'll complain that his sister took more than her fair share the day before. A college professor who claims morality is relative is outraged when his car is stolen. Darwinists who insist our morality is "an illusion fobbed off on us by our genes"[6] denounce teachers as moral reprobates for suggesting to kids that God created the heavens and the earth. Even when we're denying the natural moral law, we assume it.

Concocting a bevy of rationalizations based on a half-remembered natural law is a far cry from clear moral thinking and clear moral action. That's why God's special revelation is such a precious gift: it helps us to see the natural law with far greater clarity than we might otherwise. What we might know vaguely and confusedly by nature, we see more clearly when it is declared to us, when it is the Ten Commandments written on tablets of stone, not just the natural law seen dimly through our conscience. Deists such as Thomas Jefferson and Thomas Paine could clearly see the natural law because *they* still had the benefit of special revelation as an amplifier. But without it, natural law grows faint.[7]

The Founders were so confident in the truths of natural law that Thomas Jefferson claimed in the Declaration of Independence that they were *self-evident*. "We hold these truths to be self-evident," he wrote, "that all men are created equal, that they are endowed by their Creator with certain unalienable rights, that among these are life, liberty, and the pursuit of happiness."

Jefferson's words are true but incomplete. These truths are written on the human heart and might have been self-evident to the American Founders. It still took hundreds of years of Europeans being told that all men are created in God's image for that truth to become the cornerstone of a nation. And even the Founders didn't apply it consistently.[8]

The Founders wanted a political order consistent with natural law and natural rights. With the Constitution, they sought to establish a federal government that respected the God-given rights of man, to prevent it from gaining too much power, and to preserve space for the free exercise of religion.[9] The law of the land would not create rights, but would recognize and respect the rights we already have. "The rights essential to happiness…are not annexed to us by parchment and seals," said John Dickinson of the Pennsylvania colony in 1776. "They are created in us by the decrees of Providence, which establish the laws of our nature."

The Rule of Law Versus the Rule of Men

Sin—our tendency to do evil that separates us from God and others— is the only Christian doctrine that you can verify by simple observation. From special revelation (the Bible), we learn that God called Abraham and raised Jesus from the dead. We encounter sin when we get cut off on the drive to work, spend time in our thoughts, read the taglines on the Drudge Report, and tell our children for the thousandth time to keep their hands to themselves. Because of sin, we need governments and other institutions that can enforce a rule of law. Otherwise, the strongest and most wicked will enslave the weak.

In the book of Romans, where the Apostle Paul talks about the law written on our hearts, he also explains that government's authority comes from God:

Let every person be subject to the governing authorities. For there is no authority except from God, and those that exist have been instituted by God. Therefore he who resists the authorities resists what God has appointed, and those who resist will incur judgment. For rulers are not a terror to good conduct, but to bad. Would you have no fear of him who is in authority? Then do what is good, and you will receive his approval, for he is God's servant for your good. But if you do wrong, be afraid, for he does not bear the sword in vain; he is the servant of God to execute his wrath on the wrongdoer. Therefore one must be subject, not only to avoid God's wrath but also for the sake of conscience. For the same reason you also pay taxes, for the authorities are ministers of God, attending to this very thing. (Romans 13:1–6)

Paul wrote this when Rome was an imperial dictatorship! Apparently even bad government is better than no government.

Peter gives the same advice. In his first letter, he writes, "Be subject for the Lord's sake to every human institution, whether it be to the emperor as supreme, or to governors as sent by him to punish those who do wrong and to praise those who do right" (1 Peter 2:13–14). Does that mean Christians must always obey the dictates of government, that every government is legitimate? No. Tyranny is not government, and ought to be resisted, even overthrown. Might doesn't make right. Short of revolution, we can resist immoral commands. Peter and the other apostles recognized this. When the Jewish authorities forbade them from preaching the gospel, they replied, "We must obey God rather than men" (Acts 5:29). (Fortunately, we live in a country where we can redress our grievances peacefully.)[10]

As a practical matter, societies must have some rule of law that reflects, to some degree, natural law. A society that completely ignores the natural law has no way to suppress the worst excesses of sin and destroys itself. Any society that has lasted for any length of time has laws against murder and theft. Every society has rules for marriages. And versions of the Golden Rule can be found in every major religion.[11]

For most societies in history, there might have been a code of laws, written or unwritten, but that code was subject to the authority of a person or group of people who could overrule it. The American Experiment is different because the Founders made the basis for law a document that appealed to a transcendent source—natural rights and nature's God—rather than to a person or group of people. In the United States, all government officials and military personnel, as well as new citizens, pledge an oath not to a king or a tribe, but to the Constitution. The American Founders wanted everyone to be protected by, and subject to, the rule of law, rather than the rule of men. As Thomas Paine said in his classic *Common Sense,* "In America, THE LAW IS KING." Since most countries now have something like a constitution, it's hard to imagine how unusual this was at the time.[12]

Watching the Watchmen

The Founders saw the paradox that many earlier political experiments had failed to appreciate: Sin is the main reason we need government and also the main reason to limit government. They knew about the failed republics in ancient Greece and Rome, where the line between majority and mob rule was thin and fragile. They had studied biblical history and the history of Europe. And they took sin seriously. "If men were angels," said Founder James Madison, "no government would be necessary. If angels were to govern men, neither external nor internal controls on government would be necessary. In framing a government which is to be administered by men over men, the great difficulty lies in this: You must first enable the government to control the governed; and in the next place oblige it to control itself."[13]

The Founders didn't make up the constitutional system from whole cloth. They modeled their document on what was best in the British tradition, the Magna Carta. First issued in 1215, the Magna Carta required King John to allow his British subjects certain liberties, and established the principle that even the king was subject to a higher law.

The Founders worried about the concentration of power. They understood, as Lord Acton said a hundred years after the American founding, "Power tends to corrupt, and absolute power corrupts absolutely." They set up a balance between the president, the courts, and the Congress—the executive, judicial, and legislative branches of government. They created a further balance of powers between two chambers of Congress—the House and the Senate—elected in different ways; between the states and the federal government; and between the states themselves.

The Bill of Rights, which followed shortly after the Constitution was ratified, was designed to protect private interests—the press and religious and minority groups—against tyranny from the government and from the majority. The Tenth Amendment gave the states and the people all authority not delegated to the federal government in the Constitution. The system, called *federalism*, was an ingenious way to disperse power and limit the reach of the federal government.[14] Together, it's like a maze of booby traps designed to stop the tyrannical impulse in its tracks.[15]

The framers of the Constitution did not seek to create a heaven on earth, but to put into practice the principles they had learned as British citizens that Britain had not implemented consistently and had begun to deny to their colonial brothers in America. Slavery contradicted the ideals of the American founding, but the governing principles the Founders put in place would eventually come to include blacks and former slaves as well. The Founders' sacrifice has led, over time, to the greatest flowering of freedom the world has ever known.

A Few Enumerated Powers

The Constitution disperses power, but it doesn't leave the central government powerless. It gives the federal government "enumerated powers." As the economist John Tamny puts it, "Basically Washington is empowered to provide a military to defend us, a stable currency, protection of our property from unreasonable search and seizure, plus it must secure our right to live as we want so long as our actions don't encroach on the rights of others."[16] That's too simple, but pretty close. The Founders believed that the federal government should do a few crucial things and leave the rest to the states and the people.

The Founders saw human beings as sinners who could be shaped by society but who have a nature that men can't change. This founding philosophy could not be more different from the so-called "progressive" philosophy that now dominates our public life. Socialists and progressives assume that man can be molded and transformed like a soft lump of clay. You just need society to be set up correctly and run by really smart people. But even in an ideal environment, human beings can fall into sin. That's how we got where we are to begin with. Even when Adam and Eve were placed in a garden prepared by God, they still managed to get into trouble.

The progressive left has depended on generations of judges and justices to twist and squeeze the meaning of the Constitution to fit their vision of unconstrained state power. This is often done in the name of liberty or privacy. This tactic reached its low point when the Supreme Court reaffirmed in 1992 the "right" to kill unborn babies by proclaiming, "At the heart of liberty is the right to define one's own concept of existence, of meaning, of the universe, and of the mystery of human life."[17] When the Founders defended the "right to life, liberty, and the pursuit of happiness," they meant the right *not* to have your life snuffed out before you are born. But this view of liberty had no place with a majority of Supreme Court justices who resolved the competing interests between an unborn child and a mother by ignoring the child. This is the worst possible defense of liberty. It denies that human nature, and nature itself, has any objective reality that government must respect. It undercuts the constitutional basis on which our liberties are secured.

Outside the courtroom, the left has recently felt less need to appeal to the Constitution at all. When former Speaker of the House Nancy Pelosi was asked where the Constitution gave Congress the authority to take over health care, she didn't mount a defense; she sneered, "Are you serious?" This from an elected official who has sworn an oath to uphold the Constitution.

Legislating Morality

The primary goal of our laws is to legislate our deepest shared moral judgments—what we deem just and unjust, what can and should be coerced, if necessary, and what should be left up to personal choice. Contrary to the cliché that you can't legislate morality, morality is *exactly* what we legislate.

There is, of course, a grain of truth in that cliché. We can't legislate every jot and tittle of every moral principle, because often we would do greater evil by trying to enforce it than by tolerating it. The great medieval theologian Thomas Aquinas even argued that, in some circumstances, a government might have to tolerate an evil like prostitution! Because of human sin, we should always hesitate to give the government power beyond its core competence. That's why we don't have laws against greed, envy, anger, lust, lying other than fraud or perjury, and even private drunkenness. Any state powerful enough to prohibit such sins would be tyrannical, since it would require vast coercive power in the hands of sinful humans.

When the costs exceed the benefits of some law or regulation, or when a law gets too far removed from the natural law and public morality, it will do more harm than good. Prohibition in the United States is a good example. In the early twentieth century, Congress passed the Eighteenth Amendment, outlawing the sale and consumption of alcohol nationwide. It was ratified in 1919. Many well-meaning Christians who witnessed the scourge of drunkenness supported the amendment. It reduced public drunkenness and probably alcoholism, but it also spawned organized crime and a sprawling black market, and made criminals of millions of ordinary citizens who weren't drunkards. The Twenty-first Amendment repealed Prohibition in 1933, and alcohol sale and consumption went back to being local and state concerns. The debacle led millions of Evangelicals to drop out of politics for decades afterward.

Prohibition reminds us of the dangers of using the federal government to enforce private morality. Still, our laws will *always* reflect, to some degree, our moral beliefs, our religious and cultural ideas.

At the same time, laws *shape* our morality. Scholars refer to this as the *teaching function* of law. There is a relationship between what we believe and the laws we have on the books. As someone once said, "It's true that people support the hanging of thieves primarily because they think theft is wrong, not because theft is against the law; however, one of the reasons people think theft is wrong is they see thieves hung."

Did the abolition of slavery and the passage of civil rights laws affect people's attitudes about slavery and race? Did *Roe v. Wade*, which struck down state restrictions on abortion, influence people's views on abortion? If same-sex "marriage" is made the law of the land, do you think that will affect the sexual attitudes and actions of schoolchildren? If suicide for the terminally ill becomes widely accepted, do you think this will affect how we view the sick and the elderly? If the sale of marijuana is legalized, will that influence views on the morality of smoking pot? Yes, yes, yes, yes, and yes.

No Rule of Law, No Free Markets

If you're mainly interested in free enterprise, this talk about rule of law and morality might seem unimportant. But without the rule of law, without some public morality, neither free markets nor free enterprise are sustainable.

The stereotype of the free market is that it's "unbridled" or "unfettered capitalism." It's dog-eat-dog competition, survival of the fittest. The stereotype is seriously misleading. Sure, a free market allows competition, which is just the opposite of a monopoly; but it's competition according to rules—like the competition in a game of baseball. If the strong can steal, enslave, or kill the weak, they have no reason to trade freely. It's only when people must compete according to the rules that true economic freedom exists.

Long-term prosperity depends on the rule of law. It's the stable rule of law, as opposed to the arbitrary rule of men, that distinguishes the economies of the wealthy developed world from the corrupt and chaotic societies in much of the developing world. According to *The Economist* magazine, "Economists have repeatedly found that the better the rule of law, the richer the nation."[18] An open, independent, and reasonably honest judiciary system that can mediate contract and property disputes makes it much easier to do business because it creates a predictable environment for long-term investment. This allows more wealth to be created.

Perhaps the most tangible sign of rule of law is widespread private property rights, which are vital for creating wealth. The proof is among the poor. Where the poor don't enjoy property rights, they usually stay poor generation after generation. (More on that later.)

All of this is to say that, contrary to stereotype, a truly free market economy is not a free-for-all. It exists only where rule of law prevails.[19]

What Should We Do?

The American Founders knew that a sound government needed a virtuous citizenry. George Washington insisted that we distinguish "the spirit of liberty from that of licentiousness, cherishing the first, avoiding the last."[20] Similarly, Founder and statesman Samuel Adams said, "Neither the wisest constitution nor the wisest laws will secure the liberty and happiness of a people whose manners are universally corrupt." Without decent citizens and politicians, the Constitution is just ink and parchment. It can't secure our liberties if politicians and judges ignore it.

The rule of law depends on us, too. Adams refers not merely to politicians, but to a people. Charles Colson has often talked about the trade-off between cops and conscience. The more cops we have inside, the fewer we need outside.[21] Imagine a country where every child was born into a loving family headed by a mother and a father. All parents raised up their children in the way they should go with the perfect balance of love and discipline. The adults always did their duty, not for fear of punishment but from well-developed consciences. Even when no one was watching, everyone still did the right thing. As long as the country was sealed from outsiders, it wouldn't require any cops and prisons. The more a people freely obey the rule of law, the less need there is for the state to coerce us. The eighteenth-century Irish statesman Edmund Burke made the same point when he said, "Men are qualified for civil liberty in exact proportion to their disposition to put moral chains upon their own appetites."

If we all do whatever we feel like doing, we won't have a limited government for long. If we can't make our passions submit to our moral reason, they will have to submit to the sword. This is why Lord Acton said, "Liberty is the delicate fruit of a mature civilization." If we all do whatever we want, we won't be free to do what we ought.

Have you gotten the rule of law into your habits and conscience, as virtues, so that you would do the right thing even if you knew you wouldn't get caught? Maybe you'd never steal an iPad from the Apple store, or use your neighbor's credit card, but do you fudge on your tax returns? Have you used software that you were supposed to pay for? Have you "enhanced" your résumé when applying for a job? Have you blurred the truth when selling a house or a business, or when applying for a mortgage? Do you respect traffic rules even when you're really, really in a hurry? Have your children seen you do these things? If so, you're not just committing private sins; in a way, you're helping chip away at the foundations of freedom.

To restore freedom, we must restore respect for the rule of law. That should start with us. If those submitted to the Holy Spirit won't do it, how can we expect it from anyone else?

PART II

THE ISSUES

CHAPTER 4

God in Public

There is not a single instance in history in which civil liberty was lost, and religious liberty preserved entire.
— JOHN WITHERSPOON

You may have heard that the Constitution established a "wall of separation between church and state." But the phrase isn't in the Constitution or the Bill of Rights; it comes from a letter that Thomas Jefferson wrote to the Danbury Baptist Association in 1802. The Baptists were being persecuted by the Congregationalists—who were the state-sanctioned, *established* religion in Connecticut at the time. Jefferson was writing to Baptist ministers who were suffering discrimination by a religious establishment. He did not object to the public display of religion; he defended religious liberty. And he didn't invent the image of a wall of separation, but borrowed it from *Baptist* Roger Williams, who had founded Providence, Rhode Island, after being kicked out of Puritan Massachusetts.[1]

The First Amendment to the Bill of Rights begins with this: "Congress shall make no law respecting an establishment of religion, or prohibiting the free exercise thereof...." Those words are meant to protect religion from the encroachments of government, and prevent the federal government from establishing a single, official religion—which at the time of the Founding would have been a Protestant denomination such as Congregationalism or Episcopalianism.

Secularists today invoke a "wall of separation" to purge our public life of religious influence, especially Christian. We've almost reached the point of what Archbishop Charles Chaput calls "unofficial state atheism."[2] This is not what the Founders—including Jefferson—intended. A proper separation between the church and the state was a Christian idea in the first place. Even the distinction between a "sacred" and a "secular" realm comes from Christian history. These days many secularists fear that if too many Christians gain political influence, we will establish a theocracy, where God is the head of state and clergy control everything. This can intimidate believers who are active in politics.[3]

Christian history is pockmarked by bad behavior, of course. Christians have owned slaves, violated the Ten Commandments, misused political authority, and in a few cases, established small cultish communities. If we use the word "theocracy" liberally, some small Puritan communities, as well as England under Oliver Cromwell, and Robert Mainz in Germany, may qualify.[4,5] But there have been few theocracies in Christian history. The word doesn't just mean that a society has an established religion—that's called establishment.

Render unto Caesar . . .

When Jesus walked the earth, the Jewish homeland of Judea was part of the Roman Empire. In His earthly ministry, Jesus had little to do with politics. He said that His kingdom was "not of this world" (John 18:3), and during His forty days of fasting in the desert, He rejected the devil's offers of political power.[6] But He did voice a principle that, over the centuries, slowly transformed how Christians and much of the world understands government.

Matthew, Mark, and Luke describe an incident that occurred when

Jesus entered Jerusalem to celebrate the Passover, just before His arrest. While He was teaching in the Temple, the Pharisees tried to trap Him with a trick question:

> Then the Pharisees went and plotted to entrap him in what he said. So they sent their disciples to him, along with the Herodians, saying, "Teacher, we know that you are sincere, and teach the way of God in accordance with truth, and show deference to no one; for you do not regard people with partiality. Tell us, then, what you think. Is it lawful to pay taxes to the emperor, or not?" But Jesus, aware of their malice, said, "Why are you putting me to the test, you hypocrites? Show me the coin used for the tax." And they brought him a denarius. Then he said to them, "Whose head is this, and whose title?" They answered, "The emperor's." Then he said to them, "Give therefore to the emperor the things that are the emperor's, and to God the things that are God's." When they heard this, they were amazed; and they left him and went away. (Matthew 22:15–22)

Jesus's answer is astonishing. Just a few days before, He had entered Jerusalem to much fanfare. The crowds cheered Him as the long-awaited Messiah, who would deliver them from their Roman oppressors. Obviously such talk of a Jewish deliverer would have worried the Romans. The Pharisees, who were plotting to kill Jesus, knew this, and hoped to get Him to say something treasonous so the Roman authorities would do the job for them. Jesus managed to avoid the trap. As He handled many trick questions put to Him during His ministry, Jesus didn't directly answer. At the same time, He said a lot more than simply, "Yeah, go ahead and pay your taxes. Not much else you can do."

Notice that Jesus had to ask His interrogators for a denarius—which was worth about a day's wages for a common laborer. He apparently didn't have one. Since His interrogators had a denarius, they were *already* participating in Rome's monetary system, which involved paying taxes. They even carried the coins into the temple. Why is that a big deal? Because Roman coins not only had Caesar's image on them, but declared his absolute sovereignty and divinity![7] Jesus would not have agreed to that. Sovereignty and divinity belong to God, not to Caesar. So when Jesus says to give to God what is God's, and to Caesar what is Caesar's, He's claiming that *Caesar isn't God*, and that God's authority is outside Caesar's jurisdiction. Caesar has some legitimate claim to taxes if one participates in the Roman monetary system, but he has no claim on our ultimate allegiance. God is God. Caesar is not.

Any Roman leader who understood what Jesus was saying would have found it subversive. Religious rituals and sacrifices were a central part of Roman life. But these practices were designed to reinforce the loyalty of citizens and subjects to Caesar. Religion for the Romans needed to unify the state. So worshipping a God who was not under the authority of Rome sniffed of treason.

Rome persecuted the Jews, at times brutally. Jews understood themselves much as the Romans understood them: as a distinct nation and ethnic group with its own religion. While there was the occasional convert to Judaism, the Jews lacked evangelical zeal. Rome didn't see them as a threat.

Only with Christianity did a religion appear that transcended the boundaries of race and nation. It posed a threat to Caesar. It's no surprise that Rome brutally persecuted Christians off and on until the Emperor Constantine converted to Christianity in the fourth century.[8]

These days, everybody piles on Constantine,[9] but he did many things for which all Christians should be thankful. He ended the persecution of Christians, played a pivotal role in an early council that defended Christ's divinity, and recognized the distinct authority of the Church. He also issued the Edict of Milan in AD 313. This document didn't just legalize Christianity. It defended religious liberty for *everyone*, using arguments that Constantine had probably learned from such Christian theologians as Lactantius. So far as we know, it was the first official government document in history to proclaim religious liberty.[10]

Though paganism persisted for centuries, Christianity continued to grow until it became the most influential religion, even becoming the *official* religion of the Roman Empire. This was a reversion to the older way of doing things, since to the Roman mind, one of the main purposes of religion was to unify the empire.

Christian history after Constantine is a mixed bag. On the one hand, Western civilization slowly became more humane. On the other hand, there were dangerous entanglements between church and state. This laid the groundwork for religious persecution, which eventually led to several Christian groups establishing colonies in the New World.[11] Those colonies became the first thirteen of these United States.

Christians learned the dangers of improperly mixing church and state the hard way. For centuries, church authorities vied for political authority, and politicians vied for religious authority. Christians suffered decades of war after the Reformation in which Catholics killed Protestants, Protestants killed Catholics, and Protestants killed other Protestants. Christians—Protestant and Catholic—often treated Jews despicably.

After decades of fighting, various European countries found a compromise among its warring religious groups: The *local* prince of a city or region would determine the religion of his subjects.[12] If your prince was a Lutheran, then you were a Lutheran. If he was a Catholic, then you were a Catholic. For obvious reasons, this arrangement didn't really solve the problem. Though it reduced outright warfare, many religious dissidents who held out against the deal were persecuted as before.

The habit was hard to break. Even the early American colonists, who had fled persecution, quickly set about persecuting other Christian groups. From these bitter experiences, though, Christians began to reflect carefully on the nature of faith. They finally came to understand what American Founder George Mason said so well:

> That Religion, or the Duty which we owe to our Creator, and the Manner of discharging it, can be directed only by Reason and Conviction, not by Force or Violence, and therefore all Men have an equal natural and unalienable Right to the free Exercise of Religion, according to the Dictates of Conscience, and that no particular religious Sect or Society ought to be favored or established by Law, in Preference to others.

In other words, *real faith can't be forced*. This isn't a secular argument for mere tolerance. It's an argument for religious liberty based on our individual rights and the duty we owe to God! As we mentioned above, several of the Church Fathers made the same basic argument, as did early Americans such as William Penn, Roger Williams, and Lord Baltimore (the first proprietor of the Maryland colony). Faith works by love, not prison or thumbscrews. The point is obvious once you think of it; but it's so unlike the old way of doing things that it still took centuries to settle fully into Christian minds and habits.[13]

Religious Freedom Is a Christian Idea

Religious freedom follows what Jesus commanded. Before He ascended into heaven, Jesus told his disciples to go "and make disciples of all nations...." There's no hint that this could or should be done by force, and indeed Jesus was at pains to make Peter and the other disciples understand that they were not to spread the kingdom by the sword but by persuasion—the persuasion of reason, the persuasion of healing, and for many of them, the persuasion of their blood spilled at the hands of the Romans. For centuries, the faith grew by conviction and conversion, not coercion. Christians not only had no political power, but were hounded and persecuted by Rome. This had a profound influence on how Christians came to view politics.[14] Politics, they knew, was *important but not ultimate.*

In the scheme of things, Caesar's authority is trivial. Compared to God, the nations are like a drop in the bucket (Isaiah 40:15). The ancient custom was to have an all-powerful state with a religion to reinforce it. Judaism challenged this and Christianity eventually overturned it. If the Church has an authority separate from the state, then the state is limited by definition. *There is at least some space over which the state has no jurisdiction*, and in which people should not be coerced. It took Christians centuries to work out the logic of these ideas, but they were clearly Christian ideas.

The dangers of theocracy in modern America are more remote than winning the state lottery three days in a row. Early on, after the American Founding, some denominations—such as the Congregationalists and the Episcopalians—practiced establishment at the state level. But soon these churches were "disestablished." Their establishment had been a curse rather than a blessing. American Christianity is much more vibrant than Christianity in Western European countries, most of which still have state sponsorship of religion. Today, very few American Christians support an established religion, let alone theocracy.

Founder James Madison pointed to an additional check on any one Christian group seeking to establish itself as America's official state religion. He argued that as long as there were several religious groups seeking control, they would check each other's ambitions. Anyone who wanted Presbyterianism established would meet the resistance of Catholics. And anyone trying to establish Episcopalianism would have to deal with the Baptists. So according to Madison, for religious campaigns to succeed in American constitutional society, they would have to be based on "principles...of justice and the common good."[15] These would usually involve individual Christians, not churches, forming voluntary groups to support causes consistent with natural law.[16] So a united Christian campaign against slavery might succeed. An emergent church campaign to force all pastors and priests to grow soul patches, or an Anglican campaign to force everyone to use incense, would have much dimmer prospects.

IS THE UNITED STATES A "CHRISTIAN NATION"?

It's easy to get bogged down in a debate about whether the United States is a "Christian nation." The problem is that the phrase means different things to different people. If we're talking about the views of most Americans, then certainly we are a Christian nation. About 78 percent of Americans identify themselves as Christians of some sort. All other religions combined make up less than 5 percent, and about 16 percent are unaffiliated (though not necessarily atheist).[17] So just as we talk about "Muslim countries," where most of the citizens are Muslims, we could refer to the United States as a "Christian nation."

The phrase also makes sense if you're talking about American history. The original American colonies were overwhelmingly Christian. In fact, most started as Christian charters. Moreover, our laws and political traditions come largely from the Judeo-Christian culture of Europe, and especially Great Britain.

But when some people hear talk of America as a "Christian nation," they envision a country where Christianity is mandated, or where non-Christians are viewed as second-class citizens, or where atheists are herded out of the political process. So unless you explain what you mean by the phrase, talking about the United States as a Christian nation is liable to create more heat than light.

The Faith of the Founders

Mention the role of faith in public life, and somebody is bound to bring up the faith of the Founders. Like many debates, this one has two extremes. Many secularists (and some conspiracy-minded Christians) claim that the Founders were mostly deists or religious skeptics who wanted to keep religion on the sidelines. (Deism is the view that God created the world and established a moral law, but doesn't get involved in the day-to-day details on the ground. Strict deists rejected the possibility of miracles and the value of prayer.) They trot out skeptical quotes from Thomas Jefferson and talk about the "Jefferson Bible," in which Jefferson deleted all references to miracles from the gospels.

In response, some Christians seem intent on proving that almost all the Founders were conservative evangelical Christians. They will cite the many statements by Founders showing their Christian piety or commending the value of Christianity for society.[18] The truth is that the lines separating orthodox Christianity from deism were blurry in eighteenth-century America. We should resist the temptation to cram them into tidy modern compartments. Many of the Founders, such as Patrick Henry, John Jay, John Witherspoon, and Samuel Adams, *were* serious Christians, without a whiff of deism on them. Almost all were Protestants, though Charles Carroll, who signed the Declaration of Independence, was a Catholic.[19] None were atheists.

George Washington was an Episcopalian, though he often attended different houses of worship. He believed deeply in God's providence and in the necessity of religion for morality. In his inaugural address, he said:

> Of all the dispositions and habits which lead to political prosperity, Religion and Morality are indispensable supports.... Let it simply be asked, Where is the security for property, for reputation, for life, if the sense of religious obligation desert the

oaths, which are the instruments of investigation in Courts of Justice? And let us with caution indulge the supposition that morality can be maintained without religion. Whatever may be conceded to the influence of refined education on minds of peculiar structure, reason and experience both forbid us to expect that National morality can prevail in exclusion of religious principle.[20]

We could pile on quote after quote along the same lines from the Founders. Even so-called deists such as Thomas Jefferson and Benjamin Franklin supported prayer and religious observance.[21] Others who were Unitarian, such as John Adams, often spoke fondly of Christianity and, in particular, its moral system.

This was but the most crucial of several points of agreement among the American Founders:

- The Church has a proper authority that the state must respect.
- The federal government should neither establish nor prohibit the free exercise of religion.
- Every person should enjoy religious liberty.
- Religion, and especially Christianity, is vital to the survival and prosperity of the American Experiment.
- We know *by reason* that God and a natural law exist.
- Public displays of respect for God are right and good, and don't constitute an establishment of religion.

These views allowed the Founders to revere God in public, even officially, while still opposing a federally established church. *God's existence and the basic principles of morality, they believed, were public truths, not sectarian religious doctrines.* So when the US Congress adopted "In God We Trust" as our national motto in 1956, they were not imposing religion on the public, but publicly recognizing God—just as the

Founders did. The phrase had appeared on our coins as early as the 1850s.

Remember, it was Thomas Jefferson, a deist of sorts,[22] who wrote in the Declaration of Independence, "We hold these truths to be self-evident, that all men are created equal, that they are endowed by their Creator with certain unalienable rights...." On this point, the Founders believed, reason and revelation agreed.

Secularists insist on practical atheism as the only neutral, legitimate public philosophy. It's the idea that people can believe and practice whatever religion they choose in their private lives, but when we come together in public, whether it's to explore the origin of the universe, debate public policy, or explain why a criminal went on a shooting spree, we must assume God doesn't exist. Any reference to God or morality, on this view, transgresses the boundaries of church and state and is a dangerous step down the road to theocracy, "dominionism," or "Christian nationalism."[23]

This practical atheism is ardently promoted by groups such as Americans United for the Separation of Church and State, and the American Civil Liberties Union, and accepted by most academic elites. It is entirely alien to the thought of the Founders and most Americans. Today, our greatest danger is not a Christian theocracy, but a *secularist atheocracy* that tolerates no dissent.

Which "Religion"?

Some fans of freedom assume that all religions have historically been enemies of freedom. Whenever they see a manger scene in a park or a replica of the Ten Commandments in a courthouse, they may genuinely fear that forced baptisms and reeducation camps are just around the corner. But this fails to recognize that *not all religions teach the same thing*. Take Christianity and Islam. Both teach that there is one God who created the world. Both have a moral code. But Christianity teaches that Jesus commanded us to love our enemies. Nowhere did He command us to conquer the world at the edge of a sword. Virtually all Christians believe that faith neither can nor should be coerced. Christian martyrs are people who have died for their faith. Christian missionaries seek to win unbelievers over, not run them over.

In contrast, while it contains noble elements, force and violence have been part of the spread of Islam from the beginning. Muslim "martyrs" often kill themselves as well as innocent bystanders.[24] Fighting, conquest, and jihad seem to be baked into the pudding. Some brave Muslim scholars now argue for religious freedom, but they have to argue against much of their religious tradition and many authoritative texts.

In practice, there's a lot of overlap, since Christians don't always live up to the principles of their religion and there are many humane Muslims; but clearly, much Islamic teaching points in one direction, and Christian teaching points in the other.

Just as different religions often teach different things, not all religious traditions have developed the same way. In the West, Jews and Christians interacted with Greek and Roman thought. (Eastern Christians interacted mostly with Greek thought.) Over the course of centuries, Christian thinkers came to understand and defend the dignity of the individual, the voluntary nature of faith, and the universality of sin. On these foundations, some built political institutions that protected human dignity and freedom, including economic freedom, while balancing out the tendency of fallen human beings to consolidate power.[25] These institutions followed slowly but naturally from Christian theology. And they were nowhere enshrined more completely than in the ideals of the American Experiment, even when the Founders and other Americans failed to live up to those ideals. While other cultures adopt the free institutions developed in the Christian West, we shouldn't forget where and why they developed in the first place.

Faith in Public: Both/And

Our most cherished beliefs as Americans—equality and human rights, the value of the individual, limited government, freedom—are branches of a tree with Christian roots. The Founders believed these truths could be grasped by reason apart from special revelation. They are public, even self-evident, truths and not just sectarian beliefs.

Most of the Founders also believed that our grasp of these truths would wither unless they were constantly reinforced by faith. Because everyone can be corrupted by unchecked power, however, the Founders devised a system with no established religion but broad religious freedom. That way, separate religious institutions would hold each other in check, while believing citizens would reinforce and defend the public truths they share and on which our nation is founded.

Does that mean that we should never refer to Scripture or mention God in public debate? Not at all! Christianity is part of the American vocabulary. Practically every major freedom movement in American history was advanced not just with religious but with biblical arguments: from the American Revolution itself, to the abolition of slavery to the Civil Rights movement.

For instance, in his Second Inaugural Address, Abraham Lincoln reflected on God's judgment for the evil of slavery. It concludes with these stirring words:

> Fondly do we hope, fervently do we pray, that this mighty scourge of war may speedily pass away. Yet, if God wills that it continue until all the wealth piled by the bondsman's two hundred and fifty years of unrequited toil shall be sunk, and until every drop of blood drawn with the lash shall be paid by another drawn with the sword, as was said three thousand years ago, so still it must be said "the judgments of the Lord are true and righteous altogether."

Slavery was the norm, not the exception, for most of human history. Even in the Christian world, it took centuries for it to be eradicated. It was banned in Europe only to reappear in the colonies during the age of exploration. Now that every country has officially abolished it, it might seem inevitable that slavery would disappear. But how likely is it that slavery would have been abolished in the West and elsewhere if Christians had not become convinced, *as Christians*, that it contradicted their faith?

Biblical arguments have an established place in our political debates. Just a few years ago, a University of Chicago law professor put this point nicely:

[S]ecularists are wrong when they ask believers to leave their religion at the door before entering into the public square. Frederick Douglass, Abraham Lincoln, William Jennings Bryan, Dorothy Day, Martin Luther King—indeed, the majority of great reformers in American history—were not only motivated by faith, but repeatedly used religious language to argue for their cause. So to say that men and women should not inject their "personal morality" into public policy debates is a practical absurdity. Our law is by definition a codification of morality, much of it grounded in the Judeo-Christian tradition.[26]

That professor went on to become the forty-fourth president of the United States—Barack Obama.

What If You're Not Religious?

Even if you ignore where freedom came from, widespread Christian belief benefits unbelievers in day-to-day life. The Judeo-Christian tradition inculcates and reinforces behaviors and virtues that nurture a free and prosperous society: hard work, thrift, and delayed gratification, charity and compassion for the poor and disadvantaged, respect for the property of others and for the truth. Take that last example—respect for the truth. Unless most people tell the truth most of the time, long-term contracts, which an economy needs to create large amounts of wealth, don't work.

God, our Creator, is also a Judge of our actions toward Him and toward one another. Even non-Christian thinkers such as the German philosopher Immanuel Kant knew that belief in a divine and all-seeing judge of our actions encourages good behavior. The Founders often emphasized this. John Adams, for instance, said, "[W]e have no government armed with power capable of contending with human passions unbridled by morality and religion....Our constitution was made only for a moral and religious people. It is wholly inadequate to the government of any other."[27]

Strong Christian faith produces better citizens. If you doubt that, imagine yourself walking alone down a dark alley in the middle of the night, in a dangerous part of a big city like Chicago. You see a group of ten tough, tattooed teenage boys leave a bar known for gang activity, and they are coming your way. How do you feel? Close your eyes and think about it.

Now imagine that you know they are coming not from a gang bar but from a Bible study. Would you feel better about your situation? Of course you would! Sure, Christians can lie, cheat, and steal, but when they do so, they're violating their own beliefs. On balance, we all know society is better off if teenage boys go to Bible studies than to gang meetings.

Christian behaviors and beliefs also foster a prosperous society. Studies show that Americans who are actively religious are less likely to commit crime and domestic abuse, are less likely to abuse drugs and alcohol, are healthier, live longer, and attain more education than those who are not religious.[28] Even in already wealthy societies, religious citizens (in the Judeo-Christian tradition) are more likely to prosper over time; and this benefits their nonreligious neighbors.[29] This isn't the "prosperity gospel." The only good reason to be a Christian is because you think Christianity is true, not because of fringe benefits. If you're not a believer, though, it's nice to know that the influence of Christianity is, on balance, a good rather than a bad thing.

What Should We Do?

Don't be intimidated. You have every right to apply your faith to your politics, even to make theological arguments in public debates. At the same time, recognize that you don't *have* to do that. Sometimes, depending on your target audience, it's better not to, since you want to begin, when possible, on common ground.

If you're trying to convince a Presbyterian that he should value private property, you'll appeal to a source he trusts, such as the Bible or the Westminster Confession. You won't quote from the Koran, the Book of Mormon, or the Catholic Catechism. The same principle applies for unbelievers. If you want to convince an agnostic that he should value private property, you should base your argument on some truth that he already accepts. This might be scientific or historical evidence. You might point to studies showing that strong private property laws tend to create more peaceful and prosperous societies. *You* may support the right to private property because you think the Bible teaches it, but you're not abandoning your Christian witness by using a "secular" rather than a faith-based argument with those who don't share your faith.

Science and history aren't the only public sources you can appeal to. Remember, you can make *moral* arguments without appealing to Scripture or theology. Atheists have moral knowledge; in their hearts they recognize the natural law, even when they deny it exists. Almost every political debate involves a moral principle. And oftentimes, people on opposite sides of a debate actually agree on the underlying moral issue. When liberals and conservatives argue about how to reduce poverty, for instance, both sides assume that it would be better if no one were poor. Everyone in the health care debates agrees that health is better than illness, and would like everyone to have as much health care as needed. All sides in the education debates think knowledge is better than ignorance, and want children to get the best education they can. These are *moral* judgments, not political ones.

CHAPTER 5

Bearing the Sword

The chief duty of governments, in so far as they are coercive, is to restrain those who would interfere with the inalienable rights of the individual, among which are the right to life, the right to liberty, the right to the pursuit of happiness and the right to worship God according to the dictates of one's conscience.

—WILLIAM JENNINGS BRYAN

We'll never forget the first few days of the Iraq War in April 2003; we watched it live on TV. The US Marines rolled into Baghdad and toppled that giant, Stalinesque statue of Saddam Hussein. Iraqis dragged chunks of the statue through the streets, while young Iraqi children beat at the remains with their shoes. The world watched in real time as a dictator was toppled.

According to both the Christian tradition (for example, Romans 13) and the American Founders, this is the job of government: to punish evildoers, maintain justice at home, and protect citizens from foreign aggressors.

In the United States, the federal and state governments share responsibility for maintaining justice, while mainly the federal government carries out defense against foreign enemies. The preamble to the

US Constitution says, "We the People of the United States, in Order to form a more perfect Union, establish Justice, insure domestic Tranquility, provide for the common defence, promote the general Welfare, and secure the Blessings of Liberty to ourselves and our Posterity, do ordain and establish this Constitution for the United States of America."

The Founders wanted the government to provide so-called public goods, like defense, which private business could not provide. For instance, if your neighbors get together to pay for security for your neighborhood, you'll benefit even if you haven't paid for these public goods. If all national defense were provided through a private market, everyone would benefit, whether they paid for it or not. That's one reason why a centralized government should handle national security: so that those who benefit from the service also pay for it. "The legitimate object of government," Lincoln argued, "is to do for a community of people whatever they need to have done, but cannot do, *at all*, or cannot, *so well do*, in their separate and individual capacities."[1] Private markets work when people receive goods and services only if they pay for them. When a private market or private charity can handle a problem, the government should not tackle it, because, as we'll see in later chapters, the market is much better at delivering most goods and services.

This principle puts clear limits on what government should and shouldn't be about. "Insuring domestic tranquility" doesn't cover insurance, health care, and retirement benefits. And "welfare" doesn't refer to the "welfare" programs that swelled federal budgets in the twentieth century. With these phrases, the Founders were referring to the need for the federal government to keep the states from fighting among themselves—erecting trade barriers and whatnot—while leaving the states to handle fights within their boundaries. By protecting Americans from aggressors both foreign and domestic, the Founders hoped the government would preserve liberty and well-being both for themselves and for future Americans.

We saw in chapter three that both Saint Paul and Saint Peter suggest government's primary role is to enforce justice and punish evildoers. As Peter puts it, the Lord sends governors "to punish those who do wrong and to praise those who do right" (1 Peter 2:13–14). Most of us experience only the threat of coercion. We know that if we don't pay our income taxes, for instance, the IRS may audit us and fine us. But even this soft coercion depends on the government "bearing the sword." That's why we have courts and police and prisons. It's also why we have militaries.

The Problems with Pacifism

We both remember exactly what we were doing on May 1, 2011. That was the night we learned that Osama bin Laden had been killed by American forces. We didn't take to the streets to celebrate, like those thousands of people in Washington, DC, but we did feel a sense of relief. We didn't yet know the gory details of the mission that led to his death, but of all the deaths that have occurred in the war on terror, bin Laden's was surely the most deserved.

While many Americans felt relief when we learned that the Navy Seals had killed Osama bin Laden in a daring raid inside Pakistan,[2] not every American felt this. Some, including many Christians, were disturbed, and warned that violence only begets more violence. If we truly want peace, they urged, we can't pursue war. The path to peace they recommended was *pacifism*. The pacifist believes violence is always wrong, especially violence in warfare.

I (Jay) struggled with this question for about four years in college and seminary. As a junior in college during the mid-1980s, I had been accepted into an officer candidate program for the US Marine Corps. A couple of months before I was supposed to report to Quantico, Virginia, I realized that I hadn't considered the morality of war. I knew that God permitted and even commanded warfare in the Old Testament and told the ancient Jews to take an eye for an eye, and a tooth for a tooth. Yet He gave Moses the commandment, "You shall not kill." The Old Testament also foretold a day when "the wolf shall dwell with the lamb, and the leopard shall lie down with the kid, and the calf and the lion and the fatling together, and a little child shall lead them" (Isaiah 11:6). Isaiah described a time when the nations "shall beat their swords into plowshares, and their spears into pruning hooks; nation shall not lift up sword against nation, neither shall they learn war any more" (Isaiah 2:4).

Was Isaiah referring to the coming of Jesus, the Prince of Peace? Didn't Jesus tell us to love our enemies? Didn't He say that when someone strikes you on the cheek, you should turn the other one as well? Didn't He up the ante on the commandment that we should not kill, forbidding us even from hating someone in our heart? Didn't He tell Peter in the Garden of Gethsemane to put away his sword, since "whoever lives by the sword will die by the sword"? For that matter, doesn't the cross suggest that we should pursue a path of nonviolence? Jesus absorbed the evil done against him—even to death on the cross—rather than resist it by force. Didn't He insist that we, too, bear our cross daily (Luke 9:23)? Jesus had ushered in a new era. Perhaps, He wanted us to resist the violent ways of the world with nonviolence, even if that meant our own deaths.

By the time I graduated from college in 1989, I had decided to go to seminary rather than the Marine Corps. I started at Asbury Theological Seminary, where pacifist ideas were common. I had a New Testament professor who led a pacifist student group, and I participated for about a year. I also avidly read the progressive Christian magazine *Sojourners*, and absorbed several books by pacifist theologian Stanley Hauerwas.

But the appeal of pacifism withered on closer inspection. I can trace my doubts to a group discussion with this same professor. A student asked him what he would do if someone tried to rape his wife. He said he might try to stop the rapist by hugging him or sitting on him, but he would not use violence. Another student asked him if it was really wrong for the Allies to fight Nazi Germany during World War II. My professor said that if Christians had prayed more before World War II, then God would have prevented Hitler from coming to power. I later learned that these were common responses among Christian pacifists.

God can change the direction of history, but this answer seemed like a dodge, an assertion with no evidence to back it up. We had no reason to believe that God *would* have responded to such prayers as the pacifist supposed. Perhaps instead, He used the Allies to bring Hitler to justice.

Unsatisfied with my professor's answers, I decided to study Scripture and Church history more closely. It eventually became clear that none of the texts that I had thought of as promoting pacifism did so when read in light of Scripture as a whole. The commandment that forbids killing, for instance, uses a specific Hebrew word, *ratsach*, that is never used to refer to killing in war.[3] You might have guessed that even without the lesson in Hebrew vocabulary, since God gives the commandment in the same texts in which He commands the Hebrews to wage war. As a result, they never understood the commandment to prohibit all types of killing. (The text is probably better translated into English as, "You shall not murder.")

Jesus commands us not to return evil with evil, to turn the other cheek, to love our enemies and pray for our persecutors (Matthew 5). On the basis of such texts, New Testament scholar Ben Witherington has argued, "I do not think Christians should either serve in the military or as police."[4] But Jesus *never* denies the responsibilities of *governments* to keep the peace and protect their citizens. In these passages, Jesus isn't talking about government; he is talking about individual revenge—taking "an eye for an eye."

This Old Testament policy of retribution was better than the alternative—in which entire families or cities could be punished for the crimes of one person. But it didn't solve the spiraling problem of revenge and blood vendettas.[5] We know from history that life is miserable in societies where blood vendettas are common. If someone kills your child, and you take revenge by killing his child, that's not justice but revenge. So then the child's family retaliates against you, and your family returns the favor. Jesus is telling us how to break this cycle of revenge and violence—by choosing to forgive and absorb the evils done to us. That's why, just before Jesus tells the crowd not to resist the evil person, He says, "You have heard that it was said, 'An eye for an eye and a tooth for a tooth.' But I say to you..." (Matthew 5:38).

In contrast, in Romans 13 and I Peter 2, Paul and Peter *are* writing about the proper role of government. That's the point of the passages. Paul tells us that the political ruler is "the servant of God to execute his wrath on the wrongdoer" (Romans 13:4). This fits perfectly with what Jesus has said. Jesus commands us as individuals to break the cycle of vengeance—to absorb and forgive; but the state, as a third party, is supposed to execute justice, not revenge, on behalf of the aggrieved party. That's why criminal cases have names like *The United States of America v. Timothy James McVeigh*, since it's the state, not the individual, which exercises justice.[6]

Jesus's commands presuppose that the state should do this. Otherwise, He would be commanding that injustice prevail, since unrepentant evildoers would be encouraged by their victims' forgiveness. Translated into a foreign policy, this would lead to much greater evils than the ones it tries to prevent, since it would reward aggression. Violence in that case really would beget more violence, creating a society, in the words of Theodore Dalrymple, where "the good are afraid of the bad, and the bad are afraid of nothing." It's individual forgiveness *plus* the proper execution of justice by the state that breaks the cycle of vendetta and violence.

The pacifist reading leads to other problems. While Jesus commands Peter to put away his sword in the Garden of Gethsemane, Jesus had earlier told His disciples that the time had come to *buy* swords

(Luke 22). Jesus could have forbidden police and military service, but He didn't. In Matthew, immediately after the passage where Jesus tells His disciples to absorb evil, He visits the city of Capernaum. While there, a Roman centurion asked Jesus to heal his servant just by saying the word. This meant that he trusted Jesus to be able to heal a person who was far off and out of sight. Did Jesus say, "As a Roman centurion dedicated to keeping the peace by force, you're in a wicked profession. Go and leave your life of sin"? Remember that Jesus did tell a *paralytic* to stop sinning (John 5:14), so He wasn't above giving stern moral instruction to a person asking for healing. In the centurion's case, though, Jesus turned to the crowd and said, "Truly, I say to you, not even in Israel have I found such faith." Then He told the centurion, "Go. Let it be done to you according to your faith" (Matthew 8:10–13).

It's the same story with John the Baptist. He called the Pharisees who came to see him a "brood of vipers," so he was hardly soft on sin. Yet when soldiers asked him what they should do, he said, "Do not extort money from anyone by threats or false accusation, and be satisfied with your wages" (Luke 3:14).

We meet another Roman centurion in Acts named Cornelius, who becomes a Christian, receives the Holy Spirit, and is baptized at Peter's command. There's *no hint* that Cornelius's work was contrary to the gospel. In fact, he is called "devout."

Pacifists deal with these points by taking an isolated statement of Jesus, or constructing a principle of "radical discipleship"—and then use that to override the rest of Scripture and moral arguments against their pacifism. For instance, they may treat Jesus's commandment to love our enemies as an absolute prohibition on war and self-defense. Therefore, they must conclude that Romans 13 and the contrary statements from Jesus, whatever they mean, *can't* contradict pacifism.[7] Similarly, if you argue that human beings have a natural right to self-defense, the Christian pacifist will insist that Jesus's command to turn the other cheek supersedes that supposed right.

We're all tempted to explain away texts we don't like in light of ones we prefer. But Jesus's words in the Sermon on the Mount didn't drop from heaven as individual proverbs. They are embedded in four gospels, which are themselves embedded in the canon of Scripture. To read individual texts faithfully as the Word of God, we ultimately have to read them in light of the whole.[8] When we read the Bible carefully as a whole, it doesn't command pacifism.[9]

Pacifism versus Justice

Pacifism doesn't just violate the testimony of Scripture and historic Christian teaching (as we'll discuss below); it violates the moral views shared widely by people of every culture and religion. If, as pacifists hold, all forms of violence are wrong, then self-defense, parents protecting children, and police work are wrong as well.

Imagine an armed rapist who breaks into the home of a family of four in the middle of the night. The father has a gun, is able to load it, and gets between his family and the rapist. The rapist then raises his gun to shoot the father. At that moment, are we to believe that it would be a sin for the father to shoot the rapist to protect his wife, daughters, and himself? Everyone knows the answer to this question. You can ask a six-year-old Baptist girl in Yazoo, Mississippi, a Saudi Arabian Muslim man, a young Hindu woman in Mumbai, the guy at the checkout counter at Walmart, and a twenty-five-year-old Kenyan medical student of no particular religious persuasion, and if they're honest, they'll give you the same answer: Not only should the father be allowed to kill the rapist if necessary, but he *ought* to.

Why does this matter? Morality isn't decided by majority vote, but this conviction is grounded in our basic sense of duty, fairness, and justice—the murderer/rapist ought to be stopped; the husband ought to discharge his duty as protector as best he can; and our moral sense cries out for the family's deliverance from the intruder. If we're honest with ourselves, our deep conscience suggests that (1) killing the rapist isn't murder. It also suggests that (2) people have a right to self-defense, (3) a father (or any guardian) ought to protect his wife and daughters from rapists, and (4) the rapist in this situation *deserves* to be shot. The consistent pacifist must say that these four beliefs are wrong.

The Christian pacifist might also say that, as sinners, we all deserve to be shot; we should be gracious toward others as God is gracious toward us. This has a superficial plausibility until you realize that it isn't an act of grace to allow another man to murder and rape. It's not an act of grace to the criminal, and it's certainly not an act of grace toward the family members who will lose a father and then get raped.

We don't have space for a full discussion, but let's think about the second point. We all know that not every form of killing is the same as every other. Killing a man because he inadvertently darted in front of your car from behind a blind corner is not the same as plowing him down because he beat you in a game of bowling. The first act is an unintended tragedy; the second, premeditated murder. Not all forms of intentional killing are the same, either. Bombing an enemy tank in battle is not the same as blowing up a plane of civilians on their way to Boston.

Even when it comes to murder, we make distinctions. Killing someone in the heat of passion is not as bad as plotting his death for months beforehand. Legally speaking, killing in anger, when no other crime is involved, is third-degree murder. Premeditation makes it first-degree murder, which we punish more severely. That legal distinction reflects a legitimate *moral* distinction. The same distinctions justify police forces and at least some forms of military defense.

Pacifism levels the jagged moral landscape of reality into the parking lot of moral equivalence. There's a popular bumper sticker that boils this confusion down to three words, WAR IS TERRORISM. Um, no, it's not. Going to war to stop, for instance, Nazi Germany from taking over half the planet and wiping out the Jews may be painful, wrenching, and filled with human tragedies, but it's not terrorism. If you hold a moral principle that blurs the distinction between bombing a German tank bent on over-running a French village in World War II and flying civilian planes into the World Trade Center in 2001, you should reject the principle.

As Christians, we look forward to a future in which all wars will cease. We still live in a fallen world, however, where God's kingdom has not been fully consummated. Evil people and evil regimes still try to prey on the weak and helpless. We can't rid the world of war, and we can't be obligated to do something that we can't do. But we do have an obligation to protect the weak and defenseless within our care.

Pacifism as Pretense

Many pacifists are sincere and do their best to live out their ideals. Unfortunately, the pacifism we read the most about is a partisan posture—more opportunistic than principled. WHO WOULD JESUS BOMB? has decorated a lot of bumpers in Seattle since 2001. And evangelical pastor Greg Boyd denounced Independence Day on July 4, 2011. "So if you kill someone you don't know from a different country," he tweeted sarcastically, "it's murder, but if your president or king sanctions it, it's noble?"[10]

Many so-called progressive Christians, such as Boyd, Jim Wallis, and Brian McLaren, use pacifist reasoning against American military action abroad while supporting a highly intrusive and coercive state at home. This is inconsistent. As Old Testament scholar Lawson Stone has observed, "If one believes in government provided health-care and basic income guarantees, one believes in coercion. Violence and war are just the most conspicuous forms of coercion."[11] Exactly. Pacifism taken to its logical conclusion gives us anarchy, not a massive entitlement state.

Similarly, the pacifism of Jim Wallis and *Sojourners* seems to wax and wane depending upon who occupies the White House. When Reagan was president, *Sojourners* routinely denounced the American military, and even supported (contradictorily) the brutal communist Sandinistas in Nicaragua. Years later, when President Bush was leading the wars in

Iraq and Afghanistan, *Sojourners* didn't just disagree with Bush policy; they talked about lies, murder, and war crimes.

In contrast, when Barack Obama became president and continued the Bush policies in Iraq and Afghanistan, the cries of moral indignation from *Sojourners* and others softened into tones of regret.

This is partisan, not principled. In reality, neither the Republican nor Democratic Party is pacifist. When Barack Obama became president, he didn't dismantle the military (though some of his policies have weakened it[12]). It's intellectually dishonest to use pacifist arguments against a Republican but for a Democrat.

Since politics is about shaping government policy, and government policy is backed up by force or the threat of force, you might think that the consistent pacifist would avoid politics; but many Christian pacifists are in politics up to their eyeballs. The late John Howard Yoder, a pacifist and leading light of "Neo-Anabaptist" theology, was all-politics-all-the-time. He described Christian ethics as "the politics of Jesus," and called Jesus a "political figure" and "the model of radical political action."[13] Two other leading pacifist theologians, Stanley Hauerwas and William Willimon, insist, "Christianity is mostly a matter of politics."[14]

Patriotism, Not Nationalism

Some of the pacifism on the religious left is not so much pro-peace as anti-American. A number of Christian leftists have taken to calling fellow Christians "nationalists" simply because they defend patriotism and "American exceptionalism." Jim Wallis calls patriotic Christians *idolaters.*[15]

Idolatry is when we worship and serve a created thing rather than the Creator. Sometimes this involves politics. In the first few centuries of Christian history, Roman emperors claimed to be divine. Christians were law-abiding subjects of Rome, but they could not agree to treat the emperor as a god. No one now claims that the president or the government is divine. However, ironically, it is Wallis and his fellow leftists who have such an exalted view of the government that they invite it into every nook and cranny of our lives—except, apparently, for defense, which is one of the few legitimate functions of government.

Pope John Paul II answered the charge that patriotism equals nationalism. "Patriotism," he observed, "is love for everything to do with our native land: its history, its traditions, its language, its natural features. It is a love which extends also to the works of our compatriots and the fruits of their genius." John Paul argued that a proper patriotism is actually the antidote to nationalism. "Whereas nationalism involves recognizing and pursuing the good of one's own nation alone, without regard for the rights of others, patriotism...is a love for one's native land that accords rights to all other nations equal to those claimed for one's own. Patriotism, in other words, leads to a properly ordered social love."

Our country was chartered on the principle that "all men are created equal." To love this country is to love that principle. Just as a proper love for our family becomes the basis for our love for others, a proper love of our country and fellow Americans gives rise to a concern for others outside our borders.

We believe America is exceptional and are saddened that so many people are ashamed of our country. That doesn't mean we think it's the kingdom of God on earth. We've had our national sins—slavery and the treatment of Native Americans being the two most glaring ones—but surely we should condemn the sin and not the sinner, particularly when the sinner aspires to high ideals and has done more to spread freedom and justice than any other nation in history.

Ways of Nonviolence

We all support our military in some ways—at minimum through our taxes—yet only a small percentage of us ever see combat. God calls some individuals to lives that testify to the peaceful vision of God's kingdom in its fullness, just as He calls some to lives of solitude, singleness, or poverty. Anabaptist churches such as the Mennonites and Amish, whose members refuse to serve in combat, and religious orders that disavow the use of force are not completely misguided. Such communities of like-minded people offer a foretaste of a time when the wolf will lie down with the lamb and swords will be beaten into plowshares.

Christ clearly has called all of us, as His individual representatives, to be willing to absorb evil rather than seek retribution. If your neighbor strikes you on the cheek, your best witness to him may involve turning the other cheek. Absorbing evil in this way takes great moral courage. In the right context, it can be a powerful witness to Christ's love. It doesn't extend, however, to the government's attempt to bring to justice those who commit crimes against the innocent. We should no more consider pacifism a universal ethic than we should make every good Christian live in poverty.

Sometimes, we should use the nonviolent resistance advocated by Gandhi and Rev. Martin Luther King, Jr., rather than resorting to violence, especially when we are dealing with an opponent who is acting against his own moral code. Gandhi's methods worked with the British, as did MLK's with Americans, since they were directed at people who were not living up to the noble ideals they professed. Try the same strategy on, say, Adolph Hitler or Joseph Stalin, and you're likely to get a very different result.

Realism and Just War

At the other extreme from pacifism is so-called realism. The realist argues that since there is no larger authority to justly arbitrate the claims of different nations, the best a nation can do is to act in its own self-interest. They say that to defend ourselves against hostile foreign enemies, while trying to apply moral rules to our actions, is to tie our hands behind our back. If we try to avoid enemy civilians, our enemy will just use them as a shield. If we use our resources to care for prisoners of war, our enemies will get ahead by working their prisoners—our compatriots—to death. Realists need not be moral relativists. They simply believe it's better to do what needs to be done to win quickly, even if it means setting aside ethics. The scruples can always be picked up again after the victory has been won.

Between this "realist" attitude and the pacifist idea that all violence is wrong lies the wisdom of centuries of Christian thinking described as just war theory. This view, not pacifism, has been by far the most common Christian view of war, held by most of the great Christian thinkers throughout history. It gives us guidance on when we should go to war, how we should conduct ourselves when we do, and what we should do afterward.

Just war thinking started with such Christian theologians as Saint Augustine, but there also are secular defenders of just war.[16] Just war supporters agree that a nation has a duty to defend its legitimate interests, but unlike realists, they argue that we can, and should, use moral judgment when dealing with the details of war. They also disagree with today's conventional wisdom on the left, which seems to hold that the only just wars are those for which we have no national interest.

It helps to see the official just war criteria in a list:

1. Just cause
2. Right intention
3. Proper authority and a public declaration
4. Last resort
5. Probability of success
6. Proportionality[17]

A just war is pursued publicly, as a last resort but with good prospects for success, by the right authority for the right reasons to accomplish a just cause without using more force than is needed to win without undue loss of life. For instance, the US government, following constitutional rules, could publicly declare war against another country that has attacked the United States or one of its allies—or is about to. War should be pursued as a last realistic resort and only if it's more likely to succeed than not. It's wrong to attack an enemy if you know you can't accomplish your end. Finally, your response should fit the offense. You don't nuke a small country because of a border skirmish.

In the last few decades a presumption of pacifism has emerged among the international elite. Pacifism is treated as the path of the just. War is treated as a necessary evil that rarely seems to be necessary. According to just war theory, however, pacifism doesn't have the moral high ground. There are times when war is the most just course of action.

It can be hard to tell whether any given military effort qualifies. People who agree on just war principles can and do disagree when it comes to specific cases. We saw this during the buildup to the Iraq War in 2003, when Protestant, Catholic, and secular just war theorists lined up on different sides. Disagreements have continued during the conduct of the war. For instance, in "ticking-time-bomb" scenarios, where a prisoner has information that could thwart a deadly attack, what forms of interrogation are justified? How do we define torture? These are tough issues about which reasonable people can disagree.[18]

Disagreement doesn't excuse us from doing our best to discern the truth, however. Not every war, and every act in war, is morally equal. A war undertaken to prevent genocide, which targets an unjust regime and combatants while avoiding noncombatants, is better than a war undertaken to increase territory, with indiscriminate bombing and mass rape used to subdue the enemy population.

"Defensive Imperialism" versus "Defensive Isolationism"

Most conservatives hold the military in high regard. They know that in a dangerous world, peace and stability require that free nations have strong militaries. They're skeptical of naïve internationalist policies such as unilateral disarmament. They believe America is exceptional. They know that you can be patriotic without being nationalistic.

There is, however, one big disagreement that conservatives have among themselves.[19] You can see it right on the pages of a conservative magazine like *National Review*.[20] To exaggerate a bit, one camp tends toward "defensive imperialism,"[21] the other toward "defensive isolationism."

The former emphasize the universal thirst for freedom and America's capacity to help spread freedom. They believe that long-term security and a regard for human rights sometimes require that we intervene directly to reconstruct failed states or to protect free states from tyrants. The other group, which we might call "defensive isolationists," is more skeptical of anything that smacks of nation building. They emphasize the quirks of history and culture, point out that some cultures are implacably hostile to freedom, and that free societies have been rare in history. In their view, we shouldn't assume that we can introduce free markets, religious freedom, and democracy into every non-Western and, in particular, Muslim culture.

Both views are probably right, at least in part. Defensive isolationism is rooted in historic American ambivalence about empire. Americans have never had the taste for empire that the British, French, Belgians, and Germans had in the nineteenth century. We like trading partners, strategic outposts, maybe even a new state from time to time, but not colonies.

The defensive isolationists are right to point out that some cultures are far less open to freedom and representative government than others. Countries that were once part of the British Empire, for instance, are much more likely to be free and prosperous than ones that were not. Muslim regimes, in contrast, have a dismal record when it comes to protecting freedom. Muslim theology doesn't emphasize the human fall into sin, so Muslim cultures are less suspicious of concentrating power in the state. They've also been much slower in separating either the branches of government or political and religious institutions. Islam refers as much to a political philosophy as to a religion. We find this in shariah law. And when it is backed by the coercive power of the state, it concentrates enormous power into a few hands. The track record of this arrangement has been consistent tyranny and oppression over the years.

This does not mean the Muslim world is doomed to despotism. It *is* possible to reconstruct failed states and societies after a war. Japan and Germany were in ruins after World War II. With a military occupation, a purge of the high Nazi officials in Germany, new political structures and laws, and funds for redevelopment, the Allied victors got both countries moving in the right direction. Germany is now one of the most stable and prosperous countries in Europe (if also quite secular), and Japan, despite bad economic policies in the last couple of decades, remains the wealthiest and most advanced country in Asia.

Both countries were industrially advanced before the war, and had cultures that made them ripe for further development. Still, Japan had no history of representative government, and a radically different language, history, culture, and religion from our own; and yet they became a representative democracy. Both Japan and Germany remain under the US defense umbrella, so neither has shown that it can remain free and just while providing its own military defense. Remaining free while developing and restraining a military powerful enough to beat off a powerful adversary is the real test of reconstruction. Very few countries in history have managed to remain free and prosperous under a representative government for long. Still, Germany and Japan stand as clear refutations to anyone who insists that nation building is always doomed to failure.

There's also some reason to hope for the Muslim world. Some large Muslim countries already are somewhat free. Indonesia is no liberal paradise, but it is the country with the largest Muslim population, and it is a democracy. Turkey is also a democracy, even if a somewhat unstable one at the moment. We pray that Iraq can become a stable democracy, though we're dismayed that some Iraqi Muslims have been worse than Saddam Hussein in their treatment of Iraqi Christians.

Even though cultures can resist freedom, every person, no matter his religion, is made in God's image and longs, at some level, for true freedom.[22] The United States should support freedom movements wherever they spring up, at least with passionate official statements, and sometimes more. We should be faithful not just to our interests, but to our ideals. Even if the "Arab street" hates us, we must still desire the best for them. Maybe the Arab Spring will pass straight into a frigid Arab Winter; but it would be better if hundreds of millions of Muslims decided they were tired of the Islamists who claim to speak for them and were tired of the dictators who claim to represent them.[23] "Freedom," President George W. Bush said, "is not America's gift to the world; it is God's gift to all humanity." Let's pray that more may enjoy that freedom, and let's not get carried away by utopian fantasies. Progressive Woodrow Wilson imagined that we could "make the world safe for democracy" by an act of will. Human nature and culture are stubborn things. Not everyone will embrace freedom if given a chance. Sometimes, as strange as it seems, people may long for freedom but vote for bondage.

If We Want Small Government, Why Spend So Much on Defense?

In 2011, the United States spent at least $719 billion on defense—six times more than any other nation spends on defense.[24] Government spending tends to be far from efficient, and defense spending is no exception. Military expansion often foreshadows growth in other areas of government, as we saw in World War II; so conservatives should not give defense spending a free pass, especially when deficit spending is out of control.

At the same time, military spending depends, in part, on conditions that we can't control. After the Soviet Union collapsed, everyone hoped we would finally enjoy a "peace dividend" and cut defense spending. In 2000, President George W. Bush hoped for a "humble foreign policy."

Alas, instead of Soviet communism, we suddenly had to contend with jihadism. We are now engaged in a fight with an enemy with no fixed geography or nationality, and which is tangled up with one of the world's major religions. It doesn't fit the strategic categories built up during the Cold War. Back then, we could assume the Russians didn't want to start a nuclear war, if only because they didn't want to die. We cannot say the same thing about Iran's Mahmoud Ahmadinejad. The jihadists have declared openly and consistently that they seek to destroy the United States, Israel, and its other allies, even other Muslim countries, and establish a worldwide Muslim caliphate. We believe them.

So how much should we spend on defense? As much as it takes to make sure the jihadists don't succeed, either here or against our allies. Like it or not, it has fallen mainly to the United States to police the oceans and keep the world safe. Japan, Europe, Israel, our other allies and even our opponents benefit from an American shield of protection. Rather than gratitude, some tend to resent us, but that comes with the job of being the superpower. Just ask the British. We inherited this role from them sometime during World War II.[25] British historian "Andrew Roberts likes to pinpoint it to the middle of 1943," notes Mark Steyn. "One month, the British had more men under arms than the Americans; the next month, the Americans had more men under arms than the British."[26] Unlike most transfers of power in history, this one took place seamlessly between allies who shared a common culture and common language, while fighting alongside each other against enemies of freedom at the time: Nazi Germany, Imperial Japan, and later, Stalinist Russia. These powers have been vanquished, and a new, much more diffuse threat has now emerged: radical Islamism or jihadism. The United States leads the world in resisting this movement, and everybody knows it. To abandon this role now would be a global disaster.

We've quoted everyone from Jesus to the American Founders. But even popular culture sometimes gets what we're saying here. With great power, Spider-Man's uncle says, comes great responsibility. He was paraphrasing Scripture, "To him whom much is given, much is expected" (Luke 12:48). We find the same principle in the book of Proverbs, "Do not withhold good from those to whom it is due, when it is in your power to do it. Do not say to your neighbor, 'Go, and come again, tomorrow I will give it'—when you have it with you" (Proverbs 3:27–28). We should help and protect the weak and defenseless abroad because, in some cases, we can. This doesn't mean that we should try to depose every dictator on the planet, intervene in every civil war, and drop bombs from drones without thinking through the consequences. It does mean our foreign policy should be guided by more than narrow self-interest.

It's not inconsistent to support small, limited government and a strong defense, since defense against evildoers is what the government is for. While $700 billion is a lot of money, it's only about one-fifth of our federal budget and less than 5 percent of our overall economy.[27] In contrast, at their current rate of growth the big three entitlements—Social Security, Medicare, and Medicaid—will consume the entire federal budget and much of our economy before 2050. (We'll discuss this in the next chapter. The government would default or the economy collapse well before that could happen.) If we want to constrain government spending, certainly we can look for waste and overreach in defense spending. But we cannot solve our budgetary problems by focusing on the one-fifth of our budget that keeps our enemies from wrecking our nation and economy.

God never commanded Israel to disarm and leave herself defenseless. He fought on Israel's behalf on several occasions. The Psalms and Prophets reminded Israel that their ultimate trust and hope were in the Lord, not in a "great army" or a "war horse" (Psalm 33). Our ultimate security is in the arms of God, not the arms of men. Still, until the day that the wolf does lie down with the lamb, the United States and its allies must protect the lambs of the world from the ravenous wolves.

CHAPTER 6

How Big Is Too Big?

*There are many things the government can't do, many good
purposes it must renounce. It must leave them to the enterprise of others. It cannot feed the people. It cannot enrich
the people. It cannot teach the people.*

—Lord Acton

The birth of Tea Parties in 2009 and the 2010 election were both reac-
tions against the spendfest of the federal government. Fretting over big
government is as American as baseball and apple pie. Our Founders
sought independence, in part, because Great Britain imposed a trade
monopoly and a small but unfair tax. Public reaction will always be a
vital check on unlimited government growth.

For more than a hundred years after the founding of our country,
most people agreed that the federal government had a few important
jobs to do—maintain the rule of law and protect citizens and, otherwise,
not be part of our daily lives. Government in those years cost the average
American about $20 a year (in today's dollars). Now, it costs each of us
more than $10,000 per year on average. If you're forty years old, the vast
majority of that growth has happened in your lifetime. There are honest debates about the ideal size of government. But with such massive
growth, no one can seriously claim that ours is still too small.[1]

The unraveling of limited government began about a hundred years ago with the progressives. By the 1960s, most of the elites in both political parties had come to believe that there was no problem—no matter how large or small—that shouldn't be solved politically, preferably in Washington, DC. Now many Americans automatically look to the federal government to solve every problem—from a flood in New Orleans to poverty in Detroit to bad seventh-grade math scores in Yuma to fatty foods in Charleston. Fifty years ago, few imagined just where this mentality would lead us.

Does God Tell Us How Big Government Should Be?

Christians throughout history have lived and thrived spiritually under the shadow of large, unchecked government authority with little choice but to accept their lot. But American Christians have representative government, so political choice is not just a right, it's a responsibility. We need to exercise that responsibility with the tools God has given us.

No Proverb says, "A wise nation keeps its federal budget below twelve percent of GDP, while a foolish country keeps voting for more and more entitlements." Nevertheless, the Bible, history, and our God-given reason strongly suggest that large and unconstrained government tends to undermine the common good and lead, in the end, to bondage.

Turning Good to Evil

One way the Bible tutors us on the question of the size of government is to give us some terrifying examples of what happens when a state gets too big and intrusive.

The last chapters of Genesis tell the story of the sons of Jacob and his favorite son, Joseph. Out of jealousy, his brothers sell Joseph into slavery, and he ends up in Egypt, where his ability to interpret dreams eventually brings him into the presence of Pharaoh, the king of Egypt. Pharaoh has had a series of troubling dreams and asks Joseph to interpret them. Joseph explains that the dreams are prophetic: they describe seven years of bountiful harvests, followed by seven years of famine.

This foresight means Egypt can plan ahead and store grain in the bountiful years so they can survive the seven years of famine to follow. The famine extends to Canaan, where Jacob and his other sons have settled. In desperation, Joseph's brothers travel to Egypt to buy grain. There they encounter Joseph, who is now a high Egyptian official. They expect him to seek revenge on them for selling him into slavery; but instead, Joseph helps them. The entire family is eventually united in Egypt, where they settle down and begin to multiply. The story is so captivating that it's easy to miss another, subtle lesson: Joseph helped set up the conditions that eventually led to the Hebrews' enslavement.

The devil, as ever, is in the details. God gave Joseph the gift of interpreting dreams, but it was *Joseph* who suggested to Pharaoh that he collect "a fifth of the produce of the land" during the seven fat years (Genesis 41:34). There were other options. Pharaoh could have encouraged the farmers to store a portion for themselves to sell later. But Joseph assumed for himself the role of "policy czar,"[2] setting in motion a tragic string of events, which would take hundreds of years to come to fruition.

When Joseph made his recommendation, the text says, "This proposal seemed good to Pharaoh and to all his servants" (41:37). You bet it did! What a perfect plan to consolidate power, since everyone would eventually depend on the Pharaoh for his survival. Since Joseph suggested the plan, he was put in charge of carrying it out. Over time, Joseph's authority (given by Pharaoh) grew larger and larger over the Egyptians and the Jews, until the Jews spent all their money and all their grain and the Egyptians gave over all their livestock and finally offered themselves as slaves to Pharaoh.

Genesis ends with the death of Joseph. When the story picks up again in the book of Exodus, we learn that a new Pharaoh, who did not know Joseph, had risen to power and enslaved the Israelites. Now the story fast-forwards four hundred years from the time of Joseph, and Israel has become a nation in bondage. We all like Joseph, so we tend to miss the subtle lesson, but it's clear nonetheless: Consolidating power in the hands of a central authority, even when implemented by a good man for good reasons, can lead to tragic unintended consequences—including slavery.

Give Us a King!

In the book of Judges, another few hundred years have passed since the Jews' slavery in Egypt. The twelve tribes are now settled in the Promised Land, and have been led, off and on, by judges. The book follows a repeating pattern: The Jews initially follow God, but before long, they start to drift off and worship alien gods. God then allows them to be oppressed by their neighbors, the Philistines. In response, the Jews cry out to God, and God sends a judge to deliver them. Alas, they never remember the lesson for very long, so the cycle repeats itself over and over. Judges concludes with this: "In those days there was no king in Israel; all the people did what was right in their own eyes."

With that conclusion, you might expect to read next of a celebration at the arrival of kings to rule over Israel. But it's just the opposite! What Genesis leaves as an ironic, unstated lesson, the book of 1 Samuel shouts from the mountaintops.

Samuel is the last judge, a righteous prophet who can speak directly to God. The Bible says he "administered justice" by traveling like an itinerant preacher from town to town, always returning home to Ramah. When he grew old, he appointed his sons to help out. Talk about small government!

But all was not well. Near the end of his life, the elders of Israel came to Samuel at Ramah and said, "Behold, you are old and your sons do not walk in your ways; now appoint for us a king to govern us like all the nations." The LORD told him to accept their request, but to warn them of the results. So Samuel spoke to the people and shared God's warning:

> These will be the ways of the king who will reign over you: he will take your sons and appoint them to his chariots and to be his horsemen, and to run before his chariots; and he will appoint for himself commanders of thousands and commanders of fifties, and some to plow his ground and to reap his harvest, and to make his implements of war and the equipment of his chariots. He will take your daughters to be perfumers and cooks and bakers. He will take the best of your fields and vineyards and olive orchards and give them to his servants. He will take the tenth of your grain and of your vineyards and give it to his officers and to his servants. He will take your menservants and maidservants, and the best of your cattle and your asses, and put them to his work. He will take the tenth of your flocks, and you shall be his slaves. And in that day you will cry out because of your king, whom you have chosen for yourselves; but the LORD will not answer you in that day.

Even with this warning, the people demanded a king. So Samuel anointed Saul.

For obvious reasons, this is the favorite biblical text of many libertarians. It's the first entry in *The Libertarian Reader* by David Boaz of the libertarian Cato Institute.[3] In light of our current trouble, the text seems almost prophetic, except that we've long since passed the era when government took a mere 10 percent of our wealth!

Notice that God saw Israel's demand as a rejection of His kingship. The United States is not ancient Israel, but this should still be a warning to us: A centralized political authority with vast power is often a worldly substitute for God's rule. In both this passage and the story of

Joseph, oppressive authorities don't come in from the outside and conquer the Jews. Both times, it came on slowly and subtly. After moving to Egypt, Joseph's brothers gave up their freedom, a little at a time, out of desperation and a naïve trust that the cozy relationship between the Pharaoh and their brother would last forever.

In 1 Samuel, the Jews demanded a king because they thought he would make them secure from the other nations. While everyone may long for freedom at some level, history teaches us that people will often give up their freedom without a fight if they are promised security in return. This is a sucker's bargain. As Benjamin Franklin said, "Anyone who trades liberty for security deserves neither liberty nor security."

The Beast

Finally, let's look at the last book of the Bible, Revelation. This book, written by the Apostle John, contains a series of apocalyptic visions that has perplexed readers for two thousand years; however, Christian scholars tend to agree on how to interpret certain parts of the book. In chapter 13, John describes a great beast, which is given enormous power and authority by a dragon, which is widely seen as a figure of Satan. The beast's authority extends over every tribe and people and language and nation. It wages war on believers, and is worshipped by "all the inhabitants of the earth," except those whose names are written in the Lamb's book of life. The entire passage is terrifying—not the sort of thing to read to young children as a bedtime story.

Since John wrote Revelation as a message to the first-century Church, most biblical scholars think the "beast" refers to the murderous and idolatrous actions of Rome, perhaps under Nero, who viciously persecuted the Church. But many suspect this text refers to more than just first-century Rome. Perhaps it describes a series of "evil empires" throughout history. Perhaps it tells us something about the end times before Christ returns.

We should always live as if Christ will return soon; but we shouldn't use this or any biblical text as an excuse to avoid dealing with our responsibilities here and now. However one interprets Revelation, though, it's undeniable that the Bible ends with a horrific portrayal of a state dominating vast multitudes of people. In the twentieth century, more than a hundred million people were murdered by their own governments. And that was just in communist countries.[4] History and Scripture agree: Because of sin, governments with too much power are the worst propagators of evil and destruction known to man.

The Creeping Enemy of Freedom

The Founders imagined the Congress checking the power of the Supreme Court, and vice versa. In the last several decades, however, the Supreme Court has gone far beyond its constitutional mandate and become, in effect, the ultimate arbiter of right and wrong. Rather than interpret laws passed by Congress in light of the clear meaning of the Constitution—as determined by the stated intentions of those who wrote it—the Court has become an unchecked star chamber. As former Chief Justice Charles Evan Hughes said, "We are under a Constitution, but the Constitution is what the judge says it is."[5] If that were so, then the text of the Constitution would have no objective meaning, and no justice could misinterpret the Constitution—which is absurd. Thus does the rule of (a few) men replace the rule of law.

The reach of government now extends beyond the worst nightmares of the Founders. It's hard to think of anything it's not involved in. To some extent, it controls the mortgage market, retirement, education, and health care. It tries to cure poverty, both here and abroad (and often makes matters worse). It fixes the price that an employer must pay for labor. It subsidizes some private businesses, and punishes a host of others. It buys and sells private companies. It funds and directs scientific research, museums, art, public TV and radio, college student grants and loans, choices of lightbulbs, and billions of dollars in "aid" to foreign governments.

Rules and regulations are the stuff of government. We benefit from strong enforcement of wise rules. But most federal regulations are byzantine rather than basic, and have long since become more burden than benefit. Federal regulation touches everything. Over sixty agencies are involved, "ranging from the Environmental Protection Agency (EPA) to the Securities and Exchange Commission (SEC), and Food and Drug Administration (FDA). Together, they enforce over 144,000 pages in the so-called Code of Federal Regulations." How much is that? Think of two stacks of *Brave New World* with really thin pages reaching from the floor to the ceiling in a room with a twelve-foot ceiling, and you'll get the basic idea. But rather than a fictional story, "the rules on *these* pages are meant to protect our health and safety, to protect us from con-men and dangerous jobs, to protect (or suppress) economic competition, and to protect the environment from us."[6] All told, federal regulations cost us about $1.75 trillion in 2011 alone.[7] This hidden cost is over and above the actual federal budget, and slightly more than the monstrous 2011 deficit.

State regulations have become loony. Authorities in Texas, Georgia, Wisconsin, Iowa, Pennsylvania, and Maryland have shut down kids' lemonade stands, including ones used for charity, because they failed to get a food permit.[8] Mark Steyn tells an equally bizarre story of a 2009 raid by the Pennsylvania Department of Agriculture on a Lenten fish fry at Saint Cecilia's Catholic Church in Rochester. The inspector discovered even more criminality than he expected—some parishioners were selling *pies*:

[The inspector] swooped. Would these by any chance be *homemade* pies? Sergeant Joe Pieday wasn't taking no for an answer. The perps fessed up:

Josie Reed had made her pumpkin pie.

Louise Humbert had made her raisin pie.

Mary Pratte had made her coconut cream pie.

And Marge Murtha had made her farm apple pie.

And, by selling their prohibited substances for a dollar a slice, these ladies and their accomplices were committing a criminal act. In the Commonwealth of Pennsylvania, it is illegal for 88-year-old Mary Pratte to bake a pie in her kitchen for sale at a church fundraiser. The inspector declared that the baked goods could not be sold.[9]

You can't make this stuff up! Are we really so helpless that we need bureaucrats punishing little old ladies who sell pies at church bake sales?

Right now, there are some 1,122 aid programs to the states, for which money is taken from all fifty states, filtered through Washington, DC, and then returned with a million regulatory strings attached.[10] The benefits of this shell game do not outweigh the costs in money or loss of freedom. "A government big enough to give you everything you want," warned President Gerald Ford, "is a government big enough to take from you everything you have."

On Autopilot, Flying into a Cliff

The federal government can't abandon all of these tasks tomorrow. But government growth is out of control. We must reverse the trend and start returning tasks outside the constitutional mandate of Washington, DC, to state governments, local governments, and the private sector.

Our problem isn't just theoretical. It's mathematical. The growth of government has been fueled, not just by increased taxes, but by government borrowing beyond all restraint and wisdom, and entitlement programs that can't be sustained. The coming fiscal crisis is, as

Representative Paul Ryan has said, "the most predictable crisis in our history." Every elected official in Washington, DC, knows it's coming, but very few are doing anything about it.

Sometimes government has to borrow money. We could not have won the American Revolution or World War II without temporary borrowing. In theory, a government can borrow as long as the economy is growing faster than the borrowing. Historically, federal deficits have averaged about 2.9 percent of our GDP per year, but for a long time, our economy grew fast enough to cover the interest on the debts.

Regrettably, that's not happening now. Not even close. Government at the state and federal level has been on a spending and borrowing binge for years. On top of that, it's made all sorts of promises in pensions and entitlements—which voters like—that it can't possibly keep. According to the government's own estimates, just *two* of our federal entitlements, Medicare and Social Security, have "unfunded liabilities" of $46.2 trillion.[11]

Those deductions from your paycheck won't come close to covering them. Unlike a mutual fund, the money we're paying into Social Security and our employers are matching isn't invested. You haven't really "paid into" a fund. Your money has been passed on to current retirees. This worked when the program was started back in 1935, since the average life expectancy was sixty-two. That meant that there were forty-two workers paying in for every retiree receiving benefits. We live much longer and have fewer kids now than folks did in the 1930s. Average life expectancy is around seventy-eight. As a result, there are fewer than three workers for every retiree. And before long, there will only be two workers per retiree. Progressives and even some conservatives considered it beyond the pale when Texas Governor Rick Perry compared Social Security to a Ponzi scheme; but in its current form, it *does* function much like a Ponzi scheme.[12] Unless we reform it or find an infinite number of people to pay in, it will collapse.

The duties actually mentioned in the Constitution, such as a national defense and a justice system, are considered "discretionary," and can be cut. Because of the way entitlements are set up, though, Congress doesn't even debate them as part of the budget. They're considered "nondiscretionary" or mandatory items. Their budget is determined by how many recipients there are, not how much money there is. They even have automatic increases every year. Entitlements are on autopilot and flying us right into a cliff.

Huge and Getting Huger

The plane is gaining speed and yet taking on more cargo. Entitlements and other mandatory spending—spending that is required by law—will burden more and more of the federal budget. In 2008, the Bush administration released a report saying that, if their trajectory isn't altered, such mandatory spending would consume all the money received in taxes in about fifty years. Sound scary? Well, this fateful event actually happened in...2011! *Mandatory* spending came to $2.194 trillion in 2011, while total federal receipts from taxes were $2.174 trillion.[13]

The other parts of the budget were funded entirely with borrowed money. In 2011, forty cents of every dollar spent by the government was borrowed. "We have now gotten to the point...where if national defense, interstate highways, national parks, homeland security, and all other discretionary programs somehow became absolutely free, we'd still have a budget deficit."[14] Unsustainable debt is the evil spawn of a government that promises voters far more than it can deliver. Economist Robert Samuelson calls it "suicidal government."[15] In 2004, our total public debt (as opposed to our annual *deficit*) was around $7 trillion. That's how much debt we had accumulated since America's founding—230 years ago. A mere seven years later, in early 2011, we doubled that number and still add far more than a cool trillion dollars per year—over $4 billion every single day.[16] Our total debt is now as big as our economy.[17] And most of the money the US Treasury borrowed in 2011 was not from China or other foreign investors, but from the Federal Reserve! We're long past spending beyond our means. We're spending beyond the means of our neighbors' great-grandchildren.

Billions and trillions—what's it all mean? A billion has nine zeros. A trillion has twelve. Our minds can't really picture such large numbers. We need something more concrete, like a $100 bill. A bundle of a hundred $100 bills is not quite a half-inch thick. Imagine holding that stack in your hand. That's $10,000. Now, put a hundred of these stacks in a small grocery bag. That's $1 million. Using just $100 bills, you could fit $100 million on one wooden pallet and stick it in the back of a pickup. Ten of these pallets would equal $1 billion. Sound like a lot? A trillion is a thousand times more than that. To store $1 trillion, you'd need more floor space than you could find at an empty Costco, even if you double-stacked the pallets.[18] And remember, that's using $100 bills!

In just a few years, we will start spending more on interest payments alone than on our entire military. Current borrowing isn't temporary, as it was during World War II when we were fighting for the existence of the free world. It's not even the result of crazy one-time programs, like the "stimulus plans" where the federal government tries to borrow and spend lots of money to make us rich. At the 2011 rate, debt will accumulate beyond what any realistic amount of taxes can cover. By 2020, we'll need almost a fifth of the GDP from the rest of the world to finance our national debt.[19]

Imagine charging so much on your credit cards that it takes your entire income just to pay the interest on the debt. You don't have any money to pay down your debt, to pay rent, buy groceries, tithe, support worthy charities, get shoes for your kids, or anything else. That's where we're headed.[20] Soon, taxes would get so high that government would consume most of the output of our economy, but would provide no services, since all taxes would go to pay interest on previous debts. Then, the main options would be for the United States to default on its loans, or to print enough money to trigger hyperinflation, so that our debt wouldn't be worth much. Either of these choices would destroy our society as we know it and devastate the world economy. This has happened elsewhere—such as in Germany after World War I.[21] "There is no subtler, no surer means of overturning the existing basis of society," said economist John Maynard Keynes, "than to debauch the currency. The process engages all the hidden forces of economic law on the side of destruction, and does it in a manner which not one man in a million is able to diagnose."[22]

Trimming the budget and cutting out waste and fraud won't solve the problem. Slashing spending on defense alone won't do it. Zeroing out foreign aid won't do it. While the annual *deficit* has ballooned since 2008 in the so-called discretionary part of the budget, and has to be cut drastically, the long-term *debt* crisis is with entitlements. (Debt is the sum total of all the annual deficits.) We can't solve our spiraling debt crisis without restructuring the entitlement programs, especially the middle-class favorites, Social Security and Medicare.

Recent polls show that a majority of Americans are ignorant, delusional, or kidding themselves about this. Most voters only support cutting the budget on other people.[23] The public, and even most Tea Party activists, want smaller government with smaller budgets and deficits, but still oppose restructuring Social Security and Medicare.[24]

If a Republican or a Democratic candidate raises the issue, you can count on most in the other party to scream that the candidate wants to starve the elderly. Politicians in Washington know these programs are going to explode. They don't do anything about it because they know that most voters don't understand the problem, and the catastrophe is still a bit farther away than the next election (though not much). So they have little political incentive to reform these costly entitlement programs. They seem to think it's best just to walk softly and not make any sudden movements.

Whom Would Jesus Indebt?

During the 2011 debate over the debt ceiling and ballooning debt—which led only to trivial cuts in the *rate* of the debt increase, not real reductions—an ecumenical group called for a "Circle of Protection" around the budget. Spearheaded by Jim Wallis, along with the National Council of Churches, the group claimed to be protecting the poor, but they were really protecting failed *programs* meant to eradicate poverty. This Christian campaign for fiscal insolvency also included representatives from the US Conference of Catholic Bishops and the National Association of Evangelicals.[25] Wallis and others asked the question "What would Jesus cut?" We ask, "Whom would Jesus indebt?"

What Should We Do?

I (Jay) won't qualify for Social Security for many years. I pay into it but assume I won't be getting much out of it. I don't plan on retiring anyway.

I (James) opted out of Social Security when I was eighteen years old, because I thought it was socialistic. You had the choice at that time. When we married, Betty and I chose to secure our own future. We've never regretted that decision.

But many Americans have made different choices, or didn't have a choice. We would hate for people who now depend on retirement benefits to be cut off. That's what's going to happen if we don't reform Social Security, Medicare, and the other entitlements. The first thing we have to do is decide, as a nation, that we're willing to handle some short-term pain now to avoid catastrophe for our children. It's still possible to avoid raising taxes and prevent cutting off services to older Americans who are already receiving benefits from entitlement programs. But these programs *have* to be reworked for those of us who have time to adjust. At the least, we need to raise the minimum retirement age a little at a time, privatize and introduce competitive markets into the system—which would increase service and lower costs—and probably change the way they work for those who can do without them. The longer we wait to do this, the more painful it will be to fix it. The alternative is not the status quo ante, but fiscal chaos and millions of people suddenly not receiving the money they depend on.

We don't just have a government borrowing and spending problem. We have a personal borrowing and spending problem. Sure, borrowing money to invest can create new wealth. Entrepreneurs do this all the time. And prudent borrowing for necessities can make sense, too. But too many of us are swamped with consumer debt, paying exorbitant amounts of interest because we just couldn't resist that new Gucci purse or set of golf clubs or granite countertop. It's easy to blame the credit card companies, but they can't make us spend money. At any one time, there is almost a trillion dollars in outstanding American consumer debt. We have no one to blame for this but ourselves.

We need to recover the culture of thrift that made America great. Imagine what would happen if millions of us decided to start living *below* our means. It would take discipline, but we're going to need that discipline as individuals if we're going to have it as a nation. If we can't muster the courage as a society to support politicians of both parties who will tell us the truth about government debt and entitlements, and work to fix it before it's too late, we will destroy ourselves, which neither the communists nor the Islamic militants could have accomplished.

We're in this mess because we've looked to government to give us what it can't or shouldn't provide and what we should have gotten elsewhere or not at all. Unless we change this entitlement mentality, we'll be in deep trouble, even if we do fix the current entitlement programs. The psalmist cried, "Look to the hills from whence your help comes." Sadly, today most Americans look to the Hill and hope for help. Our coins and currency declare, "In God we trust," but it might be more accurate if they said, "In Gov we trust."

These famous words, often attributed to a Scottish statesman, should stand as a stern warning:

A democracy cannot exist as a permanent form of government. It can only exist until the voters discover that they can vote themselves largesse from the public treasury. From that moment on, the majority always votes for the candidates promising the most benefits from the public treasury, with the result that a democracy always collapses over loose fiscal policy, always followed by a dictatorship. The average age of the world's greatest civilizations has been 200 years.[26]

There's no black line that tells us exactly when government has gotten too big. But six in ten households now receive more in payouts from the federal government than they pay in taxes. Already "more Americans work for the government than work in construction, farming, fishing, forestry, manufacturing, mining and utilities combined,"[27] and government costs us five hundred times more than it did for much of its history. Most of our government budget is spent on things unrelated to its original charter and the natural duties of government. It borrows and spends with such reckless abandon that it is careening toward bankruptcy and a global economic catastrophe. It's. Too. Big.

CHAPTER 7

Choose Life

America stands for liberty, for the pursuit of happiness and for the unalienable right for life. This right to life cannot be granted or denied by government because it does not come from government, it comes from the Creator of life.
—GEORGE W. BUSH

In 1973, the US Supreme Court overturned state laws against abortion in its infamous *Roe v. Wade* decision. Since then, more than fifty-three million abortions have been performed in this country. That's almost 18 percent of our current population, and far more than the number of *worldwide* military deaths in World War II. The justices voting with the majority thought they were solving a divisive issue. Instead, they helped inflame the culture war.

If you have not had an abortion or participated in one, you may not have witnessed the direct effects of this holocaust. But we all experience it indirectly: an ever-widening gap between sex and childbearing and an ever-expanding culture of death in which human life is less and less sacred. Academics such as Princeton's Peter Singer defend the killing of handicapped infants, and most scientists think it's okay to "destroy" human embryos for their research.

The danger extends to the end of life, too. Millions of people in the

modern world now think compassion means we should kill the terminally ill. Famous British author Martin Amis recently ranted on British
TV that opposition to assisted suicide "is a residue of Christian feeling—this idea of the sanctity of life—that is holding things back, but
we have to get rid of this primitive feeling."[1]

Millions have convinced themselves that women have a *right* to
abortion, not just that it should be permitted, and many Christians,
who may believe abortion is a sin, agree. Others think that if you support individual rights, free markets, and limited government, you
should be "pro-choice." These views are mistaken.

The First Right

There is no right more basic than life. As we've discussed thoroughly,
the Declaration of Independence lists it first among those rights that
can never be surrendered; "We are endowed by our Creator with certain unalienable rights...life, liberty, and the pursuit of happiness."
Without a right to life, you can't enjoy liberty, or acquire property,
or pursue happiness. And as we've also covered in previous chapters,
the main purpose of government is to protect the lives of its citizens.
The American Founders insisted that we could discover this through
reason and conscience, apart from any particular religious faith. At the
same time, Christianity has for two thousand years tutored us to recognize what should be obvious but has all too often been ignored: This
fundamental right to life extends to the unborn, never mind that they
are voiceless and defenseless. The Church has consistently opposed
abortion because it involves intentionally killing a helpless, innocent
human being. That's murder, and murder is a sin. The logic is not very
complicated, and it applies not only to abortion but to procedures that
destroy human embryos for research as well.

While Scripture does not talk about abortion directly, it's easy
to see why Christians have always condemned it. We all know the

commandment, "You shall not commit murder" (Exodus 20:13). This applies to the unborn, since the Bible treats the unborn child as an individual human being. Through the Old Testament prophet Jeremiah, God says, "Before I formed you in the womb, I knew you, and before you were born I consecrated you; I appointed you a prophet to the nations" (Jeremiah 1:5, 6). And the New Testament treats born and unborn babies the same way. Luke in his gospel uses the same Greek word for "baby" to refer to both John the Baptist before he is born and Christ after He is born.

The earliest post-biblical records we have, such as the *Didache*, show Christians condemning abortion, which was widely practiced in the Greek and Roman worlds along with infanticide and abandonment. The *Didache* was an early Christian guide written around AD 110—not long after the New Testament was completed, and more than two hundred and fifty years before the New Testament would be officially canonized. It says, without qualification, "Do not murder a child by abortion or kill a newborn infant." Notice the word "murder." Abortion is condemned right alongside killing a newborn.

When it came to abortion, Christians—Catholic, Eastern Orthodox, and Protestant—spoke with one voice almost to the present. We could fill pages with quotes from Church Fathers, Councils, and great theologians, all condemning abortion. But none put it better than Swiss Reformer John Calvin. "The unborn child," he said, "though enclosed in the womb of its mother, is already a human being...and should not be robbed of the life which it has not yet begun to enjoy. If it seems more horrible to kill a man in his own house than in a field, because a man's house is his place of most secure refuge, it ought surely to be deemed more atrocious to destroy an unborn child in the womb before it has come to light."[2] Except when it is forced, abortion involves a mother intentionally killing her own child at its most vulnerable stage of life.

Historically, Christians have understood that life begins at conception. That's why they have celebrated not only Jesus's birth, but also His conception. Some Christians also honor the conception of Mary. Catholic, Orthodox, and Anglican Christians still have feast days celebrating these events.[3]

We live at a time when Christians no longer speak with one voice on this issue. Though most Christian bodies have preserved the historic teaching, some mainline Protestant denominations now are openly, even zealously, "pro-choice" (though pro-life convictions remain among the faithful in their pews). The president of the Episcopal Divinity School has even claimed that abortion can be a "blessing."[4] That is not just "pro-choice." It's pro-abortion. This diversity doesn't mean that there are conflicting Christian views on the subject of abortion. It means that some professing Christians have abandoned the Christian view. In every era, some Christians, including some teachers, pastors, priests, and bishops, surrender to a hostile culture, and even join forces with it.

Even pagan Greek culture, at its best, knew abortion was wrong. The Hippocratic Oath, attributed to the father of Western medicine, Hippocrates, dates from the fourth or fifth century BC. Until recently, most physicians recited a version of the oath that included this line, "I will not give a lethal drug to anyone if I am asked, nor will I advise such a plan; and similarly I will not give a woman a pessary to cause an abortion."[5] So until recently, the two main strands that make up Western civilization—Greco-Roman and Judeo-Christian—agreed that abortion was wrong.

Most elite circles of opinion now take legal abortion for granted. These are the circles of opinion that shape the thinking of most Supreme Court justices. Once elite opinion abandoned the unborn, our nation's highest court followed suit. They needed a clever legal pretense, since a right to abortion is mentioned nowhere in the Constitution or Bill of Rights, nor in any founding documents, nor in the common law tradition. So, in 1973, the US Supreme Court argued that the right to privacy, already a vague idea in itself, provided a right to abortion. Like the perverse 1857 *Dred Scott* decision, when an earlier Supreme Court determined that blacks *lacked rights that whites enjoyed, our highest court now declared that the unborn lacked rights that the born enjoyed.*

Because of *Roe v. Wade* and a few other decisions made by a handful of justices, the United States now has one of the most liberal abortion policies of any Western democracy. We restrict speech, religious practice, and arms—rights that are actually named in the Bill of Rights—far more than abortion. France and Germany, both much more secular countries than the United States, protect the unborn far more than we do.

There is, however, room for hope. We haven't yet seen *Roe v. Wade* overturned; but the faithful testimony of pro-life citizens, aided by technology that allows us to see unborn children in detail, has helped shift opinion among young Americans. Even many staunchly pro-choice people have had their minds and hearts changed. Abby Johnson, a former Planned Parenthood director, was shaken when asked to help with an ultrasound-guided abortion at her clinic. For obvious reasons, the clinic normally avoided using the revealing ultrasounds. When Abby saw the profile of the tiny, unborn baby rendered on a screen, it squashed all the lies she had told herself about abortion. She is now a pro-life author and activist.[6] Even "Jane Roe" of *Roe v. Wade*, whose real name is Norma McCorvey, has converted to Christianity, and now stands firmly against abortion. There are many such stories.

Despite more than three decades of pro-choice propaganda from Planned Parenthood, similar groups, and even bureaucrats in mainline denominations, most Americans are now either pro-life or favor legal restrictions on most abortions.[7] This is encouraging news, and we should pray that our laws might soon reflect this shift.

Why Should Abortion Be a Political Issue?

Some people object that to prohibit abortion would be to enshrine a parochial religious opinion in law. As one fiscal conservative said, "Social conservatives' positions on abortion, gay rights, etc., are seen as government intrusion on personal liberty based on a particular religious belief system."[8] Similarly, in 2008, ABC News reported on a group of young Evangelicals who were pro-life, but liked pro-choice political candidates. When the reporter asked one of them, "Doesn't that bother you?" the teen said, "Maybe a little bit, but it's all personal preference. I mean, you can't really pass judgment on someone because that's their belief."[9] As the popular bumper sticker says, IF YOU DON'T LIKE ABORTION, DON'T HAVE ONE.

We don't oppose abortion because it violates something peculiar to Christianity, however, but because it's a form of murder. If you can't make laws against murder, you can't make laws against anything. Moreover, just because we may oppose abortion on religious grounds doesn't mean there aren't also public reasons to oppose it. We oppose slavery because we believe that every human being is created in God's image and so should not be owned as property. Does that mean that our opposition to slavery, or opposition to slavery in general, violates the separation between church and state? Of course not. We could make the same arguments by appealing to the natural law, which everyone knows, at least in part.

But if antiabortion views aren't just based on religion, why is it mainly conservative believers who are so opposed to it? Sure, there are pro-life atheists.[10] If you attend a prayer rally in front of the local Planned Parenthood, though, you'll find a bunch of Catholics and Evangelicals. This doesn't prove that opposition to abortion is just a religious hang-up. Until recently there was a cultural consensus in the West that abortion was wrong. Now the centers of influence in our culture have abandoned this truth. Everyone who knows that murder is wrong ought to see that abortion is wrong. But as we mentioned in chapter three, what we ought to know by our moral reason is clouded by sin. We tend to deny what we really know deep down. That's why God had to reveal His law directly, to make clear what sin has obscured.

Those who trust God's revelation are more likely to stand firm when the culture turns against the moral truth. That's why Christians in the early Church opposed gladiatorial games and, later, slavery. They could see clearly what everyone else ought to have seen. They didn't compromise. They often died for their convictions, and eventually, Rome abandoned the games and Europe, its colonies, and the United States abandoned slavery.

A universal moral principle is at stake here, rather than just a private scruple. To say a right to privacy provides a right to abortion is akin to saying a father's right to privacy allows him to kill his teenage son provided he does it in his own home. Only by assuming that we're not dealing with human life does the privacy argument make sense. But the point in dispute is whether we are dealing with a human life.

The argument that a woman should be free to do what she wants with her own body has the same problem. We should not be legally free to use our bodies to murder other people. We don't have a right to violate the rights of others.

Abortion defenders have spilled a lot of ink trying to show that since a fetus is inside its mother, abortion is morally different from murder; but these are attempts to obscure the obvious—that the human fetus is a human being. Your right to life, unlike your right to vote, doesn't vary with location.

Other popular arguments are that the fetus is not fully human because it is quite small, or that it depends on another life and so is not really an independent life. Newborn babies are small but no less human for it. Is an eight-pound unborn baby a human while a newborn five-pound baby is not? Newborns, the weak, and the elderly all depend on others. Are they nonhuman? A person who crashes on a ski slope and is knocked out cold with a concussion would freeze to death without help. Is this person suddenly nonhuman because he is no longer independent? We all depend on others to some extent. Does that mean we are not human beings?

Changing the Subject

These days, many abortion supporters will concede that an unborn baby is human, but insist that what's important is whether it's a *person*. (This is called personhood theory.) To be a person, supposedly, one must be self-conscious, or able to get on in the world, or have meaningful relationships, or some such. But this is absurd. When people are sleeping, or in a coma, they aren't self-conscious and aren't too chatty. Does that mean they're not persons, so it's okay to kill them? Certainly not.

Philosophers point out that this argument leads to other absurd conclusions. For instance, there would be "human non-persons,"[11] since unborn fetuses would be human beings first and then become *persons* at a different time from the human beings with which they are associated. Therefore, the person and the human being are not identical. This suggests that whatever "you" are, you merely inhabit a human body. Weirder, it suggests that you, as a person, are not a human being, but merely inhabit one.[12]

The philosophical issues get more and more obscure. But if you follow the debate, it quickly becomes obvious that the whole point of getting space between "person" and "human" is to justify excluding a pretargeted group of human beings from the protection of the law. It doesn't take a lot of prophetic insight to see that if personhood theory ever becomes the basis for our laws against murder, no one will be safe.

What the Evidence of Science Tells Us

The issue boils down to one simple question: Is a preborn embryo or fetus (fetus means "little one") a human being? To settle that question, we don't need complicated philosophical discussions about person-hood or doctrines about souls entering bodies. We need only honest biology. And biologically, a distinct human life begins at conception.[13]

It's not just that this new life has its own, distinct DNA. It's an integrated, living, complete being. While dependent on its mother, it nevertheless directs its own development toward a specific end accord-ing to its nature. This marks off an embryo from any of its mother's cells. It also distinguishes it from the father's sperm, from the mother's egg, from the mother, the father, and everything else. Each of us was once an embryo, then a fetus, then a newborn, an infant, a toddler, a child, a teenager, and so forth. To say that a human embryo or fetus is not a human being, but merely some other thing called a "fetus" or an "embryo," makes no more sense than to say a teenager isn't a human being, but some other thing called a "teenager." These words just refer to different stages of development of the same human individual, a member of the species *Homo sapiens*. No stage is more human than any other. Of course, we want to see early human beings develop, to learn to speak and walk and interact with others—to flourish. But at every stage, is it is *human person* flourishing.

Science and Stem Cells

What applies to abortion also applies to scientific research that destroys human embryos.[14] In the last ten years, embryonic stem cell research has been a political hot potato. On August 9, 2001, I (James) was with President George W. Bush at the Crawford Ranch. After we had prayed together, I looked at him and said, "I trust you will always come down on the side of life." He did, and later that day he announced to the nation that he would not provide federal funding for research that destroyed human embryos. He was accused of being antiscience, even though he *increased* federal funding for related research in which no new embryos would be destroyed. When President Obama took office in January 2009, he reversed the Bush policy in the name of "science." On his third day as president, he even reversed the longstanding "Mexico City policy," freeing up taxpayer money for abortions around the world.

The issue has nothing to do with being pro- or antiscience. Nor is the issue stem cell research, since all successful stem cell research has come from sources other than embryos. It's not even about *embryonic* stem cell research, since no one would object to such research if it didn't involve destroying human embryos. Again, it's about the identity of the embryo. It's a human being, and killing human beings is not an acceptable way of advancing scientific knowledge.

Erring on the Side of Caution

In 2008, Pastor Rick Warren asked then-candidate Barack Obama, "At what point do you think a baby gets human rights?" Obama punted. "Answering that question with specificity is, you know, above my pay grade," he said. In other words, he said he didn't know the answer. *But if he were unsure, why would he zealously seek to protect the "right" to kill the unborn?* If you don't know for sure if an unborn baby is a human being and so has the right to protection, what's the best course of action? In any other situation, you would err on the side of caution.

Let's say you live in a neighborhood where the kids often play in cardboard boxes. One day, when you're riding your monster truck near your house, you see a cardboard box in the street. Would you plow over it without checking inside first? Of course not. You wouldn't risk killing a child simply because you didn't know if there was a kid in the box. Similarly, if, for all you know, unborn babies might be human beings, then surely the reasonable course of action is to assume they have human rights.

If You Love Freedom, You Should Be Pro-Life

Arguments, no matter how strong, rarely convince anyone who is determined to keep abortion legal. But there are some folks who aren't zealously pro-choice. They support individual rights, free markets, and limited government, and think that abortion should be legal for those reasons. What they don't realize is that they are striking at the root of their own beliefs.

Those who defend free enterprise almost always make a moral assumption when making their case. Take the rabidly pro-choice atheist Ayn Rand. "Man—every man—is an end in himself," she insisted, "not the means to the ends of others."[15] Rand's followers make the same argument, as do most libertarians. Whether they realize it or not, they are committed to the inherent dignity of every human being, whatever his or her race, age, or social status. They're implying that a human being is valuable because of what he or she *is*, apart from whether he or she is useful to anyone else. That's the foundation of the pro-life position, too.

The case for free enterprise—private property, limited government, and free markets—is not merely economic. The science of economics, at its best, can only describe how different policies will turn out. Economists can predict what will happen if Congress raises income tax rates to 90 percent, or slaps huge tariffs on sugar imports. But it's not the job of economics to tell us which policies are more just. That's why every defense of a free market depends on a broader moral vision that goes beyond economics.

God created us as free beings, not as robots determined by physics and programming. A society that protects our freedom allows us to exercise our creativity more fully, and more beneficially, than the alternatives. This idea is so compelling that most Americans take it for granted, even if they don't believe they have been created by God.

Pro-lifers argue on the same grounds that the government should protect the life of the unborn, the elderly, and the infirm, and should prohibit scientific procedures that destroy human embryos. Here's how the late Pennsylvania Governor Robert Casey put it in a speech at the University of Notre Dame in 1995: "Human life cannot be measured. It is the measure itself. The value of everything else is weighed against it. The abortion debate is not about how we shall live, but who shall live. And more than that, it's about who we are."

Some respond that criminalizing abortion limits choice. Yes, it limits the choice of those who seek abortions and of those who seek to provide them, in order to protect the life and freedom of unborn human beings. Libertarians support a *limited* government, as they should, not a lack of government, which would be anarchy. Anarchy is not a prerequisite for a free market but, rather, one of its greatest enemies. The central role of government—its core competency—is to maintain the conditions in which individual initiative, personal freedoms, and personal property are protected under the rule of law. Those conditions do not include the "freedom" of some to violate the basic rights of others.

Without rule of law, there can be neither free markets nor free men. And the first rule of law is to protect innocent human beings at every stage of their lives from harm and death at the hands of others. Protecting innocent, preborn, human life, then, is not only consistent with economic freedom. It is one of its prerequisites.

To put it plainly, fiscal conservatives and libertarians committed to freedom should be pro-life. "The freedom to choose is pointless for someone who does not have the freedom to live," notes Congressman Paul Ryan. "So the right of 'choice' of one human being cannot trump the right to 'life' of another. How long can we sustain our commitment to freedom if we continue to deny the very foundation of freedom— life—for the most vulnerable human beings?"[16]

Should We Be One-Issue Voters?

Pro-lifers are often accused of obsessing on abortion and ignoring other vital issues, such as the environment or poverty or taxes. It's wrong to treat abortion as the *only* concern. It's equally wrong to treat unequal issues alike. Too often, we hear young Christians say things like, "I disagree with Mr. Smith's pro-choice views, but I agree with him on global warming, taxation, and broadband regulation."

This is confused. Most political issues involve shades of gray. Should the bottom income tax bracket be 5 percent or 10 percent? Should we have an income tax or a consumption tax? Should we buy thirty more Abrams tanks for the Army, or five more F-22s for the Air Force? These aren't black-and-white issues.

Abortion is different. It deals with the first right, on which all other rights are based. It involves an act evil in itself—intentionally killing innocent human beings. So abortion policy should be far more central to our voting than virtually any other issue. If one candidate is pro-life and another is pro-choice in an election, most other issues ought to pale in comparison. You can't decide how to vote with integrity simply by making a checklist of issues and then picking the candidate who gets the most checks. Not all issues are created equal. Indeed, to treat unequal moral issues as equal is *immoral*.

A Testimony to Life

As important as abortion is in politics, it also can be a painful personal issue. Several years ago, I (James) interviewed a guest on *Life Today* who had become pregnant as the result of rape. At first, she was so horrified by what had happened to her that abortion seemed her only option. She felt as if having the baby would be an ongoing reminder of her experience. Later, when she heard a song titled "A Baby's Prayer" by Kathy Troccoli, she felt the need to pray. And as she prayed, she realized that the "little mass of tissue" in her womb was really a person with purpose and potential. She decided to keep the baby and named her Alexis Kathleen in honor of Kathy Troccoli, whose song had touched her heart and caused her to reconsider her options.

As this young woman told her story on our show, I began to weep because I also am the product of rape. My mother was an unmarried, forty-year-old practical nurse who was sexually assaulted by the alcoholic son of the man for whom she was caring. When she went to the doctor to have me aborted—because she had no husband, an inadequate income for caring for a child, and had been raped—the doctor said, "Ma'am, I simply do not believe this is best. I believe it is wrong." My mother later told me she went home, sat down alone, and prayed. And God said, "Have this little baby, and it will bring joy to the world."

My mother chose to carry me to term, and I was born in the charity ward of the Saint Joseph Hospital in Houston, Texas. Two weeks later, through an ad in the newspaper, my mother released me to a foster family, who raised me for the first five years of my life. My conception was the result of a crime, and my childhood and adolescence weren't easy, but God had a plan for this unexpected child born in difficult circumstances.

In standing against abortion, we don't want to minimize the trauma of an unexpected pregnancy—especially by rape or incest. But if we affirm the value of every life even in the tough cases, God will honor the intent of our hearts and use that choice in a way that we can't imagine beforehand. Both of us have been blessed because a mother in a desperate situation chose life. We both have a child by adoption and can't imagine life without them. Randy Robison is now forty-two, married with four beautiful children. Ellie Richards was adopted from China. She's eight and already thinks she should rule the world.

There Is a Balm in Gilead

If you have had an abortion or participated in one, you need to know that there is forgiveness, and there is a source of healing. That healing balm is the love of Jesus Christ, who died to set you free from sin and shame. He grieves with you over the loss of innocent life, and He can heal your broken heart.

Some of the most faithful Christian women we know made the tragic mistake of aborting their babies earlier in their lives, yet they will tell you that in spite of their decision, God's grace covered their sin and removed their shame "as far as the east is from the west." Denial doesn't heal pain. But you can experience God's forgiveness and find healing and redemption from a tragic mistake. If, on the other hand, you are struggling with the pain of an unplanned pregnancy right now, we encourage you to choose life for your baby, and to connect with loving Christians with experience helping women in these circumstances.[17]

What can we do to change the status of innocent preborn children who have no voice of their own? We need to support pro-life candidates. Bad laws and tragic court decisions must be changed. But we're not going to stop abortion by focusing all our attention on reversing *Roe v. Wade*. In fact, that alone could make the pro-abortion forces more militant. Unless a woman is transformed by the Holy Spirit and is living a holy life, she may find a way to terminate her pregnancy anyway.

Besides legislative action, we must take every opportunity to affirm the value of life. We must demonstrate love and compassion—not just emotionally but practically—to every woman who is pregnant, regardless of the circumstances. While we boldly proclaim the right to life, we must also help provide hope in life. We should do more of what we're doing: praying and protesting peacefully at abortion mills, and providing alternatives to mothers with tough pregnancies. Adoption, crisis pregnancy centers, homes for poor and homeless mothers—all these are part of the solution. As Christians and as Christian communities, we should lead the way in all these things. Let's focus not just on what "society" or government is doing, but on what we can do.

A nation that sacrifices its unborn children is in grave spiritual danger. God is just and He hates sin, especially sins against those who bear His image. So, above all, we should pray for an outpouring of the Holy Spirit to lead us to repentance—before it's too late.

CHAPTER 8

A Man Shall Cling to His Wife

For this reason a man will leave his father and mother and
be united to his wife, and they will become one flesh.
—GENESIS 2:24

In the Beginning

Before there were cities, before there were governments, there was marriage. Marriage was there at the creation. God makes Adam, puts him in the Garden, and then creates the woman from Adam's rib. On seeing the woman, Adam says, " 'This at last is bone of my bones and flesh of my flesh; she shall be called Woman, because she was taken out of Man.' Therefore a man leaves his father and his mother and cleaves to his wife, and they become one flesh." As long as there have been human beings, there has been marriage. It's the foundation for every other human institution.[1]

Many of the characters of the Old Testament, such as Abraham, Jacob, and especially Solomon, didn't follow the ideal of one man and one woman. They were polygamists—they had more than one wife. And though marriage was meant to be permanent, Moses gave the Israelites rules for divorce. God did not recommend but tolerated such practices. When the Pharisees asked Jesus if it was lawful for a man to divorce his wife for any reason, he pointed back to Genesis, and explained that Moses acted only because of hardness of heart, not because God approved of divorce (Matthew 19:3–12 and Mark 10:2–12).

In the spring of 2011, much of the world watched and listened as Kate Middleton and Prince William recited their wedding vows in Westminster Abbey. They committed to love and honor one another for life. But if you traveled deep into the forests of Papua New Guinea, you would find people doing much the same thing with a little less pomp and lot less television coverage.

Christians, following Scripture, have always treated marriage as sacred; but marriage is hardly unique to Christianity. Every known culture has it. Sure, there are differences here and there. Some cultures have allowed polygamy, for instance, and some have arranged marriages. Though romantic love is often part of the story as far back as Jacob and Rachel, the idea of marrying primarily for love is a more recent invention. But there is a constant, underlying theme: Marriage as a norm is a public joining of one man and one woman for life. And yet, every state in our nation is now embroiled in a debate about what marriage is. What most of the human race took for granted, judges and legislators now think they can revise. Marriage is suffering a frontal assault not just in the United States, but in the entire "civilized" world.

Where It Started

The problem did not start with the same-sex marriage debate. An epidemic of divorce, aided and abetted by the sexual revolution, began chipping away at marriage decades ago. In the early years of the American colonies, very few people got divorced for the simple reason that it was illegal—as it was in Europe. After the Founding, states established divorce laws, but divorce was still rare. In the 1960s, states enacted "no-fault" divorce laws.[2] These came in the wake of relentless assaults on marriage and chastity from academics such as "sex researcher" Alfred Kinsey and anthropologist Margaret Mead. They misled millions to believe that homosexuality and promiscuity were normal, common, and healthy. Later we learned that their work was deeply flawed,[3] even fraudulent, but the damage was already done.

Now all fifty states have no-fault divorce laws, making it much easier to divorce than it was in the past. In some ways, marriage is now even less binding than a business contract. As marriage expert Maggie Gallagher has written, "Marriage is one of the few contracts in which the law explicitly protects the defaulting party at the expense of his or her partner."[4]

Along with changing laws has come a changed culture where divorce carries little stigma. The divorce rate for first marriages—between 40 and 50 percent—is about twice what it was just in 1960. About two-thirds of second marriages, and three-fourths of third marriages, end in divorce.[5] This trend is even more startling when you realize that divorce rates have gone up while marriage rates have gone down. On average, men and women marry much later than they did just a few decades ago. For a while, divorce was much worse in cities than in the country. But now the countryside is catching up.[6]

Sixty percent of Americans in first marriages now live together beforehand.[7] "Cohabiting" is considered a good trial run that will prevent a divorce later; but statistics show that people who shack up before getting married are much more likely to divorce than those who keep two addresses until their wedding day.[8]

If the sexual revolution and no-fault divorce were dry twigs and tinder, the birth control pill and legal abortion were a blowtorch and gasoline. Together they have turned the link binding marriage, sex, and childbearing into ashes.[9] Heterosexuals have been stoking these flames for decades, long before talk of same-sex "marriage."

What Good Is Marriage?

As Christians, we may regret the collapse of marriage, but everyone else should care, too. Marriage may be personal, but it's not private. Like a rock dropped in a pond, the ripples work their way across the entire surface of civilization. The collapse of marriage and the epidemic of divorce since the 1960s have given social scientists decades of data to study, and the results are in: Marriage is good for us and divorce is not.

Men and women in their first marriages tend to be healthier and happier than their counterparts in every other type of relationship—single, widowed, or divorced. They're also less depressed and anxious,[10] and less likely to abuse drugs and alcohol. "Seventy percent of chronic problem drinkers are divorced or separated, and only 15 percent are married."[11] Married adults are more sexually fulfilled. They're better parents, better workers, and are less likely to be perpetrators or victims of domestic violence.[12]

Most men, left to their own fallen, animal instincts, would be promiscuous. Their sexual energies need to be properly channeled, so that they think and act for long-term goals rather than fleeting, short-term pleasure. George Gilder argued in the 1970s and '80s that the channeling of male sexual activity is one of the most important functions of marriage. It is crucial for civilization because it helps, well, civilize men.[13] Other scholars have confirmed Gilder's point, by showing a link between the state of marriage and the historical rise and fall of civilizations.[14]

Social scientists have concluded that married men are less likely to commit crime and more likely to hold down jobs. You don't need a PhD in sociology to recognize that unattached single men wandering the streets are more inclined to trouble than the same men attached to wives and children.

Single people can, of course, live fulfilling lives. The Apostle Paul commends the single life as a wonderful gift for those who are called to it (1 Corinthians 7:7–8). Those called to marriage, however, tend to be much better off if they are married rather than divorced. Marriage scholars Linda Waite and Maggie Gallagher sum up the results of thousands of scientific studies: "A good marriage is both men's and women's best bet for living a long and healthy life."[15] They're speaking statistically, of course, since any institution can be distorted and even destroyed by human sin. Still, all things being equal, marriage is good for us.

What *Is* Marriage?

If marriage is such a good thing, though, why should it be limited to a relationship between a man and a woman? Why can't men marry men and women marry women, if they love each other? These questions assume that marriage is about equality and about people doing what they want to do. Given the nature of marriage, though, it doesn't make any sense to refer to a relationship between people of the same sex, no matter how intimate, as marriage.

We should be careful not to confuse the question of marriage with separate issues. It's not about whether homosexuals should have the same legal rights as everyone else. (They should.) It's not about whether homosexuals should be treated with love and respect. (They should.) It's not about the origin of homosexuality. It's not about what consenting adults do in their homes. It's not about "homophobia." It's not even about whether homosexual acts are a sin. It's about the nature of marriage and its role as a public institution.

Unfortunately, it's easy to mix up issues of homosexuality and marriage because of how our language has changed. Columnist Mark Steyn observes that we once viewed homosexuality as an act—as something a person *does*. Later, activist psychologists insisted we refer to sexuality as an *orientation*. Now many people think of it as an *identity*. If one is by nature a homosexual, if one's very identity is to be homosexual, then it's easy to treat a defense of traditional marriage as a bigoted attack on homosexuals.[16]

Strip away the cultural traditions—giving dowries, exchanging rings and vows in a church, throwing parties and bouquets—and what actually *is* marriage? Let's define it clearly and precisely.

In an important article in the *Harvard Journal of Law & Public Policy*, Sherif Girgis, Robert George, and Ryan Anderson boil down the basic ingredients of conjugal marriage. "Marriage involves: first, a comprehensive union of spouses [husbands and wives]; second, a special link to children; and third, norms of permanence, monogamy, and exclusivity."[17] Notice the word "norm"—ideal. The norm is the same even if some marriages fail to fully achieve it. A proper end of the marital act is children, even if a child doesn't result from every conjugal act, just as a proper end of playing football—to take a trivial example—is to score touchdowns, even if in some football games, nobody scores a touchdown.

The word "marriage" refers to a unique relationship. We relate to our coworkers because of our jobs. We relate to our neighbors because of where we live. We relate to our friends because we have common interests. In marriage, a husband and a wife unite comprehensively, with their whole beings. We are spiritual and bodily beings. Any union that is comprehensive—all-encompassing—must include a union of bodies. But bodies can come together in all sorts of ways—dancing, shaking hands, wrestling, playing football, and cramming into a crowded subway car. The connection of bodies that is a true marital union will fulfill a true purpose that could not be fulfilled otherwise.

Each of our organs has a biological purpose. The purpose of the heart is to pump blood; of eyes, to see; of lungs, to draw in air and capture oxygen to supply the body. All of these organs also have a common purpose: They work together to allow our body to live and thrive. Moreover, they're complete: They don't need another human being to function.

Each of us, however, has one biological function that it cannot, by itself, complete: sexual reproduction.[18] That purpose can be fulfilled only by a specific kind of union with another human being of the opposite sex. That's how we're built. Male and female are "made to fit," and until recently, probably no one anywhere thought to deny this. To reproduce naturally, to produce a new human being, a male and a female must unite their bodies in the sexual act. In this one way, we are naturally incomplete as individuals and organisms. "Marriage," as one scholar has written, "proposes a reconciliation of the most fundamental natural difference among human beings—sex."[19] Men and women, certainly in our bodies but also in other, less tangible ways, complement each other.

We're not just bodies. Our minds, emotions, and souls work in harmony with our sexuality. Sex within marriage is a good thing in itself, even when conception doesn't result, but the act still naturally tends toward reproduction—children. It has the awesome power to produce new human beings. To pretend otherwise, to isolate sex from childbearing, is to court serious trouble.

The sex act is the consummation—the seal—of marriage (rather than conception or childbirth). Marriage protects, reflects, and reinforces this powerful, complementary, reproductive part of our natures. No relationship between two men or two women can qualify as marriage because ultimately same-sex pairing cannot "achieve organic bodily union since there is no bodily good or function toward which their bodies can coordinate, reproduction being the only candidate."[20]

An infertile man and woman can still marry, since it is "mating that gives marriage its orientation toward children. An infertile couple can mate even if it cannot procreate. Two men or two women literally cannot mate.... A child fulfills the marital relationship by revealing what it is, a complete union, including a biological union."[21] Same-sex unions can't bring together complementary organs and body systems that are designed to procreate.

Marriage is a comprehensive union of body, mind, emotion, and soul, a proper end of which is children. Ideally, it should also be permanent, exclusive, and monogamous. Marriage is a public commitment, an act of free will, not a fleeting emotion. Romantic love and affection can be wonderful blessings of marriage, but romantic feelings come and go. Marriage, if it is anything, must be more than that.[22]

What Harm Is There in Redefining Marriage?

Why would traditional marriages be harmed by same-sex marriage? Does it affect your marriage in Texas or North Carolina for two men to "marry" in California or New York? This is like asking if the value of a real dollar in Texas would be affected by flooding the market with counterfeits in New York.[23] Yes, it would be, because counterfeits degrade the value of all real dollars and the economy. As economists say, bad money chases out good money.

Enshrining a false definition of marriage in our laws will inevitably harm all marriages and society. Same-sex marriage does not expand the meaning of marriage, but replaces its historical meaning with a counterfeit.

If people of the same sex can legally "marry" each other, we will lose any rational basis for barring polygamy, group marriage, and incest, and for encouraging marriage to be exclusive and permanent. The reason for restricting marriage to one man and one woman is that it takes exactly one man and one woman to make a complete pair. That logic of completion evaporates if people of the same sex can marry. The arguments used to defend same-sex marriage work just as well for defending any voluntary relationship imaginable.

We're not just fear-mongering. *The jump from same-sex marriage to polygamy, group marriage, and open marriage is already happening.* Most same-sex "marriages" that have already been performed in some US states are not monogamous for long.[24] And in those places that recognize same-sex marriage, few gays even bother to "marry."[25] "Monogamous marriage," say Glenn Stanton and Bill Maier, "is democracy for the domestic and sexual lives for men and women."[26] Polygamous cultures (which are almost always *polygynous*—one husband with more than one wife) are much more competitive and unstable. Where monogamy is the norm, a man—no matter how powerful, rich, or attractive—can have, at most, one wife. With polygamy, he's free to "collect" as many wives as he can, leaving the less powerful men without prospects. History tells us what happens to cultures with large numbers of men lacking marital prospects. Typically the men turn to prostitution and are more likely to prey on the society that has not made a place for them. Polygamy also lowers the status of women, especially of the wives who must compete for the same man's attention. So rather than balancing the sexual competitiveness of men and women, polygamy makes the problem much worse. This is a Pandora's box that needs to stay shut.

Redefining marriage would foment culture wars in every hamlet, city, and school district in the country, ending with a draconian loss of religious freedom. What was once prohibited is first tolerated and then required. If same-sex marriage is defined as a basic human right, a matter of justice and equality—as its advocates claim—then no one could publicly defend real marriage for long. Government would *have* to treat traditional views as irrational bigotry. Parents who complain about their kids being forced to read *Heather Has Two Mommies* would be viewed like racist white parents who didn't want their children to attend school with black children. Everyone who holds the view of marriage heretofore held in every culture would be opposed by *this* culture. Ministries would be forced to revise their principles or close up shop. Catholic Charities already has had to abandon its adoption services in California, Massachusetts, and the District of Columbia to avoid being forced to place children with same-sex couples.[27]

If we don't reverse the trend, criticizing homosexuality could soon be illegal. It's already happened in Canada. Just months after same-sex marriage became legal there, a bill that criminalized such statements became law. "Antigay" speech crimes can now be punished by up to two years in jail![28] In 2008, the Alberta Human Rights Tribunal ordered Rev. Stephen Boisson to pay a $5,000 fine and apologize for a letter to the editor he wrote in 2002, before same-sex marriage was legalized.[29] A higher court eventually overturned the ruling, but the incident is a foretaste of the future if defenders of traditional marriage don't succeed in reversing the trend.

A Portent of Things to Come

One of us (James) experienced another such omen decades ago. In early 1979, our weekly television program was airing nationally on network and independent stations. For a few minutes on one episode, I said that homosexuality was outside of God's plan for us. I also speculated that it would prove to be a detriment to people's health. (This was prior to the AIDS epidemic.) In response, our flagship station in Dallas, a national network affiliate, cited the Orwellian "Fairness Doctrine" and took our program off the air. The next week, a gay advocacy group was given the entire 30-minute time slot.

We didn't go quietly. The Dallas–Fort Worth public rose up to support us. More than 11,000 people gathered at "The Freedom Rally" in Dallas to defend my "Freedom of Speech, the Right to Preach." Major advertisers protested the action of the affiliate and its corporate owner. The station's decision eventually became national news, making its way into *People* magazine, and onto the Tom Snyder, Jerry Rose, and Phil Donahue shows. Protests by a diverse group of citizens—Catholics, Protestants, and Jews—plus legal pressure persuaded the station to restore our program after several weeks. The incident contributed to the demise of the Fairness Doctrine. Its official purpose was to preserve freedom of speech on TV and radio, but its effect was to silence conservative voices—so it's no surprise that some liberal lawmakers want to bring it back.[30] We won the skirmish in 1979, but it is a portent of how bad laws could be used to silence us if we fail to preserve marriage as a union of one man and one woman.

If we allow the state to redefine marriage, we should expect to see marriage collapse as a public institution. Some people will still marry, but it will be like a private pact with little or no larger social effect. Several European countries in which same-sex marriage is legal show what may come. Laws have permitted same-sex marriage in the Netherlands since 2001, and rather than a marriage paradise, with straight and gay couples typically living in long-term, monogamous bliss, fewer and fewer Dutch bother to get married at all. Children are no longer connected to marriage. People just live together, and many have a hard time figuring out why marriage is even *relevant*.[31]

Many well-meaning people think same-sex marriage is just about equality and spreading the benefits of marriage. Its more radical supporters know it's about destroying marriage itself. Here's what one activist said in *Out* magazine:

> The trick is, gay leaders and pundits must stop watering the issue down—"this is simply about equality for gay couples"— and offer same-sex marriage for what it is: an opportunity to reconstruct a traditionally homophobic institution by bringing it to our more equitable queer value system, . . . a chance to wholly transform the definition of family in American culture. . . . Our gay leaders must acknowledge that gay marriage is just as *radical* and *transformative* as the religious Right contends it is.[32]

If Government Is Limited, What's It Doing in the Marriage Business?

One objection to our call to protect traditional marriage comes from some defenders of limited government. The thinking goes like this: If you support limited government and individual rights, shouldn't you oppose laws that define or favor traditional marriage? Shouldn't the state get out of the marriage business altogether, and just treat us as individuals?[33]

No. Marriage is a public institution with public consequences. If it weren't, no one would be clamoring for same-sex marriage to be legally sanctioned. Any two people can have a ceremony in their house and say they're "married" anytime they want. The reason we're having this debate is because, by definition, it's about public recognition and approval, not private vows. Andrew Sullivan, a supporter of same-sex marriage, makes that clear. "Including homosexuals within marriage," he observes, "would be a means of conferring the highest form of social approval imaginable."[34]

Redefining marriage would strike at the foundation of individual rights, too. Remember, a limited government doesn't try to redefine reality as the Orwellian governments of the twentieth century did (including the fictional government of George Orwell's *1984*). A limited government *recognizes* and defends certain culturally central realities outside its jurisdiction. Our government doesn't bestow rights on us as individuals. We get our rights from God. A just and limited state simply recognizes and protects what already exists. Marriage is another such reality. It transcends every political system. Even cultures that have accepted homosexuality, such as the ancient Greeks, still knew that marriage was for a man and a woman. Since so many different cultures and religions have recognized and protected marriage, we should conclude that it's based on human nature and is not merely a social convention that we're free to change once progressives capture the Supreme Court or the legislature of New York.

In fact, marriage is far more universal and so has more claim to be based on human nature than do our ideals of individual rights and equality.[35] We believe in individual rights and human equality, of course, but we don't accept that these are the only realities that a limited government is bound to accept. Unfortunately, many libertarians focus only on our individuality, while ignoring or rejecting the relationships that also define us. Yet even our rights depend on a relationship, namely, that we are created by God and that as social beings with both rights and responsibilities, we find our full humanity by respecting other people's rights rather than in systematically violating them.

Each of us is by nature a person in relationship. And marriage, a unique union of a man and a woman, is one of our most basic human relationships. Appealing to nature and nature's God to defend individual rights and equality, which most cultures have not recognized, while ignoring the universal testimony of nature and culture on marriage, is like sawing off the branch you're sitting on. Put another way, you can't make war on the natural law and then appeal to it for help.

So just as government can't redefine our rights as individuals made in the image of God, it has no authority to redefine marriage. Communism was totalitarian because it tried to redefine the individual, to create a new "Communist Man." We're now struggling with another totalitarian impulse to redefine reality. As the editors of *National Review* said after the New York legislature approved same-sex marriage, "There is nothing libertarian or neutral about state-imposed moral ratification of revisionist sexual ideology, especially when dissenting citizens and business owners will be forced to comply, token protections notwithstanding."[36] If the state can redefine a universal institution rooted in human nature, what *can't* it redefine?

A Right to Marry?

Some claim that laws protecting marriage violate the rights of others, that "prohibiting same-sex marriage" is like the laws that used to prohibit people of different races or ethnic groups from marrying. These are nothing alike. Racist "antimiscegenation" laws never denied the nature of marriage. Rather, they assumed that people of different ethnic backgrounds were capable of marrying. That's why the laws existed—to prevent such marriages. There were attempts to claim that interracial marriages somehow went against nature, with some even claiming that mixed-race offspring were somehow less healthy. We now know that these claims had no basis in biology. The debate over same-sex marriage isn't about preventing certain marriages, but about the nature of marriage itself.

No one—including us—has a right to marry someone of the same sex. Besides, a man attracted to other men can still marry—a woman. Any relationship a man has with another man, however, won't be marriage. Fundamentally, two people of the same sex *cannot* marry each other. The law can pretend they can. The pair can throw a big wedding ceremony, say their vows in public, but calling it "marriage" doesn't make it so. And invoking a right doesn't create a right. Rights come from our nature, and our nature comes from God. If you deny that, then you deny the basis of all our other rights.

What Should We Do?

Because most Americans support traditional marriage, few candidates running for office are going to challenge public opinion, whatever the candidate really thinks. So we have to be really discerning, even skeptical, when it comes to politicians. In 1996, the US Congress passed, and President Clinton signed, the Defense of Marriage Act (DOMA). It protects states from being forced to recognize same-sex marriages performed in other states. President Obama said before he was elected that, as a Christian, he believed marriage was between a man and a woman. As soon as he was elected, though, we learned that he was still "struggling" with the issue, and that his view is "constantly evolving."[37] Right.

In truth, Obama had already written an open letter to the "LGBT community" (lesbian, gay, bisexual, transsexual) before he was elected saying that he wanted to repeal DOMA.[38] That was his real view, which is why his Justice Department has refused to defend DOMA in court, and Attorney General Eric Holder has denounced it as unconstitutional and irrational. Unless voters replace the president with someone who will defend rather than defy the law in this area, states will soon be forced to recognize same-sex marriages performed in other states. Meanwhile, polls suggest that Americans are warming to the idea of "gay marriage,"[39] perhaps growing weary of fighting a trend they've been told is inevitable. Don't believe it! Your votes could help determine the future of marriage in our country.[40]

Pulling the right lever in the voting booth, though, is just a tiny part of the solution. It will only slow down the unraveling of marriage. To reverse the march of marriage to the gallows, we need a lot of repentance and healing. While we defend marriage with all our might, we should not stoop to hateful attacks on our opponents. Even when we're attacked as bigots or "homophobes," we need to pray for the strength to offer love and compassion in return. It's easy to demonize gay activists, but every one of them is a human being created in the image of God. They need Christ's love, not our anger. Anger is easy. Love is hard. We need to do the hard thing—show them love.

If your marriage is in trouble, even if you're in the middle of a divorce, we hope you'll do whatever you must to save your marriage, before it's too late. If there has been severe hurt or infidelity on either person's part, your marriage can still be restored and become even stronger. Please know God freely offers His forgiveness and healing if you will repent and run to Him. Early in His earthly ministry, Jesus traveled through the land of Samaria. The Jews thought of Samaritans as idolaters and mongrels and did their best to avoid them. When our Lord encountered a Samaritan woman at a well, however, He asked her for a drink. Astonished, she asked, "How is it that you, a Jew, ask a drink of me, a woman of Samaria?" In reply, Jesus revealed to her that He was the Living Water that could give eternal life.

He then told her to call her husband. She admitted that she did not have a husband; but Jesus knew the whole truth, "You are right in saying, 'I have no husband,' for you have had five husbands, and he whom you now have is not your husband; this you said truly." She already felt shame, since she was at the well at noon, rather than in the morning or evening when most women collected water. And what did Jesus do? He did not justify or ignore her sin; he *named and exposed* it, but still offered her His love. Her testimony led many of the Samaritans in her city to believe in Jesus (John 4:3–42). Talk about freedom found in true forgiveness! This woman cast off her shame, then went out publicly testifying and inviting everyone to come meet a man who knew every sinful thing she had ever done. She felt safely covered by God's grace. This was the first time that Jesus publicly announced that he was the Messiah. If He could choose to give that gift to a Samaritan woman who had been married to five men and was shacking up with a sixth, then he can certainly forgive and redeem anyone.

All of us who are married need to model what marriage is supposed to look like. Americans have surfed the no-fault divorce wave like a piece of dead driftwood.[41] As believers, we also need to repent from what *we* have done to harm marriage. Divorce is almost as common among professing Christians as it is among the general population. The stats for staying married improve a lot for Christians who attend worship at least once a week and who pray together daily as a family.[42] And for some reason, couples that practice "natural family planning," whether Catholic or Protestant, have extremely low divorce rates.[43] We can do our part to protect marriage.

Paul's advice to the church at Ephesus might as well have been written yesterday, since it's based on universal truths:

> Be subject to one another out of reverence for Christ. Wives, be subject to your husbands, as to the Lord. For the husband is the head of the wife as Christ is the head of the Church, his body,

and is himself its Savior. As the church is subject to Christ, so let wives also be subject in everything to their husbands. Husbands, love your wives, as Christ loved the church and gave himself up for her, that he might sanctify her, having cleansed her by the washing of water with the word, that he might present the church to himself in splendor, without spot or wrinkle or any such thing, that she might be holy and without blemish. Even so husbands should love their wives as their own bodies. (Ephesians 5:21–28)

Paul's command to wives to be "subject to your husbands" rubs some people the wrong way, but he also tells husbands and wives to be subject to each other. And his command to husbands is even more bracing. Remember, this was written in the first century, when women were considered property and their testimony was legally worthless. And yet we husbands are told to love our wives as "Christ loved the church and gave himself up for her." There's no taller order than that kind of sacrificial love.

If *Christian* husbands decided to take Paul's command at face value, to follow it and become real spiritual leaders of their families (rather than letting their wives do all the heavy spiritual lifting), if every married person reading this book resolved to put Paul's words into practice, to seek holiness in marriage rather than just happiness, we'd have a lot more credibility when defending marriage.

CHAPTER 9

It Takes a Family

*The family endures because it offers the truth of mortality
and immortality within the same group. The family endures
because, better than the commune, kibbutz, or classroom, it
seems to individualize and socialize its children, to make us
feel at the same time unique and yet joined to all humanity,
accepted as is and yet challenged to grow, loved uncondi-
tionally, and yet propelled by greater expectations. Only in
the family can so many extremes be reconciled and synthe-
sized. Only in the family do we have a lifetime in which to
do it.*

—LETTY COTTIN POGREBIN[1]

In the Bible, there is family from the beginning. In fact, the book of
Genesis is arranged like a family history, beginning with Adam and
Eve, and their sons Cain, Abel, and Seth. One man and one woman—
the common ancestors of every human being—give rise to a small
family, which gives rise to a larger family, which eventually gives rise to
a group of tribes, and those tribes eventually become a nation. At the
root, trunk, and branches of it all, there is a family.

The family is not just a human institution. The Bible describes Israel
as the children—the family—of God, and Paul tells us that the Church

has been adopted into this family. Paul also describes the Church as the bride of Christ. And Jesus taught us to call God *Father*. In reflecting on God's triune nature, the Church learned to refer to the Father, the Son, and the Holy Spirit as the three persons of the one God. So the concept of family allows us to apprehend ourselves, our relationship to God, and even the nature of God.

Given the important role that the concept of family plays in Scripture, we shouldn't be surprised that it is the human social unit on which everything else depends, the cells that make up the body of society. "The future of humanity," said Pope John Paul II, "passes by way of the family."

Intact Families Are Better for Kids

The natural result of sex between a man and a woman is children, and the best environment for raising children is a family headed by a married father and mother. Every society enforces marriage standards because, all things being equal, a child is much better off reared by his married mother and father. This one fact is more important to a child's well-being than his race, his parents' education, or even his neighborhood.[2] You name it—test scores, GPA, expectations of attending college—kids raised by both their mother and their father together are better off than their peers from divorced homes. Children of divorce are far more likely to get expelled from school, and later, to end up out of school and unemployed. Children raised by their married moms and dads commit less crime, have less premarital sex, and have fewer children out of wedlock than children of divorce.[3]

Kids in divorced homes are much more likely to be poor. Poverty in the United States has much less to do with jobs than with divorce. According to one Harvard professor, "The vast majority of children who are raised entirely in a home where parents are married will never be poor during childhood. By contrast, the vast majority of children who spend time in a fatherless home will experience poverty."[4] In the United States and other developed countries, by far the best antipoverty program for women and children is for the woman to be married to the father of her children. According to a recent Heritage Foundation study, "marriage drops the probability of child poverty by 82 percent."[5]

While some heroic single parents and their kids overcome the odds, in general, divorce makes kids less healthy, both physically and emotionally, and more likely to abuse drugs and alcohol. It can cause lingering health problems even when the kids become adults. And as bad as having just one parent in the home can be, stepparents don't seem to be an improvement. Kids living with adults who are not their biological parents are *much* more likely to die of maltreatment, and to suffer physical and sexual abuse.[6] God can and does heal many traumas, of course; but statistically, divorce is a disaster for children.

Not Just Two Parents: *A Mom and a Dad*

MSNBC commentator Chris Matthews once criticized black pastors in Cleveland for opposing same-sex marriage, since they were from "communities that are very much in need of more marriages—obviously, because they're unstable in many ways—some of the families."[7] This misses the point. First, since it takes a male and a female to create a child, kids raised by two "moms" or two "dads" are actually being raised by a single parent or are children of divorce or abandonment.[8] All those distressing statistics above apply to them.

Same-sex marriage advocates say children don't need a mother and a father. This contradicts everything we know. What matters is not two parents but the presence of a married mother and father. Moms and dads aren't interchangeable Lego pieces. "A father is not a male mother," says family expert Glenn Stanton. "Fathers are categorically different kinds of parents than mothers, and this is good for children."[9] Mothers and fathers bring unique and irreplaceable assets to parenting.

Their differences enrich the child's experience and understanding of the world.

While every person is unique in parenting, social science has confirmed what we know intuitively: Dads and moms tend to interact differently with their children. Dads tend to tickle and roughhouse, moms tend to cuddle and comfort; dads challenge, moms encourage. Dads stupidly throw their toddlers in the air. Moms cringe when dads stupidly throw their toddlers in the air. We also tend to communicate and discipline differently. "Dads tend to see their children in relation to the rest of the world. Mothers tend to see the rest of the world in relation to their children."[10] If a child grows up without a father in the home, he will lose out on chances to interact with a father. If the child grows up without a mother, he will lose out on the unique interactions with a female parent.

Two researchers summed up the evidence from social science this way: "If we were asked to design a system for making sure that children's basic needs were met, we would probably come up with something quite similar to the two-parent ideal."[11] A healthy culture requires a healthy marriage culture, which encourages "adults to arrange their lives so that as many children as possible are raised and nurtured by their biological parents in a common household."[12] Society has a strong interest in encouraging parents to stay married and to raise their children together. Given what we know about the importance of married parents to the well-being of children, to make the ideal anything less amounts to intentional cruelty.

The Family Limits Government

Libertarians are all for limited government, free markets, and individual rights, but some treat the family as a private matter with no bearing on public policy. Without strong families, however, we won't have freedom and limited government for long.

Remember, a limited government recognizes but does not control the social spheres outside it. The American republic was founded on the notion of the dignity, equality, and inherent rights of individuals. The state does not establish these realities but recognizes them. The government makes room for marriage and the Church, but it can't dictate what they will be. Well, the same thing is true for *the family*, which is a universal, prepolitical reality. The details may vary from place to place. In some cultures, for instance, older parents and in-laws may live with their children and grandchildren. Still, virtually all known societies have had families made up, at a minimum, of a mother, a father, and a child. By *recognizing* the perennial nature of the family in its laws, the government limits its jurisdiction over individuals and the family. If the government can't manage to acknowledge something as basic as the family, it won't acknowledge individual rights for long.

The destruction of families leads to a larger, more intrusive nanny state. Research by David Popenoe and Alan Wolfe shows a link between the breakdown of marriage and the growth in government spending in Scandinavia.[13] This isn't surprising. The family is a huge check on government power. As Mike Huckabee has said, "The most important form of government is the family."[14] The better a family functions, the less you need from local, state, and federal governments. The family exists, in large part, to protect and bring up a child during his or her formative stages. Each of us is born helpless, dependent, selfish, and impressionable. This is simply how we're designed. Parents must feed, clothe, shelter, and clean newborns. Without care, newborns can survive only a few days at most. We are more helpless in the early part of our lives than practically any animal. Some animals, such as horses and elephants, can stand hours after birth. Others, such as kittens and puppies, are born blind and helpless, but in a couple of months, they're potty trained, eating from a dish, and attacking your ankles. Newborn children won't raise their heads or use their hands for many weeks; they seldom walk before they're a year old and may still be wearing diapers on their third birthday.

At the same time, newborns are so impressionable that they normally master a language in a few years without formal lessons. They perfectly copy the language and accent they hear from their parents, though there seems to be a window of opportunity for this skill that closes a few years after birth. (That's why most adults can't master the accent of a language if they haven't heard it as infants.)

Language is just one thing children get from their parents. Ideally, in their families, children learn to love and be loved; they learn how to eat properly and feed, bathe, dress, and clean up after themselves; to brush their teeth, treat others kindly, speak clearly, share and be less selfish, consider the needs of others, negotiate, sit still, study hard and do their homework, follow the law, pray to God, resist temptation, and control their tongues and their destructive impulses. Though parents delegate some of their children's education to schools and churches, parents should still closely oversee the process. Ideally, by the time they reach adulthood, children will love God, be concerned for others, and have a properly developed conscience that steers them in the right direction. In other words, if all goes well, children eventually learn from their parents to internalize the rule of law that a free society depends on, and the discipline and knowledge that allow them to create wealth and value, rather than merely consume it.[15]

Fiscal Perks from Families

Intact families are an economic boon. Much of the "human capital" that a society enjoys is created, not in the economy, but in the family. Virtually none of the work that a mother and a father do in their own home ever shows up on an official economic report. And yet that work may create more value in the long run than the work they do that gets counted as part of the Gross Domestic Product. Imagine, for instance, two couples, the Smiths and the Joneses. The Smiths work hard raising four kids, who grow up to be successful parents and workers. Two parents have helped give society four productive citizens.

The Joneses, in contrast, neglect their four children, who grow up to be idle hoodlums. They'll be supported with tax money taken from the Smiths.

An intact family uses fewer resources such as food, shelter, and health care than it would if it were split into more than one household. The intact family can save more and invest more because it is much more efficient and enjoys greater economies of scale than either single life or a broken family. Anyone who has been single knows how hard it is to cook and save leftovers for one person. Those big bundles of ruby red grapefruit and hearts of romaine at Costco aren't really useful until you have several people under one roof. Intact families "work, earn, and save at significantly higher rates than other family households as well as pay the lion's share of all income taxes collected by the government."[16]

Families also contribute to "charity and volunteer at significantly higher rates, even when controlling for income, than do single or divorced households."[17] Arthur Brooks, president of the American Enterprise Institute, looked at American patterns of giving and concluded that "single parenthood is a disaster for charity."[18]

For the human race to survive, somebody *has* to raise children; and in the modern world, when families break down or don't form at all, the government steps in. If a father and a mother divorce, a family court will decide who has custody of the kids, when and on what days the parents get to see their children, how much the parents spend and on what, and will garnish the wages of a parent who fails to comply. Mom and Dad may both have to submit to psychological tests. The most intimate details of family life can become a part of the public court records.

The children suffer in the ways we've discussed, and though most kids of divorce survive, and some prosper, on average, they'll be much more likely to become wards of the state and to give birth to wards of the state. A study by the Brookings Institution attributes $229 billion in welfare expenses from 1970 to 1996 to the breakdown of marriage and the social problems produced in its wake, and that is just a tiny fraction of the total social costs.

This scenario gets even scarier when the parents are either abusive, so dysfunctional that they can't perform their basic duties, or abandon their children. Then the state often has to take over entirely, and either put the children in orphanages or foster care. At that point, the state becomes the all-powerful nanny, and the net effects are catastrophic. What is private, voluntary, healthy, natural, and productive in the intact family becomes political, coercive, unhealthy, artificial, and destructive when the family breaks down. The only real alternative to healthy families is not a libertarian utopia but a bloated, intrusive state.

Firsthand Experience

One of us (James) experienced just this as a child. When I was nine years old, my mother married a man twenty years older who could neither read nor write and was living on Social Security. At this tender age, I was taken into custody by detention officers after someone reported that I didn't have enough to eat. At the time, we were living in a two-room house on the banks of a dirty part of the Colorado River in Austin, Texas. We had no street address. Our home was less than modest. We were truly poor, but I was not malnourished.

At the detention center, I was put in a room with bars on the window. It was terrifying. Miraculously, I was released in a matter of days because a pastor and his wife, who had been my foster parents during the first five years of my life, traveled from Houston to Austin to get me released. (My mother didn't have a phone in her house, so they were unable to contact her.) They met with the authorities and assured them they would stock our cabinets with food. They also left money for my care. At the time, I did not know they had done this. For some reason, they were not allowed to visit with me. They told me years later that they had watched me from a window of the administration building.

It's hard to describe the traumatic effect this experience had on me. I shudder to think what would have happened if I had spent weeks or months at the detention center. No doubt the authorities meant well, but a government bureaucrat is a poor substitute for a loving parent.[19]

Socialists Don't Like Families

If you don't believe that the family is a bulwark against big government, just ask a socialist. Did you know that one of the main goals of the founders of modern socialism was to destroy the family? As soon as they took power in a violent revolution in 1917, the Bolsheviks began liberalizing Russian divorce laws. When the socialists took power in Spain in 2005, they did the same thing. Socialists want an all-powerful state that molds every individual into a new human being, the "socialist man." To do that, they need to get everyone as early as possible, while they are still impressionable. The socialist would much prefer a mass of isolated individuals all dependent on the state from the beginning, rather than having to work through a complicated thicket of family ties. Socialist states don't like other sources of authority that limit their power.

Frederick Engels, Karl Marx's coauthor, thought monogamy was capitalism's partner in crime in oppressing women. He argued that the socialist vision required the destruction of "private property, religion and this present form of marriage."[20] Feminists such as Betty Friedan, author of *The Feminine Mystique*, attack marriage as part of their broader attack on capitalism.[21] Many who practice family law in the United States would like nothing more than to see the legal status of families dissolve.

These facts alone should give libertarians pause and also explain why leftists aided and abetted the sexual revolution from the very beginning: The sexual revolution alone, if left unchecked, would swell the government without the need for a violent revolution. The sexual revolution has led our culture to separate not just sex and marriage, but sex and childbirth. Bearing children is no longer seen as an obligation and a blessing; it is now treated as a costly lifestyle choice.

As divorce laws became more and more liberal in the 1960s, and divorce more and more common, the federal government instituted massive "Great Society" welfare programs. These weren't part of a grand socialist scheme to destroy the family. Lyndon Johnson, the president at the time, saw these programs as a "War on Poverty." However, rather than reducing childhood poverty, the programs had the unintended effect of encouraging out-of-wedlock births and generational cycles of poverty. "When the federal government's War on Poverty began in 1964, only 6.3 percent of children in the U.S. were born out of wedlock....By 2008, four out of 10 births occurred outside of marriage."[22]

The trends alone have practically destroyed the black family in many urban areas—more than seven in ten black children are born out of wedlock[23]—and done serious damage to families everywhere. It's especially devastating for the poor. The sexual revolution and the Welfare State have conspired to create a vicious cycle in which family breakdown leads to a bigger, more meddlesome government, which leads to even more family breakdown.

Marriage, children, and divorce also shape people's political views. Single women tend to support bigger government and higher taxes than married women. And divorced women with children are much more likely to vote for progressive tickets than married mothers of children. "Generally, as divorce rates have increased, women voters have become more liberal."[24] Adults in intact families are more likely to support small government policies than their single and divorced counterparts.

The sexual revolution, then, isn't a private "social issue" that can be fenced off from other economic and political issues. By striking at the root of society's foundational institution, the family, it could end up destroying the free society itself.[25]

What Should We Do?

In 1996, then First Lady Hillary Clinton wrote, *It Takes a Village to Raise a Child*. The book title was taken from an African proverb, but "village" was a code word for government, since no one would title a book *It Takes a Big Bloated Federal Bureaucracy to Raise a Child*. Senator Rick Santorum answered with another book, *It Takes A Family*, which put the emphasis where it belonged.

Politicians on the left and right try to connect every policy to "the children." And those who are interested in bigger government appeal to the welfare of children to defend any and every policy that would grow the size of government. We're told we must increase spending on missile defense, education, food stamps, housing subsidies, health care, and high-speed rail to help "the children." We fall for it because we *are* concerned about children. But if we're really concerned, we have to think past the rhetoric to the reality of the policies. The word "children" or "family" in a congressional act doesn't mean it will actually help children or strengthen the family. To know what any policy will do, we have to apprehend the incentives it creates. If a policy creates an incentive for biological mothers and fathers not to marry, not to stay married, or not to stay in the home with their children, then we can safely say that policy will *not* be "good for the children," however well intended the policy may be. It will not only be bad for children; it will also grow the government and erode our freedom.

We can fix such programs, but only with political leaders committed to doing so. For instance, the Welfare Reform Act of 1996, signed by President Clinton after Republicans took control of both the House and the Senate, reformed some programs that had encouraged childhood poverty. Before the reform, Aid to Families with Dependent Children (AFDC) provided states with more funds if they got more caseloads, but cut them if the state's caseload fell. That is, the program *encouraged* states to grow their welfare rolls. AFDC was replaced with a program that gave states block grants, and allowed them to keep any money they saved. In this and other ways, the Welfare Reform Act created an incentive for states to reduce their welfare rolls.

At the time, opponents accused supporters of hating poor people and predicted that millions of poor mothers and children would end up on the streets. Instead, welfare caseloads were cut in half over the next ten years. "As the welfare caseloads fell, the employment of single mothers surged upward, and 1.6 million fewer children were living in poverty."[26] Many of the benefits of the Welfare Reform Act have been chiseled away in the last several years, but we know that incentives matter and good intentions don't magically create good results.

Part of the Problem, or Part of the Solution?

Unfortunately, many lack discernment in this area because they've taken their cues from forces in our culture that are hostile to the family. Divorce rates are only slightly better for *professing* Christians than for the general population. Our views on childbirth aren't much different, either. For instance, did you know that prior to the 1930s, *all* Christians believed that not just sex and marriage, but sex and childbearing ought to go together? While few thought that they had to have as many children as possible, historically all Christians took God's commandment to be fruitful and multiply literally.

This has radically changed, and yet few Christians ever give it much thought. You can see the effects in fertility rates. The "total fertility rate" refers to the average number of children born to a woman in her lifetime. Just to maintain a population, a country needs a fertility rate of 2.1. In 1800, the fertility rate in the United States was 7.04 for whites and 7.9 for blacks (statistics were kept separately). Except for a brief uptick after World War II, called the Baby Boom, America's fertility rate has been dropping since the Founding. It dropped by half from 1960 to 1980, and today, the fertility rate in the United States is 2.06. This is better than most other advanced nations, but it's only as high as it is because we have high rates of Hispanic immigration, and Hispanics have a slightly higher fertility rate than non-Hispanic whites. Among non-Hispanic whites, the fertility rate is 1.77.[27]

Economic and technological factors explain some of this drop in fertility rates. There was a time when about two out of ten infants died shortly after birth, so the fertility rates were not indicative of population growth. Now, only a handful of infants die for every thousand births. Also, in the past, most people lived on farms, so parents needed children to feed the chickens, milk the cows, and pick the cotton. These days, the barriers even to modest child labor are high,[28] and less than 3 percent of us live on farms, so over 97 percent of the population doesn't value young farm labor.

Finally, we now have government retirement programs, so people don't need to have children to care for them in their old age. (Ironically, as we've already seen, a lack of young workers will kill government retirement plans such as Social Security in their current form, which need workers to pay into the system to support current retirees.)

So the practical perks of having children have disappeared, while the costs—fancy day care, braces, ballet lessons, college education—have skyrocketed. There's much less economic incentive to have children, so we're having fewer and fewer of them.

The changing view of childbearing goes far beyond US borders. For decades, "world opinion" was shaped by the belief that we were running out of food and needed to reduce the world's population to survive. As recently as 1979, the worldwide fertility rate was 6.0. We still hear a lot about overpopulation, but now the worldwide fertility rate is 2.6 and dropping.[29] Even the UN predicts that while world population will go up until 2050—because developing countries are still growing—it will then level off and start dropping. This worldwide trend camouflages the trends in developed countries, most of which are already committing what some call "demographic suicide." Japan, for instance, has a fertility rate of 1.2. Soon, the Japanese population will start dropping and aging at the same time. The same thing is happening in many European countries such as Spain, Italy, and Russia. Many demographers think it is impossible to recover from such low fertility rates. Time will tell.

It's easy to blame this on snooty secularists who pass laws that discourage having children, but let's be honest. In general, Christians have been part of the antifertility trend. God didn't send a new revelation in the last hundred years telling us to stop being fruitful and multiplying and start being unfruitful and dividing, shrinking the population of Christian families from one generation to the next. The truth is, many have had their attitudes about family shaped by a competing worldview.

We say "many" because not everyone has surrendered on this issue. Statistically, religious people still have more children than nonreligious people, and the more devout (Catholic, Protestant, Mormon, and Jewish) tend to have more kids than do the lukewarm. (And they also have fewer of their children out of wedlock.[30]) Statisticians suspect that a strong religious faith may be the biggest motivation for people to have children.[31]

Childbirth is the ultimate act of hope in the future. If you're married, have faith and hope, and think of children as a duty and a blessing, then you'll probably have kids. If you're pessimistic and view human beings as parasites on the planet, wasteful carbon footprints, or a drag on your hip lifestyle, you might even think it's your duty *not* to have children, to abort the ones you would otherwise have, or at the least to have no more than one. Take a walk through some secular urban areas of Manhattan, San Francisco, and Seattle. You'll notice lots of dogs on leashes but not many babies in strollers. Some 41 percent of babies are aborted in New York City.[32]

Restoring the Culture One Baby at a Time

If conservative Christians have more children (on average) than the nominally religious and the secularists, and those children tend to retain the views of their parents, then, over time, there will be far more Christians and far fewer secularists, as a percentage of the population.[33]

Some atheists are worried. "It is a great irony but evolution appears to discriminate against atheists and favour those with religious beliefs," said researcher Michael Blume, of the University of Jena in Germany. "Most societies or communities that have espoused atheistic beliefs have not survived more than a century."[34]

Having children and raising them up in the way they should go has always been one of our most profound ways to affect the world. It is in pro-creating that we come closest to participating in God's creativity. The biblical text that says we are created in God's image also contains God's first commandment, which is also a blessing: "Be fruitful and multiply." We live at a moment when the most influential voices in our world discourage childbearing. And they follow their own advice. So in the long run, having a large family and passing on your faith and pro-family ideas to your children may be one of the most significant ways to renew our culture.

CHAPTER 10

Train Up a Child in the Way He Should Go

The philosophy of the school room in one generation will be the philosophy of the government in the next.

—Abraham Lincoln

The chief way most of us contribute to the future of society is by having children. If our children are to be part of the solution, however, we have to do what we can to prevent them from becoming part of the problem.

Proverbs says, "Train up a child in the way he should go, and when he is old he will not depart from it" (Proverbs 22:6). The proverb offers us a rule of thumb rather than an ironclad law. Even the best-raised children can go astray. We all know faithful parents who raised their children in the faith, but as soon as their kids left home, or even before, they abandoned it. According to a 2006 study by the Barna Group, six in ten twenty-somethings who were active in a church as teenagers drift off in early adulthood.[1]

Since God gives children free will, parents can't guarantee what they will decide once they leave the nest. But the proverb suggests that there's a heck of lot we can do when children are young to increase the odds of securing their most valuable inheritance. Much of that has to do with education.

The main burden of education should fall, first, to parents and families, and then to their voluntary communities. There's nothing in the Constitution about the government administering education, and there's no natural reason that it should fall under the state or federal government's jurisdiction. Over the years, however, education has become more and more a governmental function, so much so that we refer to government schools as "public schools." Our hope is that we will soon see true freedom in education. For that to happen, the government's direct control over education must diminish and the private sector must be free to let a thousand flowers bloom.

The End of Education

A proper education will impart factual knowledge: multiplication tables; the periodic table of the elements; 1066 and the Norman Conquest; 1492, when Columbus sailed the ocean blue; πr^2; Huckleberry Finn; and Julius Caesar. And it will teach kids how to think properly. A well-educated child understands that if it's raining, the street should be wet. Just because the street is wet, however, doesn't mean it's raining.

Still, the purpose of education has always been twofold: to teach and to enculturate. Education should guide children to the Good, the True, and the Beautiful. It should enlarge their minds and their souls. It should provide them not only with knowledge, but with wisdom and virtue. It should help them find not just their calling, but their purpose.

Unfortunately, secularism, relativism, cultural decay, a government near-monopoly over education, and educational theories that divorce socialization from the pursuit of truth have conspired to make a mess of American primary and secondary education. Some are skeptical that anything can be done. R. V. Young, for instance, argues, "We cannot 'reform' our system of education because it is not at all a system of education in the original, root sense but instead a curious and uneven amalgam of job training, indoctrination, and custodial care."[2]

We're less pessimistic. Education reform has broad, bipartisan support. The best single way to improve education is to create real competition. Reformers in both parties know the main impediments to reform: teachers' unions and apathy. These may seem like immovable objects, but an irresistible force is coming that will change education, by choice or necessity.

The Root Cause

To understand our current plight, though, we need to know how we got here in the first place. In 1837, Horace Mann instituted state-sponsored schools in Boston, taking his cues from the Prussian military model that influenced progressivism. Mann, more than anyone else, set our country on the course of turning public education into bureaucratic, government-sponsored, and government-controlled education.[3]

Most conservatives have also heard of the unwholesome influence of the early twentieth-century thinker John Dewey, who helped infuse American public education with his pragmatic philosophy through the Teachers College at Columbia University. Dewey dismissed the concept of truth along with old-fashioned questions like, "What is true?" He insisted, instead, that students ask, "Does it work?" or, "Does it work for me?"[4] Public schools, for Dewey, were not about imparting truth but making practical citizens.

Our problems with public education didn't start with Mann or Dewey, however; they started with enmity among Christians. In the early American colonies, education was an overwhelmingly Christian affair. Most of the early colonies had established religions (that is, Christian denominations), and education reflected that. In response to immigration in the early 1800s, though, legislators in New York and elsewhere grew worried about the type of education that students were receiving in their states. Illiteracy wasn't the problem. In New York, 93 percent of school-age students were already attending private schools. But with waves of immigration from Ireland, Italy, and Germany, many worried about Catholic kids going to Catholic schools and becoming criminals or secret agents of the Pope. Lawmakers reasoned that if "Protestant schools could be made less expensive through government subsidies...some Catholics would transfer their children there."[5]

In the 1850s, there was even a semisecret, anti-Catholic organization called the "Know-Nothings" (because they would say "I know nothing" if asked about their activities). The Know-Nothings pushed anti-Catholic policies such as requiring public school teachers to be Protestant and requiring Bible readings only from the Protestant Bible.[6] This, of course, encouraged Catholics to set up more Catholic schools.

At the same time, the various and sundry Protestant schools that enjoyed government subsidies competed with each other to attract Catholic students. The effect was to water down their religious instruction, instruction that would have seemed Protestant and, therefore, threatening to Catholic immigrants. (By this time, education for children between certain ages was more or less compulsory.) In response, lawmakers started limiting subsidies only "to the approved Protestant school nearest to a student's home," to prevent competition between them. The precedent of government control and geographical restrictions on schools had been set.

Here's what happened next, according to economist John Lott, Jr., an expert in the history of American education:

> As government programs tend to do, over time the subsidy scheme grew until it began eliciting complaints that the subsidized schools were getting most of their money from the government while being protected from competition. With the Free Schools Act of 1867, the state simply took over the subsidized schools, which then became public institutions.[7]

In other words, our problems with education started with Christian discord. We'll never know what would have happened if Christians had made common cause against the forces of statism and secularism that were already quietly gathering strength, rather than using the power of the state as a weapon against each other.

You know the rest of the story. As time has passed, government education has become more secularized and more centralized. The high point of this trend was probably 1980, when the National Education Association badgered President Jimmy Carter into elevating the Department of Education to Cabinet-level status, a lobbying campaign it started in 1867!

We won't spill a lot of ink on the moral and cultural rot of so many public schools. Christians have been complaining about it for decades. Over the years, Supreme Court justices have decided, suddenly, inexplicably, that prayer, talk about God, even a hint that there might be some purpose to the universe or human life, violate the First Amendment. Of course, education is still supposed to inculcate virtue. So moral training is reduced to lessons on how to get informed consent before performing a sex act—followed by a demonstration of how to perform the sex act "safely."[8] Vices are transformed, *via* consent, into virtues.

Most secular elites are still interested in academics but not soulcraft. In 2011, "Tiger Mom" Amy Chua, a professor at Yale Law School, ignited a firestorm by writing in *The Wall Street Journal* that Chinese moms are superior to Western moms because Chinese moms push their kids much harder academically.[9] In a book and follow-up pieces, she described ways to reshape US education.[10] She wrote passionately, if provocatively, about academic achievement, which America must have if we are to grow our "human capital." In the United States, poverty and poor education go hand in hand. According to a recent study, "census data show that if all Americans finished high school, worked full time at whatever job they then qualified for with their education, and married at the same rate as Americans had married in 1970, the poverty rate would be cut by around 70 percent."[11] Notice the part about stable marriage. Much of what Amy Chua said rang true. It also rang incomplete. She focused on academics, but said nothing about the spiritual dimension. True, life-changing education doesn't leave that out.

Freedom on the Fringes

Despite these problems, we should be thankful that the American educational system has never been completely centralized. Local school districts and states still mostly run the show, so many government schools don't resemble the little Prussian factories of secularist indoctrination that you might expect if you just read about Mann and Dewey. There are many good, hardworking teachers, and still many good public schools. They are good in spite of the system, not because of it.

All taxpayers have to pay for the system, and freedom has been drastically limited at certain times in certain states, but today, most parents can send their children to a private school, or they can homeschool them—*if they can afford it*. What drives people away from the public schools? Christians and other people of faith tend to be worried about the moral rot; upper-middle-class achievers are disappointed in the academic quality of the public schools in their area. These concerns create demand, which is met by thousands of good private schools around the country. There are also about a million and a half homeschooled students. Compare that to nice tolerant countries such as Sweden, where you can go to prison for homeschooling your kids.[12]

The freedoms to privately educate and homeschool were hard won, though, and things could have turned out differently. Oregon's 1922 "Compulsory Education Act" would have forced all students to attend a *government* school; but the US Supreme Court struck it down in 1925. In their decision, the Court said, "The child is not the mere creature of the state; those who nurture him and direct his destiny have the right, coupled with the high duty, to recognize and prepare him for additional obligations."[13] The Act, incidentally, was sponsored by the Masons, the Ku Klux Klan, and the state's Democratic governor to prevent Catholics from sending their children to Catholic schools.

In recent years, through the tireless efforts of parents and organizations such as the Home School Legal Defense Association, parents who can afford it—whatever their faith—have lots of options. If we want all parents, regardless of income, to enjoy freedom and justice in educating their children, then we still have a long, hard slog ahead of us.

We Must Have Choice

In the stirring documentary *Waiting for "Superman,"*[14] director Davis Guggenheim follows the plight of several kids, most in failing inner-city schools, who seek to get into charter schools. Anthony is a black boy being raised by his grandma in Washington, DC, trying to get into a SEED school. Daisy, a young Hispanic girl in Los Angeles, hopes to get into a KIPP school. Francisco, from the Bronx, and Bianca, from Harlem, are trying to get into Harlem Success Academy. Emily, a white high school student in an upper-middle-class district in California, is trying to get into Summit School. In the climax of the film, we watch these children and their families anxiously await the outcome of a lottery in a public auditorium. We won't spoil the ending, but if you haven't seen the film, you should.

Charter schools are public schools that aren't limited to one neighborhood. Students throughout the district can enroll there. They're usually better than the average school in their districts, though, and that creates a problem: Far more students want to attend these schools than the schools can accept. So interested students and their families are left to the caprice of a bingo cage.

As school reforms go, charter schools are among the most modest. They're still public schools connected to the school district and look, at least on the surface, like other public schools. But since they're subject to competition and expose the problems with the system, teachers' unions viciously oppose them. As a result, they're still not available to most students.

Imagine if we had a system like the public school system for cars and clothing. We all paid into a general fund managed by the government. The government then redistributed that money to a single car lot and clothing store in our individual neighborhoods, and forbade us from shopping in other neighborhoods! Not only would it be a grotesque violation of our freedom, the lack of competition would lead to cars and clothes that were shoddier and more expensive. There would be a revolution at the ballot box in the next election, forcing the politicians who thought up the scheme to find other employment.

When private businesses fail, they normally go bankrupt. When public schools fail, or commit fraud or gross negligence,[15] they often get more funding. Anyone who gives the issue five seconds' thought knows that choice and competition rather than restrictions and ever-increasing funding by taxpayers would drive down costs and improve education, both public and private.[16]

Those who believe in limited government tolerate a government semimonopoly on something as personal as a child's education for two reasons: teachers' unions and public apathy fueled by what we might call the *things are different in my district* syndrome.

The teachers' unions—especially the two big ones, the National Education Association and the American Federation of Teachers—are reactionary forces against reform. NEA and AFT together are the largest campaign contributors in the country. More than 90 percent of that money goes to Democrats in national elections. (They manage to cow many Republican politicians, too.)[17] Some brave Democratic politicians resist; but for the most part the Democratic Party is, in the words of liberal *Newsweek* writer Jonathan Alter, "a wholly owned subsidiary of teachers unions."

Unions are not to blame for all our country's education problems. We admire the hard work of so many public school teachers, including Christian ones; but we agree with Alter, who says, "Teachers unions are generally a menace and an impediment to reform."[18]

These unions have made it nearly impossible to fire terrible teachers. Most teachers achieve tenure almost instantly, which means that only one teacher in 2,500 loses his teaching credentials. A district is almost always better off paying a teacher to do nothing rather than suffering an expensive, drawn-out legal battle with a union.

Compensation for public school teachers resembles a socialist state, in which performance bears little or no relation to salary. And since public schools enjoy a semimonopoly with almost exclusive claim to tax money for education, the quality of their service has little to do with cost. In real dollars, we've doubled the average amount of money we spend on primary and secondary public education since 1970—it's now around $11,000 per student per year[19]—but student achievement has "flatlined."[20] It's either stayed the same or gotten worse, depending on the school and the district. In Washington, DC, one of the most abysmal systems with a US address, the average cost per student is almost $25,000! That's about what it costs for a student at the prestigious private Sidwell Friends School, where Malia and Sasha Obama attend. The average private school in DC costs about $15,000 a year.[21]

Teachers' unions aren't all-powerful, and we understand that the near total destruction of the family among urban minorities feeds the problem and the costs. If a child has never met his father, has a mostly absentee mother working full-time, and is surrounded by all manner of crime and social pathology, he's fighting an uphill battle. We can't expect teachers to be miracle workers. Parental involvement is crucial. But the very same children often *improve* dramatically when moved to better schools.[22] So the schools *are* part of a vicious cultural cycle.

What do you think would happen to the education of DC public school kids if the District just gave a $15,000 voucher to the parents or legal guardians of every child in the system, and required them to spend it on their child at the school of their choice? We won't answer that, since it's so painfully obvious.

The Real Victims

The other reason this creaky, unjust system hasn't already been replaced is that millions of Americans in the middle and upper classes don't feel the urgency of the problem. Parents in nice neighborhoods can challenge their public schools. If they don't see improvement, they can move to a different district or remove their kids from the system. That freedom functions as a release valve. These parents don't suffer enough from the system to fix it.

Children at every level in the public school system can suffer in some way. But the people most likely to suffer under the current regime are the poor, especially minorities, in urban areas, who have neither the money nor the political clout to challenge the system. As a result, they languish in failing schools, where they become victims of every silly educational fad and social dysfunction. This is grossly unjust. Those who have options have got to muster the courage to make educational choice a priority, not just for ourselves, but for those who need it the most.

Our Education "System": It Will Not All Die, but It Will Be Transformed

The way we do K–12 education is not much different from how it was done a century ago: a large class of students about the same age with a teacher at the front of the classroom, equipped with a white- or blackboard, textbooks for separate subjects, in a school building or complex with other students segregated by other grades/age groups. Almost everyone reading this book had this type of education. Most of us were in public, that is, government schools. Some of us attended private schools organized in the same way, and a few of us were homeschooled.

For those who had miserable public school experiences filled with bullies and classes poorly matched to their skill level, it's easy to imagine other ways to educate children. But for many of us, our public school experience wasn't all that bad, and it's easy to attach nostalgic feelings to it. We remember the smell of that red kick ball, the spelling bee where we got stuck with the word "gnarl," those high school football games in October as the days grew shorter, the cute boy or girl who unexpectedly gave us the time of day, the prom date that came together at the last minute, the friends we met in band or choir.

As nice as all of this is, you can educate and be educated, socialize and be socialized, without any of it, certainly without having it bundled together and delivered by an arm of the government. Our education delivery system is obsolete. As education policy experts Fred Hess, Olivia Meeks, and Bruno Manno put it, "Twenty-first-century reformers have inherited a model of K–12 public education that dates from the early-twentieth-century progressive movement and was borne of an era marked by lurching, bureaucratic, black-box provisions."[23] It makes no more sense in the twenty-first century than do big radios the size of refrigerators.

School choice reforms have been picking up steam—from educational savings accounts in Arizona and a voucher program in Colorado to new or expanded tax credit plans in Georgia, Indiana, Iowa, and elsewhere.[24] Unfortunately, these reforms help only a tiny fraction of the public school students nationwide. Most places are still struggling to get "school choice." Even getting access to public charter schools is a challenge. What all parents of school-age children need are flexible vouchers, or something like vouchers. These will turn the people most interested in and responsible for their children into free, discerning, involved consumers, rather than passive victims of a lumbering bureaucracy.

Untying the Knot

To have real freedom, and real progress, we really need to go beyond school choice to *educational choice*, where we unbundle the parts of education. Math, basketball, band, science, and history don't all have to be taught in the same way, at the same place, or at the same pace, to groups of kids about the same age. We do these things because of an economy of scale, but there are far better ways to teach a human being.

In the near future, millions and millions of Americans will be opting for something either slightly or radically different from what we have now. For at least four reasons, education will be far more customized: (1) the current system is not nearly as good as it should be—and it's *much* worse than it should be for the cost, (2) the demand for change is growing, (3) entrepreneurs will find ways to meet that demand, and (4) new technology will make it possible, if not inevitable.

Although we spend more on average per student than any country in the world,[25] US public schools consistently rank around thirteenth on tests that combine reading, math, and science.[26] When the competition is limited to math and/or science, the United States drops to around twenty-fourth.[27]

For years, polls have shown that most Americans across the political spectrum support "school choice."[28] But it's not a high priority for the middle and upper classes, and most of the worst victims of the current system vote for politicians who oppose school choice. Moreover, when vouchers are put to statewide votes, voters tend to vote *against* them—falling for the monopolist arguments of the teachers' unions.[29]

The good news is that we're seeing a historic creation of new modes and sources of education, in part because of technology, in part because of entrepreneurs seeking to meet the pent-up demand of frustrated parents, reformers, and educators. We'd love to provide a lengthy guidebook to these new resources, but we'll have to be content with giving a few examples.

The Near Future

Schools have been offering distance-learning programs for years. But the advent of high-definition video, cheap video cameras, easy editing software, lightning-fast computers with cameras and microphones, and broadband access to most homes is as much a game changer for education as was Gutenberg's invention of the printing press—if not more so. These and related technologies will transform every form of education, from kindergarten to med school.

Rosetta Stone and Mango software have helped millions of people learn foreign languages using old-timey DVDs. Free courses and seminars from leading institutions such as Oxford University are proliferating at iTunes University and elsewhere.[30] You can download entire courses as video podcasts with slides, watch them on your computer, smartphone, or tablet computer. Savvy Internet surfers are already bundling courses from different schools to create entire, if unofficial, degree programs, such as "How to Receive a Theological Education through iTunes U."[31]

Other free and paid courses are offered through live streaming video. In fall 2011, Stanford University professors Sebastian Thrun and Peter Norvig taught "Introduction to Artificial Intelligence (AI)" to a class at Stanford, but they also made the class available online as an experiment in online education. Now you could have paid to take a course like this from some guy at your local community college. *Or* you could get it free (plus the cost of the textbook) in your living room from Thrun and Norvig. Thrun is a Google Fellow, a member of the National Academy of Engineers and the German Academy of Sciences. Norvig is director of research at Google Inc., a Fellow of the American Association for Artificial Intelligence and the Association for Computing Machinery. You don't have to be a rocket scientist, or an AI expert, to guess how that experiment turned out. The online course lacked a mechanism for online students to get credit and a credential—though they did take an online test and evaluation and could compare their progress to other online students. Still, over 150,000 students registered for it.[32]

These examples are technical tweaks on older ways of doing education. But technology provides a way for clever entrepreneurs to break the mold entirely.

Salman Khan was born in New Orleans to a Bengali family. His father emigrated from Bangladesh, his mother from India. He was valedictorian of his high school and has a BS in mathematics, a BS in electrical engineering and computer science, and an MS in electrical engineering and computer science, all from MIT. He also holds an MBA from Harvard Business School. Until 2009, he was a hedge fund analyst in Boston.

Several years earlier, he was tutoring his younger cousin Nadia back in Louisiana and decided to put up some videos on YouTube for her to watch. His videos are pretty simple. The student sees a computer screen or virtual blackboard with a cursor or a colored marker moving around the screen, accompanied by Khan's voice explaining what's going on. It might be a map, a complicated equation, or a picture of a galaxy. Khan's is not the voice of a computer nerd. He's engaging, energetic, sympathetic.

When Khan put the first videos up, his cousin informed him that she preferred him "on YouTube rather than in person."[33] It wasn't an insult. With the videos, she could pause her cousin Sal, or play his explanation over and over until she figured out what he was saying. She could get her tutorials when it was most convenient for her, and she knew he would never get annoyed.

Without any marketing, people started stumbling onto his math videos and sending him e-mails. One, responding to one of his first calculus videos, wrote that it was "the first time I smiled doing a derivative."

This inspired Khan to start a not-for-profit organization, Khan Academy, to provide videos for "anything that can be taught in this format." That's the plan, anyway. As of this writing, this so-called

YouTube channel has more than twenty-four hundred lessons, plus an incentivizing "badge" system. Lessons run the gamut from addition and subtraction to vector calculus, biology, chemistry, astronomy, cosmology, development economics, physics, SAT prep, and on and on and on. All free! Good teachers around the world are already using these videos as lessons in their own classrooms. Bill Gates uses them to tutor his kids.[34] Under our public school system, Khan couldn't be a teacher, since he doesn't have a teaching certificate. But thanks to new technology and Khan's entrepreneurial streak, parents, students, and even other teachers can benefit from his obvious gifts.

We can't venture to guess how education will be transformed and improved with new technology and human genius. But we have hope that our current calcified system will either reform, or be reformed.

Bad Philosophy

Despite a costly "education bubble" that will pop at some point,[35] the United States has some of the most competitive and sought-after colleges and universities on the planet. Students can get a terrific education. At the same time, modern colleges and universities (including some Christian ones) are often unsanitary brothels of bad ideas that can poison minds and spirits. If people of faith want to restore our culture, however, we have to excel in academia.

Colleges and universities are overwhelmingly left-wing,[36] so you can expect your children to be exposed almost exclusively to the entire political spectrum from left to far left. They'll be told every which way that America and the free market are bad for the poor, bad for their health, and bad for the environment. They'll be told that faith and reason are at odds, and that the history of Western progress is a series of moves away from Christian superstition and prejudice. Ideas so absurd that only an intellectual could defend them—like Marxism—will be treated sympathetically.

The left-wing politics are easy to spot. The really awful ideas are not so much political as philosophical. In the sprawling zoo of bad ideas, the five-hundred-pound gorillas are *relativism* and *materialism*.[37] Sending your children off to college without thoroughly arming them against these simian behemoths is like pushing them into a jungle river filled with parasites and piranhas and expecting the experience to toughen them up. No one should be surprised if they get killed by an infection or eaten alive.

Relativism is the idea that our knowledge, religious beliefs, and moral judgments are just "social constructions" we've picked up from our parents or culture. They have no more claim to the truth—whatever that is—than do other, equally narrow beliefs of other cultures.

No one really believes relativism consistently (after all, relativism is itself a truth claim), but professors often use relativist mantras to get rid of the ideas that students arrive with, so that the professors can replace them with the ideas they favor. And they rarely hold up a big neon sign saying, HEY, GUYS, I DON'T BELIEVE IN TRUTH; I BELIEVE WE JUST MAKE IT UP AS WE GO!

Materialistic ideas, like microbes, are everywhere but mostly invisible. They are rarely defended or even discussed. This makes them all the more pernicious. But you can be almost certain that in a class on history, biblical studies, biology, or cosmology, materialism will be treated as the only reasonable belief for smart, sophisticated people of the twenty-first century.[38]

What Should We Do?

There's no unique type of education that fits every child and every family. We've made a variety of choices ourselves. Every parent's case is a bit different. Through prayer and counsel, seek out what works best for you; but don't rationalize and tell yourself that the *easiest* choice is the best one. All parents have the *same* responsibility, until our kids leave home—we must try to give them what they need to grow in character and faithfulness, a broad knowledge of the world that prepares them for adulthood, and a way for them to develop a marketable skill and find their vocation. Many people are on a tight budget and have limited options. That's why we need educational freedom.

If you have the means to homeschool, hire the best private tutors you can and customize a curriculum to fit your children's interests, strengths, and weaknesses, then be thankful. The emperor Alexander the Great had Aristotle as his private tutor! Not everyone is so lucky.

If you send your children to a public school, no matter how rigorous the academics, you *have* to supplement their education if you want them to see how God and their faith are relevant to all those subjects they studied in school. Help them connect the dots during the normal school years, and perhaps consider giving them a "thirteenth year" after they graduate from high school, where *you* devise a curriculum designed to help them prepare for life and for college. We'd suggest that they study critical thinking and logic, apologetics, Scripture, theology, some basic American history (if they don't know it), speed-reading, and some classic books they probably won't read in college. If they haven't developed spiritual disciplines—prayer, Scripture and devotion reading, spiritual direction—then focus on that. You might include some spiritual seminars and retreats in the mix. There are an amazing number of quality resources to help with all of these subjects. Finally, strongly encourage them to get plugged into a serious accountability group in college. Be nosy. Don't leave it to chance.

Inoculation, Inoculation, Inoculation

Whatever you do, you should avoid two extremes: quarantining your children on the one hand or overexposing them on the other. Instead, do your best to *inoculate* them against bad ideas and bad peers.

When doctors inoculate children, they give them a less dangerous form of a pathogen, such as a virus. Billions of children, for instance, have received the smallpox vaccine. They don't get the full-blown smallpox virus, but the much less virulent cowpox virus injected under their skin. This causes their immune system to kick in and build up a resistance to the virus. That resistance keeps them from contracting the much more deadly smallpox virus. The human race managed to (mostly) rid the world of smallpox in this way, and most of us were left with little more than a small scar on our arms.

Millions of parents, including Christians, expose their children to deadly ideas and influences for dozens of hours every week. They assume that an hour or two of church a week plus some short conversations at dinner should be enough to counteract thirty-five hours of TV per week,[39] another thirty-five hours of secular schooling—a place where God is "He who must not be named"—another few hours of Internet surfing, and several more hours breathing in the ambient secular culture, not to mention the often unwholesome influence of classmates and friends. Exposing your children to all this bilge defies common sense.

Maybe overexposure isn't much of a danger for your kids. Unfortunately, conservative Christian parents sometimes use the opposite approach: quarantine. Most of us know adults whose parents "protected" them from the world—or thought they did. Their parents home-schooled them or sent them to Christian schools, and in many cases, even sent them to a Christian college. These kids were told what they were supposed to believe, but never given good reasons to think these things were true. As a result, their "Christian" education didn't take. They read a book by an atheist such as Richard Dawkins or Stephen Hawking, or got to graduate school or seminary, and realized they had been given caricatures of what their parents called "worldly ideas." They were recruited by the very cultural forces that their parents tried to protect them from.

In some cases, the parents thought they were inoculating their kids; but they lacked discernment and taught things about science or history that fell apart when exposed to the evidence or intelligent objections. It was as if the parents opted for mysterious herbal remedies rather than a real smallpox vaccine. In other cases, the parents spent so much of their energy helping their kids see the flaws in other Christian traditions that they neglected to help them see the glories of Christian history and the debilitating intellectual weaknesses of secularism and atheism. The ranks of prominent atheists are filled, not just with people who were raised in liberal mainline denominations, but with people who were raised in sheltered homes as conservative Christians. They tend to be the angry ones. Some even lost their faith during their time at Christian colleges that cost their parents a hundred thousand dollars.

Inoculation means that we expose our children to the best and strongest ideas that the world has to offer, but expose them in a way, and in an environment, that allows them to build up intellectual immunity. We must acquaint them with the best arguments on all sides of an issue, and teach them to evaluate the arguments critically. That's easier said than done, of course, and we can't offer a complete kit of vaccines here. But we can give some examples (see the Notes for more).

I (Jay) know about overexposure not only from direct experience as a former college and graduate student, but also because I visit many state universities and private colleges every year. As a freshman at a formerly Methodist liberal arts college, I found myself awash in relativism, materialism, and Marxism. Marxist and socialist ideas took me years to shake off; but I got over the spell of relativism and materialism quickly because someone gave me the "C. S. Lewis six-pack." These are six little books, often bundled together as Signature Classics, by the great twentieth-century scholar and apologist: *Mere Christianity, The Screwtape Letters, A Grief Observed, The Problem of Pain, Miracles,* and *The Great Divorce.* There are thousands of good books in circulation, but Lewis's books have helped millions of people, including me. Don't let your children leave home until they've read them. And while you're at it, get them a copy of J. Budziszsewski's *How to Stay Christian in College*[40] and the DVD *Toughest Test in College.*[41]

There are now dozens of groups that deal with Christian apologetics—the reasoned defense of the faith. They have thousands of articles, interviews, and lectures available free online. We all have more high-quality information available at our fingertips (with a computer and an Internet connection) than anyone in history. Look in the Notes for some examples.[42]

Students in high school and college often encounter materialism in their science classes.[43] We have nothing to fear from scientific evidence. Unfortunately, since the nineteenth century, that evidence has been packaged with bad materialist philosophy, and lots of people, including many Christians, can't tell the good evidence from the bad philosophy. They assume that what "science says" (according to *Newsweek* or *The New York Times*) is the same thing as the evidence of science. It's not. Science doesn't *say anything*. Scientists and science writers say things, and sometimes what they say has more to do with their assumptions than the evidence. Informed citizens, and informed parents, must learn to tell the difference.

While materialistic glosses are present in physics and other scientific fields, the materialist's holy of holies is biology. Since 1859, Charles Darwin's theory of evolution has been used as a battering ram against the fortress of faith. Darwin sought to explain design not by chance alone but by a blind process of natural selection, which would preserve beneficial, random changes in a reproducing population. This process, Darwin argued, would make things look designed without a designer.

What is remarkable about Darwinism is how little evidence there is for it. Sure, natural selection and random mutations[44] can explain little tweaks, such as bacteria losing some feature, the loss of which helps them resist certain antibiotics (while never becoming anything but bacteria) and finch beaks getting thicker or thinner depending on the climate. The problem is, we don't need to know how bacteria lose features and finch beaks vary slightly. We need to know where bacteria, finch beaks, and finches themselves, came from. It's often said

Darwin's mechanism can explain the survival of the fittest, but can't explain the arrival of the fittest. It can't even explain the organs, cells, or proteins of the fittest.[45]

Unfortunately, bad counterarguments gather around this subject like lint on a ball of tape. Many Christian children, for instance, are taught that Darwin said life "just happened," or is purely the result of chance. That's not true. So you have to be discerning in what you teach your kids. You may not have the time to absorb the growing literature on this subject and teach it to your children; but at the very least make sure they have read *Darwin on Trial* by Phillip Johnson. If possible, have them study the textbook supplement *Explore Evolution* while taking biology.[46] Other good books include *The Edge of Evolution* by Michael Behe and *Icons of Evolution* by Jonathan Wells.

This is to say nothing of the positive evidence for intelligent design in cosmology, astronomy, origin of life studies, biology, and elsewhere. Some important books on design include *Darwin's Black Box* by Michael Behe, *Signature in the Cell* by Stephen Meyer, *The Design Revolution* by William Dembski, *A Meaningful World* by Benjamin Wiker and Jonathan Witt, *The Privileged Planet* by Guillermo Gonzalez and Jay Richards, and many others.[47]

Anyone who reads these books carefully and with an open mind will be immune to the simplistic arguments that other students find so compelling.

Not every challenge a student faces will deal directly with the big cosmic questions, of course; some, as we mentioned, involve politics and economics. Imagine an eighteen-year-old freshman named Karl at a Christian college. He finds himself in a history class where the professor tells him that the early Church was communist, that the free market is all about greed, where the rich get richer and the poor get poorer, that "capitalism" destroys the environment and is responsible for pretty much everything bad in the world. Since he's at a Christian college, his guard is down. He's never heard these things before. Maybe his dad is a banker, and his professor's arguments feed Karl's need to rebel against his dad. Maybe his dad wasn't the best Christian either, so this allows Karl to feel self-righteous, too.

If this is the first time he's heard these claims, what are the chances that he'll get out of the class intact? Not very high. Karl's in trouble.

On the other hand, what if his parents not only had been powerful role models, but had had him read and discuss *The Communist Manifesto* and work through a sixteen-week course such as *Economics in a Box*,[48] which combines solid, accessible economics with Christian theology? What if they had him attend, or watch online, seminars by think tanks such as the Acton Institute, the Discovery Institute, the Heritage Foundation, the Intercollegiate Studies Institute, or the Foundation for Economic Education? At the least, his parents would have decreased the odds that Karl would become an avid fan of Michael Moore or that other Karl who wrote *The Communist Manifesto*.

Preparing our children for the world isn't all about inoculating them from bad ideas, of course. Parents shouldn't isolate or indoctrinate their children, but they should inoculate and *insulate* them with personal attention, love, truth, wisdom, and virtue. We want to help our children become stout of mind, body, and spirit.[49]

CHAPTER 11

Culture Matters

Let me write the songs a nation sings, and I care not who writes the laws.

—Attributed to PLATO

Culture includes practically everything. But that doesn't help us get a handle on it. A simple way to understand culture is to think of it as one of three overlapping but distinct realms in society—the political, the economic, and the cultural. Politics, more than the other realms, involves or threatens coercion. The economic realm involves competition, cooperation, and exchange, and includes local, national, and international markets, banks, businesses, employers, and employees. The cultural realm includes pretty much everything else—church, family, *The New York Times*, the symphony, Teen Challenge, the Knights of Columbus, Bible Study Fellowship, the Boy Scouts, the Red Cross, LIFE Outreach International, Sarah Lawrence College and Biola University, Suzuki music programs, *The Simpsons*, *The Sopranos*, Montessori preschools, and on and on and on.

Talking about public and private realms, as we often do, just doesn't capture these contours of society and culture. The distinction is especially misleading because of how we now use the word *public*. The word used to refer to things that apply or are open to the community as a whole. But now, when we talk about public libraries, public roads, public utilities, and public schools, we're referring to *government-run entities*. We've lost the idea of a society that is larger than the state. Eminent political scientist James Q. Wilson observed, "Once politics was about only a few things; today, it is about nearly everything."[1]

This should trouble you if you believe in limited government. Politics is important; but it's not everything. It's not even the most important thing. Politics is a reflection of our culture.

Moral and cultural bodies such as churches and private charities are often called mediating institutions because they mediate between individuals and the government. They're vital for sustaining a free market economy and a limited government,[2] because they create a public sphere, often called civil society, that the state doesn't control. They keep our life from becoming all politics all the time.

Mediating institutions cultivate personal virtues and cultural values, without which a society cannot survive. The family is the most important mediating institution for instilling these qualities, but most families delegate some of their authority to schools, church groups, athletic teams, and so on. It is these institutions, plus family life, that socialize us, that teach us to be responsible. Without citizens who accept responsibility for their actions, liberty quickly descends into license.

Many mediating institutions serve purposes that would otherwise be handed over to the state. Think of charities that help the poor, the ill, the addicted, the disenfranchised, and the orphaned. Most Americans believe that we should help our less fortunate neighbors. That doesn't mean that the federal government should administer such help. On the contrary, if you can do something voluntarily, it should not be imposed coercively. And studies have shown that private charities are usually much more effective than their government-run alternatives.

Those committed to a limited government need to do more than talk about individual rights. We also must defend vibrant cultural institutions that shape who we are, instill in us a sense of virtue and responsibility, and help us fulfill Christ's mandate to help our neighbors.

How Do We Change the Culture?

While it's useful to distinguish the cultural sphere or civil society from the economy and politics, we shouldn't go to the opposite extreme and fail to see how related they are. Our ideas shape the culture, but the culture shapes our ideas. And culture doesn't just affect our politics. Our politics also affect our culture. If we forget this, we'll end up with a simplistic understanding of how to restore the culture.

"Transformed people," Charles Colson has said, "transform culture." Dozens of Christian organizations work to change the culture by changing people. Some of them, such as Campus Crusade for Christ and Catholics Come Home, focus on evangelism. This is all to the good. A few decades ago, though, many Evangelicals thought evangelism *alone* was the answer. If we could just get people to accept Jesus as their personal Savior, then we would heal our culture. But just because you become a Christian doesn't mean you influence others or have the slightest idea how to apply your faith to your job or your family life or the tax code or environmental policy or the fight against poverty. That's why many groups now work to help Christians think through and apply a Christian world-and-life view.

We've all heard the old chestnut that *ideas have consequences.*[3] We're in a culture war in which the clash is not over territory and the weapons are not bullets. The clash is over ideas. Anyone who studies history can see that ideas give rise to movements, policies, even civilizations. To make positive changes in culture, then, you have to make positive changes in people and their ideas.

We've suggested that believers fully committed to God, thinking clearly, applying their thinking correctly, and persuading others of their good ideas can make a difference in the world. Bill Bright, the late founder of Campus Crusade for Christ, said, "Spiritual revival is the key to changing America.... In my opinion, the only way to change the world is to change individuals." Mother Teresa said, "People ask me: 'What will convert America and save the world?' My answer is prayer." And Pope John Paul II said that "if man allows himself to be prompted by God, if he walks together with Him, he is capable of changing the world."[4]

Standing athwart this great cloud of witnesses is Christian sociologist James Davison Hunter. In his recent book *To Change the World*, he criticizes the idea that "changing hearts and minds will change culture." "This account [of how to change the culture]," he says, "is almost wholly mistaken."[5] He argues that even if we experienced a third great awakening, in which half of the American population was "converted to a deep Christian faith," we would still probably not make a dent in the culture.

Hunter doesn't oppose evangelism, spiritual renewal, worldview training, or applying faith to politics. He just thinks we don't understand cultures and how they really change. "Only indirectly do evangelism, politics, and social reform affect language, symbol, narrative, myth, and the institutions of formation that change the DNA of a civilization."[6] According to Hunter, the main drivers of cultures, both now and in the past, have been elites—cultural gatekeepers—and the overlapping networks that they lead.

We find Hunter's argument unpleasant. Since all men are created equal, we want to believe that everyone can have some influence on the culture; but like it or not, culture is disproportionately influenced by a small number of "elite" individuals and institutions.

History, including Christian history, confirms this truth. God used Moses, who was raised in Pharaoh's household, to deliver the Jews from slavery in Egypt. Jesus had a motley group of disciples, and some, such as Peter, had profound influence. But Jesus chose Paul to proclaim the gospel to the Gentiles. Paul was a Roman citizen with a strong grasp of Greek and a wide-ranging education, who was taught by the revered Jewish rabbi Gamaliel.

The Church Fathers and the leaders of the Protestant Reformation, the American Founders, and the Abolitionists were well-educated, well-connected leaders. While many ordinary people supported abolition, the game changers were men such as William Wilberforce and his network of other abolitionists. God can and does use ordinary people, but God often chooses to work through elites.

Secular Elites

Networks of *secular* elites now dominate large parts of our culture, even though they're out of step with the public. As we've said previously, most Americans think that most abortions should be illegal. As a result, prior to 1973, most states had laws prohibiting most abortions. Yet seven justices of the US Supreme Court declared such laws unconstitutional, so now we have some of the most permissive abortion laws in the world.

Most Americans go to church, but few movies or TV sitcoms reflect this. The vast majority of Americans believe that God created the heavens and the earth, even if they differ on how they understand the details. But *all* of our public institutions (that is, government institutions)—elementary, middle, and high schools; universities; public museums; the National Science Foundation—maintain a strict allegiance to Darwinism and materialism, vigorously denying any role for a Creator. Even raising scientific criticisms of Darwinism is dangerous. If a scientist or a public school teacher suggests that there's evidence of design in nature (apart from any biblical issues), he'll soon find himself on the receiving end of a witch hunt.[7]

Most Americans are either moderate or conservative politically. But overwhelming majorities of faculty and administrators at universities are left-wing. Most Americans believe in God, but 95 percent of the members of the National Academy of Sciences are atheists.

A few years ago, the California Supreme Court proclaimed that people have a right to "marry" people of the same sex. Californians responded by voting in 2008 to amend the state constitution to preserve marriage as every civilization has understood it. *One* US district judge, Vaughn Walker, overturned the vote, and later disclosed that he had been in a same-sex relationship for the previous ten years.[8] Now the status of marriage in California hangs in the balance pending opinions from higher courts.

The bitter reality is that 299,900,000 Americans might believe one thing—might have history, reason, and revelation on their side—but the 100,000 with influence can set the cultural agenda. Worse, many ordinary Americans get their beliefs about the world from those elites, without even realizing it.

Hunter notes, "Under specific conditions and circumstances ideas can have consequences."[9] The ideas that really make a difference, that shape the culture, are the ideas held by elites and propagated by their networks and institutions. A culture is "about how societies define reality—what is good, bad, right, wrong, real, unreal, important, unimportant, and so on. This capacity is not evenly distributed in a society."[10] The most influential people and institutions are usually the ones with the highest symbolic status. They're in the cultural center, or at least close enough to the center to influence it.

For instance, a story in *The New York Times* has more influence than a story in the *Skagit Valley Herald*. A story in *The New York Times* probably even has more influence than a blog post that goes viral and gets twice as many reads, since the *Times* story is read by more influential people. A degree from Yale opens more doors than a degree from the University of Minnesota Morris. *The New York Times* and Yale are in the cultural center. The local paper and the obscure state university are on the periphery.

Over the last few generations, conservative Christians and our ideas have moved, or been moved, farther and farther from the cultural center, and more and more toward the periphery. We've been marginalized. Sure, there are Christians teaching at Princeton, Yale, and Harvard. There are Christians writing screenplays in big Hollywood studios and opinion pieces at *The New York Times*. There are well-known Christian TV personalities and musicians, and Christians in key positions in the federal government. But they are in the minority, even the extreme minority.

The commanding heights of culture have changed. Just think of the contrasts: from Michelangelo to Mapplethorpe, Bach to the Beastie Boys, puritan Harvard to pagan Harvard, the Cathedral of Notre Dame to the modernist Cube marring the Paris skyline.[11] Wander into almost any art museum in any major city and look for a single piece of sacred art dated after, say, 1900. Unless you're in the Vatican Museum, you'll do a lot of searching.[12]

All of this raises a question. There are millions of Christians in the United States. How have we survived culturally? We've created subcultures and parallel institutions—Christian colleges, publishers, magazines, music labels, radio and TV networks, even art. Many institutions, including most private colleges, were founded by Christians—Harvard, Princeton, Yale, Georgetown, and many others. But most of these surrendered to secularism long ago. In fact, Yale was founded after Harvard went belly-up theologically. And Princeton was founded after Yale went belly-up.

Hundreds of formerly Christian institutions suffered from such mission creep, so conservative Christians had to start new institutions. Evangelicals started doing this in the nineteenth century—founding Biola, Calvin, Wheaton, Taylor, and many other colleges—to compete with mainline schools that had given up the ghost to liberalism. This has continued up to the present. Catholics have started doing the same thing more recently—with schools such as Christendom, Ave Maria, and Thomas Aquinas College.[13] These and many other institutions have helped sustain Christians, and have surely kept our country from becoming as secular as Europe; but their very existence shows that we've been pushed to the cultural margins. If conservative Christians still occupied the cultural center in large numbers, we wouldn't have needed to build new institutions.

The Major Networks

James Hunter stresses the influence not just of elites but of their overlapping networks. This is another painful reminder that Christians' failure to love one another as Christ has loved us has helped marginalize us. We don't even have one big alternative Christian network where we can pool our resources. We have all sorts of separate, nonoverlapping, and even hostile Christian institutions and networks. It hardly matters if 80 percent of the population is Christian if we're so riddled with divisions that we can't work together. Our divisions have allowed secularists to fill the leading cultural space. Ironically, they seem much more functionally unified and connected than believers are.[14] We're reminded of Joel's prophecy, which describes the judgment of consuming locusts working in unity. "They each march in line...do not deviate from their paths. They do not crowd each other; they march every one in his path. When they burst through the defenses, they do not break ranks" (Joel 2:7–8). People who value faith, family, and freedom need to come together in focused harmony if we are to restore the culture.

Sociologist Peter Berger once said that if India is the most religious country and Sweden the most secular, then the United States is a country of Indians ruled by Swedes. To stick with the metaphor, the United States' legal, moral, and artistic traditions are Indian, but those traditions have been largely translated into Swedish. Though Hindi and dozens of other Indian languages are still spoken, sung, and written in many homes and private settings, most public conversations take place in Swedish. There are a few cable stations that transmit in some or another Indian language, but all the major networks and news stations are Swedish, as are the major newspapers and magazines. The newer buildings, art museums, state-sponsored universities, and symphonies have a strongly Scandinavian feel. Even many private Indian colleges have had recent Swedish makeovers. The Swedes still depend on Indians for their jobs since they have elections, so they often hire translators well versed in the various Indian languages.

We won't make a dent in our current politics or culture without overcoming this Indian-Swede problem. But don't despair. Restoring a culture is not impossible; it just takes a lot of hands and a lot of concentrated, thoughtful work.[15] If cultures normally change through overlapping networks of elites, then we must influence these elites, penetrate their networks, and/or create networks that overlap or compete with them. That's the lesson of Hunter's argument. If we hope to influence our culture, believers have to be high achievers in many fields—business, academics, science, literature, technology, art, music, politics, journalism, publishing, and philanthropy.

We can't allow our Christian subcultures to be assimilated by a hostile culture or to become dilapidated ghettos isolated from the rest of the culture and from each other. We need to *create* our own culture, not just complain about popular culture or copy secular culture with a patina of Christianity thrown in for marketing purposes. To quote the overused phrase, we have to be fully in the world but not of it. Wise as serpents; innocent as doves (Matthew 10:16). Working together as allies, not fighting apart as rivals or enemies.

Weirdly, Hunter completely disavows this obvious lesson of his book. "The worst possible conclusion," he says, "is that what Christians need is a new strategy for achieving and holding on to power in the world—at least in the conventional sense."[16] Instead, he calls for Christians to take a break from politics and adopt a "postpolitical view of power" that he calls "faithful presence." "It is not likely to happen but it may be that the healthiest course of action for Christians, on this count, is to be silent for a season," he writes, "and learn how to enact their faith in public through acts of shalom rather than to try again to represent it publicly through law, policy, and political mobilization."[17]

This advice "to be silent for a season" is deeply misguided. Christians have been marginalized from large swaths of our culture; but politics is one of the *few* places (along with business and the military) where we still have some influence. The US Congress and US Supreme Court, despite their problems, represent the views of the American public and its Christian majority far more than practically any elite institution that is insulated from the electorate. If believers had stayed on the sidelines since 1980, do you think the Supreme Court would include Antonin Scalia, Clarence Thomas, John Roberts, and Samuel Alito, men who have consistently defended human life and constitutional limits? Probably not. We'd have nine justices who think there's no stable meaning in the Constitution and who feel free to discover new rights in the text that nullify the rights it guarantees. *If we followed Hunter's advice, we would marginalize ourselves even more. It amounts to preemptive surrender.*

Don't Fall for Mere God Talk

Besides, we have some effect on culture already. Or perhaps we should say that Christians could be having more effect, if we would think clearly and strategically, and not fall for the Christian camouflage worn by so many politicians. Consider this: Most elite institutions are overwhelmingly secular, while only 16 percent of the US population identifies itself as religiously unaffiliated, agnostic, or atheist. Yet not one member of the US Congress does so.[18] In fact, 97.5 percent of the members of Congress identify themselves as either Christian or Jewish. The House and the Senate are probably not more religious than the American population as a whole. Rather, politicians feel pressure to profess the form of faith even if not its substance. For example, Nancy Pelosi, a Catholic, staunchly defends abortion rights and same-sex marriage. This means we can't take politicians at their word when it comes to faith. We have to look closely at their policy choices—what they do in office—not what they profess or their photo op in front of a church with a big Bible in hand.[19]

That almost all politicians profess a Judeo-Christian faith shows that believers aren't marginalized politically. If we were, then many politicians probably wouldn't sound so religious, and Democratic activists wouldn't work so hard to persuade Americans that their party is friendly to faith.[20] Irreligious leftist billionaire George Soros, for instance, has donated hundreds of thousands of dollars to *Sojourners*, Jim Wallis's organization, and to the liberal National Council of Churches.[21] Clearly *he* thinks that his favored policies need Christian camouflage to be palatable to most Americans.

Despite our failure to transform the culture, therefore, we may have more effect in the political realm than elsewhere. But we need to exercise it more wisely.

Politics isn't everything, but it can play a powerful role in shaping culture. Think of North and South Korea. Both countries share the same language, history, ethnicity, and geography. South Korea is prosperous and free, and Christianity is now its largest religion. North Korea, in contrast, is oppressed, famine-ridden, and poor, with no freedom of religion. Less than 2 percent of the population claims to be Christian. The difference is politics. South Korea has representative government and a market economy. North Korea is controlled by one party—the communists.

We have emphasized the cultural power of elites, but in democratic societies, public policy is still influenced by public opinion. Some elites understand this, and will bend over backward to appeal to the common man. In 2011, Paul Krugman wrote a column called "The Unwisdom of Elites," panning his usual opponents—Bush tax cuts, the war in Iraq, and "deregulation" that supposedly led to the financial crisis.[22] Krugman took the side of "the man on the street" who suffered from these "elite" policies. Coming from Krugman, this is bizarre. The very liberal Krugman attended MIT and Yale, is a professor at Princeton University and the London School of Economics, a winner of the Nobel Prize in economics, and has a weekly column in *The New York Times*. About the only way he could get more chits on his elite scorecard would be to get elected Secretary General of the UN. And yet he still recognizes the rhetorical value of identifying with ordinary people and denouncing elites. Krugman certainly knows that public opinion matters.

Take the example we've already mentioned. Seven justices of the Supreme Court, or even five, can overturn well-established laws on matters such as abortion. This looks like a clear case where a tiny elite can single-handedly overrule the majority. But public opinion on abortion is notoriously muddled. Imagine, instead, if 85 percent of the population were staunchly pro-life, and voted accordingly. Over time, this would lead to a federal government that was overwhelmingly pro-life, with pro-choice congressmen relegated to a tiny caucus from a few pro-choice cities. Harvard and Yale law professors might be donating to Planned Parenthood and the National Abortions Rights Action League, but they would not be sitting on benches in federal courts.

Christ and Culture

In the 1950s, American theologian H. Richard Niebuhr wrote a famous book, *Christ and Culture*, in which he described the sundry ways Christian thinkers have related faith to culture.[23] He talked about the accommodating "Christ of culture" model, the separatist "Christ against culture" model, and a couple of others, before defending his favorite, "Christ transforming culture." But there is no pat answer to how Christianity relates to culture, because culture isn't one simple thing. Almost every culture will have something that Christians should affirm. We support the American commitment to human rights and equality, a limited government, rule of law, and economic freedom. But as our mainstream culture becomes more hostile to Christianity, Christians should become more countercultural, rejecting materialism, relativism, abortion, secularism, promiscuity, consumerism, pornography, and so on. Discernment consists in figuring out which parts of our culture to preserve and defend, and which parts to resist and defeat.

Interceding for Our Culture

Relating our faith to *American* culture is rewarding as well as complicated, since one of its roots is Christianity. In 1630, the Puritan preacher John Winthrop told the pilgrims of the Massachusetts Bay Colony that the world would look upon their experiment as a shining city upon a hill. Generations of Americans have seen our country as that shining city. We've seen our struggle for freedom as an example for other nations. At times, we have even imagined America as a New Israel, and expected God to deal with us as He dealt with ancient Israel. As God promised Israel in Deuteronomy 28, if we follow Him, we will be blessed. If we reject Him, we will be cursed.

God was behind the founding of our country and has blessed us for a special purpose. That doesn't mean His relationship with the United States is the same as it was with ancient Israel. God elected Israel from all the peoples of the earth to be a priesthood for all nations. He has now extended His covenant to the Church. As Paul says in Romans, the Church has been grafted into the tree of God's covenant (Romans 11:17). But nowhere are we told that God has dealt with any other nation in quite the same way as He dealt with Israel, or with the Church.

God doesn't follow a tidy formula in dealing with other nations and cities. Sometimes, He blesses them, or uses them despite their unbelief. The prophet Isaiah refers to Cyrus, the King of Persia, as God's servant, because Cyrus returned the Jews to the Promised Land after they had been exiled in Babylon. In other cases, God destroyed cities and empires because of their sin. Since God's ways are mysterious, we should be very careful about connecting the dots between tragedies such as 9/11 and God's judgment, or between our prosperity and God's blessing. As Jesus tells us, God sends His rain on both the just and the unjust (Matthew 5:45).

Despite the stereotype of a vengeful Old Testament God, the Lord shows a heart of forgiveness throughout Scripture. God's forgiveness even extended to Israel's enemies, such as Nineveh, the capital of ancient Assyria. It was the Assyrians who captured the northern tribes of Israel and dragged them into exile. And yet God commanded the prophet Jonah to go to Nineveh and "cry out against it" because of its wickedness. Jonah disobeyed God and tried to flee to Tarshish; but God compelled the prophet to go to Nineveh. When Jonah finally did preach in the city, the king put on sackcloth and ashes and called on his people to repent.

Jonah didn't like this one bit. "O Lord!" he complained. "Is this not what I said while I was still in my own country? That is why I fled to Tarshish at the beginning; for I knew that you are a gracious God and merciful, slow to anger, and abounding in steadfast love, and ready to relent from punishing" (Jonah 4:2). Apparently the repentance was short-lived, since the prophets Nahum and Zephaniah proclaimed God's punishment on Nineveh and Assyria for its sin. But the message is clear: Although God punishes evil, He also forgives the repentant. As He instructed Ezekiel to tell Israel, "I have no pleasure in the death of the wicked, but that the wicked turn from his way and live; turn back, turn back from your evil ways" (Ezekiel 33:11). He expects His people to name sin, but still to hold out the possibility of forgiveness.

One of the biggest surprises comes in the Old Testament book of Jeremiah. Jeremiah was a prophet in Jerusalem when it was sacked by the Babylonian emperor Nebuchadnezzar (around 589 BC). Jeremiah had the thankless job of telling the Israelites that this was God's judgment on them for turning away from Him. Worse, he had to tell them that they would have a long exile in Babylon. Rather than telling them to pray for a quick return to the Promised Land, Jeremiah said this:

> Thus says the LORD of hosts, the God of Israel, to all the exiles whom I have sent into exile from Jerusalem to Babylon: Build houses and live in them; plant gardens and eat their produce. Take wives and have sons and daughters; take wives for your sons, and give your daughters in marriage, that they may bear sons and daughters; multiply there, and do not decrease. But seek the welfare of the city where I have sent you into exile, and pray to the LORD on its behalf, for in its welfare you will find your welfare. (Jeremiah 29:4–7)

The Israelites' welfare is to be found in the welfare of Babylon? Surely that was a surprise!

Of course, we Christians aren't ancient Israelites. We haven't been told like Jonah to preach to the capital city of our enemy. And we're not exiles in a foreign land, though we are partly exiled from influential pockets of our culture.[24] Still, there's a lesson for us here: Christians should intercede for our country, even when it violates God's laws. We should follow the example of Abraham when he interceded for Sodom and Gomorrah,[25] and the Jews in Jeremiah's hearing who were commanded to pray for the city of Babylon. It's not our job to decide the time of God's judgment. Like the Jews in Babylon, we should plead for God's mercy on our country. We all have something to lose if God gives us what we deserve. As the old Russian proverb says, "God hurries not, but misses not." Let us hope and pray for God's patience and long-suffering for our country.

The Church is God's emissary to the world. Maybe our own lack of righteousness—our unwillingness to suffer and sacrifice and stand in the gap—is part of the problem. We should spend more time soul searching. If the United States, which has been richly infused with Christianity from the beginning, is on the highway to hell, what does that say about us Christians? It took centuries, but a tiny minority of persecuted Christians managed to transform the Roman Empire and world history. Why can't a majority of people of faith in the United States get things moving in a better direction?

Maybe God will deal with our nation in light of how the Church in its midst conducts itself. Whatever we do, we should never act like Jonah, withholding the offer of God's forgiveness because we want to see our "enemies" punished for their sins.

CHAPTER 12

Am I My Brother's Keeper?

Help one person at a time, and always start with the person nearest you.

—MOTHER TERESA

In the early chapters of Genesis, Cain and Abel—the first two sons of Adam and Eve—each present an offering to God. God approves of Abel's offering but rejects Cain's. Out of jealousy, Cain kills his brother. God, of course, knew what had happened to Abel, but rather than accusing Cain, the LORD asks, "Where is your brother Abel?" Cain replies, "I do not know; am I my brother's keeper?" (Genesis 4).

Cain's question never receives a direct answer from God. Instead, it hangs in the air and echoes inside our heads, so that we might ask it of ourselves: *Are* we responsible for our brothers, for our fellow human beings?

Most readers suspect the answer is "yes," and if they keep reading, that suspicion is confirmed. Throughout Scripture, God shows His care for the poor, orphans, and widows, and He expects His people to share His concern. The Psalms are filled with references to God as a deliverer of the needy and the oppressed. Alongside God's command to treat the poor justly, God commanded ancient Israel to make provisions to alleviate poverty. They were commanded to leave some grain in their fields after the harvest, so that poor sojourners might have something to eat. "And you shall not strip your vineyard bare, neither shall you gather the fallen grapes of your vineyard; you shall leave them for the poor and for the sojourner: I am the LORD your God" (Leviticus 19:10). Ruth, the great-grandmother of King David, was one widow who benefitted from these "gleanings."

God commanded the Jews not to be "hardhearted" or "tight-fisted" toward the poor (Deuteronomy 15:7), and Jesus extends that command. In His parable of the sheep and the goats, Jesus describes a time when the "Son of Man comes in His glory" (Matthew 25:35–40). The sheep are invited into God's rest while the goats...are not. The King (representing God) tells the sheep:

> "Come, you that are blessed by my Father, inherit the kingdom prepared for you from the foundation of the world; for I was hungry and you gave me food, I was thirsty and you gave me something to drink, I was a stranger and you welcomed me, I was naked and you gave me clothing, I was sick and you took care of me, I was in prison and you visited me." Then the righteous will answer him, "Lord, when was it that we saw you hungry and gave you food, or thirsty and gave you something to drink? And when was it that we saw you a stranger and welcomed you, or naked and gave you clothing? And when was it that we saw you sick or in prison and visited you?" And the king will answer them, "Truly I tell you, just as you did it to one of the least of these who are members of my family, you did it to me."

Jesus cares so much about the poor and the outcast—the losers— that He identifies Himself with them. He couldn't have emphasized God's regard for the poor and downtrodden more strongly.

Jesus's listeners assumed that wealth was a sign of righteousness. Jesus reverses that assumption. "Blessed are you who are poor," he tells a crowd, "for yours is the kingdom of God" (Luke 6:20). He tells his disciples that "many that are first will be last, and the last first" (Matthew 19:30). When we see the world through the eyes of faith, we realize that a person's wealth alone tells us nothing of his status in God's eyes. A poor man might be first in God's kingdom. Indeed, as the parable of the sheep and goats makes clear, when we minister to that poor and suffering person, he is—in some mysterious sense—Jesus himself.

Many of the biblical commands to care for the poor are directed to Jews helping other Jews and to Christians helping other Christians. But our responsibility to assist the poor reaches beyond our faith communities. Jesus's parable of the Good Samaritan, for instance, shows us that to be a good neighbor we must love and aid even those outside our religious and social group.

We could easily cite a hundred biblical texts showing God's concern for the poor, along with countless theologians and Christian statements throughout the centuries affirming the same, but no one seriously disputes that we should care for the poor. Even most unbelievers agree. The pressing question is *how best* to alleviate poverty.

Is It the Government's Job to Eliminate Poverty?

In well over a hundred biblical passages about the poor, not one mentions the government. Yet practically everybody has gotten the idea that it is the government's job to eliminate poverty. One of us (Jay) goes to a church in the Seattle area where we have corporate prayer. Someone leads with a prayer intention, such as, "For the orphaned and the widowed in our community we pray," and the congregation responds, "Lord, hear our prayer." It's a solid, conservative church, and normally these prayers aren't controversial. One Sunday in July 2010, however, a woman leading prayer asked our congregation to pray "that the president and Congress would succeed in eliminating poverty." I've probably prayed along similar lines before; but this time, the prayer troubled me. After thinking about it, I realized that it rested on a couple of doubtful assumptions.

The first assumption is that it's even possible for us to "eliminate poverty." Sure, we have ways of reducing poverty and creating wealth. And God could work a miracle and eliminate poverty; but insofar as poverty is part of the fallen human condition—like sin, death, and disease—perhaps it's presumptuous to think that anyone can literally eliminate it on this side of the kingdom of God to come. Jesus did say, "The poor you will always have with you" (Matthew 26:11). This is not a counsel of despair, but it should temper our hopes for eliminating poverty.

The more troubling, and unquestioned, assumption in the prayer is that the president and Congress can eliminate poverty. Nothing in the US Constitution suggests this. Nothing in Scripture or Christian theology justifies the assumption. We should pray that our public servants will act wisely and justly. But why think that they can vanquish poverty? We should pray that the poor will have their needs met, and that poverty will diminish; and we should follow our prayers with action. But if we want our prayers to get beyond vague and even misguided generalizations, we need to think about how poverty is normally alleviated in the world God has created.

Social Justice

Before discussing how poverty is overcome, we need to clear some fog and confusion. The idea that the cure for poverty is found in government can be blamed, in part, on progressivism, or statism, which tends to see government as the cure for everything. It's now so far advanced that many Christians have a hard time distinguishing care for the poor from the government forcibly redistributing the wealth of citizens. Many people who know that government doesn't create wealth still think it's a jolly idea for government to take Peter's wealth and give it to Paul. This is often called "social justice."

The term has a noble pedigree in Catholic Social Teaching.[1] Even today, many people refer to efforts to help the poor and outcast as "social justice." Catholic churches, for instance, often have "Social Justice Committees" that oversee food pantries, homeless shelters, and homes for poor, pregnant women. Unfortunately, the left has cleverly hijacked the phrase to refer to government redistribution of wealth, gay marriage, environmental activism, and their other pet causes. "'Social justice' is one of several terms," John Leo observes, "that has been given in-group meanings by the wordsmiths of the cultural Left."[2]

Appropriating the phrase "social justice" makes it easier for the left to demonize people who oppose "spread the wealth" schemes. In 2010, conservative talk radio host Glenn Beck urged Christians to leave churches that preach social justice. He meant that Christians should look out for churches and religious leaders that use the phrase "social justice" to mean wealth redistribution or watered-down socialism. He didn't make that point clearly, though, so he provided an opening for Jim Wallis to challenge him to a "civil dialogue" on "how Christians are called to engage in the struggle for justice."[3] Notice the word switch. Beck was talking about "social justice" as a euphemism for "socialism." Wallis then challenged Beck for opposing "the struggle for justice."

Another problem with using "social justice" when talking about poverty is that it implies that poverty is always caused by injustice. Sometimes it is. The developing world is filled with grotesque violations of justice by governments that keep people trapped in poverty. But not all poverty is due to injustice. A small tribe of aborigines in Australia in the twelfth century could be dirt poor even if no one was treating them unjustly.

We're from the Government, and We're Here to Help You

Hundreds of private charities worked to eliminate poverty throughout the United States in the early twentieth century, but government started crowding out private charities based on progressive attitudes that politics could fix everything, as long as the right experts were in charge.

A few government programs got their start in the 1930s under President Franklin D. Roosevelt. These programs were supposed to end the Great Depression, but we now know that they made the Depression worse and longer lasting than it would have been otherwise.[4] Most programs that we identify with the welfare state, though, started in the mid-1960s with President Lyndon Johnson's War on Poverty, as part of his Great Society agenda. There are now over seventy-seven different federal, "means-tested," welfare programs.

Since 1965, the United States has spent over $16 trillion on welfare. In fiscal year 2008, federal, state, and local governments spent some $714 billion on welfare programs. That's more than we spent on defense, including the cost of the war in Iraq. This huge price was not a short-term surge: it follows a steady four-decade growth in spending. Originally, at least most of the expense went to the poor, but now the majority of the costs go to the Welfare State bureaucracy.[5] We now spend about thirteen times more on welfare than we did in the mid-1960s. The Welfare Reform Act of 1996 helped a bit, but it reformed only one of those seventy-seven federal programs.[6] So welfare costs have continued to grow.

This might have been worth the price if poverty had been eliminated or even reduced. The poverty rate, alas, has stayed roughly the same, although it was steadily dropping *before* we started the "War on Poverty."[7] From 1959 to 1965, it dropped from 22 to 15 percent. In 1965, it started to level off, and now stays in the 12 to 15 percent range. It stood at 14.3 percent in 2009.[8] Worse, these programs have created social problems like rampant out-of-wedlock births and cycles of dependency that didn't exist before. Our government-run welfare is well meaning, but it hasn't worked.

Foreign Aid

Ditto with government attempts to solve poverty on the international stage. For half a century, our weapon of choice in the battle against international poverty has been foreign aid—loans and grants given either directly government-to-government or through the UN, the World Bank, and the International Monetary Fund. These efforts went viral in the last decade through publicity efforts such as the ONE Campaign—led by stars such as Bono—the lead singer of the band U2. Bono even spoke to the National Prayer Breakfast in 2006, and many Christians got behind the campaign.

The ONE Campaign draws attention to the Millennium Development Goals set by the UN to "make poverty history." Many of these are laudable goals—such as clean water, reduced sickness and death from malaria, diarrhea, AIDS, and other diseases, and economic development in Africa.[9]

Contrary to popular opinion, foreign aid money is not a large part of our federal budget—it's much less than 1 percent. The goal of the ONE Campaign is to get foreign aid raised to 1 percent of the federal budget. If you go to the ONE Campaign website, they ask you to do three things: Write President Obama, call the White House, and attend an event to put pressure on politicians to boost foreign aid.[10]

If we could really make world poverty history with 1 percent of the federal budget, few Americans would begrudge the expense. Before pestering the president to grow the budget for foreign aid, though, we should see whether it helps people. After all, it's not a new idea. Developed countries including the United States have spent nearly $2.5 trillion over the last half century in this effort, and have very little to show for it.

Scholars have criticized foreign aid for years. They tell a sad story of money siphoned off by bureaucrats and corrupt dictators, who use the money to line their pockets and keep their populations oppressed. For instance, Haiti's Papa Doc and Baby Doc Duvalier received the most credit endorsements from the International Monetary Fund from 1957 to 1986.[11] One World Bank study revealed that in some cases 85 percent of aid was diverted from its intended uses. An early World Bank deputy director said that "when the World Bank thinks it is financing an electric power station, it is really financing a brothel."[12] Despite trillions of dollars in foreign aid, millions still die every year in places such as Africa for want of medicine and bed nets that cost a few cents apiece.[13]

There are smart, well-meaning people on all sides of the "aid debate." But one thing is clear: There's no correlation between receiving foreign aid and economic growth.[14] Foreign aid doesn't make countries prosperous.

In fact, according to Zambian economist Dambiso Moyo, the aid system has made things *worse*. It has created a perverse and corrupting dependency that prevents many poor countries from developing. In her book *Dead Aid*, Moyo says that it's "time to stop pretending that the aid-based development model currently in place will generate sustained economic growth in the world's poorest countries. It will not." She calls on Africa "to rid the continent of aid-dependency, which has hindered good governance for so long."[15] This is true even of aid in more recent years, which has officially been tied to practices of good governance and economic reforms. As Moyo says:

> The notion that aid can alleviate systemic poverty, and has done so, is a myth. Millions in Africa are poorer today because of aid; misery and poverty have not ended but have increased. Aid has been, and continues to be, an unmitigated political, economic, and humanitarian disaster for most parts of the developing world.[16]

Maybe foreign aid in some form could help some people, but there's no reason to believe that it will ever eliminate poverty.

A Compassion Connection

Long-term foreign aid to governments is mostly harmful, but emergency and humanitarian aid after tsunamis and earthquakes have probably saved millions of lives over the years. And we don't want to disparage programs that have made life-saving food and medicine available to the poor in Africa and elsewhere.[17]

Many private charities are doing wonderful work overseas. As a rule, the most successful endeavors have a local connection. Rather than trying to "end poverty as we know it" from an office in New York, they focus on specific tasks in specific places. For instance, one nonprofit, Population Services International, has managed to get bed nets treated with insecticide distributed in Malawi by selling the nets through birth clinics, and allowing the nurses involved to keep part of the proceeds of every net sold to a poor mother. This strategy has not only worked better than government-funded efforts that give the nets away, but has also gotten nets into the hands of the people most likely to use them.[18]

A project of the ministry I (James) founded, LIFE Outreach International, is called Mission Feeding. It works with local ministries in famine-ridden communities to feed some 500,000 per month. Another one of our projects, Water for LIFE, helps poor communities in many third world countries dig wells to provide clean water. Every day, children all over the world walk miles down a road of death to fetch unclean water filled with waterborne pathogens that cause disease. The diseases caused by contaminated water kill 1.8 million children every year. Because of unclean water, up to 50 percent of all people in poverty-stricken nations suffer severe health problems. Those trillions of dollars in foreign aid spent in the last six decades haven't solved this tragedy.

In Matthew 10:42, Jesus urges us to give water to the thirsty. Taking this call to heart, Water for LIFE drills wells that not only stop disease and promote healthy bodies, but also provide the means for families to grow their own gardens and care for their own animals.

Three thousand wells are now in use. With each serving an average of a thousand people, the estimated number of changed lives reaches three million. In mid-2012, the twelfth year of Water for LIFE, there will be 415 new wells in needy areas in twenty nations around the world. The average cost of each well is $4,800. So a child can receive a lifetime of clean water for as little as $4.80. What a bargain! Through *Life Today*, our television program, and many others emphasizing the importance of clean water, numerous organizations, businesses, and churches have been inspired to start drilling fresh water wells. This is just one example of what a ministry can do to help the suffering and inspire others to do so. There are many great NGOs (nongovernmental organizations) worthy of our support.

These efforts are possible only because of an intricate web linking funding and ministries with people on the ground who have local connections and local knowledge. We're convinced a compassion connection is essential to assist effectively those who suffer in poverty or crisis, or who are recovering from natural disasters.

What Should We Do?

Thousands of domestic charities also have a winning track record. One of the most insidious ideas of the left is that government-run welfare programs can take the place of private—that is, non-government-run—charity. But they're not the same thing. Charity comes from the Latin word meaning "love." Love can only be given voluntarily. So charity is different from "help" given impersonally and mechanistically by a government agency using tax money.

Charity has to be well thought out and not just well intentioned. Unfortunately, people often give based on intentions rather than results. A famous study published in 2007 revealed some startling information about what motivates people to give.[19] In the study, three different groups were presented three different scenarios, each involving the work of an organization called Save the Children. The first group heard about a seven-year-old girl in Mali (in western Africa) named Rokia, who suffered from hunger and malnutrition, and was at risk of starving to death. However, with financial support, the group was told that Save the Children could help feed her, educate her, and treat her medical needs.

The second group was not told about Rokia, but received instead some horrendous statistics, "Food shortages in Malawi are affecting more than three million children. In Zambia, severe rainfall deficits have resulted in a 42% drop in maize production from 2000. As a result, an estimated three million Zambians face hunger. Four million Angolans—one-third of the population—have been forced to flee their homes. More than 11 million people in Ethiopia need immediate food assistance."[20]

The third group got both the story about Rokia and the statistics.

Guess which group responded most generously? The people in the first group, who just heard the story of Rokia, were much more likely to help, since the need involved an "identifiable victim." The group that heard just the stats gave the least. Surprisingly, the group that heard the story and the statistics gave only a bit more than the stats-only group.

This study confirmed what many charities have known for years—donors are more likely to respond to a concrete story about a person with a concrete need than to an abstract list of depressing statistics. Development ministries wisely give prospective donors stories and pictures of individuals like Rokia. Several even have adopt-a-child programs, which pair a donor with one recipient.

According to the researchers, people tended to give based on emotion rather than a rational evaluation of what would do the most good for the most people. They even went so far as to say that most donors give "irrationally." News stories about the study reported that charities should tug on the heartstrings of donors rather than appeal to their reason.

It's true that well-meaning people often provide help based on emotions without thinking through the effects of their giving. This can be

a tragic mistake. Jesus told us to love the Lord with all our hearts, all
our souls, and all our *minds*. Millions of Christians have hearts for the
poor; but very few have minds for the poor. If we really want to help
people, then we need to think through the consequences of our giving.
Does a ministry empower recipients, or make them weak and dependent? Will the help make things better off in the long run, or will it
create unintended consequences? Will it encourage what it is meant to
cure? If our emotions keep us from thinking through these questions,
then we need to check our emotions.

The researchers showed that people give emotionally, but did
donors give *irrationally*? No. The study suggests that donors don't find
statistics very compelling; but the donors who were told about Rokia
assumed that their money would help someone, namely, Rokia. Emotional giving is not necessarily less rational than giving on the basis of
abstract statistics. People in the second and third groups were given no
reason to believe their donations would help more *overall* than the first
group, which heard only about Rokia. Money is fungible. If you give
$10 to the Union Gospel Mission, and the shelter helps a hundred men,
you could think of the $10 as going to help one man you know, or you
could think of ten cents being disbursed to help one hundred men you
don't know. It's no more nor less rational to give under either scenario.
That one is more emotionally compelling doesn't make it less rational.

In fact, the study may reveal a hidden logic. Perhaps donors sense
that the more personal and concrete a gift is, the greater its chances
of success. Imagine, for instance, a married man with two children in
Detroit who loses his job. He and his family go to a large church with
a ministry to help unemployed members. The ministry provides the
man with temporary financial support, which is overseen by an experienced group of volunteers; it also connects him with a mentor who is a
successful and well-connected businessman from the church.

Now imagine the same man in a different scenario. He never enters
a church. He loses his job and signs up for unemployment insurance.

He has to show that he's applying for jobs, but that's not too hard. When the insurance payments end, he applies for several federal welfare programs. He lives in Detroit and the check comes from Washington, DC. Now, in which situation do you think the man is more likely to get back on his feet quickly? Clearly the first one. All things being equal, smaller, voluntary, local sources of help are better than large, distant, government-run alternatives.

The Web of Responsibility

One reason that local and private is better has to do with information and incentives. A centralized government knows less about individual problems than does someone closer to the problem. Normally, knowledge is lost with distance. Charity is less effective when it's made a commodity. Generally, things work better if people are most responsible for the matters they know the most about. Think of responsibility as a cluster of overlapping circles or jurisdictions, like a really complicated spiderweb. The person or group with the narrowest jurisdiction has the most knowledge and responsibility. The narrowest jurisdiction is the responsibility you have for yourself. You know when you're tired, hungry, thirsty, and sleepy. Therefore, unless you get sick or pass out or lapse into a coma or dementia, you are primarily responsible for yourself. It would be stupid and unfair to expect some guy down the street or at the Department of the Interior to feed you, breathe for you, and make sure you go to bed when you're supposed to. Talk about a nanny state! If this went on too long, you might even forget how to take care of yourself.

Young children are under their parents' jurisdiction. If parents fail in their duties, a grandparent or an aunt may have to step in. If that doesn't work, then a local church or aid group can help. It's only when these options are exhausted that government should be involved. Even then, it should be incremental, starting locally. The federal government is the jurisdiction of last resort.

Little Jieshu was found in Foshan City outside Guangzhou, China, in April 2003, when she was just a few days old. When the authorities found her, as they were meant to do, since she was placed in a conspicuous place, she had no known family. So they sent her to a local orphanage. By Chinese standards, it was a very good orphanage.

Providentially, the Chinese government, which created such heart-wrenching scenarios with its one-child policy, also knows that children do best in actual families, and made it possible for people around the world to adopt children like Jieshu. For months, the local orphanage gave her the basic care any toddler needs—a crib, formula, someone to change her diapers and keep her from wandering out in the street. But that was the extent of her care. Many Chinese orphans do not survive this period. Jieshu was a fighter, though. She survived; but she did not prosper. At twelve months, she was pale, thin, couldn't crawl, and spent most of the time on a plywood "mattress" in her crib.

No matter how caring the family service workers in faraway Beijing were, the most they could do was to identify her and handle the paperwork so that she could be connected with a family. The nannies at the orphanage were as caring as they could be, considering that they were employees who had some *sixty* infants to tend.

Jieshu finally got her "forever family" on June 6, 2004—called "Gotcha Day"—and the family—from Seattle—received a wonderful blessing. She crawled within a week after Gotcha Day, and was walking by July. Her full name is Ellie Jieshu Richards. Her parents, Jay and Ginny Richards, know exactly what she likes, and exactly what she needs. We are grateful for the joy and responsibility Ellie has brought into our lives.

The same dynamic is true with charity. Over time, government welfare tends to do more harm than good because it tears through an intricate web of overlapping jurisdictions of responsibility, and assumes knowledge in a context of ignorance. When the federal government jumps in and overrules this intricate web, it violates the principle of subsidiarity. That's a big word for a simple idea that Christian moral thinkers have discussed for centuries.

Here's how Pope Pius XI explained the principle:

> Just as it is wrong to withdraw from the individual and com-
> mit to a group what private initiative and effort can accomplish,
> so too it is an injustice for a larger and higher association to
> arrogate to itself functions which can be performed efficiently by
> smaller and lower associations. This is a fundamental principle.
> In its very nature the true aim of all social activity should be to
> help members of a social body, and never to destroy or absorb
> them.[21]

When the state or any larger entity takes over a task that is better handled by someone closer to the problem, it violates its proper boundaries and creates more problems than it set out to solve. When helping those in need, voluntary, private, and informed is better than government-run and distant.

Another way to put this is to say that effective charity will tend to be compassionate in the proper sense of the word. "Compassionate" doesn't mean that you feel warm fuzzies in your heart. It means "to suffer alongside." You can't really suffer alongside people without knowing them and knowing what they need.

We could give many examples of compassion, but we'll mention just one. Some of the most effective charity starts with one person, or one family. Our (the Richards') good friends, Geoff and Tami Biehn, had felt glimmers of a call to help orphans for years, but weren't sure what to do. They were wide open to God's prompting, though, and as they prayed, they independently received strong impressions about an orphanage, and selling their house. That last part was a hard word. Geoff is a financial advisor, and through a turn of events, the Biehns had been able to buy their house without a mortgage. It was in an idyllic, mature neighborhood in a suburb of Columbus, Ohio. They loved everything about it. Besides, they had always dreamed of having extra money to buy a beach house for their children to enjoy.

Still, they kept listening and praying. They asked trusted family members and friends for prayer and advice. Their seven-year-old daughter, Brianna, began sensing that God wanted them to sell their house and help orphans, even though moving would mean she and her older brother, Braydon, would have to leave their school and friends.

Through these independent confirmations, Geoff and Tami finally concluded that God was indeed asking them to sell their house, even though the depressed 2011 housing market seemed like a terrible time to do so. Within three weeks of putting the house on the market, however, they received a full cash offer from a buyer. Meanwhile, the Biehns found a smaller version of their beloved house in another neighborhood nearby. Their daughter, Brianna, told her parents, "I think God has a house for us on the Big Hill and it would be great if it was on a court." Without knowing it, she had described the house.

The price of the new house was about 60 percent of the selling price of their old house; so after the move, they had a hefty balance to help orphans—somehow. They used keen discernment in deciding what to do. Before they started their research, they knew they wanted to work with (1) a Christ-centered organization that was tied in with a local church, that (2) had a passion to continually do more for the children, (3) was operating in a country where there was a strong need, (4) was safe for their young children to visit, and (5) close enough that their whole family could visit regularly. These criteria led them to VisionTrust. As it happens, the ministry had an immediate need in the Dominican Republic. The Biehns flew to the Dominican Republic to learn everything they could about the orphanage and VisionTrust.[22]

They found that the orphanage was home to about thirty young girls and was being run by Ketty Figueroa, a local pastor's wife. When the Biehns visited, VisionTrust was renting the property, but the landlord had needed to sell it. The landlord offered Ketty a discount if she could come up with a few thousand dollars for a deposit. She had managed to scrape the money together on faith that God would bring the rest of the money to buy the house. He did, and He used Geoff and Tami Biehn to deliver it.

Because of the Biehns' willingness to pray, listen, and sacrifice, God used them to help bless thirty orphaned little girls. But the Biehns will tell you that God blessed *them*. They can now visit the orphanage every year as a family, help out, and then spend a few days vacationing on a beach in the Dominican Republic—much better than their dream beach house.

God does not call every family to sell their house; but He does call each of us, in our unique circumstances, to help those in need. We just have to listen.

How Is Poverty Eliminated?

The Biehn family will spend years tuned in to the needs of a group of orphans in the Dominican Republic. Their story is a crystal-clear example of how charity can work, of how it ought to work. Unfortunately, charity doesn't always work—it doesn't always help—at least on large scales. Haiti, which shares the island of Hispaniola with the Dominican Republic, has more aid workers per capita than any country in the world, and yet it's still the poorest country in the Western Hemisphere and one of the poorest in the world. Many individual Haitians are alive because of these workers, but the country as a whole remains in abject poverty. Even when charity is effective, it has never lifted an entire culture out of poverty. We have no reason to believe it can. We're both affiliated with nonprofit organizations and have every reason to emphasize the good work of charities, but we know the reality.

We need to support good charities, but we shouldn't expect them to do more than they can do. Charity is like the gleanings on the edge of a field. It helps in emergency situations. We can deliver vaccines and hydration packs, and dig wells for the poor in Africa and elsewhere. We can volunteer at homeless shelters in our neighborhood. We can even buy an orphanage for little girls in a Caribbean country. But all these acts are gleanings—they're funded by wealth produced elsewhere. There must be fertile fields and an abundant harvest before there can be any leftover stalks of grain for the sojourner. The greater the bounty, the greater the gleanings. But where does the bounty come from?

Wealth has not been the usual state of affairs for human beings. Most people for most of history have been extremely poor by US standards. Imagine a family with a tiny plot of land cking out just enough food to stay alive, and you'll have a picture of how millions of people in poverty have lived their lives. The only cure for material poverty is, obviously, wealth. While the government is vital for maintaining the conditions under which wealth is created, almost all wealth is actually created in the nonpolitical spheres, by entrepreneurs, inventors, laborers, farmers, builders, bankers, and businesses. We give some of that wealth to charity. And government garnishes some of it with taxes and indirectly with regulation; but government doesn't create the wealth.

That prayer that looked to the president and Congress to eliminate poverty ignored the normal way poverty is eliminated in the world. God can create wealth directly if He wants to, just as He can make bread—manna—fall from heaven. But business and trade are the normal ways God gives us wealth, just as farmers and bakers are the normal ways God gives us bread. If we want to alleviate widespread poverty, rather than just offering platitudes and good intentions, then we need to understand how wealth is created in the real world. We'll do that in the next several chapters.

CHAPTER 13

A Place to Call Our Own

The moment the idea is admitted into society, that property is not as sacred as the laws of God, and that there is not the force of law and public justice to protect it, anarchy and tyranny commence.

—JOHN ADAMS

Most Americans say they believe in the right to private property, but few can explain why exactly they should have such a right. This lack of understanding would be okay if private property were not under attack, at the extreme, by socialists and communists who violently oppose it for creating haves and have-nots, rich and poor, slave and free. Even Christians in the mainstream who would never claim the socialist label worry that it is selfish to insist on a right to own things. They know the story from the book of Acts, where members of the early church in Jerusalem sold their personal belongings and shared everything in common. If this describes the Christian ideal, they wonder, why should we worry about the erosion of private property rights?

Was the Early Church Communist?

Let's look carefully at the text from the early part of Acts:

> Now the whole group of those who believed were of one heart
> and soul, and no one claimed private ownership of any posses-
> sions, but everything they owned was held in common.... There
> was not a needy person among them, for as many as owned lands
> or houses sold them and brought the proceeds of what was sold.
> They laid it at the apostles' feet, and it was distributed to each as
> any had need. (Acts 4:32–35)

This was the first church to form after the gift of the Holy Spirit at
Pentecost. The church was formed in the city of Jerusalem. Acts says
that these believers were "filled with the Holy Spirit and spoke the word
of God boldly" (Acts 4:31). If this is communism, it would be a big
deal. But "communism" is not just a big word for "sharing." Communism in its modern form treats private property rights as a system that
oppresses the poor. It is based on Karl Marx's theory of class warfare,
in which the capitalists (bourgeoisie) slowly extract most of the wealth
from the workers (proletarians), at which point the workers revolt
against the capitalists—those who own the means of production—and
forcibly take control of the means of production, that is, productive
property. The state becomes the owner of all property on behalf of the
workers, but eventually, this socialist state withers away and a communist utopia emerges where everyone is free and has everything he
needs.

There's not one word about bourgeoisie or proletarians in Acts. Private property is not condemned for oppressing the poor. These early
Christians are selling their possessions and *sharing* freely and spon-
taneously. The state isn't confiscating anything. No one is coercing or
being coerced. The church in Jerusalem had no political or economic

power. The early church in Jerusalem is nothing like the modern communist state. As Ron Sider notes, "Sharing was voluntary, not compulsory."[1] Sharing must be voluntary. If you're being compelled to share, you're getting mugged.

Neither does what happens later in the book of Acts with Ananias and Sapphira confirm a communist reading of this text. At first glance, it appears that Peter condemns the couple for keeping back some of the money they got from selling their land. "Ananias," Peter asks, "why has Satan filled your heart to lie to the Holy Spirit and to keep back part of the proceeds of the lands?" A few seconds later, Ananias is dead on the floor, apparently struck dead by God. You might think Ananias was condemned because he didn't give up everything he owned, that ownership was a violation of community rules; but study the rest of Peter's statement: "While [your lands] remained unsold, did it not remain your own? And after it was sold, were not the proceeds at your disposal? How is it that you have contrived this deed in your heart? You did not lie to us but to God!" (Acts 5:3–4).

Peter says outright that the property was rightfully theirs, and so was the money they got from selling it. Private property is clearly not the problem. Peter condemns Ananias and Sapphira not for keeping back part of the proceeds of the sale, but for lying about it.

The communal life of the early church in Jerusalem is never made the norm for all Christians everywhere. The early chapters of Acts describe a unique situation—the very beginning of the church in Jerusalem. Churches in other cities appeared after the gospel was preached by Paul or one of the other apostles. The church at Corinth was made up of Corinthians. The church at Galatia was made up, we can assume, of Galatians. The day of Pentecost in Jerusalem was quite different. On that occasion, Peter preached the gospel to thousands of Jews who had come to Jerusalem from all around the Roman Empire, speaking various languages. And this was no ordinary sermon. When Peter preached, the Holy Spirit descended with such power that flames of fire appeared on the heads of the gathered, and they began communicating in languages they didn't know, while hearing foreigners speak meaningfully to them in their own language.

Thousands were added to the Church on this one day. Normally, Jews visiting Jerusalem would return home after the holiday since they were away from their jobs, extended families, and homes. Now suddenly they were part of a brand-new community. New Christians needed to stay in Jerusalem much longer than expected in order to be properly discipled; thus, the local believers began selling their property so they could share with these new, temporarily displaced brothers and sisters. They were in a unique and short-term situation. At some point, many of the new Jewish Christians returned to their homes, taking their faith with them.

Other churches in other cities did things differently. When some Thessalonian Christians took advantage of the generosity of fellow believers, Paul ordered them to "earn their own living." He even laid down a stern rule: "Anyone unwilling to work should not eat" (2 Thessalonians 3:10, 12).[2]

In short, communism is not the Christian ideal.

The Roots of Private Property

Scripture nowhere says explicitly that property is a right; but a right to acquire property is one of those truths that is assumed everywhere in Scripture, so much so that it probably didn't occur to anyone that they needed to defend it outright. Two of the Ten Commandments assume the right: You shall not steal, and you shall not covet your neighbor's possessions (Exodus 20:2–17 and Deuteronomy 5:6–21). Neither of these commandments makes sense unless there are some things that rightly belong to other people. One of the fifty chapters of the book of Genesis (chapter 22) is devoted to describing—in detail—Abraham's purchase of a plot of land to bury Sarah. This suggests that standards for buying and selling property were already well developed in 2000 BC in the ancient Near East.

As Westerners, we benefit from four thousand years of laws, customs, and thinking about the concept of property. Drawing on ideas from Christian theology and Greek philosophy, the Western world slowly developed a highly sophisticated system of property law and titling that, without intention, resulted in a system that protects property rights, reinforces our other rights, and encourages widespread wealth creation.

Property Protects Our Other Rights

The Founders insisted that if you don't enjoy a right to property, you won't enjoy the other ones, either. They understood that our right to property is an extension of ourselves and our liberty. John Adams said that property "implies liberty because property cannot be secure unless he have his personal liberty of life and limb, motion and rest for the purpose."[3]

The right to property not only protects our freedom; it also limits government. Property rights protect you from others and dictate how the government may interact with you. If millions of people own their own homes, cars, land, clothes, and labor, then much of our daily life is outside the government's jurisdiction. If the government wants to take your land to build a road, for instance, it has to compensate you fairly. It can't just push you and your family off the property. If we enjoy no right to property, we're at the mercy of either the strongest person or an all-powerful state.

If You Care about the Poor, Defend Private Property

Although the concept of private property has been part of Western culture for thousands of years, in the nineteenth and twentieth centuries, many prominent intellectuals argued that private property laws harmed the poor, and that we ought to prefer "public" ownership of property. The first plank of *The Communist Manifesto,* written in 1848 by Karl Marx and Frederick Engels, calls for the "abolition of private property." And the 1917 Russian Revolution, led by Vladimir Lenin, tried to put Marx's ideas into action.

The revolution, as it turned out, provided a trainload of evidence that Marx didn't know what he was talking about. By 1920, industrial production in Russia had dropped to 18 percent of its 1913 level.[4] When Lenin tried to collectivize farms in Russia in the 1920s, over five million peasants died of starvation. It got so bad that Lenin had to tweak the policy. Although hard industry and most of the land continued to be state-owned, he allowed families to cultivate small private plots.[5] These plots made up only 2 percent of the cultivated land, but they contributed one-fourth of the output of Russian agriculture. That is, "the output per acre of the private plots was about sixteen times the per-acre output of the state-owned farms."[6]

The Communist Chinese discovered the same thing in the 1970s, but not before trying their hand at creating a so-called "new heaven and earth for man." Attempts to collectivize both farms and industry led to the deaths of some 20 million Chinese from famine, and another 20 million in labor camps.[7]

These are just two of dozens of horrific examples of communist catastrophe in the twentieth century. The evidence proves that abolishing and collectivizing private property helps neither the economy nor the poor. Property laws are one the most basic conditions for reducing poverty and creating wealth. Pope Leo XIII put this point well in his 1891 encyclical *Rerum Novarum*, "The first and most fundamental principle...if one would undertake to alleviate the condition of the masses, must be the inviolability of private property."[8] To help the poor, protect private property.

The Founders understood that if people enjoy the fruits of their labor, they're more likely to be good stewards, to work hard and produce wealth for themselves and others. The only way you can really enjoy the fruit of your labor is if you have a right to property. In a communist setting, everyone gets the same compensation no matter what they do. All have an incentive to be free riders—to do as little as possible. People will find ingenious ways to look busy without actually working. Communists learned this lesson the hard way in the twentieth century. One of the best ways to destroy the productive industry of peasants, factory workers, and everyone else, is to collectivize their efforts.

In contrast, if hard work pays better than free riding, everyone has an incentive to work harder. The Greek philosopher Aristotle knew this twenty-four hundred years ago. "That which is common to the greatest number has the least care bestowed upon it," he said. "Everyone thinks chiefly of his own, hardly at all of the common interest; and only when he is himself concerned as an individual. For besides other considerations, everybody is more inclined to neglect the duty which he expects another to fulfill."[9] We can count on most people to act in their own self-interest. That doesn't mean everybody always does the *selfish* thing. It just means that if you can acquire property, then your self-interest will orient you to provide something for others—whether you're selfish or not—since you'll want to have something to trade in the marketplace (more on this later).

The Founders understood the power of legitimate self-interest so well that they even provided in the Constitution for writers and inventors to have "exclusive Right to their respective Writings and Discoveries." This right to intellectual property is the basis of our patent system, which is one reason there have been so many great American inventors. As Abraham Lincoln explained, by protecting intellectual property, our Founders "added *the fuel of interest to the fire of genius* in the discovery and production of new and useful things."[10]

The Mystery of Property

Only recently have we begun to realize how fortunate we Americans are to have robust property laws that cover not just land and material things, but intellectual property. Perhaps the best way to see this is to compare our lot with those in the developing world.

There, people often live and work on land that they don't really own. A dog may have a sense of where his master's land ends and the neighbor's begins, but the people don't have titles representing ownership, which the police and the government will protect and neighbors will respect. As a result, a farmer might work on the same plot of land for decades but never get beyond hand-to-mouth subsistence farming, producing just enough to survive. The land serves only its immediate physical purposes, and that very poorly. The farmer has little incentive to tap the land's untold potential. He acts for the short term, not the long term. He prefers crops that come quickly to harvest to crops that are more profitable in the long run but take several years to mature. This "dead capital," according to Peruvian economist Hernando de Soto, is held informally or "extralegally."

Contrary to old communist arguments against private property, de Soto argues that what the poor in the third world need to improve their standard of living are *strong private property laws*. Sophisticated property laws and titling, he argues, are the "mystery of capital" that has allowed the West to create vast wealth and raise the living standards of the poor. The problem is not that people in the developing world are stupid or predestined for poverty but that they don't enjoy the property and contract laws we do.[11]

In the 1990s, de Soto sent research teams to several South American and Caribbean countries to study their property laws. What they found was astonishing. You might guess that the lack of property laws is the result of a government that is too small and standoffish. What they found was that the same governments that fail to protect property rights also erect bureaucratic roadblocks that seem designed to keep citizens from opening businesses or owning property legally. What the governments should do, they didn't do. And what they shouldn't do, they did.

To buy a home legally in Peru, for instance, a Peruvian has to track through a five-stage maze, with 207 steps in the first stage alone.[12] Haitians have it really bad. They must jump through 65 bureaucratic hoops just to lease land from the government. If they want to buy the land, they have another 111 hoops ahead of them. It would take a Haitian 19 years to pull this off.[13] Still, imagine that some poor Haitian manages to steer his way through this Haitian House of Horrors. The Haitian still lacks secure property since Haiti tends to go from one dictatorial regime to the other with alarming speed. Who's to say that a land contract secured under one regime will be recognized by the next? Can you imagine conducting business, investing in, or developing property in such a climate of uncertainty? No one else can, either.

De Soto compares this lack of solid property and contract laws in the developing world with the laws in countries like the United States. In the developed world, "the same assets also lead a parallel life as capital outside the physical world," he explains. "They can be used to put in motion more production by securing the interests of other parties as 'collateral' for a mortgage, for example, or by assuring the supply of other forms of credit and public utilities."[14] In contrast, "the total value of real estate held but not legally owned by the poor of the Third World and former communist nations is at least $9.3 trillion."[15] That untapped wealth is more than all the foreign aid ever given to these countries, much of which has done more harm than good. Third world people, says de Soto, may "have houses but not titles, crops but not deeds, businesses but not statutes of incorporation."[16]

Let's say you buy from its previous owner a cozy 15,000-square-foot bungalow in Medina, Washington—a suburb of Seattle, home to Bill

Gates and other really rich people. What's happened exactly? Nothing magical. The house and the land it's on haven't gone anywhere. There's no chemical reaction of the dirt with the air at the moment the property changes hands. In changing owners, the house just comes to be represented in a new way; and that way of representing it changes how everyone else treats it. Your ownership of the house is recorded—on paper, computer, and the "cloud."[17] The new reality of your ownership is embedded into a much larger system of laws, agreements, and symbols that give it meaning and force.

In response, relationships change. You're now accountable to the bank that provided your mortgage (or the bank they sold it to). Your credit rating hangs in the balance, just waiting to drop the moment you forget to make your house payment on time. You now have to obey lots of touchy and costly city ordinances that only billionaires could take in stride. The same ordinances protect you, too. Your neighbor won't be able to put up a three-story barn, paint it tarp blue, and block your view of Lake Washington. And he certainly won't be able to steal your property. Ditto for the government. If the state of Washington wants to expand the Route 520 bridge near your house and take out part of your yard, they'll hear from your lawyers, and they will have to compensate you for your loss.

These rules, representations, and perceptions also create new opportunities for you. You can receive mail and hook up utilities. The value of your home can now be compared with the value of other assets all around the world. You might even use the equity on your house to get a business loan to invest in your neighbor's new company, which is supposed to build quantum computers. Without that collateral, the investors probably wouldn't take such a risk—since no one has ever built a quantum computer.

Do you see what has happened? Your house has been *transformed* into more than just a house. It's an asset. It's capital. It's *property*. All of

this is due to an intricate way of representing something and then consistently adjusting our behavior and perceptions accordingly.[18] If you
don't find this mysterious, go back a couple of pages and read it again.
Rules, symbols, meanings, contracts, attitudes: These ethereal things
turn dirt, wood, Sheetrock, and concrete into assets and wealth, which
in turn can be used to create more wealth. Of course, a formal private
property system doesn't solve every problem known to man. It's not the
only thing a culture needs to grow prosperous. We should think of it as
the beginning, the first rung on the ladder to creating wealth (or perhaps the second rung after people stop killing each other at the drop of
a hat). Without it, an economy will tend to stagnate with much of the
population living hand-to-mouth while a few lucky kings, princes, and
scoundrels get fabulously wealthy. In contrast, places that have robust
ways for ordinary people to acquire and keep property tend to get rich
in the long run.

The right to property channels and orients our behaviors in wealth-
enhancing ways. It alters not just our actions but the very way we view
ourselves and the world around us. We see this with squatters who gain
property rights. Squatters are people who live on land that they don't
own or rent. Cities in third world countries are often surrounded by
shantytowns where thousands of squatters live in dilapidated shacks.
In 2007, a team of economists studied a settlement of squatters in a
shantytown in Argentina. One section of town was granted title to their
small properties. The other part was not. The economists compared the
squatters who had acquired legal right to their land with their neighbors
who had not. They found that the property owners were more opti-
mistic. The owners tended to trust others and to believe people could
achieve something good if they worked hard.[19] As a result, they pursued
their longer-term economic interests, and tended to grow more prosperous as a result.

Most ordinary squatters know that any day, the police could come

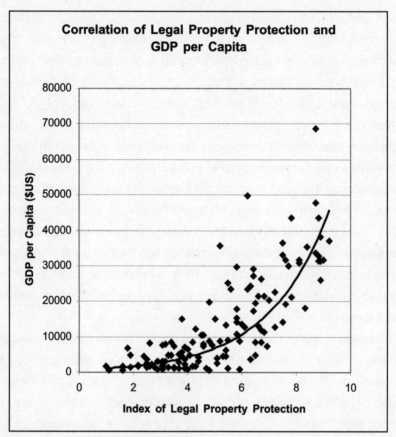

Correlation of Legal Property Protection and GDP per Capita

Sources: James D. Gwartney and Robert A. Lawson, Economic Freedom of the World: 2006 Annual Report, *September 2006. GDP per capita (PPP) 2004 CIA World Fact Book, https://www.cia.gov/cia/publications/factbook/rankorder/2004rank.html.*

For decades, there has been a close correlation between the wealth of a country's citizens and the strength of that country's property laws. In general, the more a country (which includes the government and its citizens) protects private property, the more prosperous the citizens of that country will be.

in, bulldoze their ramshackle house of corrugated fiberglass, tarp, and wood, and leave them homeless and destitute. It makes sense that they just try to get by from day to day; they don't think about creating long-term wealth.

The Financial Crisis: Why Ownership Can't Be Forced

The right to property is not a right to have someone give you property. It's a right to acquire and keep property by your own productive efforts. Still, once you see the benefits of owning property, you might think that the government can improve the lot of poor Americans by making it easier for them to own homes. As we learned in 2008, however, the devil is in the details. There's a difference between merely *having* property and disciplining yourself so that you can *acquire* property, and we get nothing but trouble when we mistake one for the other.

It's easier for us Americans to acquire property in our country than it is for practically anyone in any other country to buy property in theirs; but poorer Americans can still have a hard time securing a mortgage to buy a house. In a normal market, to get a mortgage loan from a bank, you would need a stable job with a big enough salary to make the monthly payments. You also would need a good credit history and enough money for a down payment. To a bank, these are all signs that you'll probably repay your debt rather than default. A lender assumes that if you don't have any skin in the game, you'll be less motivated to uphold your end of the bargain.

If you have a plump down payment, say, 20 percent of the loan, and a stellar financial history, you can usually get a loan with a relatively low interest rate. The riskier you are as a borrower, the higher your rate of interest will be (to offset the risk to the bank). If, for instance, you have $78 in savings, $17,516 in credit card debt, no property for collateral, and a bad habit of ticking off employers—then normally, you wouldn't be able to get a loan at all.

But what if some of these less-than-ideal borrowers could get a mortgage loan? Wouldn't that help them and everyone else in the process? People take better care of homes they own rather than rent. They tend to take more interest in their community. They're more law-abiding and do more long-term planning, since they slowly accumulate an asset—the house—as they pay off their mortgage. For these reasons, many politicians—Republican and Democrat—have supported policies for decades to make it easier for lower-income people to buy homes.

Unfortunately, in the process, they caused the underwriting standards on mortgages to be degraded for high-risk borrowers. (These are the guidelines that banks use to make sure the loans they issue and maintain are safe and secure, and which they use to determine the interest rate they charge to offset the risk of giving a loan.) Few imagined what would happen as a result—the 2008 financial crisis. If you feel you don't understand the crisis, don't feel bad. It's really complicated, and the powers-that-be generally avoid explaining the crisis accurately, since they were a big part of why it happened.

There were several factors that led to the crisis. One was the Federal Reserve's policy of increasing the money supply and keeping interest rates artificially low.[20] There was also the government's known tendency to bail out financial institutions that are deemed "too big to fail."[21] But a major part of the story is the millions of risky "subprime" mortgages that entered the system in the years leading up to the 2008 disaster.

The federal government has been fiddling with the mortgage market since the 1930s, mainly via the tax code.[22] But the 1977 Community Reinvestment Act (CRA), "which currently requires all insured banks and [Savings & Loans] to make loans to borrowers at or below 80 percent of the median income in the areas the banks service"[23] set "borrowing guidelines" for lenders, subtly coercing them to weaken the standards they use to evaluate loan applications.

The "government-sponsored enterprises," Fannie Mae and Freddie Mac,[24] also played a key role. They were first established to create a national market for mortgages. They're for-profit banks, but enjoy special favors from the federal government, which, among other things, allows them to borrow money at a lower interest rate than other banks. Years after they were chartered, "Affordable Housing Goals" were set for lower-income, risky loans. Over time, these quotas got bigger and bigger. By buying millions of loans that originated with other lenders, Fannie and Freddie allowed those lenders to get the risky loans off their books. The rate of borrowers defaulting on their home loans and their homes going into foreclosure is "seven to ten times the parallel rates for conventional loans to prime borrowers."[25] As a result, lenders, which were already under pressure to weaken their standards, now had even less reason to resist the pressure—since they could hand off their loans on someone else. Fannie and Freddie came to dominate this secondary market for mortgages. "During the decade prior to their insolvency, Fannie Mae and Freddie Mac purchased more than 80 percent of the mortgages sold by banks and other originators."[26]

Fannie and Freddie ended up competing with another government agency, the Federal Housing Administration (FHA), which was officially set up to provide loans to lower-income Americans. As a result, by 2008, about 27 million loans, half of all mortgages in the United States, "were subprime or otherwise risky loans."[27] When you consider that borrowers were putting less and less into down payments, the amount of residential real estate actually owned by households, as opposed to being financed with debt, *went down* from 2001 to 2009.[28] The housing boom, in other words, didn't provide households with more assets. It was nothing but debt.

Temporarily, this strange policy brew stimulated demand, leading to a surge in new construction and home prices. Returns on real estate were much better than many stocks, and those returns in turn drew more money into the real estate markets. This encouraged experts to create new financial instruments to take advantage of the booming real estate market. Mortgages began to be "securitized." That is, millions of subprime mortgages were chopped up, bundled, turned into securities, and sold around the world. The idea was to allow investors to diversify risk by holding just a tiny bit of the lender's right to interest payments on a given mortgage, but holding a tiny bit on many mortgages. That way, if one loan went bad, it wouldn't wipe out the investor, since he had diversified his risk across lots of mortgages. The problem, however, was that the whole mortgage system was now rotten, thanks to government interventions. The problem wasn't an irresponsible banker or borrower here or there. The problem was systemic, and the system was now global.

A smidgen of a subprime mortgage in, say, Detroit, could end up being held by a pension plan for city employees in a little town in Norway. So a wave of defaults in Detroit, Tallahassee, Las Vegas, Key West, and so on, could cause bankruptcy in that little Norwegian town. In hindsight, some of these financial practices seem crazy, especially when combined with all the bad policies; but a lot of smart people trusted their fortunes to them before the crisis.

To make things worse, the whole system, to some extent, suffered from "moral hazard," that is, the big financial firms, certainly Fannie and Freddie, expected that if they got into trouble, the federal government would jump in and provide a soft landing. For the most part, that's exactly what happened, with the government passing the trouble on to present and future American taxpayers.[29]

There's more to the story—it's actually worse than we've described here—but the lesson is clear: Even really good intentions don't suspend the laws of economics and incentives. Government policies didn't encourage lenders to find qualified borrowers with bad luck— a laudable goal. Rather, they pushed, prodded, and in some cases, coerced lenders to *degrade* their lending standards for lower-income and minority applicants, to the point that they were making loans not merely to poor people but to poor people with a track record of irresponsible financial dealings. This corrupted the whole system from top to bottom, and drew into its web not just Wall Street and bankers but Realtors, mortgage brokers, homebuilders, and buyers. Millions of people received loans who wouldn't have qualified—for good reasons—if the mortgage market had been kept free of government tampering.

A Virtuous Circle

Politicians left, right, and center made the classic mistake of confusing correlation with causation. As we've mentioned, homeownership, all things being equal, is *correlated* with good behavior. Homeowners tend to keep up their homes, to have more interest in their community, to be more law-abiding and plan more for the future, than people who don't own their homes. But ownership doesn't automatically make people financially wise and virtuous. In a country with stable property rights and other basic rights, wise and virtuous behavior tends to lead people to accumulate enough capital so that they can buy a home, which in turn further encourages them to behave wisely toward their hard-earned property.

In a healthy mortgage market, people get a mortgage loan because of what they've already done—they've worked hard, kept their jobs, paid their debts, delayed gratification, and saved for a down payment.[30] For decades in the United States, these habits allowed millions of people to get loans to buy a home. This was a central part of the American Dream that has drawn immigrants to our shores from around the world. They dreamed of owning the walls around them, of owning a home that no landlord could kick them out of, that could be passed on to children or used for collateral to start a business (many businesses started as home-based businesses). This dream of buying a house encouraged good financial practices, hard work, and thrift. Once people had the homes, they valued them, in part, because of what they had to do to get them in the first place. The equity they put into the loan spurred them to stay on the straight and narrow. It was a virtuous circle. Wise behavior made it possible to acquire a home, and then acquiring a home reinforced wise behavior. When government short-circuits that loop of incentives, a vicious rather than virtuous circle results.

The Same Story, Simplified

Maybe we've given you more than you wanted to know about the financial crisis. Let's boil it all down. Imagine a nurse, Jan, who has worked hard, scrimped, paid her bills on time, and saved for ten years to get enough money for a down payment on a house. She eventually saves $50,000 and uses it to get a loan to buy a $200,000 house. If she defaults on her loan later, she'll lose her house, her down payment, whatever principal she's accumulated, and her well-earned credit rating.[31]

Now imagine a guy, Jason, who discovers that he can get a so-called NINJA loan (*no income, no job, or assets*, a type of loan which was available as late as 2007[32]). He has no money for a down payment, bad credit, and an iffy employment history. He's spent the last seventeen months sleeping on his sister's couch, working odd and unreliable jobs. Still, he can just barely make the monthly mortgage payments on a $200,000 loan because he doesn't need to make a down payment, he's getting an artificially low interest rate that doesn't represent the real risk of the loan, and he can get a "negative amortization loan" in which his monthly payment doesn't even cover the interest on the loan, leaving a big fat payment looming out in the future.[33] This might seem crazy, since he will get deeper in debt over time; but he's not worried about defaulting. Since housing prices are going up fast, he figures that if he gets into financial trouble, he can quickly sell the house for a profit and pay off the loan. Jason's actions are risky but logical, *as long as housing prices keep going up faster than he is going into debt.*

So which of the borrowers, Jan or Jason, is more likely to default on a mortgage when the housing market stalls? Yeah, it's pretty obvious.

In a *normal* market, loans will go to people like Jan but not to people like Jason—at least until Jason starts behaving like Jan. No rational lender is knowingly going to provide a loan to someone who's likely to default. In the mortgage market sullied by the federal government, though, there were *millions* of Jason loans, sold and then resold, chopped up, and held by people and institutions all around the world, most of whom didn't realize they were keeping time bombs in their safes. The crisis was inevitable.

We would like to report that the Congress learned its lesson and fixed the problem. Unfortunately, the official investigation was politicized, so millions of Americans now blame "unfettered capitalism" and greedy fat cats on Wall Street. The Dodd-Frank Act that Congress passed after the crisis puts severe restrictions on the market without solving the problems—which is what we should expect from a bill named after Senator Charles Dodd and Representative Barney Frank, the two politicians most responsible for pushing through many of the policies that led to the financial crisis. As a result, the same thing may happen again.[34]

Still, the crisis can be a good lesson for us. It shows how the subtle details of property and contract laws can direct people's behavior—for good and for bad.

What Should We Do?

The right to property is not legal selfishness. It's the right that protects many of our other rights. When laws and customs properly protect that right, we can create wealth. We must zealously guard our right to acquire property. As we learned in the financial crisis, however, when politicians try to manipulate and short-circuit the market process by which property is acquired, they do far more harm than good.

One thing we know: When people can't acquire property, they can't expect to enjoy the fruits of their labor and the benefits of a global economy. Nor can they create much new wealth. If we really want to fight poverty *overseas*, therefore, we need to support policies that strengthen rather than weaken the property rights of individual citizens and families. This will probably take the combined efforts of missionaries, ministries, development groups, and enlightened foreign policy over many years, but we believe it *can* happen.

CHAPTER 14

Free to Win-Win

If our present order did not exist we too might hardly believe any such thing could ever be possible, and dismiss any report about it as a tale of the miraculous, about what could never come into being.

—F. A. HAYEK

Many well-meaning people believe free markets follow the law of the jungle, where the strong are free to prey on the weak. The protestors of "Occupy Wall Street" in 2011 implied that "unfettered capitalism" had allowed the richest 1 percent to get richer by making the bottom 99 percent poorer.

Christians are just as likely to think this way. Jim Wallis and his organization *Sojourners* pay lip service to the market. But Wallis accuses his critics of believing in "free market fundamentalism,"[1] and seems to treat communism and the free market as morally equivalent.

Meanwhile, Brian McLaren, who drifts farther left with every book he writes, accuses fans of the free market of making capitalism God. He calls for some sort of hybrid between capitalism and communism. One of McLaren's recent books is called *Everything Must Change*.

Wallis, McLaren, and many other "progressive" Christians may mean well, but when it comes to economics, they don't seem to know much.

In fact, every one of these popular complaints about the free market is based on simple economic confusion. If we want to see things change *for the better* rather than just chanting "everything must change," then we can't skip over the basic insights of economics. They're unavoidable if we want to translate our good intentions into policies that do good rather than unintended harm.

The most important of these insights concerns *freedom*.

Freedom Economics

J. D. Foster and Jennifer Marshall of the Heritage Foundation use the term "freedom economics." It reminds us that our economic freedom isn't a special case but is of a piece with our other freedoms. You can't have free markets or free enterprise without free men: "In contrast to these other terms, freedom economics situates the human person at the center of economic discussion, reminding us that the market is for man, not man for the market. Moreover, freedom economics tells us about the human ends that it ought to serve. Economics should serve human freedom in all its dimensions—political, social, physical, spiritual."[2] Our freedom, in other words, is indivisible. It's about us, first of all, not about an ideology or some abstract system. "Freedom economics is the expression of millions of people, each freely making hundreds of daily decisions that have economic implications."[3] We love this description, because it gets us focused on human persons living out their God-given capacity as free but fallen creatures made in the image of the Creator.

Champions and critics of the free market often misrepresent it because of the words we use. Some people talk about "capitalism."[4] Others prefer to defend "free enterprise," the "free market," or just "private property." These aren't exactly the same thing. "Capitalism" focuses on the savings that accumulate over time and then get invested. "Free market" focuses on uncoerced exchanges between two or more people in the marketplace of goods and services. "Free enterprise" emphasizes the role of creative, risk-taking entrepreneurs. Each of these terms captures part of the whole, but each is incomplete by itself. Like everyone else, we use "capitalism," "free enterprise," and "free markets" synonymously in this book, but what we defend is freedom economics. (We'd like to call this "free-conomics,"[5] but that might get confusing.)

The Trading Game

Keeping this terminology in mind, let's deal with some of the confusions that lead many believers to think that economic freedom is a bane rather than a blessing.

I (Jay) grew up in Amarillo, Texas, which is known for its extreme weather. It can be 110 degrees in the summer and still get freezing ice storms in the winter. When I was in the sixth grade, we had one of those ice storms. The weatherman must have predicted it the day before, because our teacher, Mrs. Hubbard, came to school prepared to deal with rowdy students trapped inside during recess.

She had apparently shopped the dollar section of a store, because she brought us a bunch of cheap toys and told us we were going to play a "trading game" as she passed out the goodies, one to each student: a paddleboard with one of those red rubber balls tied down with a rubber band, an egg of Silly Putty, a set of Barbie trading cards. Nobody got the same toy, and we could all see what everybody else got.

She then asked us to write down, on a scale from 1 to 10, how much we liked our gift. We didn't have to consult anyone. Mrs. Hubbard then had us call out, one by one, the score we had given our toy. She added them all up, and she wrote down the total on the board.

Next, she told us that we could trade with the others in our row. So everyone had four other potential trading partners. (I don't remember exactly how many students were in the class, but let's assume there were five rows of five—twenty-five in all.) No one had to trade, and no one could steal; but if one kid had the Silly Putty, another had the paddleboard, and each preferred the other's toy, then they were free to trade. Some students kept or got stuck with their original gift, but a lot of us ended up with a toy we liked more. Again, we wrote down how much we liked our toys then, on a scale of 1 to 10, called them out, and Mrs. Hubbard added up the scores. Guess what happened? The total went up after the trade.

For the second round, she told us that we could trade with everyone in the room. Now we all had twenty-four possible trading partners rather than just four. Everyone, including the kid in the back row who hadn't said a word all year, suddenly snapped to attention.

The room was abuzz for several minutes with trades, trades, and more trades. Some toys changed hands several times. But the commotion died down once no new trades were possible. We again graded our toys and added up the scores. The total score Mrs. Hubbard wrote on the board was much, much higher than the first two scores. Almost everyone ended up with a toy he liked more than the one received at the beginning. (I ended up with the paddleball.) No one had a score that had gone down.

Win-Win

A free trade isn't utopia. It can't solve the problem of scarcity; but it is a win-win exchange. If I traded Barbie trading cards to Suzie for my paddleball, Suzie (who doesn't give a rip about paddleball) and I both win. In positive-sum or win-win games, nobody loses. Some players may end up better off than others, but everyone ends up better off than if they'd taken their toys and gone home. An exchange that is free on both sides, in which no one is forced or tricked into playing, is a win-win game. It's a positive-sum game. The trading partners wouldn't trade unless both saw themselves as better off as a result. Even though nothing new was added to the system, the total value goes up; the outcome is a win-win. If you understand this one concept, you understand the free market better than most of its critics.

There are other kinds of games. Win-lose games are often called zero-sum games, because if your opponent takes one unit from you, he's at 1 and you're at –1. The sum of 1 and –1 is zero. If the game is, say, a form of gambling, you may have both started out with some money, but you haven't added any money to the total. The sum total of what you have added is zero. No new wealth or value has been generated (though, perhaps, you value the game itself, however it turns out). To have a winner in a zero-sum game, you have to have a loser. Monopoly, tennis, chess, and football are zero-sum games because a win for one side means a loss for the other. In a Super Bowl pitting Dallas against Pittsburgh, if the Dallas Cowboys win, the Pittsburgh Steelers lose, end of story. (Unfortunately, that hasn't happened very often.)

Even some economics courses misrepresent this fact. An outfit called the Teacher's Curriculum Institute has Advanced Placement high school students play a different game with an entirely different lesson.[6] The teacher is told to pass out tokens to all the students. Three "wealthy" students get ten tokens each, and the rest of the students—the "workers"—receive one token. Then the students play rock-paper-scissors over and over. You know the game: Rock beats scissors, scissors beats paper, and paper beats rock. In every round, the winner gets a token from the loser. Students play until they either run out of tokens or can't win any more. The curriculum helpfully explains that within a few minutes, "three students will have most of the tokens, a few students may have one or two tokens, and most students will have nothing."[7] *Voilà*, a zero-sum game.

The game is intended to illustrate Marx's *theory* of capitalism, which it does well—the kids who start out with more tokens usually end up with the majority of them—like the wealth in an economy moving from the proletarians to the bourgeoisie. Unfortunately, students subjected to this curriculum aren't told there's a difference between Marx's theory of the free market and reality. They leave the classroom thinking they understand "capitalism," when all they've gotten is Marxist propaganda.

In a free market, when you walk into a grocery store with twenty dollars, there's not a rock-paper-scissors officer waiting there to force you to play the game with the grocer, with the winner getting twenty dollars and the groceries. No, you buy Wonder Bread, Cheez-its, Goober peanut butter, Slim Jims, All Bran, star fruit, or whatever you prefer more than the money in your pocket. If you don't find anything, you leave and go to a store with better prices or better groceries. The only function the rock-paper-scissors game should serve is to illustrate that a free market isn't like it!

A free market is not a free-for-all where the strong always prey on the weak. It requires a rule of law that allows only certain kinds of trades, like the Trading Game. Students can't threaten or steal from each other. And since every class has a bully, you need an authority like Mrs. Hubbard. With these rules in place, free trade ends up being win-win. If free trade were like one party gaining a token and the other losing a token, there would be no trades that are free on both sides and no uncoerced trades would happen. *Free* trades can happen only if both traders see themselves as better off as a result of the trade.

We saw in the trading game that the total value of the toys, that is, how much everyone liked what he had, went up with the increased number of possible trading partners, but not everyone graded theirs the same. Some students graded their final toy as a 9, while others graded theirs as a 6. Still, almost everyone ended up with a gift he liked more than the gift he started with, even though nothing new was added to the game and the players were competing against each other.

Economic Value Is in the Eye of the Beholder

All the toys cost Mrs. Hubbard about the same, but we students valued them differently. For centuries, economists and philosophers often defined economic value in terms of labor or cost of production—called the *labor theory of value*.[8] They thought that something was worth what it cost to produce it. This sounds right when you first hear it, but the Trading Game shows that economic value is in the eye of the beholder. This may seem like a subtle point, but understanding it is vital if we are to avoid disastrous economic policies.

To see why the labor theory is wrong, imagine you decide to open a home baking business because your friends keep telling you that your chocolate torte recipe is to die for. You sink your savings into an industrial oven, buy hundreds of pounds of ingredients at Costco, and start cooking. You make a hundred tortes on your first run. Then, to find out how much you need to charge to cover your costs, you add up the cost of the ingredients, throw in a fraction of the cost of the oven, an average hourly wage (to account for your labor), and so forth. Because you use a variety of boutique specialty ingredients, you learn that, just to cover your costs, you will need to charge $100 per torte. Of course, you don't just want to break even. Otherwise, what's the point? So you decide to charge $110 per torte, figuring you deserve a 10 percent profit for your trouble.

So how much is one of your tortes worth—$110? Well, no. If its value is determined by the total cost to produce it, then it would be worth $100. But is it even worth $100? Well, let's say you build a website, post signs around town, and even put up a stand outside to try to sell your chocolate tortes, and no one buys. You launch an investigation to find out why. After a while, you discover that anyone can buy a really tasty torte for $20 at that popular bakery and latte bar down the street. And Costco sells pretty decent ones for $9.99. Yikes!

You've suddenly realized that just because it cost you a hundred bucks to make one torte, that doesn't mean anyone is willing to pay that much for it. So how do you find out how much your tortes are worth economically? Assuming you already have a good marketing plan, you have to start dropping the price until you find the sweet spot where your torte is worth more to someone than the money he has to give up to buy it. The good news for you is that, as it turns out, many people do find your torte slightly superior to the neighborhood bakery torte. The downside is that you discover that they are only willing to pay an additional $5 over the $20 charged by the bakery. In your market, people will pay you only $25 for a torte that cost you $100 to make. That's too bad for you; but at least now you've found out what it's worth. *The economic value of something is determined not by its cost of production but by how much someone is willing to give up freely to get it.* Of course, labor often adds value, as long as it creates what someone wants. But you can't *define* economic value in terms of labor. If you mess up your torte by mistaking the salt container for the sugar, you haven't made a hundred-dollar torte, no matter how much labor you've poured into it. You've made a mistake.

Again, economic value is in the eye of the beholder; but the beholder's eye can be fickle. If you're taking a cross-country road trip, find yourself desperately hungry, and come to a gas station with the sign out front that says, LAST FOOD AND GAS FOR 120 MILES, you'll be glad to see a Subway sandwich store attached to it. You will value that toasted, foot-long, double-meat club on honey wheat a lot more in that situation than if you were walking around downtown Seattle, where there is a Subway on every third corner. You'll also be willing to pay more for the first sandwich than for every subsequent one. If one sandwich fills you up, you might not buy another, even if it cost only five cents.

But how can the second sandwich be worth so much less (to you) than the first one just because you're full? Scottish moral philosopher Adam Smith tried to resolve this paradox in his book *The Wealth of Nations.* It seems like a paradox if you're looking for economic value in all the wrong places. It makes perfect sense once you realize that economic value is subjective: it has to do with how much you, and lots of other people, value some particular good or service in a market.

Economic value is subjective but that does not mean "everything is relative." Economic value is not ultimate value. Your ultimate value in the eyes of God is not the same as your economic value.

Imagine a society that ignored this insight about economic value and instead based its laws on the labor theory of value. In that society, the "just price" for one of your tortes would be $100. Even if you could get more than that, it would be unjust to charge more than it's worth. It would also be unjust for anyone to pay you less than $100. But there's a problem: Since nobody is going to buy your tortes freely, a free trade won't happen. If someone pays you $100, it will only be because he was *forced* to do so. Win for you, loss for him.

If you're making the tortes, you might like this arrangement, since you wouldn't lose any money on a sale. But this policy has unintended consequences: No one has any incentive to be efficient or to think about what people might actually want to buy, and at what price. People usually won't go to the trouble of anticipating what people want or would buy if they can make others buy their product. That's the beauty of a free market. Whether people are selfish, selfless, or indifferent, it will channel their economic behavior toward producing things that other people want, at a price they're willing to pay. That's a win-win.

This doesn't mean that in a free market, no one ever loses. You might still lose a sale of tortes to the local bakery. A free market doesn't guarantee that everyone wins in every competition. Rather, by coordinating our choices, it allows many more win-win encounters than any alternative. Free markets are win-win for everyone in the marketplace because every producer is also a customer. Competition reduces cost and improves quality for you and everyone else. If the word "competition" sounds cruel and Darwinian to you, keep in mind we're talking about competition under rule of law where people are protected from theft, violence, and fraud.

The alternatives to free markets are, as discussed, socialism, lawless anarchy, and, another alternative that is pretty bleak, too—an oligarchy or monopoly controlled by the powerful and politically well connected. In a monopoly, producers have little incentive to improve their product or cut costs, since consumers have no other choices.

History supports this conclusion. Any time a producer has managed to work hand-in-glove with the government to establish an artificial monopoly on a good or service, the quality of the good or service stagnates and prices are higher than in free markets where the same product is produced. The laborers working for the monopoly might have higher wages than in a competitive market; but even so, their income won't go nearly as far because, in a monopoly economy, virtually every good and service is shoddier and more expensive.

Market competition is *far* better than monopoly, since competitors, buffered by the rule of law, will tend to focus on meeting the wants and needs of customers rather than stealing from them or forcing them to buy their products.[9]

The Mystery of the Market

A free market not only sets up win-win exchanges; it distributes goods and services far better than any distribution system planned out by human beings. This is what Adam Smith had in mind when he described the market as an "invisible hand." His idea is that a free market will guide the acts of individuals "to promote an end which is not part of [their] intention."[10] The butcher, brewer, and baker don't need to know all the outcomes of their work, and they don't need to visualize world peace or think nice thoughts in order to benefit the world. They could just as well be thinking about their electric bill, their car insurance, or their desire to win the "best business owner of the year" award from the Chamber of Commerce. They might even be selfish. Nevertheless, they will still work to provide something that others will freely buy. Smith saw this invisible hand as God's providence over human affairs, since it creates a more harmonious order than any human being could contrive. The great Austrian economist F. A. Hayek also marveled at what he called the "spontaneous order" of the market.[11] Common sense might lead you to suspect that a free market, where no government entity determines prices, production quotas, and the like, would lead to chaos. To get an orderly distribution of goods and services, you might think that somebody will have to be in charge of the whole operation. This is more or less what socialists and progressives thought in the twentieth century, and because they gained control over whole nations, they could test their beliefs on a broad scale. The result was misery and oppression, food shortages, overproduced products that gathered dust on store shelves, widespread poverty, and at the extreme, death.

In the 1980s, the last premier of the Soviet Union, Mikhail Gorbachev, traveled to Great Britain and met British Prime Minister Margaret Thatcher. According to a popular story, when Gorbachev was touring with Thatcher, he was surprised to see how well off the British seemed to be. He asked Thatcher who made sure that the British people got fed. "No one," she told him. "The price system does that." The British people got fed far better than the subjects of the Soviet Union, who languished under a planned economy.

Think of the Trading Game again. What if, instead of the students getting to trade freely, Mrs. Hubbard dictated or tried to guess which toy each of her twenty-five students preferred? Would all the kids have gotten what they liked best? Probably not. The fact that they freely traded when given a chance proved that most of the kids hadn't gotten what they preferred at the beginning.

The random distribution by Mrs. Hubbard illustrates the dilemma that would beset any centralized economic planner. Such planning simply can't work because human planners are not all-knowing. To plan a whole economy, a planner would have to know the value of every product for every person in the economy at every time and place, since the value of things can change drastically depending on the situation. Remember the Subway sandwich. The first one you eat is worth more to you than every subsequent one, at least until you get hungry again.

Much to the surprise of socialists, planned economies create all sorts of crazy distortions. For a time in the Soviet Union, glass factories were paid according to how many tons of sheet glass they produced. Since they didn't have to concern themselves with what people actually wanted, the factories started producing glass so thick that it was useless. The planners then changed the rules and paid factories by the square meter. Guess what happened? Factories started producing glass that was so thin that it broke at the slightest provocation.[12]

If you've followed us this far, you might be wondering: If economic planners can't know the right price of anything before the moment of free exchange, how is free trade possible?

This is the central mystery and wonder of the market order: We *can* learn the value of any economic good—a one-hour aromatherapy session in Monaco on June 6, 2012, a cantaloupe at Trader Joe's in Santa Monica on May 5, 2013—but *only* through the market process in which free choices are channeled by rule of law.

The purchased price of a good or service in a free economy is like a label packed with information. It tells us what that thing is worth (economically) at that moment. This price compresses a huge amount of information since it represents thousands of underlying realities. On the basis of current prices, savvy entrepreneurs can make educated guesses about how and where to invest. Savvy suppliers and producers can do the same.

In a free market, prices have an amazing power to summon goods, services, and resources to the place they're most valued. If there's a housing boom in Houston, Texas, the prices for lumber, bricks, concrete, and construction skills will go up, and before long, supplies will appear there to meet the higher price. But other parts of the country don't necessarily end up with a shortage. If there's any demand for these things in Poughkeepsie or Pawnee, the prices will rise there, drawing some of the needed resources back there. Unless there is a literal shortage where a good just isn't available, the freedom of prices to go up and down will keep supply and demand for scarce goods in an exquisite equilibrium.

This is not utopia, but it is a more complex, efficient, and just order than any that human planners can or ever have devised. If we're interested in freedom *and* helping the poor, we have to recognize the power of the free market—at home and abroad.

CHAPTER 15

Going Global

Free trade is not based on utility but on justice.
—EDMUND BURKE

Free trade is not only a win-win game; the larger the pool of trading partners, the greater the benefits for everyone involved. The Trading Game in the previous chapter illustrated this even though we only had toys to trade. A real market allows people and companies to specialize, to focus on those tasks in which they have a comparative advantage and thus will receive the greatest rewards. In their agricultural sectors, Costa Ricans are wise to focus on growing and exporting bananas and Icelanders on catching and exporting Arctic fish. That part of the story is simple. When specialization goes global, the results are astonishing. The supply chain that gives rise to iPads, cell phones, Boeing 747s, and the Internet is the outcome of international markets plus specialization, with billions of people involved. These webs of cooperation have, in the last few centuries, allowed vast wealth to be created and enjoyed, much of it enjoyed by even relatively poor people.

Large markets and specialization are important. Imagine the alternative: The citizens of Fargo, North Dakota, decide they are only going to buy local. They resolve not to wear, eat, drive, or live in anything that originated anywhere outside the Fargo metropolitan area (which includes a few hundred thousand people). They want to keep their wealth at home rather than transferring it to "foreigners" in Duluth, Topeka, and Salt Lake City. To live like they do now, they would need to have mines and smelters of all sorts, steel mills, oil wells, oil refineries, car manufacturing and computer chip fabricating plants, lightbulb factories, leather tanners, farms, ranches, butchers, dairy farms, fruit orchards, paper and textile mills, chemical factories, pharmaceutical factories, movie studios, and on and on and on—all in and around Fargo. Few citizens of Fargo have the skills to perform the tasks required for such a wide variety of industries. Farms and orchards in Fargo don't produce in the cold winters. There would be no citrus, no seafood. Many commodities and metals just aren't available in Fargo. Fargo has a major Microsoft contingent, which provides a lot of software experts; but they're in oversupply since there's no trading outside Fargo.

Without large markets that accommodate specialization, most of what the folks in Fargo now take for granted would disappear, and their lives would start to resemble the lives of villagers prior to the Industrial Revolution. They would work much harder and less productively, everything would be much more expensive, and everyone would be vastly poorer. Their lives would be nasty, brutish, and short.

Most Americans understand that specialization and free trade inside US borders leads to a much higher standard of living, for everyone; however, even many "conservative" Americans who claim to believe in free markets and limited government violate their own principles when it comes to trading with our fellow human beings from other countries.

I, iPad

Leonard Read's famous story "I, Pencil,"[1] delightfully demonstrates the benefits of free trade. We'll update it a bit.

*   *   *

I am an iPad—a smooth, flat, rectangular tablet computer produced by Apple. You can watch streaming HD movies on me, talk to friends and siblings on the other side of the country with audio and video display, surf the Internet, and download hundreds of thousands of audio and video files from iTunes. You can use me to guide you to your destination by downloading a 99-cent application from the App Store. With various apps, you can check weather, traffic, and the headlines, and read dozens of different versions of the Bible and thousands of books. I can help you translate a foreign language, or scan a bar code on almost any item and then find the store nearest to you that has it, and tell you how much it will cost. You can download the Liturgy of the Hours and pray the Psalms in the mornings and evening with people around the world. These are just a few of the more than 200,000 apps available to you with the click of a touch screen.

I only weigh about one and a half pounds. I can connect to the Internet using both cellular and Wi-Fi. I'm lightning fast. I have a 1-gigahertz, dual-core A 5 chip for a processor, a ten-hour battery, two cameras—one on front and one on back—a 9.7-inch (diagonal) LED-backlit glossy widescreen Multi-Touch display with IPS technology, with 1,024-by-768-pixel resolution at 132 pixels per inch, with finger-print-resistant oleophobic coating.[2] These are just the superficial specs. I'd love to tell you about my flash memory chips and my aluminum casing, but I know this stuff gets boring.

You probably have no idea how my touch screen works or what is going on inside me. You may feel technologically illiterate because you could never build me from scratch. But I'll let you in on a little secret: No one at Apple, indeed, *no one on the planet, knows how to build me from scratch*. Even if you broke me down into my smaller systems—the touch screen, cameras, processor, memory chips, casing, whatever—no one person could make these components from scratch, either.

My casing is made from aluminum, which has to be processed from bauxite ore at a mine in Africa or Australia. It has to be refined, smelted, and fabricated in a very complicated process.[3] Then the aluminum is shipped to China, where it's molded. Thousands of people are involved in creating this one simple piece. Wintek in Taiwan makes my glass touch screen and bezel assembly. The liquid crystal display underneath comes from South Korea. Some folks in Irvine, California, were also involved. My audio chip is from Austin, Texas. My flash memory is made by Toshiba at the Yokkaichi factory in Japan, just five hundred miles south of the terrible tsunami-triggering earthquake that struck Japan in 2011.

I could spend hours telling you what is involved in making any one of my other parts. Though I am "designed in California and manu-factured in China," millions of people all over the world play a part in getting me to an Apple Store. Many millions more are involved in the technologies—cellular, fiber optics, Internet, Global Positioning Satel-lites, power generators, computer programmers—that make it possible for me to do what I do. No one person or even one company knows how to do all these things. That knowledge and information isn't stored in one place. It's dispersed in the minds of millions of people, including the minds of people no longer living. If you trace the network of knowledge back historically, you'll discover thousands upon thou-sands of patents secured over decades that came before me. No one has all that information or the needed skills to implement it. And yet, here I am, downloading the latest version of the Angry Birds app because you forgot to password-protect me from your children.

Not only can no one build me from scratch; most of the people involved weren't intending to make iPads or maintain the infrastruc-ture so that I can work. Certainly not the miner in Australia and the oil rigger on a platform in the Gulf of Mexico drawing up oil from the sea floor. Not even Steve Jobs and Steve Wozniak had thought of the iPad when they founded Apple back in the 1970s.

No human being oversees the whole process. Rather, people work-ing freely in specialized jobs, speaking dozens of different languages in different countries, following the prices of just the goods and services closest to their part of the operation make me a reality. If I didn't already exist, you might assume such a feat was either impossible or magical.

Of course, I'm not the only tablet computer. The Hewlett-Packard TouchPad, the Dell Streak, the Fujitsu Lifebook, and many more tablets have a similar story to tell. I'm not impressed, but I must admit that these competitors push Apple to make me more fabulous, while still pricing me affordably. If Apple had a monopoly on tablet computers, I can assure you that I would be much less impressive and much more expensive.

You might think that only high-tech gadgets like iPads need international supply chains, but even something as humble as a yellow number two pencil depends on the coordinated work of many thousands of people around the world. That was the point of Leonard Read's "I, Pencil." No one could make an iPad, but no one knows how to make that simple pencil from scratch, either! This global market is one of the greatest wonders in the world; it deserves at least to be admired. Woven into market competition is a magnificent efflorescence of free cooperation, coordination, and creation. It channels human creativity into unparalleled feats.

Globalization, Not Globalism

Even Christians who defend the free market are often wary of global markets because they link them to the rise of a one-world government. There is a world of difference between economic globalization and one-world globalism. "Globalization" refers to the growth of trade and specialization among the countries of the world. On balance, this is a good thing. There are still a billion people languishing in severe poverty, and billions more who could be doing much better. These people will stay impoverished unless they can get plugged into global markets.

One-world *globalism*, on the other hand, is a political ideology.

Globalists consider nation-states obsolete and seek to establish trans-national entities to manage seven billion world citizens. Globalization is about the spread of economic freedom. Globalism is about the spread of political control—of one world government. The words look alike, but they refer to opposites. We should support globalization, not globalism.

But What About Outsourcing?

Globalization is a sore spot for many Americans, especially those in manufacturing, who worry about competing with cheap foreign labor. If you have a manufacturing job in Detroit, and your plant closes and relocates to Mumbai, that's painful and disruptive for you. But that does not mean the change is unjust or bad overall.

No one—no business and no person—*likes* competition if they can have monopoly control instead. If you're getting paid $50 an hour to build motherboards for computers, you're not going to like it if someone in another country is willing to do the same job just as well for $12 an hour. You'll probably like policies that protect your job by making it harder for those foreign workers to compete. If the government slaps steep tariffs on imported motherboards, for instance, you're less likely to face competition from Mexico City or Mumbai.

Is the computer company obligated to keep paying you $50 an hour, even if it makes the company less competitive, when an Indian does the same job for a lot less money? Are you entitled to the job, and entitled to prevent the poor Indian from having the job? And should your neighbor be forced to buy a higher-priced motherboard made by you than purchase a more economical one produced by the guy in Mumbai? This amounts to subtly coercing your neighbor to give up some of his property (the extra cost of your motherboard).

What if the government put a tariff on imported motherboards to raise their costs, and used the money to subsidize the American company? Lots of Americans support policies like this. This amounts to a government official making your neighbor give some of his money to you. Labels like "just wages" don't seem just in this light.

Economic change always leads to some temporary displacement. Joseph Schumpeter called it *creative destruction*. If a company doesn't provide something people will freely buy, it will be transformed or cease to exist (unless the government props it up). The buggy whip industry was displaced by the auto industry, the electric typewriter by the personal computer, and whale oil industry by petroleum refining.

More recently, everyone in the floppy disk industry was displaced when the technology became obsolete. Ditto with the eight-track tape industry when cassettes and then CDs displaced them. Still, no one would argue that the Department of Commerce should have subsidized floppy disk and eight-track tape manufacturing, just to avoid displacement. This would have been a huge waste of resources. Despite the pain, those making floppy disks and eight-track tapes needed to move to other jobs that provided something people wanted.

The question is not, how can we avoid all painful change and job displacement, but rather, what's the best arrangement for everyone overall? Are free and open international markets better than protectionism in the long run, despite displacement of jobs? We know the answer: yes.

Adam Smith, the father of modern capitalism, explained why over two hundred years ago:

> What is prudence in the conduct of every family can scarce be folly in that of a great kingdom. If a foreign country can supply us with a commodity cheaper than we ourselves can make it, better buy it of them with some part of the produce of our own industry, employed in a way in which we have some advantage.

Buying a product such as coffee from another country is *not* a "wealth transfer" from us to them, if they can provide it to us less expensively

than we could produce it ourselves. Both sides are better off as a result
of the trade. With the time and effort we save by not growing coffee
inefficiently, we can be employed more fruitfully.[4] If, instead, we think
we're entitled to our jobs at their current salary, and we support politicians who promise to "protect" our jobs, we'll all end up worse off in
the long run.

It's often hard to think clearly about this issue when we have a personal stake in it. So consider Israel. The government there imposed
heavy tariffs and protections on its citizens for decades after its founding in 1948. Once these were reformed in the late 1980s and '90s, Israel's economy exploded. No doubt every person benefitting from the
earlier protectionist policies at the time thought they were better off as
a result. But they weren't looking at the long-term costs and benefits of
the policies.

The benefit of international trade is not just theory; it's fact. In the
last thirty years, per capita income and life expectancy have gone up in
most countries around the world. Total income has increased worldwide, including in many developing countries. The exceptions are
communist and other oppressive countries such as North Korea that
have remained mostly outside global markets.[5] Generally, the more
freedom a country enjoys, the better it does economically. Every year,
places such as Hong Kong, New Zealand, and Australia rank near the
top in rankings of economic freedom. Zimbabwe, Cuba, and North
Korea land at the bottom.[6] Free trade between nations, on balance,
allows its participants to be better off economically than they would
have been otherwise.

Perverse Protectionism

Unfortunately, the United States and other Western countries still *protect* many industries such as agriculture, shielding them from competition with poor countries. We subsidize parts of our farm industry

with tax money and add punitive tariffs (taxes on goods produced in other countries) on imports such as sugar and cotton. Many subsidies were originally put in place to help struggling family farms during the Depression, and to stabilize food prices. We know farmers personally who benefit from these programs, and we understand their fear of losing their livelihood. And as long as they're in place, it makes sense for farmers to accept them. But, again, we need to look at these policies in a principled way, rather than personally.

Though American farmers receiving subsidies benefit in the short term, they harm all of us—including farmers—over the long term, since they make food more expensive and prevent many Americans from channeling their efforts into work that would create more wealth for everyone. According to a recent study, the parts of the country that are most highly subsidized are economically decrepit.[7] Though subsidies should be phased out slowly to allow those affected to adjust, we would all be better off, long term, to eliminate them. Because of our stable climate, rich soil, and the growing market for local produce and other foods, it's highly unlikely that a freer market would mean all agriculture would move offshore. It would just fix the current economic distortions that inflate food prices and misallocate resources better employed elsewhere.

The policies are not only uneconomical but also unfair to the developing world. We cannot claim to care about the poor in the developing world while preventing them from competing fairly in our markets. Africa loses about $500 billion a year because of trade restrictions— "largely in the form of subsidies by Western governments to Western farmers."[8] That's a huge amount of money in Africa. Every cow in the European Union gets around $2.50 per "day in subsidies, more than what a billion people . . . have to live on every day."[9]

We salve our consciences with government-to-government aid, but in reality such foreign aid often does more harm than good. By subsidizing goods such as cotton and sugar, these crops get overproduced, and then the United States, Europe, and other rich countries flood the international market with crops that are artificially cheap or simply given away to poor countries as foreign aid. We mean to help, but dumping free goods can actually be harmful, making it impossible for African farmers to compete. Imagine if the federal government gave Target hundreds of billions of dollars but didn't do the same for Walmart. Walmart couldn't compete since Target could sell its stuff much more cheaply. That's what we often do to farmers in many poor countries with our subsidies and tariffs.

This is one reason the entire continent of Africa contributes a mere 1 percent to worldwide trade. Tariffs between African countries make them poorer, too, as many African countries have steep tariffs on goods from other African countries.[10] We in the United States would all be much poorer if every state had tariffs on goods from every other state.

Protectionism, however plausible it may seem at first glance or however personally it touches you, doesn't protect wealth. It reduces it.[11]

CHAPTER 16

Crossing the Border

Give me your tired, your poor, your huddled masses
*   yearning to breathe free,*
The wretched refuse of your teeming shore.
Send these, the homeless, tempest-tossed to me,
I lift my lamp beside the golden door!
                              —EMMA LAZARUS

Closely related to international trade is immigration. International trade allows goods and services to go where they are most valued. Open immigration allows the same thing with people. For years, Microsoft has had to petition the government to make it easier for them to hire foreign employees, when they could not find qualified domestic applicants. This suggests the priorities in our immigration policy are out of whack. Our immigration laws often make it hard for legal immigrants to maneuver, while doing little to prevent illegal immigration.

Views on immigration don't divide up neatly into "liberal" and "conservative." Some people focus on the economic benefits to the free flow of labor. The editorial page of *The Wall Street Journal*, for instance, tends to be pro-immigration. Just as capital in a free market will flow to the places it is most valued, labor will do the same. This is a good thing, and it has always happened within US borders. In the nineteenth century, farmers moved west in search of soil more fertile than the rocky ground available in New England. "In 1870, Iowa's farms were producing 40 bushels of corn per acre, while Maryland farmers were making do with 22 bushels."[1] Right now, there is an exodus of workers from California to Texas, because Texas has a much better business climate. If Californians couldn't move out of their state in search of jobs, the state government in Sacramento would have even less reason to avoid stupid economic policies. In the long run, this freedom of movement is not just good for Texas and for workers, but for California as well.

The problem with *foreign* immigration is not so much economic as social and cultural. Labor can't be transferred by wire or shipped by FedEx. Labor is people—families, religious beliefs, political histories, and cultures. That's why some worry about the long-term cultural impact of undisciplined immigration. In order to maintain our laws and culture, they want the flow of immigration to be gradual enough to allow immigrants to assimilate.

Others focus on human rights and so want to grant blanket amnesty to illegal immigrants. Some are even cynical and want to grant blanket amnesty so that the new citizens will then vote for the candidate who granted amnesty.

Labor unions, however, usually don't like immigration (legal or otherwise) because they fear that immigrants will undercut their union wages.

Love the Sojourner

Christians must remember that God commanded the Jews to treat the *sojourner* with kindness. In Deuteronomy, Moses said to the assembled Jews, "[G]od executes justice for the fatherless and the widow, and loves the sojourner, giving him food and clothing; love the sojourner therefore; for you were sojourners in the land of Egypt" (Deuteronomy 10:18–19). God has special compassion for sojourners and we should, too.

Immigration Policy Is the Main Problem

Recently, both the US Conference of Catholic Bishops[2] and the National Association of Evangelicals[3] have called for "immigration reform." While both have important things to say, neither, in our opinion, has offered a politically viable solution.

The problem is not with immigration itself, but with the illogical immigration policy the United States has stumbled into in the last few decades. Immigration doesn't mean what it meant when the pilgrims sailed from England by way of the Netherlands, the Irish immigrated here during the Irish potato famine, and Chinese immigrants sailed to California. These immigrants often abandoned everything in hope of a better life for their children. They came here legally and worked hard when they got here.

In 1956, a certain man and woman met in an English language class in New York City. The man had just immigrated from Germany, and the woman from Greece. They married and had a family. Though neither of them attended college, their son attended Yale and eventually became a writer—our friend Eric Metaxas, author of *Amazing Grace* and *Bonhoeffer*. This is just one of countless immigration success stories.

In the last few decades, this pattern of immigration, which made America great, has changed. The United States has grown lax in securing its borders. It's also become a vast entitlement state, so that even immigrants who want to make a life for themselves can end up on the public dole. Many of our institutions now discourage assimilation and encourage cultural relativism. These policies often have turned immigration into a liability rather than an asset. No plan for immigration reform that ignores these facts has a prayer of passing muster with voters. Nor should it.

James C. Bennett managed to boil down the dilemma with

immigration to a short proverb: "Democracy, immigration, multi-culturalism…pick any two." These three policies are like territorial cats. You might get two to live under the same roof, but not three. Democracy and immigration can coexist as long as immigrants are assimilated and adopt the same constitutional values as their adopted country. Immigration and multiculturalism (that is, cultural relativ-ism) can coexist in a brutal dictatorship (without democracy) because, even if a million *Mayflowers* arrive with pilgrims and don't assimilate, they lack the political power to transform the country. And democ-racy and multiculturalism can coexist if the cultural variety was pres-ent at the beginning, and no new immigrants with contrary values are admitted afterward.

The key point, for us, is that immigration plus multiculturalism plus democracy will give rise to dangerous ethnic and religious factions, eventually tearing apart our democracy. The point is obvious in the extreme: Imagine granting American citizenship to 305 million people, all at once, from cultures that are *opposed* to individual human rights, representative government, and religious freedom. How do you suppose the next election would turn out? And the one after that?

Illegal Immigration

Confusing immigration with illegal immigration is "like saying that because you don't like people breaking into your home, you are anti-guest."[4] Opposing illegal immigration does not make you anti-immigrant. It's easy for those of us who live hundreds of miles from our southern border with Mexico to accuse ranchers there of being racist and anti-immigrant. Just because some have racist attitudes doesn't mean racism and hatred of foreigners are the main problems. Many of those harmed by illegal immigration are legal immigrants and Hispanic Americans whose ancestors have been here for generations.

More Demand Than Supply

The flow of illegal immigrants isn't surprising. American citizenship is a valuable commodity and millions seek to immigrate here. American employers, for their part, often see the economic advantages of immigrant labor.

We could open our borders and solve the immigration problem right away. But that would be like abolishing all private property to eliminate theft: it would trade a problem for a disaster. In the long run, we would support a policy to make it easier for people to immigrate legally, although most Americans will not support more open immigration policies until the problems with the current policy get fixed. Real reform is tough because we don't have the luxury of crafting an immigration policy from scratch, like the founders of a new nation. Some twelve million people currently live in the United States illegally: either they entered illegally or got here legally but stayed after their permit expired. Millions of these illegal immigrants have been here for years, have jobs, are settled in a community, and have children in public schools. That makes the problem different from ordinary crime such as shoplifting. Richard Land, president of the conservative Ethics & Religious Liberty Commission of the Southern Baptist Convention, illustrated the point by recounting a discussion he had with a congressman:

> [The congressman] said to me, "It's immoral to break the law." "Agreed," I replied, "but it is also immoral to not enforce the law for two decades and then decide arbitrarily one day that you are going to do so retroactively."
> Suppose the government informed me that they had been monitoring my driving and now they were going to fine me for every time I had exceeded the speed limit for two decades.

I would owe a tidy sum, whereas if they had stopped me the first couple of times, I would have slowed down permanently. Most Americans would reject such a policy as unfair.

Government inaction has allowed undocumented workers to work here, yet their illegal status has kept them from assimilating to the majority culture as rapidly as previous immigrants. This is rending the social fabric in ways that are far easier to rend than they are to mend.[5]

Our immigration problem is partly due to immigrants being here illegally, and partly due to decades of lax enforcement of our laws. That, combined with desperate circumstances in parts of Mexico and other countries to our south, means that no solution is going to be perfect. What we do with illegal immigrants who are already here is one thing; how we handle future illegal immigration is another.

It's utterly unrealistic to think we can deport twelve million people. That would be like moving the entire population of Washington State—twice. Let's assume we could round them all up. How would we deport twelve million people—men, women, and children. In freight containers? Buses? Trains? A long march south? Even if this were feasible, the human tragedy would be horrendous. We're not a nation who could commit such an act.

On the other hand, to grant blanket amnesty to illegals would be to reward the lawbreakers, discourage the law-abiding, and encourage even more illegal immigration. It would be unfair to the millions who have entered, live, and work here legally and millions of others still waiting in line. Amnesty could lead to widespread unrest and more resentment of immigrants, since a majority of the American public is opposed to amnesty.

So we should quit talking about blanket deportation on the one hand and blanket amnesty on the other, and focus on realistic options between these two extremes.

A Way Forward

In our opinion, any viable proposal should include the following elements, and in the right order.[6]

Enforce the Law

First—and we do mean first—the government needs to secure the borders both to gain the trust of the American people and to prevent more illegals from arriving. Many countries, including Mexico to some degree, treat illegal immigrants into their own countries as foreign enemies of the state. The least we can do is secure our borders. Keeping people from crossing our borders illegally is different from deporting people who have already been here for years. We're surely capable of slowing the amount of illegal immigration down to a trickle through some mix of fences, walls, border guards, National Guard, private citizens, and surveillance technology—but it hasn't been a priority.

Many illegal immigrants didn't sneak across the border, but came here legally and stayed when their visas expired. This is more a problem with law enforcement and record-keeping rather than border control. If the federal government can keep track of Social Security checks and income tax returns, however, surely it should be able to keep better track of these immigrants. It just hasn't been a priority.

Assimilation, not Multiculturalism

Second, we must pursue an energetic policy of assimilation with immigrant populations, enforced by law, which includes civic education and training in English. There's nothing magical about English. But English is the primary language in the United States. A common language unites people. Immigrants are much more likely to succeed if they learn English, which is the language of international trade.

We're *not* saying we should forbid the use of other languages or make Spanish road signs illegal. In fact, we would all do well to learn other languages. (You've probably heard the old joke: If someone who knows three languages is trilingual, and someone who knows two languages is bilingual, what is someone who knows one language? An American!)

The alternative to assimilation isn't live-and-let-live, but what Mark Steyn calls "reverse assimilation," whereby the immigrant culture displaces the native culture. This is already apparent in Muslim immigration to Europe. We're not talking about well-assimilated Muslims who are delighted to be free of oppression in Iraq or Iran, and who are committed to freedom and individual rights. We mean large, unassimilated, hostile Muslim populations living in enclaves. Unreconstructed Islam is both religious and political, and secular Europe is ill prepared to handle it. According to a poll by the London *Telegraph*, "40% of British Muslims want shariah implemented in predominantly Muslim parts of the United Kingdom."[7] If hostile Muslim populations in Europe come to predominate, we could see a stark example of reverse assimilation in the next generation.

So far, most mainstream European politicians have turned a blind eye to this problem. That leaves the nonmainstream, including extremists, such as Anders Behring Breivik, to respond. Breivik is the terrorist who killed dozens of his fellow Norwegians in July 2011. He was motivated, at least in part, by hostility to Muslim immigration. After the massacre, author Bruce Bawer, an Oslo resident, wrote, "Several of us who have written about the rise of Islam in Europe have warned that the failure of mainstream political leaders to responsibly address the attendant challenges would result in the emergence of extremists like Breivik." Predictably, Breivik's evil rampage gave leftists a golden opportunity to denounce reasonable concerns as "Islamaphobia."

We have our problems, of course, but nothing as serious as this. In the 2011 United States versus Mexico soccer championship in Los Angeles, for instance, the US team was "smothered in boos" by the crowd. It was so loud that the US team felt as if they were playing an away game.[8] These boos came not just from Mexican spectators, but from Mexican *Americans* rooting for the Mexican team. This made a lot of people angry, because it suggested that these Mexican immigrants opposed their adopted country. We understand the frustration, but we should keep in mind that many immigrants from our south are Christian and see themselves as heirs of Western civilization in the broad sense.

Teach American Culture

Third, we must pass on American culture to immigrants. We're all for cultural and ethnic variety, but many of our institutions are now training schools for cultural relativism. These days, if a woman immigrates here from Vietnam or Venezuela and enrolls in an American history class at a nearby community college, she's likely to learn that America is the incarnation of evil but never learn the story of America. This is not the way to cultivate new citizens. We must roll back the influence of cultural relativism and anti-Americanism in our public institutions. These trends harm immigrants by preventing them from embracing and assimilating into American culture. There are already many ministries that work with immigrants and refugees, and they should play a role in this effort. This is one of those areas in which private organizations, ministries, and the government could work together.

Work, Not Entitlements

Fourth, we must reform entitlements and welfare programs that tend to suck immigrants into a cycle that discourages work. As Milton Friedman once said, "You cannot simultaneously have free immigration and a welfare state."9 We have seen immigrants come to the United States as political refugees with help from Christian ministries. Rather than seeking gainful employment, however, they are tempted to get Social Security Income and other benefits from the federal government that they have not earned. This is false compassion. It prevents immigrants from integrating into society and contributing to it. It also creates resentment. Christians should take the lead in helping immigrants find jobs and get on their feet, and help them fight the temptation to become wards of the state.

Legal Status and a Path to Citizenship, Not Amnesty

Fifth, we should develop a program that gives illegal immigrants a legal status but not automatic citizenship. Employers of illegals need an incentive to identify their employees. I (James) have talked to employers who suspect that some of their employees are illegals. They would jump at a chance to resolve the situation without losing their livelihood or their employees. Some type of fine and guest-worker program could provide this.

To keep reform from being mere amnesty-on-the-installment-plan, legal status must come at a price, not just for employers, but for the illegals themselves. Richard Land, summarizing the 2006 resolution of the Southern Baptist Convention, suggests this:

> Proper reform should consist of a "guest-worker" program that requires an illegal immigrant to undergo a criminal background check, pay a fine, agree to pay back taxes, learn English, and get in line behind those who have legally migrated into this country in order to apply for permanent residence after a probationary period of years.[10]

America Means Freedom

If the government will do its job and prevent the flood of illegal immigration, and we will all help assure that immigrants become productive and loyal citizens, most Americans should come to see the value of immigration and view immigrants as valuable consumers and important creators of wealth. The United States has always been an immigrant nation—a beacon of hope for the oppressed peoples of the world.

While immigrants no longer pass through Ellis Island, the Statue of Liberty still stands in the New York Harbor, raising her torch high in her right hand, and holding a tablet in her left. It reads, "Give me your tired, your poor, your huddled masses yearning to breathe free."[11] In 1989, when Chinese dissidents protested in Tiananmen Square against the communist government, they chose a replica of the Statue of Liberty as their symbol. As much as we hear about how much the rest of the world dislikes us, America still symbolizes freedom to the oppressed people of the world. This is surely one of the greatest compliments a nation can receive and one to remember in our current struggle with illegal immigration.

CHAPTER 17

All Men Are Created Equal

Equality, rightly understood as our founding fathers understood it, leads to liberty and to the emancipation of creative differences; wrongly understood, as it has been so tragically in our time, it leads first to conformity and then to despotism.

—BARRY GOLDWATER

During the budget debates in Washington, DC, in 2011, the Public Religion Research Institute ran a poll on capitalism and Christianity. According to the poll, a large chunk of Americans—both religious and nonreligious—said that "capitalism" and Christianity were incompatible. The numbers were especially high among women and Democrats, with 50 percent and 53 percent respectively saying that Christianity and capitalism were at odds.

Since the word "capitalism" brings to mind, for many people, the image of the portly, cigar-smoking, tuxedo-wearing guy on the Monopoly game, we're not sure how significant the poll is. Still, the follow-up questions are telling. More than six in ten Americans think that "one of the biggest problems in this country is that more and more wealth is held by just a few people."[1]

We suspect the stats are not far off. Not a day goes by without some pundit wringing his hands about the "gap between the rich and the poor." Lots of people *do* think that fairness and "social justice" require that the government "spread the wealth around." We understand this impulse.

We are troubled that in a world in which some are richer than kings, there are still billions who can barely scrape by. We want everyone to make enough to avoid poverty. We want everyone to have the chance to pursue their best opportunities, and to earn more as a result. What's frustrating to us is that many people oppose the very economic system that comes closest to realizing these goals. They think that Peter is poor because Paul is rich. The best antidote to poverty, however, is freedom, not wealth redistribution.

Justice Doesn't Mean Equality of Outcome

Equality is one of the bedrocks of the American Experiment, which we inherited from the Judeo-Christian tradition. We should be treated as equals before the law. We merit equal protection from wrongdoers, no matter our status, and no one should get special favors just because he's rich or well connected. But that does not mean everyone should have the same amount of money and wealth. Not a single passage of Scripture, or a single theological principle, suggests this.

Jim Wallis claims that "God hates inequality,"[2] but no biblical text supports that. Jesus tells His Apostles that they will sit on twelve thrones (Matthew 19:28) in the kingdom of God. So far as we know, nobody else will get those thrones. While it can rain on both the just and the unjust (Matthew 5:45), God does not disperse His gifts uniformly to his creatures. He gives gifts in various ways. Some folks are strong; some are weak. Some are smart; some are dimwitted. Some can pitch a ball as if they got throwing lessons in the womb; others throw so poorly that it's painful to watch. God has given blessings to all, but our gifts differ both in degree and in kind.

In Jesus's parable of the talents, a rich man gave his slaves different amounts of money. One gets five talents, another two, and another one. No equality of gifts there. The man leaves to go on a long trip. When he returns, he judges his servants based what they've done with what each had been given (Matthew 25:14–30). The one who earned nothing is even called a "wicked servant."

The parable of the landowner who hires laborers for his vineyard looks as if it *does* teach an equality of outcome—if you don't read it carefully. To the workers the landowner hires first thing in the morning, he offers them the going rate—a denarius. Before long, he realizes he's shorthanded. So he hires more workers at nine o'clock, then again at noon, and again at three o'clock. He even finds a few potential workers around five o'clock just lollygagging around, so he hires them, too. At the end of the day, the landowner pays all the laborers one denarius. Here we get equality of outcome, but in exchange for unequal amounts of work. The outcome isn't really equal, since the workers are getting paid different *hourly* wages.

The guys who worked all day don't like this, of course, since they did so much more work. When one of them complains, however, the landowner says, "Friend, I am doing you no wrong; did you not agree with me for a denarius? Take what belongs to you, and go; I choose to give to this last as I give to you. Am I not allowed to do what I choose with what belongs to me? Or do you begrudge my generosity?" (Matthew 20:13–15).

The rich man and the landowner represent God in these parables, so we can assume that what they do is just. Justice-as-the-Son-of-God-understands-it—which we can call "justice" for short—apparently doesn't require that the rich man give his servants the same amount of money. And justice doesn't require that the landowner pay the workers the same hourly wage. He's free to pay them equally for unequal amounts of work. Justice has to do with what each of us is rightly owed. *If what is owed is equal, then justice requires equality. If what is owed is not equal, then justice requires inequality.* In the parable of the landowner, the landowner was obligated to pay the workers what each worker had agreed to, not what the others had agreed to. As long as he honored his agreements with the individual workers, those payments could be equal or unequal.

Neither of these parables is first and foremost about economics. They illustrate a mystery about the kingdom of God: where "the last will be first, and the first will be last." The parable of the landowner is also about God's generosity and grace. Like the father who runs out to meet his prodigal son who has returned, the landowner goes out looking for workers. That tells us of the abundance of God's grace, but there's no hint of absolute equality. If we won't get an equality of outcome in the kingdom of God to come—when all sin has been vanquished—then we're surely off base if we think justice requires it here below.

For a hundred years, the left flank of our culture has been feeding us the lie that justice means sameness or equality in everything. Although this has the patina of morality, it is just reinforcing a sinful impulse called envy. Envy leads us to think that if somebody somewhere has something we don't have, or has more than we have, then we're entitled to have it as well. In the parable of the landowner, all the workers should have been glad that they got what they were promised, and that they were better off than when they started. Instead, the early workers were grumpy because of what *other* workers received. Probably the only workers who were content were the ones who worked the least.

If none of the workers had known about the workers hired at other times, though, they would not have felt cheated. So their attitude was *entirely* the result of knowing what others had received. That is *envy* masquerading as moral outrage. If we want to think correctly about these matters, we have to learn to recognize the difference between envy and justice.

Freedom and Fairness

Economists have come up with experiments to test how people see fairness when it comes to money. One of the most interesting is called the "ultimatum game." The game has two players—strangers—who are told they can split $10. Let's call them Bonny and Clyde. Bonny is given $10, and she gets to decide how much to give Clyde. If Clyde accepts the offer, then they both get to keep whatever money they have. But if they can't come to an agreement on how to divvy it up, then neither of them gets any money. This game has been played thousands of times. How do you think it normally turns out?

If Clyde were rational and free of envy, then he would see that no matter how much money Bonny offers him—even a penny—he's better off than he was before. It makes sense that he would hold out for the best deal he can get, but he would not refuse a final deal out of spite, even if he would like to have more. And he wouldn't think he was a victim of injustice, since Bonny has simply been given some money and told that she's free to share however much she wants with Clyde, with the one proviso that if they don't come to an agreement on the amount, they'll lose it all. If Bonny and Clyde are like average people, however, then Clyde will probably refuse Bonny if she just offers him a dollar. In other words, he'd be willing to lose the dollar, no doubt because he would think it unfair for her to get $9 and him to get only $1. This attitude is common enough that the average offer for the ultimatum game is about $4. And even then, it's only "accepted about 85 percent of the time."[3] So envy can lead people to cut off their nose to spite their face.

Notice that in the ultimatum game, the money is just given away. Neither player earned the money. That may partially explain the outcome. In a competitive market, however, this isn't how things normally work. Remember what we learned about prices in chapter fourteen. In a market, a price tells us how much something is worth at that moment—that is, how much others are willing to give up in exchange for it. This holds whether we're talking about a 72-ounce Big Gulp, Lasik surgery, or a job selling copy machines. The value of your labor will depend on where you live, what you can do, and how much others value that. You can spend your days picking dandelions and singing old Beatles songs to yourself. If you want to make a living, however, you have to do something that somebody else values.

This might mean that you're stuck doing something you don't really enjoy. Nevertheless, in large modern societies, most people have far more options than most people did in history. A society in which people seek out jobs that provide goods and services that others want is surely better than one where John is forced to pay James a certain amount no matter what James wants. That's basically reverse slavery, and it's not only morally dubious; it's a terrifically bad way to get the goods and services that people want created and distributed. Recall our earlier discussion of how economic value is in the eye of the beholder. People often think inequality is unjust because they aren't thinking correctly about value. Without realizing it, they're thinking like Marxists.

In *The Communist Manifesto*, Karl Marx and his coauthor, Frederick Engels, predicted that capitalism would ultimately self-destruct. Over time, they claimed, more and more of the wealth in an economy would move from the laborers—called the proletariat—to the capitalists—the bourgeoisie. At some point, a few rich capitalists would have most of the wealth, leaving the laboring hordes in poverty. The few rich get richer and fewer; the many poor get poorer and more numerous. It's like the rock-paper-scissors game we talked about in chapter fourteen. At that point, the laborers would revolt—according to the theory. Marx's argument was based on the labor theory of value.[4] According to Marx, when a factory owner hired a worker to make a shirt, and then sold the shirt for a profit, the owner sold it for more than it was actually worth. This profit, what Marx called "surplus value," was a form of theft. For Marx, the shirt was worth exactly what it cost to produce it.

But as we saw earlier, the labor theory of value has no basis in reality.

Labor by itself doesn't create value in the marketplace. And without that flawed definition of value, Marx's argument collapses. The workers have received what they agreed to. The factory owner has made a good business decision, combining his employees' labor with his resources. He then markets and sells the shirts for more than they cost to produce but not more than others will freely pay. The profit is what he earned through his entrepreneurial effort, and an incentive for him to keep finding ways to produce what people want, at a price they will pay. This isn't unjust.

Many Christians look at the high salary of a business owner or an entrepreneur, or a corporate CEO, and denounce it as unjust. But in a market economy, wages and salaries tend to reflect the economic value of their roles. Business owners and entrepreneurs bear the risk for their venture, and CEOs make decisions that can make or break a company. The skills of a good executive are extremely rare and extremely valuable.

Jim Wallis has said, "It's a 'fraud' when the average CEO of a Standard & Poor's 500 company made $13.5 million in total compensation in 2005, while a minimum wage worker made $10,700."[5] Notice that Wallis didn't make an actual argument. He's counting on readers to assume that "unequal wages" are unjust by definition.

In a free and just society, disparity of wages is not proof of injustice. Basic to a just society is our right to the fruits of our labor. We can exchange labor—our time, knowledge, skill, willingness to risk, and effort—for other things we value. Your own labor varies by time and place. Why would you assume that the value of everyone else's labor should be more or less equal to yours?

Again, justice requires equal treatment for equal cases, and unequal treatment for unequal cases. Imagine a university in which you could get a bachelor's degree and a 4.0 no matter what you did. The really smart high school valedictorian who attended every class, took careful notes, studied for hours and hours before every test, and got perfect scores as a result found that she always got A's. And the guy who can't remember the difference between "there" and "their," spent most nights drunk and passed out in his dorm room, skipped half his classes, never studied one minute for any test, and failed every test as a result, also got A's on his transcript. If justice always required an equal outcome, then that would be a just way of grading. Obviously, though, it would be unjust because they should be getting different grades that represent the very different results of their work and their skill.

Spreading the Wealth Around

Our politics are often based on envy and a distorted understanding of justice, rather than clear thinking on economics. During a 2008 presidential primary debate, Charles Gibson of ABC asked Barack Obama if he would raise the capital gains tax even if he knew that cutting the tax would bring in more revenue. Obama reacted as a player of the ultimatum game. He said that because of "fairness" he would still want to raise the rate.

Later in that same campaign in Toledo, Ohio, a man named Joe Wurzelbacher, who became known to America as "Joe the Plumber," approached candidate Obama. Joe asked, "Your new tax plan is going to tax me more, isn't it?" Amid a flurry of words, Obama eventually answered, "I think when you spread the wealth around, it's good for everybody."[6]

Um, who's the "you" that's spreading the wealth around? It ain't Santa Claus. By *you*, Obama meant the government. And where does wealth come from? Is it in a pot or a safe somewhere in Washington, DC, where Treasury officials can go scoop it up and spread it around like hot tar on a flat roof? Of course not. The government must first *extract* wealth from private citizens before it can spread it around. Let's forget that for a minute and just focus on his claim that it's "good for everybody." No doubt President Obama believes that, but it's not true.

Attempts to spread wealth around do more harm than good. "Just wage" or minimum wage laws are a prime example. It's hard to notice the effect of these laws when they're set pretty low, as in the United States. (It's hard even to find babysitters in Seattle for minimum wage.) But imagine that the federal government decided everyone should be paid $100 an hour. Then, everyone would be rich, right? No. The law would benefit some people in the short term, namely, those doing unique, indispensable work who were already getting paid almost $100 an hour. But what about everyone else? If the value of your labor were less than $100 an hour, then you wouldn't keep your job for long. And most new hiring would grind to a halt. The law would create huge unemployment and black markets for labor. As Henry Hazlitt wrote, "You cannot make a man worth a given amount by making it illegal for anyone to offer him anything less."[7]

In 2007, the US government imposed a minimum wage law on the American territories of American Samoa and the Commonwealth of Northern Mariana Islands (CNMI). The purpose was to raise the living standards of the islanders. The result, according to our General Accounting Office, was that within a couple of years there was a 19 percent drop in the employed workforce, almost entirely due to this law. It increased the costs for Chicken of the Sea and Starkist, who were forced to make huge layoffs.[8] The value of the Samoans' labor is what it is. The minimum wage law didn't change that. It just made the Samoans poorer and less competitive.

Employers know labor is a cost of doing business, and wage laws are price controls on labor. These price controls harm the poorest of the poor: the untrained, unlucky, inexperienced, and handicapped workers. No matter what the minimum wage is, the labor value of these people will be the farthest from it. These are the people who need to grab the bottom rung of the economic ladder. If you raise it too high, they can't reach the bottom rung.

Few Americans stick with low-wage jobs for their entire career. In a diverse and competitive economy, low-paying jobs are entry-level jobs. These jobs tend to improve the value of one's labor over time. This is just what the poor need to get out of poverty. Some people need entry-level jobs very close to ground floor. Minimum wage laws eliminate those opportunities, and thus favor the politically powerful and fortunate who retain jobs over the vulnerable workers who least can afford it.

Spreading Wealth with Taxes

The other way to "spread wealth around" is with taxes. Taxes have a legitimate purpose: to raise revenue for government expenses. For decades, though, politicians have used the tax code for social engineering. Think of our income tax. If we had a flat income tax that was fixed at a specific percentage for all taxpayers, more tax revenue would still come from higher income brackets. After all, 10% of $1 million is $100,000, and 10% of $100,000 is $10,000. We have a *progressive* income tax, however, which means there are higher rates for higher marginal incomes. As a result, in 2008, the top 1% of income earners had a 20% share of the total income but paid 38.02% of the income taxes, and the top 50% of income earners had 87.25% share of the total income but paid 97.30% of the income taxes.[9] The bottom 50% had 12.75% of the total income paid but only 2.7% of the income taxes. Talk about progressive.

Since everyone gets to vote, in theory the bottom 51% of income earners could elect politicians who promise to extract most of the income tax from the top half. Fortunately, many Americans in the bottom half reject that idea as morally repugnant. Unfortunately, they have been more than counterbalanced by confused people in the top 50% (Warren Buffett and George Soros come to mind), who think this business of "spreading the wealth around" is virtuous and beneficent.

In the 2011 poll we mentioned at the beginning of this chapter, "two-thirds (66%) say that it's fair for wealthier Americans to pay more taxes than the middle class or those less well off."[10] Politicians exploit the fact that some voters like sticking it to people who make more than they do. In the cliffhanger debate over the budget and the debt limit in the summer of 2011, President Obama never offered a plan, except to say that richer people ought to pay more. Well, that's what we have: The top 50% of income earners pay over 97% of the income taxes.

There are several tolerable ways a society can impose taxes. Government can tax people's productivity, using a flat tax (with one rate). Or it could impose a consumption tax, often referred to as a fair tax rather than an income tax. Something has to be taxed, so why not tax our consumption?[11] Consumption taxes encourage saving and investing, rather than punishing hard work and productivity. Those who consume more goods pay more in taxes. The rich who consume luxury items would still pay the most in taxes.[12] We'd rather see a consumption tax, but even a flat tax would be less morally offensive than what we have now.

There is bipartisan agreement that our tax code needs to be reformed and simplified. Even liberal Congressman Charles Rangel recently said, "The income tax is too damn complicated."[13] Worse, it's a moral perversion when politicians seek votes by pledging to tax one person, usually someone richer than us, more than they're going to tax us. If, as voters, we reward this political theft, we won't have a more equal society but a more vicious one.

Spread the Wealth to Spread Power?

The American Founders created a political system that separated power between three branches of government, and balanced power with the branches themselves. Progressive Evangelical Ron Sider argues that we need to do the same thing with economic power, by preventing wealth from getting concentrated in the hands of the few. Otherwise, the rich will wield too much political power. "Concentrated wealth," Sider contends, "equals concentrated power."[14]

What Sider has in mind is that "we" should disperse economic power by having the government disproportionately separate the wealthy (however we define them) from their wealth. The government will then distribute that wealth to the poorer members of society (however we define them).

We're so accustomed to redistributionist schemes that we might forget the obvious: It's unjust to take one person's property and give it to others. It's unjust for the government to pit the interest of one group of citizens against another group. But even if you ignore these injustices, Sider's argument is absurd. To prevent power from getting too concentrated in the hands of the rich, he suggests that the government—the entity with the tanks, missiles, army, and unique coercive power to make and enforce the laws, and to print money—should confiscate the legal wealth of some citizens and give it to others. So Sider's solution to concentrations of power in the private sector is to concentrate yet more power in the state.

The wealthy do often use their wealth for political influence, but his argument treats the rich as if they were a unified voting block with identical interests. Rich people disagree with each other as much as do those in other income brackets. Financier George Soros and singer Barbra Streisand support different candidates and causes than do oil and gas tycoon T. Boone Pickens and venture capitalist Peter Thiel. Power is much better balanced and divided when wealth is under the stewardship of the millions of diverse, private citizens who earned it, than when it is confiscated and used as a tool by politicians who didn't earn it.

The Gap

When we talk about poverty, we often compare the poverty of some with the wealth of others, as if the wealth of some causes the poverty of others. "The problem with our international global economy," argues Bishop Thomas Gumbleton, "is that the wealth of the world goes from the poor to the rich. The rich get richer and richer. The poor get poorer and poorer."[15] But the "gap between the rich and poor" does not automatically mean that wealth was just transferred from the poor to the rich. In a market economy, it's as wrong as saying the health of some causes the illness of others, or the intelligence of some leads to the ignorance of others. Steve Jobs and his many well-paid employees didn't get rich by stealing iPads from homeless people! In fact, this "gap" thinking can actually prevent us from helping the poor.

What Is Poverty?

As Christians, we must do what we can to help the poor. To do that well, we first need to know what poverty is. In our work at LIFE Outreach International, we often send pictures to our supporters of our work in impoverished nations.[16] Since we provide basic nourishment and clean water, these may be pictures of young African children, with little or no clothing, drinking out of dirty puddles of water or foraging for scraps of food. These children are often emaciated, with skinny arms and legs and distended stomachs—the telltale signs of extreme malnutrition. These images provide a simple, concrete illustration of *absolute poverty*.

International organizations often define "absolute poverty" as living on less than one or two dollars a day.[17] But a better definition focuses on human needs—calories, essential nutrients, clean water, shelter, basic health care, and so on. If you can meet these basic needs, you may be poor, but you don't suffer from absolute poverty. If, however, your body is using your muscle for fuel, you have a disease that would be cured with a multivitamin or a three-dollar antibiotic, you're barefoot, sleeping in a lean-to, and have worn the same long T-shirt for a year, then you're probably suffering from absolute poverty.

In a poll that asked Americans to define "poverty," most named familiar problems such as homelessness, hunger, lack of basic nutrition or other material needs. Less than 1 percent defined it in terms of relative income.[18] Regrettably, our government sides with the 1 percent. If an individual or a family makes less than some income threshold, the US Census Bureau by law must define them as poor. The number varies by year and family size, but the basic idea is simple. For example, in 2009, the poverty threshold was $26,245 for a family of five.[19] Based on this way of dividing up the population, we're told that about one in seven Americans is poor.

Unfortunately, this method exaggerates the problem and takes our focus off the small percentage of people in the United States who are living in extreme poverty. It also makes it look as if the living conditions of the poor have stayed virtually the same for forty years. In reality, the average poor child in the United States consumes the same proteins and nutrients as kids in the upper middle class. (That's not to say that any of them are eating as nutritiously as they should be!) Moreover, "poor boys today at ages 18 and 19 are actually taller and heavier than middle-class boys of similar age in the 1950s, and are a full one inch taller and 10 pounds heavier than American soldiers who fought in World War II."[20] A big problem with today's poor is obesity, so mere calories are no longer an issue.

If we look at thirty basic household amenities (refrigerators, computers, DVD players, flatscreen TVs, dishwashers, and so on), "poor" households in the United States, on average, lag behind all households by only about ten to fifteen years. In other words, on average, if you're below the poverty line, you probably have about the same number of amenities as the average American did in the late 1990s. You may not get a big flatscreen TV as quickly as the bank executive across town. Within a few years, however, prices will drop and you'll probably have one. (Whether that's a good thing is another question.)

As a result, in 2005 the *typical* poor household with children had air-conditioning, a computer, cable or satellite TV, three TVs, a DVD player, and a game system like Xbox, Wii, or PlayStation. The kitchen had a fridge, stove, oven, microwave, and automatic coffeemaker. They have a cell phone, cordless landline, and clothes washer.[21] And these families normally were not packed into a tiny, dilapidated shack with a hoard of consumer electronics. "The typical poor American has considerably more living space than does the average European." In fact, even after the housing crisis, "forty-three percent of all poor households own their own homes. The average home owned by persons classified as poor by the Census Bureau is a three-bedroom house with one-and-a-half baths, a garage, and a porch or patio." And only 2 percent of these homes had "'severe' physical problems."[22]

These are averages. We're not saying that American poverty is no big deal. We need an accurate picture of poverty in the United States if we want to reduce it. There are many Americans who go through periods without enough to eat, and without adequate shelter, health care, and clothing. I (James) know this firsthand. As I mentioned in chapter nine, I was placed in foster care with a pastor and his wife until I was five years old. For the next ten years I lived in poverty with a stepfather who couldn't read or write. After that, my mother married my biological father—an alcoholic who had raped her. I moved fifteen times during that chaotic period. We were always dirt poor. Most of the homes we lived in did not sit on a normal street. One was on a dirty river in which I bathed and another was on the backside of a garbage dump. Our mail had to be delivered to other people's homes.

I know all about material poverty. I also know that the poverty I experienced was like most American poverty: it was not so much an economic problem as an economic symptom of moral and social problems. Even as a child, though, I never resented people who were better off than I was. I knew that I was not poor because other people were rich.

Forget the Gap

An income gap, by itself, is a nonissue. If you earn $100,000 one year, and some big stock investor earns $100,000,000 during the same year, there's a huge gap between your incomes. In absolute dollars, the gap is $99,900,000. As a ratio, the investor earns a thousand times more than you. *So what?* Assuming it wasn't illegally gained, then he earned it, probably by making several risky but wise, wealth-creating choices about where to allocate capital.

Now imagine a poor fruit picker in Costa Rica, with a wife and four kids, earning $1,000 a year. The gap between his income and yours is much less significant: $99,000. Your income is a hundred times greater than his. So the gap between you and the fruit picker is much smaller than the gap between you and the investor. And yet the latter case is more troubling. Why? It can't be the size or the magnitude of gaps in income. If it were, we should be ten times more troubled by the gap between you and the investor. We're much more troubled by the gap between you and the fruit picker because we assume that if the picker is only bringing in $1,000 a year, then he's extremely poor.

The problem with defining poverty in relative terms is that the bottom 10 percent of income earners could be *much* better off than the bottom 10 percent were forty years ago, but they would still be labeled "poor." Using this logic, if you make $100,000 a year (with the purchasing power of 2012 dollars), but 90 percent of the population makes at least $1,000,000 a year, you'd be defined as poor. This is absurd. Rather than helping us grasp a complicated reality, our statistical method blinds us to it.

When we talk about material poverty, we need to focus on real deprivation. Gaps are not the problem. Poverty—real, hope-crushing, disease-inducing, absolute poverty—is the problem. Alleviating real poverty should be our goal. Getting rid of gaps should not be.

Not a Pie Either

Kevin Drum of the left-wing magazine *Mother Jones* recently commented on some recent statistics. "This income shift is real," he complained. "We can debate its effects all day long, but it's real. The super rich have a much bigger piece of the pie than they used to, and that means a smaller piece of the pie for all the rest of us."[23]

In a market economy, however, wealth is not a physical object like an apple pie. The pie image is just as misleading as the gap image. Wealth is not fixed; over time, free economies grow. Even when the gap between rich and poor grows, the poor may not have become poorer, because the total amount of wealth may have increased. If the pie grows, someone can get a bigger slice without taking someone else's piece.

And when people grow their own slice, they almost always grow others as well. Needless to say, this is not like any pie we've ever eaten. It's more like a farmer raising geese that lay golden eggs, some of which hatch into other geese that lay golden eggs. He has room for only one such goose, though, so he sells the goslings.

We're not sure if that analogy works, either. Whatever wealth creation in a market is like, though, it's not like a pie.

The Real Issues

The important questions, then, are not about gaps or slices of pie, but poverty. For instance: (1) Is there statistical evidence that the rich are getting richer by making the poor poorer? (2) How well are the people at the bottom doing (compared to absolute poverty)? And (3) Do the people at the bottom of the economic ladder have opportunities to move up that ladder; can they create more wealth for themselves and their families? Does study and hard work tend to pay off, or does it not make any difference?

The answer to (1) is no. If you look at the Census Bureau stats, you don't find that the top 20 percent are getting richer and richer and the bottom 20 percent are getting poorer and poorer. The answer to (3) is yes, hard work pays off, though our current economic policies don't do enough to encourage entrepreneurship. The answer to (2) is that even the bottom 20 percent of the population gets better off over time, and few Americans suffer absolute poverty. *Every* income category has gone up from 1967 to 2009, even though the population has nearly doubled and there has been stagnation in the middle incomes for the last several years.[24] In other words, the wealth of individual families *and* the total amount of wealth have gone up. The rich did get richer, but they didn't do so by making the poor poorer. Every income category got richer.

The truth is still better than that. For even if 15 percent of the population is below the ever-rising poverty line at any one time, that doesn't mean that that segment is always populated by the same people. Upward and downward mobility are common in dynamic market economies. Except for those who inherit a fortune, most of us are in the lower income brackets early in our careers, but we don't stay there.[25]

In other cases, an industrious immigrant comes to the United States, scrimps and saves working low and medium skill jobs his whole life, but his kids learn higher skill trades and move up the income ladder, and their children go to college and move up another notch. The possibility of this American Dream is what draws millions of people to our shores and borders.

Think of the Great Red Spot on the planet Jupiter. It's a swirling oval-shaped storm sort of like a hurricane, thousands of miles in diameter. Human beings have been observing the spot for many decades— it may be more than two hundred years old—but the hydrogen and helium atoms that make up the spot are changing constantly.

Income categories are like the Great Red Spot. In 1980, there was a bottom 15%. In 1990, there was a bottom 15%. In 2000, there was a bottom 15%. Lo and behold, in 2010, there's a bottom 15%. That bottom 15% is always there, but its *members* are constantly changing. Jesus's statement that we will always have the poor with us is practically a logical truth, if that means there will always be someone in the lowest income category. There are some people who get stuck in the vicious cycle of a dysfunctional underclass. That should bother us. But to imagine that the bottom 15% of income earners in America always contains the same people, or even the same families stuck in poverty generation after generation, is to fall for a statistical illusion.

Moreover, as technology develops, more and more amenities are available to more and more people at lower income levels. A hundred and fifty years ago, you could only listen to great orchestral music if you were rich and could go to a live concert. Now even the poorest people have access to first-rate recordings of all kinds of music, classical and otherwise, on the radio, the Internet, CDs, and iPods. For most of history, people spent a large chunk of their income on food. Yet even though food prices have gone up in the last few years, Americans spend on average less than 10 percent of their disposable income on food.[26] As recently as 1930, Americans spent about a quarter of their income on food.[27] Even early in the last century, rich and poor alike were dying of tuberculosis, pneumonia, and polio. Now we have cheap, universal cures. Income does not fully measure wealth and can be vastly unequal, but over the long haul, well-being has improved for everyone.

Because all men are created equal, we should seek a society of widespread opportunities, not equality of incomes or outcomes. We should *not* use the coercive power of the state to confiscate the wealth of some and give it to others. Rather, people should be free to pursue their lawful endeavors, to create wealth for themselves and others, because human beings, under the right conditions, *create wealth*.

CHAPTER 18

Be Fruitful

When God fashions man from the dust of the earth, and breathes into him the breath of life, and speaks those first words of vocation to the human family, He, in effect, is inviting the human family to be co-creators with Him, not "co" in the sense of "equal," but "co" in the sense of "cooperating," "working with Him" in the continuation of the creation of the world....

—Rev. Robert Sirico

"In the beginning, God created the heavens and the earth," says the Bible's opening verse. Genesis 1 goes on to describe God creating everything over the course of a workweek. During each of His days, God calls forth new things from what He has created, saying, "Let there be...light...waters...living creatures." And at the end of each day, Genesis says, "God saw that it was good."

The sixth day starts like the previous ones, with God saying, "Let the earth bring forth living creatures of every kind." But then there's an encore. Rather than simply saying, "Let there be," God speaks to Himself, saying, "Let us make man in our image, after our likeness; and let them have dominion over the fish of the sea, and over the birds of the air, and over the cattle, and over all the earth, and over every creeping thing that creeps upon the earth." Then God blesses the man and the woman, saying, "Be fruitful and multiply, and fill the earth and subdue it; have dominion over the fish of the sea and over the birds of the air and over every living thing that moves upon the earth." On the previous days, God said that what He has created is good. Only after He creates human beings, though, does He say everything is "very good."

The idea of the image of God—the *imago dei*—has given theologians gainful employment for two thousand years. Theologians have often equated the image with our reason or our soul; but the text simply says that human beings, all of us, male and female, are true icons of God. In the text, God is acting as the sovereign King over the heavens and the earth. This Divine King, in turn, appoints us to have dominion as kings and queens over the tiny part of creation we can affect. God creates simply by calling things into existence. He then commands us to create according to our power, to "be fruitful and multiply, and fill the earth and subdue it." All our creativity comes from God. It doesn't compete with Him. As Creator, though, God has made us *creators*.

Where Genesis 1 gives the cosmic overview, Genesis 2 zooms in tight. God fashions man from the ground, breathes into him the breath of life, and puts him in a garden "to till it and keep it."[1] We aren't ghosts trapped in bodies. We're made of dirt, we're made to work with dirt— and yet we have in us the very breath of God. Work itself is part of God's original blessing, not his curse after the fall. We are a unique mixture of heaven and earth, so the way we work should reflect the fact that we are a unity of matter and spirit, neither pack animals nor angels.

We learn more about the image of God in the first chapter of John, which parallels Genesis 1. "In the beginning was the Word," it begins, "and the Word was with God, and the Word was God. He was in the beginning with God; all things were made through him, and without him was not anything made that was made." Before everything else, there was mind, reason, *Logos*. It was through this Logos that God created everything.

Though these biblical texts are not drawn from an economic

textbook, they cast light on the most important truth of economics. With our hands and our minds, we can create wealth, and in the right circumstances, that human-generated wealth becomes the basis of more wealth. We are made in the image of the Creator God, so we should expect this of ourselves.

The Origins of Wealth Creation

Humans were created and first roamed the earth as hunters and gatherers; then they began to domesticate sheep and cattle and to cultivate plants such as wheat and barley. These farmers started with what God had provided—seeds, land, rain, animals—and enriched it. In Medieval Latin, *capital* referred to head of cattle or livestock.[2] Today, economists list the three factors of production as land, labor, and capital. After man developed ways to store food and irrigate land, cities appeared with growing populations not tied directly to agriculture. From cities grew much larger civilizations. Metal plows and wheeled carts slowly replaced stone and wood tools, horses replaced oxen for plowing, and tractors replaced horses. A thousand and one innovations—from seed drills, reapers, combines, and hybridized grains, along with countless new farming techniques—made farming much more productive. Even though the human population is many times larger than it was for most of history, we don't suffer global famines.

As recently as 1900, 80 percent of the world population still lived on farms. By the 1970s, though, that number had dropped to 50 percent. Millions of people still engage in primitive subsistence farming, as they have for centuries—growing just enough to feed themselves, if they're lucky. With solid private property laws and high technology, however, less than 2 percent of the American population now lives on farms, and yet they produce enough not only to feed the American population, but to export abroad. Most of history was marked by scarcity, but we now live amid both great abundance and scarcity.

Better farming opened the way to developments in art, music, philosophy, literature, and all sorts of new technologies. From mastering fire and inventing the wheel, building levers and pulleys, learning to draw metal ores from the earth with mining and smelting, to harnessing the energy of rivers and wind with water and windmills, our ancestors slowly transformed the material world around them to create new wealth. But technology is only the tip of the iceberg.

More and More Mind

Though the word "capital" originally referred to cattle, it also looks like the Latin word for head, *caput*.[3] In modern economies, the mind matters more than matter. Hernando de Soto points out that property laws make capital "mind friendly," since they allow physical assets such as land to take on a parallel existence in the realm of representation. For instance, if a farmer owns 100 acres in the Mississippi Delta, his relationship to that chunk of land translates into other avenues for wealth creation; his ownership is fungible. He can take the title to that rich soil and get a loan to buy a tractor, because that title represents, among other things, his legal right to farm that land year after year and recoup the income from the harvest, or to sell the land to someone else. He can translate his ownership of that land into a line of credit with a banker or a loan for farm equipment and start farming.

Most of the vast new wealth created in our economy derives not from land, however, but from intellectual capital, information—encoded on servers, riding radio waves, microwaves, lasers, tiny fibers of glass, etched in tiny wafers of silica. Knowledge is being applied to knowledge itself, said the great management guru Peter Drucker. "It is now fast becoming the one factor in production, sidelining both capital and labor."

This hints at a startling trend. Over time, we can create more and more wealth with less and less matter, and less and less significant matter. It took some six thousand years to go from the first farms to the invention of the wheel. Everything from cars, toilets, and telephones to electric lights, cars, planes, rockets, computers, the Internet, and antibiotics were invented in the last four generations. We now use virtually free material, silica, like the sand on the beach, to make computer chips and fiber-optic cables—the memory banks and nervous system of a telecommunications revolution. A fiber-optic cable made from 60 pounds of cheap sand can carry 1,000 times more information than a cable made from 2,000 pounds of expensive copper.[4] God gave us sand but gave to us the dignity of transforming it into chips and cables. Though we inform matter, information is not mere matter. Information comes from minds.

In certain high-tech corners of advanced societies, the creation of wealth now follows an exponential trajectory in which human creativity transforms matter. Futurist Ray Kurzweil has popularized this idea with his law of accelerating returns.[5] Kurzweil deserves credit for calling attention to something profound. The evidence is all around us. We now measure everything from increases in wealth to changes in technology in months rather than millennia. One way to see this is to consider the number of patents granted in the United States since 1870.

At the end of the nineteenth century, Charles H. Duell, commissioner of the US Office of Patents, announced, "Everything that can be invented has been invented." He peered into the future and saw diminishing returns. The future thought otherwise. Inventions not only kept coming, but came at a faster rate. Around 1870, the US Patent Office granted about 15,000 patents per year. The annual total now exceeds 150,000. That's a tenfold increase, and it keeps going up. When Google acquired Motorola Mobility in 2011, the company commanded about 17,000 patents![6]

Another common example of accelerating returns is Moore's Law, named for Intel cofounder Gordon Moore. In 1965, Moore observed that the number of transistors on an integrated circuit *doubles* every

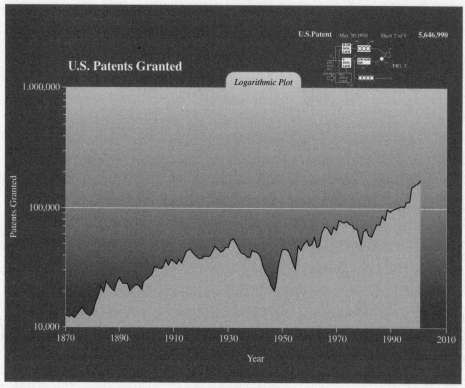

Courtesy of Ray Kurzweil and Kurzweil Technologies, Inc.[7]

twenty-four months, while the cost for the new circuit stays the same. Moore noticed one stage of a trend of increasing computer calculations per second, which has been in effect for over a hundred years. And the trend isn't limited to the integrated circuit; it can be traced backward in time to transistors, vacuum tubes, relays, and even nineteenth-century electromechanical computers. When we take in this wider historical framework, we see that the trend transcends any one technology or material structure. Even if we reach the end of the line for one type of technology, such as the integrated circuit we have now, that doesn't mean we've reached the end of the line. The movement is carried along not only by tweaks to a preexisting technology but by a spiral of human ingenuity building on the ingenuity that came before it.

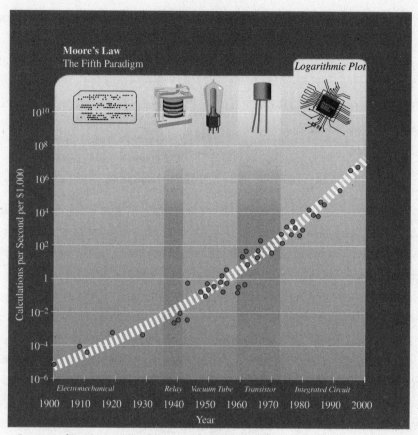

Courtesy of Ray Kurzweil and Kurzweil Technologies, Inc.

The graph above describes the growth of computer technology in terms of how much computational power can be bought for $1,000 at different times.

These are real trends, not just future projections—and they're happening in the high-tech, information-dense parts of the economy—the places where mind predominates. At the moment, there are accelerating returns not just with computing speed, but in many other high-tech areas as well, such as memory storage capacity. You have probably noticed how much more you can store on thumb drives or camera cards now, compared to five years ago.

We don't know if these growth *rates* will continue indefinitely.[8] But we have no reason to think that our ability to create new wealth will come to a halt tomorrow. New wealth comes not from matter alone, but from how we represent, inform, and transform matter—from mind. This most profound truth of economics is just what Christians should expect, since we know that each of us is created in the image of God.

A Wealth-Creating, Not a Wealth-Hoarding, Culture

Wealth isn't created automatically or universally, like learning to walk or speak a language. People differ both in what they can do and to what degree their environment amplifies or diminishes their innate creative gifts. If Apple cofounder Steve Jobs had been born and raised in Haiti, he would not have created the wealth that he did growing up in the United States. Jobs has been called "America's greatest failure."[9] He's credited with iTunes, iPod, iPad, and iPhone. But Jobs was also the architect of Lisa, a disaster that's been long forgotten. Jobs and Apple cofounder Steve Wozniak also gave the world Apple I and Apple II, which early on, were commercial flops. Jobs lived in a society where he could learn from his failures, however, and turn them into a foundation for fabulous future success. There are still large swaths of the planet where this just doesn't happen.

A wealth-creating culture can be a sign of human flourishing, especially when a culture once in extreme poverty begins to create enough wealth to move beyond destitution. We should celebrate it when cultures reach a point where they can feed, clothe, and shelter themselves and begin educating their children to use their God-given abilities more fully. Still, we shouldn't forget that the Bible and the Christian tradition repeatedly warn about the dangers of wealth.

"Do not store up for yourselves treasures on earth," Jesus says to his disciples, "where moth and rust consume and where thieves break in and steal, but store up for yourselves treasures in heaven.... For where your treasure is, there your heart will be also." Elsewhere, Jesus insisted, "You cannot serve God and mammon" (Matthew 6:19–24). And when the rich young ruler asks Jesus what else he can do to inherit eternal life, Jesus tells him to sell everything he has, give it to the poor, and come, follow Him. When the man turns away, Jesus tells His disciples, "It is easier for a camel to go through the eye of a needle than for a rich man to enter the kingdom of God" (Luke 18:18–25).

The Apostle Paul describes greed as a form of idolatry (Ephesians 5:5) and says "the love of money is the root of all evil" (1 Timothy 6:10), and James tells certain greedy people in one church that the rust from their ill-gotten bullion will eat their flesh (James 5:3–6)!

Scripture is chock full of warnings about money and wealth. And contrary to extreme versions of the prosperity gospel, the Bible *never* says that all believers will be materially rich if they just have faith. We should never reduce God's blessing or the meaning of a fulfilled life to material riches. This idea that faith must produce material riches is false. Nevertheless, the Bible often does treat material wealth as a *blessing* from God. This is a recurring theme in much of the Hebrew Scriptures. If wealth can be a blessing, then it can't be bad in itself. In the New Testament, Jesus didn't avoid the wealthy. He often stayed in their homes and associated with people like Mary and Martha, who were apparently far from poor. And Luke, who records the story of the rich young ruler, also informs us that wealthy women provided for Jesus and the disciples (Luke 8:3).

The prosperity gospel is one extreme. The opposite extreme is to treat involuntary poverty as a blessing. The poor are blessed, as Jesus says in Luke, not because poverty in itself is good, but because they know how dependent they are on God. In the Sermon on the Mount, Jesus says, "Blessed are the poor in spirit." To be poor in spirit is to be so free of false attachments that God can fill you with His Spirit. That's why missionaries and monks can be so blessed spiritually when they embrace material poverty voluntarily. That doesn't mean we should welcome mass poverty. Fasting is a path to spiritual growth, but we don't pray for famines.

These warnings concerning money and wealth refer either to misplaced loyalty or to hoarding. The Bible never treats money and wealth as evil in themselves. Paul says the *love* of money is the root of all evil, not money itself. To love money, to serve Mammon, is to make it your top priority—to value your hoard more than God. That's why greed is a form of idolatry. Since money and wealth mean power, they can easily be a stumbling block.

Jesus commanded the rich young ruler to sell everything he had, but He didn't issue that command to everyone—as He commanded us all to love our neighbors. Jesus knew that this man's wealth was a profound hindrance to his salvation.

When James warned the rich that their money would eat their flesh, he was speaking to wealthy people who were defrauding the poor of their promised wages—the rich stealing from the poor. Talk about idolizing money!

If a person is *hoarding* his wealth, then the wealth is a stumbling block. The classic hoarder, of course, is the miser, like Ebenezer Scrooge, who fondles and counts his coins, usually with bony fingers and a hoarse cackle. The Bible has nothing good to say about the miser; but free economies discourage miserliness, and encourage its near-opposite: enterprise.

"The grasping or hoarding rich man is the antithesis of capitalism, not its epitome," writes George Gilder in his classic *Wealth & Poverty*, "more a feudal figure than a bourgeois one."[10] The miser prefers the security of his possessions to the risk of investment. Entrepreneurs prefer the opposite. They embrace uncertainty in the hope of greater gains in the future. For the miser, money is the end. For the entrepreneur, the money he has is the means to another end, even if that end includes future gain.

Great entrepreneurs succeed, not by amassing fortunes but by anticipating the desires of others, and then risking whatever fortune they've acquired to meet those desires.[11] Unlike the greedy miser who clutches his money,[12] entrepreneurs use money to create or deliver something they imagine will fulfill some need or desire—an axle that makes it easier to turn a carriage; a new institution that allows many investors to take on a small amount of risk in a huge business venture; a leaf that tastes delightful and delivers caffeine when dried and boiled in water; melted and dried sand that allows walls to become transparent windows; on and on the list could go. Long before these things exist, they appear as vague flashes of inspiration and imagination in the mind of an entrepreneur.

From Waste to Wealth

The documentary *The Call of the Entrepreneur*[13] tells the story of dairy farmer Brad Morgan. For the first five years of his career, Morgan rented a farm near Evart, Michigan. He was eventually able to get a loan to buy the farm. In the early years, his efforts paid off, and he led the region in milk production per cow. In 1999, however, milk prices plummeted and he was in danger of losing his farm. Morgan could have given up at that point and tried to sell the farm. Instead, he developed, against the odds, a way to make a profit composting cow manure. All the experts thought this would never work. It would cost far more to produce than he could sell it for. But Morgan was sure he could find a way to make it work, and he did. Before long, he had developed a way to compost the manure more quickly, and was hauling in dairy manure by the truckload. As Morgan's son explained, "We're speeding up this process from what everybody thought would take two years, and we're doing it in sixty days."

With paid help from a soil expert, Morgan kept tweaking the formula until he had developed very high quality compost. Then he set about marketing his "Dairy Doo" to gardeners, farmers, and golf courses. His organic fertilizer sells out before it even hits the market. Morgan, whether he realizes it or not, is fulfilling God's original command and blessing to man—to be fruitful. He's creating wealth—from waste.

No one, not even Brad Morgan, knew how popular his fertilizer would become, but he did anticipate it. That's the nature of enterprise: risk, initiative, and invention precedes supply. And supply of a new good or service precedes demand, even creates demand. At the base of the free enterprise system is not greed or consumption, which are everywhere, but intuition, imagination, and creation.

Free enterprise, or entrepreneurial capitalism, requires a whole host of virtues. Before entrepreneurs can invest capital, for instance, they must first accumulate it. So unlike gluttons, entrepreneurs must save rather than consume much of their wealth. Unlike misers, they risk rather than hoard what they have saved. Unlike the self-centered, they anticipate the needs of others. Unlike the impulsive, they make prudent choices. Unlike the robot, they freely discover new ways of creating and combining resources. Unlike cynics, they trust their neighbors, their partners, their culture, their employees, and "the compensatory logic of the cosmos."[14] This cluster of virtues is the essence of what Rev. Robert Sirico of the Acton Institute calls the "entrepreneurial vocation."[15] Not everyone is cut out to be an entrepreneur, but everyone can benefit in a society where entrepreneurs are free to pursue their calling.

No one can predict what an entrepreneur will create ahead of time— not even the entrepreneur! We see the work of entrepreneurs after the fact. Supply and demand kicks in after there's a supply. And in a modern economy, supply depends on enterprise, and enterprise, on freedom— the freedom of entrepreneurs to save, gather, and risk capital in pursuit of their visions. Only in this way can they create new wealth.

For all its wonders, the invisible hand of the market would not emerge without the visible hands of the entrepreneurs who first create new value. Land, labor, and capital are still important, but in the modern age, it is entrepreneurs who are largely responsible for orchestrating those resources, with the human laborer voluntarily entering into the entrepreneur's orchestra as part of a win-win exchange. When this happens, even somewhat unskilled labor can generate more wealth than in other settings. A maid, for instance, can make far more money in the vicinity of a Bill Gates or Michael Dell than in a rural US setting or a developing country. The result of entrepreneurial orchestration is a wealth-creating zone that extends beyond the entrepreneur.

Israel Inside

One of the most stunning stories of entrepreneurial creation in recent years involves not just a person or an industry, but an entire country: Israel. Several books have recently appeared touting the "economic miracle" of this "start-up nation."[16] Although minority Jewish populations have excelled in every country where they have enjoyed some freedom, Israel's success was slow in coming. In fact, the country's short history is a perfect illustration of how bad economic policies can stymie even the most gifted entrepreneurs.

After the founding of Israel in 1948, Israel suffered from wars and heavy defense spending, but that's only part of the story. Many Jews emigrating from Europe brought socialist beliefs with them. Israel is one of our most important allies, and yet, for decades, the country indulged in utopian schemes, such as kibbutzim, which "put intellectuals to work with hoes and shovels," communities that looked a lot like "a voluntary version of Chairman Mao's Cultural Revolution."[17] These experiments in communal living, with no private property and communal parenting, dotted the wadis of Israel for years. Some still exist, but most have long since been reformed and privatized.

Unfortunately, kibbutzim weren't the isolated experiments of a few eccentric philosophers. Israel's entire economy languished in socialist torpor for decades. "Before July of 1985," writes George Gilder in *The Israel Test*, "Israel was a basket case with wage and price controls making everything scarce. Inflation rates were spiking from 400 percent to nearly 1000 percent by 1985."[18] During this time, Jews were much more likely to succeed in the United States than in Israel.

As Gilder further explains, Israel was, to a large extent, socialist, even into the 1990s:

> In a general enthusiasm for public ownership of the means of production and finance, the government through the 1990s owned four major banks, two hundred corporations, and much of the land. Stifling any private initiatives that might miss these sieves of socialism, Israel's taxes rose to a confiscatory 56 percent of total earning, close to the highest in the world.[19]

So what happened? The government began to reduce tax rates and, at the end of the 1980s, started to absorb almost a million immigrants, mostly from the Soviet Union. "The influx of Russian Jews into Israel represented a 25 percent population increase over a period of five years, a tsunami of new arrivals tantamount proportionately to the United States accepting the entire population of France."[20] Many of these immigrants were trained in science and engineering, and—having seen the failures of Soviet socialism firsthand—were vehemently anti-socialist. This meant not only new people but new policies, ones that allowed the entrepreneurial spirit of Israelis to transform Israel and the world.

This tiny country on the eastern shores of the Mediterranean has just over seven million people, of which five and a half million are Jewish. It is surrounded by hostile powers who want to drive it into the sea. Yet it is now a world leader in high technology—medical technology, biotech, telecom, software, microchips, and more. Israel is the leading country other than the United States in start-up companies and technologies. In innovations per capita, it stands alone. Germany's population is ten times larger than Israel's, yet the two countries were roughly equal in 2008 in launching companies backed by venture capital. There is Israeli technology in computer microprocessors, such as Intel's "Core i7" chip, as well as in iPods, GPS systems, Internet routers, cell phones, thumb drives, and on and on and on. In a nod to a popular Intel advertising campaign, George Gilder quips that "most of Intel's key products could be stamped *Israel Inside*."[21]

The Israel Test

Gilder's book, *The Israel Test*, is an incandescent exploration not only of modern-day Israel, but of the uncanny success of Jews throughout history, against hostile and even deadly opposition. But what exactly is the Israel Test? It's a test of how one responds to the economic success of others: "What is your attitude toward people who excel you in the creation of wealth or in other accomplishment? Do you aspire to their excellence, or do you seethe at it? Do you admire and celebrate exceptional achievement, or do you impugn it and seek to tear it down?"

Do you see people as creators of value and wealth, and recognize those exceptional few who create vast wealth? Do you think that wealth created by a few can benefit the many? Or do you assume that anyone with exceptional wealth has extracted it from others, that "poverty is a major side effect of wealth"? Are you oriented toward human creativity or vicarious envy?

In *The Israel Test*, Gilder discusses how Jews were treated for centuries in non-Jewish cultures. When they were persecuted, or not allowed to own land, they would become merchants and bankers. They then succeeded, creating wealth and new possibilities for their economies in the process. Unfortunately, their success then became an excuse to attack the merchants, bankers, and middlemen who were supposedly leeches on the real economy. Envy, ignorance about how wealth is created, and anti-Semitism have traveled hand in hand for centuries. Even when they've been tossed out, they're always looking for ways to rejoin the party.

What Should We Do?

We need to purge our culture, our language, and our thinking of this bias against wealth creators. We can't expect unbelievers to retire the rhetoric of envy when even *Christian* leaders encourage it. We need an economic system that allows the poor to work their way out of poverty and allows entrepreneurs the freedom to create wealth for themselves and others. Only free economies do both.

CHAPTER 19

Have Dominion

Perhaps God is strong enough to exult in monotony. It is possible that God says every morning, "Do it again" to the sun; and every evening, "Do it again" to the moon. It may not be automatic necessity that makes all daisies alike; it may be that God makes every daisy separately, but has never got tired of making them. It may be that He has the eternal appetite of infancy; for we have sinned and grown old, and our Father is younger than we.

—G. K. CHESTERTON

It's hard to imagine how anyone can observe the beauty of the fields and the forests and the mountains and not see beyond their majestic splendor to grasp the greatness of nature's God and their Father. Psalm 19 says the heavens declare God's glory, and Paul told the Roman church that something of God's nature can be "clearly seen" in the things God has made. The creation, Saint Augustine said, is one of the two books by which God reveals Himself to us. As Christians, thinking of Nature as God's work of art is perfectly natural, yet only in the last few decades has the environment become a huge moral and political concern. We're now aware that we can have an impact on the environment, for good or for ill. For instance, our technology makes it easy for us to overfish a lake, or even an ocean.

Many claim the Bible and the Christian tradition are against the environment, and that to save the earth and its climate, we must replace the biblical idea of human dominion with a more nature-centered faith, and must surrender our freedoms to the UN. They're wrong.

Dominion

In Genesis 1, God blessed the man and the woman He created, saying, "Be fruitful and multiply and fill the earth and subdue it; and have dominion over the fish of the sea and over the birds of the air and over every living thing that moves upon the earth" (Genesis 1:28). Some read *dominion* as domination. In a famous 1967 paper in *Science*, Lynn White blamed the biblical idea of dominion for the "ecological crisis." "By destroying pagan animism Christianity made it possible to exploit nature," White argued, adding that "we shall continue to have a worsening ecologic crisis until we reject the Christian axiom that nature has no reason for existence save to serve man."[1] No such Christian axiom exists. Neither in Genesis nor anywhere else does the Bible state or imply that "nature has no reason for existence save to serve man."

It says just the opposite. When God confronts Job and his accusers, for instance, God asks, "Where were you when I laid the foundation of the earth?...Can you bind the chains of the Pleiades, or loose the cords of Orion?...Who provides the raven its prey?...Who has let the wild donkey go free? Behold, Behemoth, which I made as I made you....He is the first of the works of God." God continues on in this vein for three chapters (Job 38–41). The point is God has all sorts of purposes in the world, involving creatures and objects great and small, of which we know nothing!

In Genesis 1, at the end of each of God's days of creation, God looks at what He has made and pronounces it good. He does this five times before man ever arrives on the scene. It's hard to imagine a more blatant contradiction of White's slander on the Bible and on Christianity.

White, like many people, didn't read the Bible carefully. In Genesis 1, God called the universe into existence, created man in His image, and then gave him responsibility over a tiny part of creation. God is the true King, but He delegates some of His dominion to us. Our dominion over the earth and its creatures, then, is derived from the benevolent King of the Universe. We are responsible for how we treat the earth. Dominion doesn't mean destruction. Since all the earth is God's creation, it has value on its own, apart from what we do with it.

We should care for the environment and seek to protect it from being destroyed. Unfortunately, the environmental movement includes ideas that may be the greatest threat to human freedom and dignity in our culture today.[2] They're especially insidious because almost everyone agrees that we should be good stewards and should trust good science. So environmental activists couch their arguments in the jargon of environmental stewardship and science. But Christians and all people of goodwill should oppose these bad ideas tied up with environmentalism.

Some environmentalists package their arguments in the language of the Bible and Christian theology. Christian groups have received funding from secular, left-wing foundations that support abortion and population control.[3] Just because a group has received money from such a source doesn't mean we should dismiss its arguments, but neither does a claim festooned with Bible verses deserve a free pass. The only clear difference between the statement on climate change from the National Religious Partnership for the Environment (NRPE) and Greenpeace International is that the NRPE folks talk theology.[4] When Christians talk about "creation care," we have to do more than baptize the conventional wisdom of the environmental movement.

Environmental stewardship is about a lot more than global warming. Still, the issue is important and brings into focus many of the problems we Christians face as good stewards of the world God has entrusted to us.

~~Global Warming~~ Climate Change

Imagine if the UN held a meeting in a Scandinavian city attended by hundreds of presidents, heads of state, government leaders, nongovernmental organizations, science groups, and UN officials. At this meeting, a former president of Ireland says, "The future of the world is being decided."[5] The participants seem to agree that institutions of "global governance" need to be established to reorder the world economy and massively restrict energy resources. Hundreds of them applaud wildly when socialist dictators wearing red shirts and berets denounce capitalism.[6] Exotic New Age ceremonies adorn the gathering. Finally, our president insists that the motivation for the meeting is based, not on fiction, but on science—that is, a scientific consensus that human activities, particularly greenhouse gas emissions, are leading to catastrophic climate change. Pundits herald the gathering as the most important meeting since the end of World War II.

It may strike you as ridiculous—like a scene from a pulp fiction novel written by a conspiracy theorist. Alas, this scenario isn't from a book, and it isn't fiction. The event described above occurred in Copenhagen, in December 2009. And it might have gotten some traction, except that it was scheduled during a global recession, when few people had an appetite for climate regulations that would further dampen the global economy. It also occurred when no net global warming had been measured for a decade, a fact inconvenient enough that everyone started calling global warming "climate change." That made it possible to count everything from a late spring freeze to a dust devil moving across a West Texas cotton field as evidence for the theory.[7] It also took place a month after the so-called Climategate[8] scandal revealed that prominent climate scientists, and a leading research organization responsible for much of the important data, had shamelessly manipulated key evidence and the sacrosanct process of peer review. A rare snowfall occurred in Copenhagen during the conference, and Washington, DC, was hit with a nasty blizzard, forcing American politicians to leave Copenhagen early to get home ahead of the storm. God certainly has a sense of humor.[9]

Two years earlier, former vice president and eco-activist Al Gore and the UN's Intergovernmental Panel on Climate Change had won a Nobel Peace Prize. Gore's climate change documentary, *An Inconvenient Truth*, had won an Oscar. In 2006, the Evangelical Climate Initiative had publicized a document signed by eighty-six Evangelical leaders, calling for the federal government to restrict carbon dioxide emissions.

But then the movement started unraveling, and the public began to grow more skeptical of the hysterical warnings.[10] Many Americans still think we may be contributing to global warming, but are much less inclined to panic about it. Of course, NPR is still doing the same story over and over about how "science" is absolutely certain we're causing severe climate change.

When the media talk about climate change, that phrase is shorthand for the claim that man is causing abnormal, even catastrophic changes in the climate, mainly by adding carbon dioxide to the atmosphere, and that we need a political solution—fast!—to prevent the submersion of our coasts and low-lying islands, megahurricanes, and on and on. This means we need to slow down or reduce how much carbon dioxide we're belching into the atmosphere. Since we won't do that voluntarily, the government or the UN has to make us do it.

Unfortunately, there are several *different* claims here masquerading as one. They should be considered one at a time.

1. Is the earth warming?

To answer to this question, we must ask: Has the earth been warming since _____? If you start with 1998, then our best evidence suggests we've had no significant net warming. If you measured from 1940 to 1979, and took the average, you'd say the earth (that is, the average global temperature) was cooling. If you're older than forty, you might even remember that the big scare in the mid-1970s was the looming threat of runaway global cooling, a reality that much of the media treated as a near scientific certainty. If you measured from AD 1000 to the present, there's been a bit of cooling (since it was probably warmer then). And if you pick a baseline of, say, 1850, and aren't overly skeptical of the data, it looks like we've had some mild warming since then—about 1½ degrees Fahrenheit. There's pretty good evidence for this mild warming since 1850.

2. If the earth is warming, are we causing it (especially through carbon dioxide emissions)?

The global temperature seems to have risen about 1½ degrees Fahrenheit in the past 160 years. Humans have been adding carbon dioxide to the atmosphere during that time, thanks to the industrial revolution. In 1960, there were about 320 parts of carbon dioxide per million (ppm) in the atmosphere. Now there are about 390 ppm. Is this causing the warming?

Effect and cause—the warming and the *cause* of the warming—are two different things. This is a point of logic, not science. Retreating glaciers in Alaska, polar bears looking mournfully at the ocean from the edge of a chunk of sea ice, shorter winters year after year, may be evidence of warming, but can't tell us *why* the earth has warmed.

Still, we know that carbon dioxide is a greenhouse gas because of basic chemistry—it's good at absorbing infrared radiation.[11] But by far the most important greenhouse gases are water vapor and methane. Almost all climate scientists agree that by itself, carbon dioxide won't contribute much to global warming. We would have to *double* the carbon dioxide in the atmosphere just to get 1 degree (centigrade) of warming. We've added only about 20 percent in the last sixty years, far short of the 100 percent increase needed to raise the temperature 1 degree. Then we'd have to double what had already been doubled just to get another degree of warming. Very quickly, it would get exponentially harder to raise the temperature another degree.

So why do many scientists assume that catastrophic warming is just around the corner? They assume that various feedback processes are enhancing the warming effects of the extra carbon dioxide. Since they plug those assumptions into computer models, the models show more drastic warming in the near future.

But extreme warming is not what scientists have actually observed. This has led some researchers to suspect that the models are wrong, that some of the feedbacks are actually negative—that is, they counteract the modest warming effect of the extra carbon dioxide rather than magnify it. Several recent scientific papers suggest that certain clouds are doing at least some of the counteracting.[12]

This makes sense. The earth has experienced warming and cooling trends throughout its history. It has suffered major assaults, with the amount of carbon dioxide in the atmosphere varying widely. If tiny changes in carbon dioxide in the atmosphere led to huge changes in the earth's temperature, we would see that in the earth's records (such as the ice cores from Antarctica). Those records show major changes in temperature, but these don't follow slight increases in carbon dioxide in the atmosphere.

On the contrary. When the global temperature has varied in the past, changes in carbon dioxide in the atmosphere have changed several hundred years *afterward*.[13] We know why: The warmer the oceans, the less carbon dioxide they can hold. So when the earth warmed in the past, the oceans would slowly release carbon dioxide into the atmosphere. Yet this process did not lead to a runaway greenhouse gas disaster with warmer temperatures releasing more carbon dioxide from the oceans, which then warmed the planet further, which then released more carbon dioxide from the oceans, and so on. This suggests that the changes in carbon dioxide that are in view today won't lead to major changes in climate, either.

The hockey stick diagram showing unprecedented warming in recent years was the star in Al Gore's *An Inconvenient Truth*, and in the 2001 Report by the UN's Intergovernmental Panel on Climate Change (IPCC). It misrepresented the facts. Scientists such as Michael Mann (of Climategate fame) used sophisticated statistical techniques to get meager and probably cherry-picked data to fit in a hockey stick pattern. It told the story that many people wanted, so the experts didn't check it carefully. Smart independent scholars figured out that it was a huge mistake.[14] In its more recent 2007 report, the IPPC dropped the hockey stick entirely. Whether the result of zeal or willful misrepresentation, it was a mistake that resulted in far-reaching misinformation.

The current changes in global climate aren't unprecedented.[15] For all we know, our slight warming trend may be perfectly normal. Certainly there are other possible causes for the warming. Some scientists argue that changes in the sun's energy output or magnetic activity are the main actors in Earth's changing climate.[16] Others point out that it's also gotten warmer on Mars in recent years.[17] Earth and Mars don't have Exxon, BP, and Chevron in common. They do have the sun in common.

It's plausible that human activity has some effect on the climate, but to say we are the main driver of climate change, you have to assume that the climate is supersensitive to changes in the concentration of carbon dioxide in the atmosphere. And there's plenty of reason to doubt that.[18]

3. If the earth is warming, and we're causing it, is that bad overall?

Even if we are causing the earth to warm, it doesn't follow that this is all bad, or even mostly bad. It might lead to droughts or floods in some places, but to warmer, wetter, more productive weather in many others. People seem to prefer warm to cold weather. All the landmass in the far north of the globe could be fertile, pleasant territory in a warmer world. Also, we use less energy when it's warm than when it's cold. Some warming might be a net positive.[19,20]

To know whether warming is good or bad, we'd need to know what the optimum global temperature is, and then we could see whether we're moving toward or away from it. But we don't know what that optimum is.

What we do know is that carbon dioxide is plant food—*not* a toxic pollutant—and that different plants increase their growth in the face of rising levels of carbon dioxide—surely a good thing. These plants, in turn, sequester carbon dioxide that would otherwise be in the atmosphere, creating another feedback that tends to dampen or neutralize rather than amplify warming.[21] All this gives us plenty of reason to doubt that moderate warming, even if we're causing it, is a catastrophe.

4. If the earth is warming, we're causing it, and that's bad, would any of the proposed "solutions" on carbon dioxide emissions make any difference?

Most informed experts agree that any politically feasible policy would not make much difference. For years, the international favorite was the Kyoto Protocol. This UN treaty called for participating nations to restrict their carbon dioxide emissions to 5.2 percent below 1990 levels. According to the official estimates, it would have reduced the rate of warming an undetectable 0.05 degree centigrade after about 50 years. And yet complying with it would have cost the worldwide economy a huge amount of money—in the trillions of dollars. Imagine what it would cost to reduce carbon emissions by 80–90 percent, without an abundant and affordable alternative (we don't have one yet). This *would* be catastrophic.

In contrast, a few years ago, a group of scholars that make up the "Copenhagen Consensus" estimated that it would cost about $200 billion to outfit the rest of the world with water sanitation capacity. That's many times cheaper than the estimated cost of Kyoto, and would be vastly more helpful to poor people suffering and dying from unclean water than would a predicted and almost imperceptible slowing of global warming.

During the 2009 UN meeting in Copenhagen, there were hopes of getting a new international treaty to replace Kyoto, which has now expired. The conferees flew home without any agreement. No surprise there. The costs to "doing something" are insanely high, and the benefits, negligible.

Even if we assume the worst about human-induced climate change, the extreme costs and minuscule benefits lead us to oppose attempts to restrict carbon emissions by political fiat.[22] Such attempts would increase the cost of energy—that's the point of restrictions—and so would hit the poor the hardest. It's all pain and no gain.

Beware of *Political* Science

The official solution for environmental problems is always more political control, less freedom. Sometimes that might be necessary, when no market solution is possible, but coercive restrictions on economic freedom should be the last resort.

Patrick Moore is a Canadian environmental scientist, a cofounder and former president of Greenpeace. He loves the environment, continues to write books about how to be a good steward, and has virtually the same views he had when he helped found Greenpeace.[23] He left the organization after he concluded that it had become more about political activism than protecting the environment using sound science and economics. His epiphany came when his colleagues wanted to lead a campaign to ban chlorine, one of the life-essential elements on the periodic table. Moore argues that the collapse of the Berlin Wall and the Cold War led many communists to seek cover in the environmental movement. "Many of its members moved into the environmental movement," he recalls, "bringing with them their neo-Marxist, far-left agendas. To a considerable extent the environmental movement was hijacked by political and social activists who learned to use green language to cloak agendas that had more to do with anti-capitalism and anti-globalization than with science or ecology."[24]

Neither ecology nor climate science should be more political than any other science. But the bitter reality is that environmental controversies are shot through with politics, and politics leaks into the science and the way it's reported. Ottmar Edenhofer, the cochair of the UN's IPCC Working Group III, explained that the goal of climate policy "is redistributing the world's wealth and natural resources."[25] Like it or not, much large-scale environmental activism is more about left-wing politics than protecting the environment.[26] As a result, we have to exercise extreme caution and discernment. If you're told that "science says" something or even that there's a scientific consensus behind a claim, always look for the dissenting view.

The late author Michael Crichton put it best. "I regard consensus science as an extremely pernicious development that ought to be stopped cold in its tracks," he said in a famous lecture at Cal Tech. "Historically, the claim of consensus has been the first refuge of scoundrels; it is a way to avoid debate by claiming that the matter is already settled. Whenever you hear the consensus of scientists agrees on something or other, reach for your wallet, because you're being had."[27]

Wealth Is Good for the Environment

Our environmental problems are not getting worse. Some Americans imagine that poor villagers are in harmony with nature while rich Westerners are mindlessly riding in smoke-belching, tree-felling bulldozers; but the facts tell a different story. Almost any way you measure it, we are healthier and our environment is cleaner than it has been even in the recent past.[28] Nothing is risk free, but over time, we use more efficient and less environmentally destructive forms of energy—uranium or oil extracted from deep in the ground rather than wood from forests.

In the developed world, most of the important trends have improved, not declined, in the last several decades: wealth, infant mortality, life expectancy, nutrition, and the leading environmental indicators such as air and water quality, soil erosion, and toxic releases.[29] In general, the wealthier a country is, the more environmentally sustainable it is.[30]

Long-term trends in life expectancy are also good, not bad. Those trends are the fruit of technology and techniques developed in societies that enjoy political and economic freedom.[31,32] A *New Yorker* cartoon captured the irony of our situation. Two cavemen are sitting together in a cave, in characteristic shredded fur tunics. "Something's just not right," one man says to the other. "Our air is clean, our water is pure, we all get plenty of exercise, everything we eat is organic and free-range, and yet nobody lives past thirty."

The have-nations forget about the environmental ills still afflicting the have-nots in the developing world, since we solved them decades ago. Societies start to worry about the environment *per se* once they have solved basic problems of survival and comfort. Americans with two or three cars per household, automatic heating and cooling systems, nontoxic air and water, safe streets, and too much to eat are more likely to fret about separating paper and plastics, protecting salmon runs, and preserving the habitats of the Karner Blue butterfly than are people who live in villages without plumbing or clean water. Those villagers aren't heartless. They just have more pressing matters on their minds. The developing world will become more environmentally conscious if and when it becomes wealthier.

There's a growing literature in economics on what is called the Environmental Kuznets Curve. The basic idea is that, while in the early stages of industrial growth a country can be quite hard on the environment (think China and India), this trend levels off after a country reaches a certain per capita income, and then the environmental indicators start improving.[33] Not only does technology become more efficient; environmental cleanness becomes a higher priority.

The wealthier you are, the easier it is to adapt to change. You can buy different clothes, move, add insulation to your attic, go on vacation, install an air conditioner or heater, work inside, or whatever. The poor have far less flexibility. Any change in the economy or the climate is going to hit the poor harder because they have fewer means to *adapt*. So even if the planet gets warmer, or the weather gets harsher (though there's no evidence of that), it's much wiser for us to help them to become wealthier rather than to stage misguided campaigns to restrict energy use, restrictions that will do little or nothing for the environment, trap billions of people in poverty, and so, make them much less likely to become environmentally friendly.

What Should We Do?

Do not throw up your hands in despair. Think, pray, and investigate before you adopt fashionable eco-trends. Find the best arguments for and against a policy.[34] Reject false dilemmas. Tackle real environmental problems with gusto, especially at the local level, where we see the effects and can make course corrections more easily. In Texas, fresh water is a big deal. In Washington State, it's salmon. These are real problems that need hard thinking and tangible solutions.

We should look for market solutions to environmental problems whenever possible.[35] Regulations should be a last rather than a first resort, since they are coercive. Strong private property laws are often the best ways to encourage people to act in environmentally friendly ways. We tend to act less responsibly when we enjoy a benefit but don't suffer the cost, or when our bad behavior doesn't directly affect us. We're more likely to treat our backyard better than the grass at a city park.

Ever wonder why buffaloes almost went extinct as Americans spread west? Nobody owned them. Cattle are not in danger of extinction because they're owned and bred. Neither are buffalo in danger now that ranchers own them. When people have a strong motivation not to eradicate a species, they don't.

Sometimes, though, as with some types of pollution, the problem is what economists call an externality. That refers to a cost not fully accounted for in an exchange. If you buy some lumber from a sawmill, for instance, that's a win for the mill and win for you. But what if the mill dumps a lot of sludgy pollution in a nearby stream as part of its work? That's a cost that someone else has to pay. Well-crafted environmental regulations can make sense in such cases.

In the case of the polluting sawmill, the simplest solution might be for the mill to bear the cost of cleanup—along with a penalty premium to discourage other sawmills tempted to pollute. For the long term, sawmills would do the cleanup automatically, and then raise the cost of their lumber to compensate. In this way, what was an externality would be internalized in a market transaction.

In short, let's look at long-term historical trends and think clearly about real problems before we act. We *can* preserve the environment for our children and also give the impoverished world a chance to develop as we have.

CHAPTER 20

Till It and Keep It

If you want one year of prosperity, grow grain. If you want ten years of prosperity, grow trees. If you want a hundred years of prosperity, grow people.

—CHINESE PROVERB

When British soccer star David Beckham and his wife, former Spice Girl Victoria Beckham, had a baby girl, bringing their number of kids to four, the Beckhams were attacked by pundits. Reporter Tracy McVeigh reported that population experts complained that "the birth of their fourth child make the couple bad role models and environmentally irresponsible."[1]

Experts propose sundry solutions to what they view as a problem. Some recommend changing the tax code to punish overbreeders. I (Jay) once had a prominent scientist write to me, "From where I sit, Planet Earth could use another black death, and pronto!"[2] This isn't a brand-new idea. In 1989, a biologist working for National Park Service, David Graber, let this fly in the *Los Angeles Times*:

Human happiness, and human fecundity, are not as important as a wild and healthy planet. I know social scientists who remind me that people are part of nature, but it isn't true.

Somewhere along the line...we quit the contract and became a cancer. We have become a plague on ourselves and upon the earth. It is cosmically unlikely that the developed world will choose to end its orgy of fossil-fuel consumption, and the Third World its suicidal consumption of landscape. Until such time as Homo sapiens should decide to rejoin nature, some of us can only hope for the right virus to come along.[3]

This thinking is in the mainstream today, but it is inspired by a nineteenth-century Anglican priest and amateur scientist, Rev. Thomas Malthus. Early in his career, Malthus compared human population growth, which was increasing exponentially, with food supplies, which were not. He concluded that worldwide famine was on the horizon, and this would bring the population back to a manageable size. (Charles Darwin got some of his ideas from Malthus.) Doomsday never came, so Malthus changed his tune later; but his original song is still sung.

In the 1960s and '70s, the Club of Rome warned that we were using up our natural resources. And in 1968, Paul Ehrlich wrote in *The Population Bomb* that England had just a 50 percent chance of making it to the end of the twentieth century.[4] "The battle to feed all of humanity is over," Ehrlich wrote. "In the 1970s the world will undergo famines— hundreds of millions of people are going to starve to death."[5] It didn't happen, of course, and this gave Ehrlich time to release new editions of his book. Same basic argument, different dates for doomsday, more book royalties.

Here's the reasoning: The earth's surface is finite, as are the number of trees, the amount of water, oil, copper, fertile land, and so on. The earth now holds seven billion people—to say nothing of all the beetles and spiders. There must be some limit, some point beyond which we exceed the feeding capacity of the planet. And when scientists calculate that point, columnists like Thomas Friedman announce that "the Earth is full," as he did on June 8, 2011.[6]

The doomsday predictions are always wrong, decade after decade, century after century, because they're not looking at the full picture.

It was an understandable mistake when Thomas Malthus made his argument in the early nineteenth century, when there *was* an exponential increase in human population under way.[7] Malthus's error was that he extrapolated the trend out into the future, and assumed that all organisms always reproduce until they meet the limit of available food, and then start dying off in mass numbers. Bacteria will do this in a Petri dish, but human beings don't breed like bacteria. When you take a longer view, human population growth follows what is called an S curve rather than a hockey stick curve. Early on, human population was pretty low and didn't change much over time. Industrialization allowed us to become much more productive, and the population started to grow very fast. But as societies become more technologically advanced, their fertility rates drop. As we mentioned in chapter seven, most industrialized countries are not even replacing their current populations. The UN expects world population to level off at about 9 billion in the year 2050, and to start declining after that.[8]

What Is Man?

That there's a known carrying capacity to the earth, and we've already passed it, is as baseless as the assumption that human beings will keep breeding to infinity and beyond. Both assumptions are based on false beliefs about man. When God blessed Adam and Eve, and told them to "be fruitful and multiply," he put them in a garden, not in the desert or a rain forest. They were then commanded to "till it and keep it." So from the very beginning, our dominion, our stewardship, was meant to involve us in transforming the world around us for fruitful purposes.

This happened before the fall—when the first human pair defied God. The fall didn't create work; it turned work into often frustrating toil. The fall has affected the entire natural world. Paul writes that "the creation was subjected to futility" (Romans 8:20). In exercising our stewardship, we can mess up, pollute, and destroy. Nevertheless, God intended us to work, to create, to tend the garden, to transform the earth. If you've ever seen a Japanese garden, you know how much human input can add to a natural landscape. The best gardeners work with the natural tendencies of the plants, the land, the climate, even the koi fish, to create something that nature without man would never have produced. Words such as "nature," "humanity," "environment," and "stewardship" mean one thing to someone who sees human beings mainly as consumers, destroyers, locusts, or aliens, and quite another to someone who has fully imbibed this biblical view.

It's easy for antihuman assumptions to creep into our thinking as Christians. A few years ago, *The Green Bible* was published to much fanfare. It prints all the texts having to do with the environment in green. In Psalm 8, for example, the first verse is printed in green, "O Lord, our Sovereign, how majestic is your name in all the earth!" But verse two is not in green: "Out of the mouths of babes and infants you have founded a bulwark...."[9] In Scripture, however, human beings are a part of the environment. That every text referring to a human being isn't printed in green in *The Green Bible* illustrates the problem. We don't think the editors did this intentionally. Still, if we want to think Christianly, we must train ourselves to include humanity at every point. And we must oppose the antihuman population control partisans, who see human beings as mere consumers of resources rather than valuable in themselves and potential creators of value.[10]

We are not saying there are no limits to how many humans the earth can sustain, that we can blithely squander resources, that technology will always save us. We are saying the common beliefs about the earth's carrying capacity and sustainability are based on false assumptions about man, about nature, and about resources.

Understanding Resources

When we see the word "resource," we think of stuff we can weigh or count: oil in the reservoir, land with barbed-wire fence around it, water in a lake or an aquifer, gold coins buried in a mattress. Some resources, such as water, wood, and fish, are renewable as long as we don't overdo it. Other resources aren't renewable: oil and coal, for instance. Oil reservoirs don't refill, so far as we know.[11] That's why we all tend to believe reports that we're past the peak of oil reserves and they're now dwindling, even though those arguments have been made for decades and don't have a good record of success.

The problem with these warnings is that they are based on proven or known oil reserves. Discovering an oil reserve costs money. BP or Exxon Mobile or Arco has to spend millions digging dry holes before they find a new reserve. "How much of any given natural resource is known to exist," notes Thomas Sowell, "depends on how much it costs to know."[12] It also depends on how much it is worth to know it.

As the current supply dwindles, or as demand spikes, the price per barrel goes up. If it gets high enough, it encourages oil companies to look for new reserves in more costly locations (since they can make a profit at the new, higher price). When they find a new reserve, they still have to tap it, transport it, refine it, market it, and deliver it. The price represents all of those things put together. When it reaches the market, the new supply regulates the price. Known reserves tell us how much it's worth to know about right now, not how much total oil there is to discover or exploit. If we were about to run out of oil, the price of gasoline would be a lot closer to a million dollars a gallon.

There are other forms of oil deposits, such as oil shale and oil sands, which are different from the crude oil coming out of oil wells. As long as crude oil is abundant and cheap, it doesn't make economic sense to figure out how to extract these deposits. If the price of oil gets above a certain point, however, lots of mining and petroleum engineers will turn their attention to these more exotic deposits. In fact, that's already happening.

Still, if there's only so much oil, won't we *eventually* run out of it? The surprising answer is no, and the reason has to do with how people respond to changes in the price for a good or service. Imagine we're still using oil for energy in fifty years. We've found new ways to recover oil, and found more oil than we ever dreamed possible; but it has become so costly to tap new reserves that it costs $1,000 (in today's dollars) to recover and bring just one barrel to market, and the price doubles every year. The cost of getting the oil, in other words, has overwhelmed the marginal cost of bringing it to market once it's extracted. Before conditions reached this point, the high price would signal to everyone that it was time to carpool, hitchhike, take the bus or train, and pour extraordinary amounts of mental and physical energy into discovering, developing, or improving other sources of energy. That's what prices do, if they're allowed to fluctuate to represent changing market realities. This isn't happening now because for many uses, especially transportation, oil is still the best and cheapest source of energy available.

The amount of matter hiding in the ground in Canada or Saudi Arabia is less important than human beings devising new ways to access and exploit it. Because we develop new ways of exploring, mining, and refining, future resources are often cheaper to acquire than current resources, even under pressures of greater demand.[13, 14]

Many of us, including Christians, adopt zero-sum, even materialist, ways of thinking when it comes to resources. We will always fear that we're running out of resources if we think of them merely as some finite amount of physical stuff. But resources aren't just there in a lake or tank or the ground. We *create* resources.

We stopped using whale blubber for oil not because we killed off the last whale or that every salty harpooner suddenly developed a soft spot for all of those leg-chomping white whales roaming the seven seas, but because whale oil was pricey and creative humanity kept its eyes open for alternative forms of energy suitable for heating and lighting. And that's just one page in the sprawling history of human innovation.

The alternative, of course, was petroleum. For centuries, humans ignored the stuff. In the mid-nineteenth century, though, someone figured out how to refine oil into kerosene, and someone else figured out that kerosene was useful for heating cold houses and lighting dark rooms. The discovery helped save the whales.

Black gold really took off with the invention of cars and the internal combustion engine. Since then, we have devised all sorts of ways to explore, refine, and use it more and more efficiently. Oil became a resource through the vision and ingenuity of man.

Most resources are only resources because human beings are involved in some way. This is even true for something as simple as water. Most of the water that we drink is mediated by human minds and hands. If it's freshwater from a deep aquifer, someone had to dig and maintain a well. Other water is recycled and purified. Most of it has to be transported by pipes and plumbing. Since it's pretty much odorless and colorless when we get it, it's easy to imagine that the water is just there. But little of it would be there unless someone brought it from somewhere else.

We don't create from nothing, as God does. We use the material world that God has given us. Nevertheless, over time, the matter in some material resources matters less than how human beings creatively transform them for some use—wolves are transformed into sheep dogs; wood into fuel, lumber, and houses; stones into walls and arrowheads; clay into pots, bricks, and ovens; fur into coats; fields into farms; manure into fertilizer; oil into gasoline and kerosene; iron ore into spearheads; cotton into clothing; copper into phone lines and electric generators; sand into computer chips and fiber-optic cables; light into lasers; plastic into DVDs bearing software read by lasers.

The Green Revolution

Consider the work of just one man, Norman Borlaug, who, for years after his official retirement, was a professor at Texas A & M University. Most Americans have never heard his name. He died to too little fanfare in 2009 at the age of ninety-five. In an obituary, science writer Gregg Easterbrook called Borlaug "arguably the greatest American of the twentieth century." Borlaug received the Nobel Peace Prize in 1970, the Presidential Medal of Freedom in 1977, and the Congressional Gold Medal in 2007—one of only six people ever to receive that triple honor. Why? He was the father of the Green Revolution.

"As a young agronomist," Easterbrook explained:

Borlaug helped develop some of the principles of Green Revolution agriculture on which the world now relies including hybrid crops selectively bred for vigor, and "shuttle breeding," a technique for accelerating the movement of disease immunity between strains of crops. He also helped develop cereals that were insensitive to the number of hours of light in a day, and could therefore be grown in many climates.

Green Revolution techniques caused both reliable harvests, and spectacular output. From the Civil War through the Dust Bowl, the typical American farm produced about 24 bushels of corn per acre; by 2006, the figure was about 155 bushels per acre.[15]

Borlaug's methods have allowed much farmland to revert back to forests.

A billion or more people may be alive in India and other parts of the developing world today because of the work of this man, and others who gave us the Green Revolution. On news of his death, the prime minister of India Manmohan Singh and the president of India Pratibha Patil said, "Borlaug's life and achievement are testimony to the far-reaching contribution that one man's towering intellect, persistence and scientific vision can make to human peace and progress."[16] Ah, how the image of God is reflected by such men who are given the grace to transform humble seeds and soil into historic and bountiful harvests!

The men and women of the dim and distant Stone Age were acquainted with the raw materials of Borlaug's Green Revolution, but the innovations occurred in the blink of an eye in the twentieth century AD. In other cases, we do not find new ways to harness old resources, or to use them more efficiently; we discover, and create, fundamentally different types of resources. This is especially true with energy.

Energy Everywhere

People for centuries have feared they were running out of whatever resource they happened to be using at the time. First it was wood; then it was coal. We've still got plenty of both. What happened in both cases was that hard work and ingenuity were spurred on by rising prices responding to scarcity. Scarcity, labor, and creativity conspire to get us to the next level, to the next resource, or to the next technological breakthrough. Necessity is indeed the mother of invention; but humanity is the father. Together they make a very fruitful pair. "The Stone Age came to an end not for a lack of stones," someone once said, "and the oil age will end, but not for a lack of oil."[17]

The lesson of history is clear: Just because there's a fixed supply of dung or wood or coal or oil or uranium doesn't mean that we are doomed to run out of energy. The image conjured up is of a bright electrified pot of stuff called "energy," where the big kids are getting more than their fair share, and the obvious moral is that we need to use less so that others can have more. "Our world is characterized by an alarming discrepancy," says the National Religious Partnership for the Environment, "between those who consume too much and those who do not have enough."[18]

This is like the story we tell children who won't eat their peas. "Listen buster, you need to eat what you're served, because there are children starving in Africa." Sometimes the jolt of guilt works on sensitive children. But as a diagnosis of the problem, the claim is misleading, since the uneaten peas in Schenectady don't cause the starvation of a child in Sierra Leone. The lack of gratitude of the American child is a problem, but it pales compared to the really serious problem: that starving child in Africa! Gluttony, wastefulness, and consumerism in our part of the world are serious moral problems, but they're not causing want and hunger elsewhere.

Fixed pie thinking, as discussed earlier, distorts our view of reality, especially regarding energy. The amount of energy latent in matter is almost unimaginably high (it's an unimaginably big pie). At any time, we're using only the tiniest fraction of that. Besides, the earth isn't a closed system. We get energy from the sun. There are vast amounts of plants, trees, uranium, sunlight, hydrogen, wind, waves, geothermal heat, river currents, etc., which we're not using for energy. The humble hydrogen atom packs a powerful punch when forced to fuse with another of its kind. The challenge is figuring out how to extract and use the energy, without using even more energy or causing big problems in the process. That can be a huge hurdle, but it is, in essence, an intellectual and technological one.

Somebody has to produce, capture, and channel energy. So unless the energy producers have violated the property rights of others to retrieve and extract the energy, or the energy consumers have stolen from the energy producers, what's the problem? Some places produce, buy, and consume more energy than other places. Wastefulness and gluttony are common sins, but the problem with respect to energy isn't that some places are able to produce or buy ample energy. The problem is that other places are not.

A Reasonable Hope

Thinking of resources in static terms, such as the (presumed) volume of oil in the ground, can be a deceptive projection of a limited imagination. We have to learn to think of resources in light of human creativity in a free economy and how that creativity builds upon itself over time. We have to be willing to trust that free human beings in free societies will be able to do in the future what they've done in the past. This is an act of faith, but it is a rational faith.

We view human beings and our relationship to the rest of the creation as fallen creatures who can really mess things up, who must consume to live, but who nevertheless have in us the breath of God, and have been given a spark of creativity from the Creator of heaven and earth.

Trusting isn't an act of blind faith, because we can look at past trends. If we keep the long-term past trends in mind rather than just the moment we happen to be walking the earth, we should expect scarcity and creativity to conspire to give us ample new supplies of usable energy, just as they have in the past. We suspect we'll discover alternatives long before that happens.

It may be something we can easily imagine, such as converted natural gas or coal. Maybe we'll go electric, and beef up our power grids with clean nuclear plants with improved safety features. Maybe we'll find ways to develop cheap geothermal heat pumps for every home.[19] Maybe the future's main energy source will be fusion reactors using deuterium culled from seawater, and tritium converted from lithium, harnessing a type of atomic reaction even more energy-rich than fission, and whose radioactive waste becomes inert in a matter of a few decades. A matter-antimatter reactor? Hyperefficient wood-pellet-burning furnaces? Paint you can put on anything that captures usable energy from the sun? Who knows? It will probably be something we can't even imagine yet, perhaps arising from a new discovery in physics.

If we can keep in mind how prices and inventors have worked

historically in a free economy, we have far more reason to expect a solution than a calamity.

The Ultimate Resource

As we discussed earlier, people everywhere have the potential to create. In some situations, however, that potential is stymied, and people remain mainly consumers. Impoverished peoples can consume as much or more than they produce. They do this through no fault of their own, and certainly haven't chosen their lot.

Profligate governments and consumers in advanced economies can do this, too—though in their case, it's sinful farce rather than tragedy. As a society, we have been on a consumption binge for a quite a while—by choice rather than necessity. Compared to the Chinese, who on average are much poorer than we are, we hardly save. No matter how prosperous we are, we can't consume indefinitely more than we save and invest.

Most people in free societies can produce more resources than they consume. Free societies allow human beings to be fruitful and multiply, to till the garden and keep it, rather than merely consume. Whether they choose to do so is another matter.

In free markets characterized by the rule of law and limited government, our labor, even our low-skill labor, becomes more productive over time. We know market economies can grow. So why do we often fall for claims that contradict what we already know? Because we forget what the late economist Julian Simon called the ultimate resource— the creative vision and imagination of human beings living in freedom. The more human beings in free societies there are, the more laborers, inventors, producers, builders, farmers, problem solvers, and creators there are to transform material resources and to create new resources. Man, not matter, is the ultimate resource.[20]

In 1991, Pope John Paul II wrote an encyclical, *Centesimus Annus*, on the heels of the collapse of the Iron Curtain and the Soviet Union.

In the encyclical, he reflected on the twentieth-century battle between two different ways of understanding the economic order. While it's not an economic treatise, the Pope's words were eerily reminiscent of Julian Simon. "Indeed, besides the earth," he wrote, "man's principal resource is *man himself.* His intelligence enables him to discover the earth's productive potential and the many different ways in which human needs can be satisfied."[21] Read that again. Let it sink into your bones and color how you look at your fellow human beings.

Man's principle resource is man himself. We should not be surprised that two great minds, one an agnostic American economist, the other a Catholic Polish philosopher, should alight on the same truth. Economists see the effect of a truth that God's Word has long revealed. It is only when we understand the truth about man that we fully understand the nature of resources.

Of course, we don't spring from our mother's womb at our full potential—transforming stone into gold with the touch of a hand. We must be taught, and corrected, and nurtured, and planted in the right cultural setting to become even a fraction of what we can be. Nevertheless, "there are no *ordinary* people," C. S. Lewis said. "You have never talked to a mere mortal. Nations, cultures, arts, civilization—these are mortal, and their life is to ours as the life of a gnat. But it is immortals whom we joke with, work with, marry, snub, and exploit—immortal horrors or everlasting splendors."

All of us can be everlasting splendors. This is why, as long as we enjoy the freedom to exercise our God-given creativity, and take seriously our call to steward the earth, we need not fear that we will exhaust its resources.

Living Within the Truth

*And do not suppose this is the end. This is only the begin-
ning of the reckoning. This is only the first sip, the first
foretaste of a bitter cup which will be proffered to us year
by year unless by a supreme recovery of moral health and
martial vigour, we arise again and take our stand for freedom as in the olden time.*

—WINSTON CHURCHILL

Americans often say that they vote for the person rather than the party.
There's something to this. We should look at the individual candidate
rather than just pulling a lever based on whether there's an "R" or a "D"
next to the candidate's name. In practice, though, this turns elections
into popularity contests. If we were electing the national homecoming
king or queen, this wouldn't be a problem. When we're voting for a
president, senator, or representative that will be making national decisions, however, it's a mistake. Party affiliation is no guarantee, but it
gives voters a sense of what a candidate is likely to *do* in office: which
policies he'll probably support, and which he'll oppose. That is far
more important than whether a particular candidate has good hair or
makes your leg tingle.

Policies are important, but they stem from something more basic:

principles. To distinguish good from bad public policies—the *what* and not just the *who*—we have to connect time to eternity. That is, we have to apply unchanging, timeless *principles* to the constantly changing real world. Identifying the principles is hard; applying them is even harder.

You also need more than one principle. If you know some, such as *all men are created equal*, but not others, such as *wealth can be created*, you still might end up supporting policies that do more harm than good.

For instance, if you believe we're all created equal but think that wealth can only be transferred from one group to another, then you might want the government to "spread the wealth" around. If you know that people can create wealth, however, and that wealth redistribution schemes discourage that, then you'll likely support policies that encourage wealth creation, not wealth redistribution.

If you believe we're all created equal but don't know that evil exists and must be restrained, then you might think that war is just an artifact of a primitive age and that diplomacy and reason will always prevail with enough time and patience. If you know that evil exists and can't always be vanquished by kind words, you'll probably think that war is a tragic but sometimes necessary means to protect a nation's liberty.

If you know evil exists but don't realize we're *all* sinners, then you might be fine giving unchecked power to politicians and bureaucrats as long as they're the right kind of people. If, however, you know that everyone eligible for public office is a sinner who is easily corrupted by power, then you'll want checks and balances so that no one can get too powerful.

Is it any wonder that it's hard to find an ideal candidate for political office?

Still, if we can learn to *think* clearly, we can increase our odds of making the best choices available. What we need is a small set of mutually reinforcing principles, along with guidance on how to apply them in the real world.

In this book we decided to show these principles at work in policy debates before spelling them out. Now we'll do that so they can serve as anchors to sound thinking about public policy.

You won't be surprised to learn that the principles don't segregate themselves neatly into moral and economic baskets. Plenty of pundits in New York and Washington, DC, claim just the opposite. They advise Republican candidates to avoid the pro-life and marriage debates, or abandon them altogether. In 2009, author Amity Shlaes bluntly told her fellow Republicans, "Junk the social conservatism."[1] Wrong. Defending individual rights, limited government, and free markets while rejecting the sanctity of human life is a sign of deep confusion, not political acumen. An economic issue is rarely just about economics, and values aren't limited to abortion and marriage. In fact, so-called social and economic issues often hang on the same principle.

It's also foolish to jettison some basic moral principles, such as the sanctity of marriage, but defend others, such as the sanctity of life. Before the 2008 elections, Meghan McCain, John McCain's daughter, said, "I am a pro-life, pro-gay-marriage Republican."[2] Ms. McCain may be able to hold two conflicting ideas in her head; but this thinking is ultimately misguided, since both issues—marriage and life—depend on recognizing natural and prepolitical realities. A government that rejects one won't protect the other for long.

Just as there's more than one way to skin a cat, there's more than one way to describe first principles.[3] We can't give an exhaustive list of what you need to know in every situation. Still, we *can* isolate some of the principles and suggest some ways these ought to guide our policy choices.[4]

If we can etch these on our hearts and minds, seek a life of holiness and wisdom so we can discern them, teach them to our children, and apply them wisely in our personal lives and politics, then with God's help, we'll have most of what's needed to restore faith, family, and freedom in the twenty-first century.

THE FIRST PRINCIPLES OF FAITH, FAMILY, AND FREEDOM

1. Every human being has equal value and dignity.
2. We are inherently and specifically social.
3. Marriage and the family are *the* fundamental social institutions.
4. We can know God and moral truth.
5. Judeo-Christian religious faith guards our freedom.
6. We're all sinners.
7. We need a state strong enough to protect and maintain the rule of law but limited enough not to violate it.
8. We are meant to be free and responsible.
9. When we're free, we can create wealth.
10. Culture comes before politics.

---

1. Every human being has equal value and dignity.

If you want your political and economic views to be based in reality, glue them to this principle. It's right there in the Declaration of Independence, described as a self-evident truth, "that all men are created equal, that they are endowed by their Creator with certain unalienable rights, that among these are life, liberty, and the pursuit of happiness." Life is the first right. Without it, you can't enjoy liberty or any other right.

Everyone knows vaguely that man is more than a mere animal, but most ancient cultures had a much lower view of human life than we do. America emerged from a culture that had been taught for centuries the biblical truth that each of us, male and female, is created in the image of God. Pope Benedict XVI put it beautifully in his inaugural sermon as Pope: "We are not some casual and meaningless product of evolution. Each of us is the result of a thought of God. Each of us is willed, each of us is loved, each of us is necessary."[5] We still have a hard time applying this truth consistently, and the culture of death seeks to erase it from our cultural memory. Yet the truth still haunts the minds of Americans, even those who insist there is no God.

Unfortunately, secularism and progressivism have eroded this belief. Progressive Charles Merriam once wrote, "Rights are considered to have their source not in nature, but in law."[6] Alas, what the government giveth, the government can taketh away, as we have learned in spades since *Roe v. Wade*. A culture once committed to life now risks being consumed by the culture of death.

Against this, we must proclaim, until we have no voice, that the twelve-week-old unborn baby sucking its thumb, the handicapped infant, the grouchy old widower hooked up to an oxygen tank, the *losers* that we don't think contribute to society, are valuable simply by virtue of being human. They don't earn their value, and the government does not bestow it upon them. A just and humane government recognizes, in its laws, the equal value of every human being. The first duty of government is to protect the right of innocent human beings not to be destroyed by others. Pull out that thread and eventually the whole tapestry will unravel.

The right to private property, to enjoy the fruits of our labor, is closely linked to our right to life. Our property is, in a sense, an extension of ourselves; it is intimately wrapped up in our God-given role as stewards, so a right to property also protects our right to life. This is why no coherent defense of the right to property will deny the right to life.

Because we believe that every human being has value, we treat extreme poverty, disease, and death as enemies rather than just bad karma. We can't create heaven on earth, but we should support policies that can lift people out of extreme poverty in the long run.

None of this is to say that we all have, or even should have, the same skills, motivation, or economic value. In announcing his Great Society initiative, President Lyndon Johnson asserted that "we seek not just equality as a right and a theory but equality as a fact and equality as a result."[7] No. This is to seek what cannot be had—unless we merely want equality in misery. Bitter experience teaches us that trying to establish an "equality of outcome" among diverse individuals not only is counterproductive, but also it violates justice and our dignity as individuals. If you doubt that, read up on the history of the Soviet Union. While insisting that we are created equal, we must also protect our diversity.

This is the first of our principles. Still, it won't always guide us reliably without the principles that follow it.

2. We are inherently and specifically social.

Each of us has value by virtue of being human, but as God said of Adam, it is not good for man to be alone. No man is an island. *Our many, diverse relationships also define us.*

Our relationship with God is the most fundamental one, even if we fail to recognize it. God does not need us, but He created each of us, He loves us, and He sustains us at every moment. Our value comes from this unique relationship. "For you formed my inward parts/you knitted me together in my mother's womb," says Psalm 139. God is closer to the unborn child than that child is to his mother.

After our relationship with God come our relationships with other people. Here, there are more varieties than there are flavors of ice cream. As children, we depend on our parents. Our relationship with our father is not the same as our relationship with our mother. As parents, we're responsible for our children; we love them, sacrifice for them, and can't imagine life without them. As spouses, we give ourselves to another person uniquely. Marriage is so profound that Paul compared it to Christ's relationship to the Church!

As Christians, we are members of Christ's body, surrounded by the great cloud of witnesses that have gone before us (Hebrews 12).

We seek communion with others and develop natural ties among our fellow countrymen. We pray, live, learn from and with others. We work with others, trade goods and services with others, and, when we are free, create value for ourselves and others.

Just as we have rights that others are bound to recognize, we also have obligations to our fellow human beings, especially for those in need—the poor, the orphaned, the widowed, the outcast.

We're belaboring this point because it's easy to distort this principle. We can best help the hurting when we practice well-thought-out acts of charity, not random acts of kindness. Moreover, when charity is replaced by political coercion, it tends to hurt rather than help.

Some libertarians view individuals as isolated atoms and miss this principle altogether. *Social*ists make a near-opposite mistake: they confuse society with the state. Socialism can appeal to well-meaning people who seek community; but it destroys real community. Under socialism, the quirky variety of real relationships—spouses, parents, children, friends, coworkers, trading partners—is dissolved and confused by a coercive state, leaving poverty, enmity, and envy in its wake.

It might seem paradoxical, but *policies that do not respect the natural diversity of our relationships end up violating our rights as individuals.* A well-known twentieth-century politician said approvingly, "In fundamental theory socialism and democracy are almost if not quite one and the same. They both rest at bottom upon the absolute right of the community to determine its own destiny and that of its members."[8] These words belong to President Woodrow Wilson, an ardent progressive.

Just policies, in contrast, respect the natural diversity of our relationships. The way the federal government ought to relate to citizens, for instance, is not the same as the way a mother relates to her children. The government is charged with protecting our rights. It's not our mommy.

Today's secular left makes a hash of relationships because it is a confused hybrid of libertine individualism and collectivism. On matters of sexuality, it's every man and woman for him- or herself. If it feels good, do it. Yet the secular leftist wants the coercive state involved in pretty much everything else. In fact, most leftists, President Obama included, are infatuated with *international* governance. On this view, taken to its logical conclusion, ordinary patriotism is not a healthy, natural expression of our social natures, but a dangerous and jingoistic nationalism.

Finally, while most of our relationships involve other persons—God and other human beings—we also depend on the earth and its creatures for our sustenance. The earth is the Lord's, and we are made from its dust; but the Lord has made us stewards over it. So we should treat the creation responsibly while never mistaking it for the Creator.

3. Marriage and the family are *the* fundamental social institutions.

Conjugal marriage and the family are the two most basic human institutions. They exist in every time and place, and they precede the state. The state and other institutions don't define or determine what marriage and family are, but they must recognize them. That's why political attempts to redefine marriage and family are not tolerant but totalitarian. They are wars against the creation itself. We must oppose the trends in our culture and in our politics with all our might.

At the same time we must support policies that encourage healthy families. This requires discernment, since every half-baked bill proposed in Congress claims to be pro-family. As we've seen, however, many policies create incentives that harm the family. Remember what the welfare state did to marriage and family in poor communities in the United States? Divorce rates, out-of-wedlock births, and fatherless homes have risen in every class in the United States in the last fifty years, but the decay has been catastrophic in poor communities, where the welfare state has mostly replaced the traditional roles of the father and the Church. This tragic unintended consequence suggests a rule of thumb: If a policy surrenders territory to the state that ought to be part of civil society, that policy will harm rather than help families in the long run.

4. We can know God and moral truth.

Contrary to today's fashion, the American Founders understood that everyone has a general knowledge of the natural moral law and the Lawgiver. From the starry heavens above to the moral law within, the world points to its Creator. That's why even atheists know that murder is wrong, experience feelings of gratitude and guilt, bristle at injustice, and get mad at the God they don't believe in when unjust things happen around them. We can discern enough of the law "from the things that have been made" so that we can be held accountable for what we do (Romans 1).

The existence of a Creator and a natural law are *public truths*. This is why the Founders appealed to the "Laws of Nature and Nature's God," though they still took pains not to establish a specific religion. Even the Supreme Court, which hasn't always respected this part of our history, reiterated these points as recently as 1984, stating, "We are a religious people whose institutions presuppose a Supreme Being."

Secularism and progressivism, however, deny that we can know God and morality.[9] They seek to quarantine both to a ghetto of private religious faith. This has created a secular and relativistic public square, which is exactly the opposite of what the Founders intended. We must reverse this trend and defend the truth that man has real moral *knowledge*, which is the foundation of just government.

5. Judeo-Christian religious faith guards our freedom.

Though everyone has some knowledge of God and morality, that knowledge is darkened by sin. It tends to wither away without vibrant faith to reinforce it. We should stand with the Founders, who both opposed the establishment of a specific religion and supported robust expressions of religious faith in the public square. That's not a contradiction. It is, quite simply, the free exercise of religion guaranteed by the First Amendment.

Contrary to secularist myth, faith in the public square need not imperil our freedom. It's true that in the past, Christians have persecuted others, including fellow Christians. But they were violating the spirit and content of their faith in doing so. While not every religious belief is friendly to freedom, the basic tenets of Christianity reinforce political, economic, and religious freedom. As we've seen, we owe our freedoms, in large part, to the Judeo-Christian tradition. It's where we get our belief that individuals have equal value. It's also where we get the idea of sin, which inspired the Founders to establish a limited government and a separation of powers.

Faith encourages the virtues that help sustain the free society. It gives us hope in the future, which is under the providence of God, while preventing us from falling for utopian fantasies like the communist illusions that killed scores of millions of people in the twentieth century.

We must do our best to correct the false stereotype that faith feeds theocracy and defend the freedom of believers to apply their faith to the concerns of the day.

6. We're all sinners.

Evil is not just in our imaginations. We can't eradicate it with the right amount of social engineering or positive thinking. We sin. Though we can know God exists, we forget. Though we can know the truth, we fail to uphold it. We do the very things we don't want to do. We are tempted by wealth, power, prestige, lust, gluttony, and greed, and often give in to those temptations.

We not only fail to do what we know we ought to do, but we also get confused about what we ought to do. Politically, this puts us in an awkward position. On the one hand, we need a government to punish evil and bear the sword. On the other hand, the very sin that needs to be restrained can only be restrained by other sinners. J.R.R. Tolkien, author of *The Lord of the Rings* and *The Hobbit*, once told his son, "The most improper job of any man, even saints (who at any rate were at least unwilling to take it on), is bossing other men. Not one in a million is fit for it, and least of all those who seek the opportunity."

The solution is a government limited in scope but strong enough to restrain sin that harms others.

7. We need a state strong enough to protect and maintain the rule of law but limited enough not to violate it.

The American Founders understood this paradox of power. That's why they established checks and balances in the Constitution. Between the Founders and us, unfortunately, came the progressives. They sought to expand government without limit, so they viewed the Constitution not as a guide but an impediment. Progressivism came to dominate all branches of government and most elite institutions in the twentieth century. This created a conspiracy of consensus, which has devastated the checks and balances established by the Constitution. The federal government is now a Leviathan. *We must support policies and candidates committed to restoring constitutional wisdom to our political institutions.* This means that we must be willing to see unsustainable programs cut, even programs that we like and depend on.

While the government helps provide the conditions for prosperity and the creation of wealth, it's not their source. When government tries to substitute itself for the proper functions of business, enterprise, and the market, it does more harm than good, distorts natural incentives, encourages cycles of dependency, replaces the happiness of earned success with the subtle indignity of a handout, hinders the creativity of entrepreneurs, and turns the win-win game of a free exchange into a win-lose game of coercion and redistribution.

Some Christians think that because of sin, the federal government should have even more power over the economy and our lives, as if the way to disperse power is to give *more* power to the most powerful entity. As we've seen, however, a free market limits the power of the state. A free market exists only where there is a rule of law, private property, and business institutions that, while certainly not perfect, at least channel our creativity, legitimate self-interest, and even vices such as greed into ventures that meet the needs of other.

Since everyone in a market is sinful as well, laws and economic policies should, as much as possible, be set up to channel selfish motives into actions that benefit others. We know from experience that a free market does this better than the alternatives. That's why we should defend policies that advance economic freedom rather than extend the reach of political control ever farther into the economic realm.

Still, a free economy can't long exist unless a people are at least minimally virtuous. "Liberty," said Lord Acton, "is the delicate fruit of a mature civilization." Our economic freedom won't last long unless certain institutions, especially churches and families—are free to instill virtue.

As important as government is for preserving the rule of law, history teaches us that it can also be the worst violator of the rule of law. We must oppose attempts to expand the role of government beyond its constitutionally enumerated duties. Given our current debt crisis, for instance, we should especially oppose attempts to add or expand entitlement programs. These programs entice citizens to vote for more and more services for themselves with borrowed money that must be repaid by our children and grandchildren. As people become more and more dependent on these programs, it becomes almost impossible for elected officials to reform them, even in the face of fiscal ruin. That's why we must support policies and politicians that deal with this looming disaster honestly, and do whatever we can to explain this problem to our fellow Americans.

We should have a strong defense as part of a limited government, since defense is one of the things government is limited *for*. One reason to limit the tasks of government is so that it can focus on its most important jobs. Defense, like all other expenses, is subject to budget constraints. But we should oppose attempts to weaken our military and defense capabilities, and reject claims that supporting the military amounts to nationalism and militarism. In a fallen world, protecting life and liberty requires that, at times, we take up arms against aggressors. Pretending otherwise is naïve, utopian, and ultimately unjust.

8. We are meant to be free and responsible.

We are created to be free. God valued our freedom so much that He even gave us the power to reject Him. And we did. This put us under the bondage of sin. But God did not leave us in our bondage. By bearing the brunt of sin, He reconciled us to Himself. Ultimate freedom is freedom in Christ. But God in His common grace also has revealed ways for societies to restrain evil and achieve some measure of freedom.

In free societies the government both *protects* and *submits* to the rule of law. It conforms to those realities outside it, including to the roles of individual persons, families, the Church, and other institutions of civil society. Free societies protect private property. They allow their citizens to participate in the political process, to make basic economic choices, and to freely exercise their religious faith. These freedoms are indivisible. A regime such as the People's Republic of China may try to provide some measure of economic freedom while retaining a strong grip on politics and religion. But in the long run, political, economic, and religious freedoms stand or fall together.

Freedom doesn't mean we can do anything that strikes our fancy. With freedom comes responsibility—for our choices, our children, our actions, our neighbors, our faith, for seeking the truth, and for the natural environment that God has given us to steward. If we hope to preserve freedom in the twenty-first century, we must embrace these responsibilities.

9. When we're free, we can create wealth.

Every person is made in the image of God, and every healthy person can create wealth. We do so by specializing, transforming matter into resources, inventing new technologies and better ways of organizing businesses, and providing service to others. And as we saw in the Trading Game, we can create value in another way. Exchanges that are free on both sides allow us to create value for ourselves as well as for others—even when no new material has been added to the system.

To create new wealth and value depends not only on how hard we work, but also on where we are. The same hardworking person is likely to create far more wealth in an advanced, law-abiding society filled with creative entrepreneurs than in a lawless and oppressive society filled with despair. As we saw, one of the best ways to predict economic growth in a country is to look at the economic freedom its citizens enjoy.

Because human beings are wealth creators, we should reject the false idea that the prosperity of some must come from the poverty of others. We should oppose policies that punish wealth creators and seek to eliminate poverty by taking wealth from those who have earned it to redistribute it to those who have not. The best antipoverty programs allow and encourage wealth to be created rather than forcibly redistributed.

10. Culture comes before politics.

Politicians who violate these principles must be replaced with politicians who defend and apply them properly, especially now, when the stakes are so high. If we want lasting change, however, we have to restore the rest of the culture, too. Politics shapes the culture, to be sure; but ultimately, politics is a part of the culture. People of faith can still vote, but we have been culturally marginalized, and that has had a devastating effect.

Unfortunately, in the twentieth century the political realm absorbed much of the territory that once belonged to civil society. We will only be able to reform unsustainable entitlement programs if we can rekindle the cultural virtues of thrift, prudence, personal responsibility, and delayed gratification, even while financial incentives pull many Americans in the opposite direction.

If we can't do that, these programs will collapse—at least in their current forms—and drag the world economy with them. We don't know exactly when all this will happen; but it will happen during the lifetimes of most of the people reading this book. We need to prepare. Either way—courageous reform or disastrous collapse—there will be a growing need for nongovernmental charitable programs that can *really* help the elderly, the poor, the handicapped, and the otherwise disadvantaged. Increasingly, Christians will need to play a larger role in helping the needy in our communities.

Let's hope we can restore the culture before we have to rebuild it.

Pray

Of course, the most profound cultural change will come from outward expressions of inward change—a moral and spiritual renewal of our hearts and minds, our churches, communities, and cultural institutions. *Besides principles and policies, we need people and prayer.* Wherever the Church—the Body of Christ—is aligned with the Spirit and willing to suffer for truth, the kingdom of God breaks through in the here and now. We must live within the truth.

As Archbishop Charles Chaput explains:

> Living within the truth means living every day and every moment from the unshakeable conviction that God lives, and that his love is the motive force of human history and the engine of every authentic human life.... Living within the truth also means telling the truth and calling things by their right names. And that means exposing the lies by which some men try to force others to live.... We are ambassadors of the living God to a world that is on the verge of forgetting him. The form of the Church, and the form of every Christian life, is the form of the Cross.... Let us support each other—whatever the cost—so that when we make our accounting to the Lord, we will be numbered among the faithful and courageous, and not the cowardly or the evasive, or those who compromised until there was nothing left of their convictions; or those who were silent when they should have spoken the right word at the right time.[10]

The history of our country is but a short, small chapter in God's grand, unfolding cosmic drama. Yet it is the chapter in which we live and choose and act. We have been told how the story ends, but not how our chapter ends, perhaps because, mysteriously, it is given to us to help write it. Our hands are feeble, our eyes are dim, and our resolve is weak. Yet we *must* face the trouble now if our children are to live in peace. So let us pray, more fervently than we have ever prayed, for a historic outpouring of the Holy Spirit on us, His Church. Not an outpouring that merely moves us to tears, but a cascading waterfall of God's suffering and abiding love, which will lead us to act with bravery, to walk with integrity, and to stand in unity for the renewal of our culture and the restoration of our nation—one nation, under God, indivisible, with liberty and justice for all.

NOTES

Acknowledgments

1. See the article about the 2011 Summit meeting, "Supernatural Gathering," at: http://www.jamesrobison.net/?q=node/88.

Introduction. Where Were You When Freedom Died?

1. This statement is from *Planned Parenthood v. Casey*, 505 U.S. 833, 851 (1992). The Court, of course, understood itself in *Roe v. Wade* and later abortion-related cases merely to be applying the right to privacy consistently, rather than denying the inalienable rights of any human beings. As we discuss in chapter five, seven Justices in *Roe* found a legal pretense for decriminalizing abortion in the concept of privacy. Even on its own terms, the argument is absurd. The right to privacy of one cannot trump the right to life of another.
2. Tony Evans, *Oneness Embraced* (Chicago: Moody Publishers, 2011), p. 262.
3. Contrary to stereotype, divorce rates have leveled off in recent years. But this gives the false impression that things are improving. Far more people are now living together and having children without getting married, so fewer children are being raised by married parents, even though divorce rates per se aren't going up. See detailed statistics at: http://www.familyfacts.org.
4. Lev Grossman, "2045: The Year Man Becomes Immortal," *Time* (February 10, 2011), at: http://www.time.com/time/health/article/0,8599,2048138,00.html.
5. This is in the context, of course, of some fifty million legal abortions since 1973. See "Abortions by Year" at the *National Right to Life* website, at: http://www.nrlc.org/abortion/facts/abortionstats.html.
6. Jonathan V. Last, "America's One-Child Policy," *The Weekly Standard* 16, no. 2 (September 27, 2010). We discuss the details later in the book.

Chapter 1. Principles, Policies, and Prayer

1. This quote is from the "comments" section below the article by David Paul Kuhn, "Some Social Conservative Leaders Feel Scapegoated," *RealClearPolitics* (May 11, 2009), at: http://www.realclearpolitics.com/articles/2009/05/11/social_conservatives_leaders_feel_scapegoated_96435.html.
2. Quoted in the post by Rick Moran, "We're Going to Need a Bigger Tent," *PajamasMedia* (June 13, 2009), at: http://pajamasmedia.com/blog/were-going-to-need-a-bigger-tent/.

3. Michael Duffy, "Jerry Falwell: Political Innovator," *Time* (May 15, 2007), at: http://www.time.com/time/nation/article/0,8599,1621300,00.html#ixzz1CeYbuaPg.

4. In describing the Status of Global Mission Report, George Weigel notes: "There were 1,600 Christian denominations in 1900; there were 18,800 in 1970; and there are 42,000 today." George Weigel, "Christian Number Crunching," *First Things* (February 9, 2011), at: http://www.firstthings.com/onthesquare/2011/02/christian-number-crunching.

5. For instance, Paul Weyrich, a conservative Catholic and early leader of the Heritage Foundation, was an early organizer of the religious right.

6. For an excellent summary and critique of the earlier ecumenical movement, see Jordan J. Ballor, *Ecumenical Babel: Confusing Economic Ideology and the Church's Social Witness* (Grand Rapids, MI: Christian's Library Press, 2010).

Chapter 2. What Is Freedom?

1. Quoted in C. Bradley Thompson, "John Adams and the Coming of the French Revolution," *Journal of the Early Republic* 16, no. 3 (Autumn 1996), p. 361.

2. For an excellent discussion of this richer Western concept of freedom, see the essays in Roger Scruton, editor, *Liberty and Civilization* (New York: Encounter Books, 2011). See also Samuel Gregg, *On Ordered Liberty: A Treatise on the Free Society* (Lanham: Lexington Books, 2003).

Chapter 3. The Law Is Written on the Heart, Stone, and Parchment

1. J. Budziszewski, *What We Can't Not Know* (Dallas: Spence, 2003). This is the best single book to read on the concept of natural law.

2. The sermon was entitled, "On the Right to Rebel Against Governors." For this and similar quotations, see Matthew Spalding, *We Still Hold These Truths* (Wilmington: ISI Press, 2009), pp. 136–39.

3. Promiscuity is wrong not because it leads to venereal disease; rather, venereal disease is a natural consequence that can remind us that promiscuity is wrong.

4. Some believe that natural law is just a Catholic idea. That's not true. See, for instance, Stephen J. Grabill, *Rediscovering the Natural Law in Reformed Theological Ethics* (Grand Rapids, MI: Eerdmans, 2006), and Greg Forster, *The Contested Public Square* (Downers Grove, IL: InterVarsity Press, 2008). While many twentieth-century Protestant theologians, such as Karl Barth, Stanley Hauerwas, and Reinhold Niebuhr, rejected natural law, the early mainstream Reformers such as John Calvin did not.

5. For more on biblical texts that describe the natural law, see Budziszewski, *What We Can't Not Know*, pp. 227–34.

6. This is what Darwinists Michael Ruse and E. O. Wilson said of our belief in ethics. Since they assume that all of our traits are the product of blind natural selection and random mutations, our morality gets us to act in ways that enhance our (or our species's) chances of survival. But our moral judgments aren't *true*. Michael Ruse and E. O. Wilson, "The Evolution of Ethics," *New Scientist* 108:1478 (October 17, 1985), p. 51.

7. God gave the Ten Commandments to Moses on Mount Sinai. The commandments seem to mix the general (don't murder) with the particular (keep the seventh day holy). But traditionally, they've been seen as a type of summary of the moral order

that should govern our actions, first toward God, and then toward our fellow human beings. They're distinct from the ceremonial laws that God gave to the Jews for their specific time and place. For more on the relationship of the Ten Commandments and natural law, see Budziszewski, pp. 28–50.

8. The Founders were steeped in the biblical tradition, so it's no surprise to find references to Scripture and the Ten Commandments in historic American documents and in government buildings. There is a carved relief of Moses and the Ten Commandments on the back of the US Supreme Court Building, for instance, and similar images inside the Courtroom. This doesn't mean they intended to establish Christianity as the national religion. Secularists often want to purge American history of all Christian influence, and some Christians react by overstating things in the opposite direction. We'll talk more about this in chapter twelve.

9. The Constitution did allow established religions at the state level, which existed at the time. For more on the purpose of the Constitution, see Matthew Spalding, *We Still Hold These Truths*, pp. 99–116.

10. We don't need to delve into the complex issue of revolution against a tyrannical government. For a discussion of John Locke's theory of when revolution can be justified, see Greg Forster, *The Contested Public Square* (Downers Grove, IL: InterVarsity Press, 2008), pp. 182–201.

11. C. S. Lewis gives examples of common moral themes in different cultures in his book *The Abolition of Man* (San Francisco: HarperOne, 2001), first published in 1943. He refers to natural law as the "Tao" in the book, to avoid giving the impression that natural law was exclusively Christian. This is a book that everyone should read at least once.

12. Even now, many countries ignore their constitution. For instance, the new Afghan constitution assures religious freedom, but Afghans are still executed if they convert to a religion other than Islam. To be precise, the Afghan constitution is contradictory. It cites the UN's Universal Declaration of Human Rights, which includes religious freedom, but insists that everything be subsumed under shariah law, since Afghanistan is an Islamic state. And shariah law requires death for "apostasy." See Andrew McCarthy, "Death to Apostates: Not a Perversion of Islam, but Islam," *National Review* (February 19, 2011), at: http://www.nationalreview.com/articles/260155/death-apostates-not-perversion-islam-islam-andrew-c-mccarthy.

13. This is from *The Federalist* #51. Madison exaggerated a bit. Even if we weren't sinners, we would still need some rules for traffic and whatnot; but without sin, we wouldn't need a government to bear the sword and coerce us.

14. Even if a task is given to the government, it doesn't follow that it need or ought to be given to the *federal* government. Federalism provided a way for political ideas to be tested without being imposed on the entire country. In 1932, Justice Louis Brandeis described it this way: "It is one of the happy incidents of the federal system that a single courageous state may, if its citizens choose, serve as a laboratory; and try novel social and economic experiments without risk to the rest of the country." The problem, unfortunately, is that bad policies tested in one state, such as California, have a mysterious tendency of spreading to other states.

15. The Founders' realism about human nature is why the American Revolution turned out so differently from the French Revolution.

16. John Tamny, "The State of the Union: An Excessive Amount of State," *Forbes.com* (January 30, 2011), at: http://blogs.forbes.com/johntamny/2011/01/30/the-state-of -the-union-an-excessive-amount-of-state/.

17. This is from the 1992 case *Planned Parenthood v. Casey*, 505 U.S. 833, at 851.

18. "Order in the Jungle," *The Economist* (March 13, 2008).

19. See discussion in ibid. Unfortunately, it's hard to implement the rule of law in places that don't have it. What good is property law reform with a populace that won't respect the property of others? Similarly, a transparent and predictable legal system is an economic plus. But how can policy makers, or development economists at the World Bank, impose such a system on a deeply corrupt population and political culture? People interested in economic development have often acted as if we get the policies and infrastructure right, then prosperity will follow. But with some minimal public morality, policies probably won't have much effect. We talk more about the role of property later in the book.

20. Spalding, *We Still Hold These Truths*, p. 137.

21. Philosopher Peter Kreeft even calls this "Colson's Law." See his discussion in *How to Win the Culture War* (Downers Grove, IL: InterVarsity Press, 2002), pp. 46–54.

Chapter 4. God in Public

1. See discussion in Richard Land, *The Divided States of America* (Nashville: Thomas Nelson, 2011), pp. 116–22. There is a difference between an institutional separation of church and state, and the prohibition of religious belief in public. Jefferson supported the former, not the latter. For an excellent scholarly study of this issue, see Daniel L. Dreisbach, *Thomas Jefferson and the Wall of Separation Between Church and State* (New York: New York University Press, 2002).

2. In remarks at World Youth Day 2011, in Madrid, Spain. Reported in Michael W. Chapman, "Archbishop: New York Times, Newsweek, CNN, MSNBC Not 'Trustworthy' on Religion," *CNS News* (August 19, 2011), at: http://www.cnsnews.com /news/article/new-york-times-newsweek-cnn-msnbc-not-tr.

3. There is a type of "reconstructionist" or "dominionist" theology in certain quarters of Reformed theology, which seeks a sort of theocracy or, rather, Christian authoritarianism—though even here, we're not dealing with the violent overthrow of a democratically elected government. Be that as it may, dominionism is an extreme minority view, even among conservative Calvinists. Unfortunately, secularists often treat this as the majority view of conservative Christians. See, for example, the website: http://www.theocracywatch.org/. In fact, most conservative Christians have never even heard of this theology. Its main practical function is to serve as a foil for far left critics of Christianity.

4. Another instance might also look like some sort of theocracy: the Papal States of Italy. For centuries, these were under the official authority of the Pope, as the result of a series of donations to the Church. But anyone familiar with the history of the period knows how tenuous the Pope's political authority was. There continued to be kings and emperors. And from 1305 to 1378, the Popes had to reside in Avignon in southeastern France. The average Italian living in a Papal State during these years

was more likely to experience the despotism of some local chieftain, and would probably have liked the Pope to have more practical authority rather than less.

5. Mainz's shenanigans led to some of the abuses that so infuriated Martin Luther. As our friend Greg Forster reminds us (in private correspondence), "Albert of Mainz was simultaneously the elector (civil ruler) and archbishop (religious ruler) over a big swath of Germany. The Tetzel indulgences campaign that sparked the Reformation was a direct result of Albert's desire to maximize the opportunities for exploitation afforded by his simultaneous control of both civil and religious offices."

6. In fact, all three of Satan's temptations to Jesus describe the presumed powers of a Roman emperor. This makes it hard to avoid the conclusion that the point of the temptation narratives is to show that Jesus rejected a purely political fulfillment of his Messiahship, which was what most Jews at the time were expecting.

7. During Jesus's ministry, Tiberius, the son of Augustus, was emperor. So the denarius that Jesus was referring to had an abbreviated inscription on it that said: "Tiberius Caesar, Worshipful Son of the God, Augustus." Although we can easily miss these theological undertones when reading the story in the gospels, the original audience would have understood them immediately.

8. In fact, early on, the Romans called Christians "atheists." In AD 155, Polycarp, the bishop of Smyrna and a disciple of the apostle John, was captured by an angry mob. The Roman proconsul tried to persuade him to save himself by saying, "Away with the atheists!"—which was the official denunciation of Christians that the Romans required. When Polycarp uttered the phrase, though, he pointed to the crowd, which then bound him and burned him alive. He had said, in effect, that the God he worshipped was real, while the worship of the Roman gods was atheism, since those gods didn't exist. Greg Forster, *The Contested Public Square* (Downers Grove, IL: InterVarsity Press, 2008), p. 20.

9. Almost everything we learn and read is critical of Constantine, so it's nice to see a recent book by a Presbyterian scholar that corrects the stereotype. See Peter Leithart, *Defending Constantine: The Twilight of an Empire and the Dawn of Christendom* (Downers Grove, IL: InterVarsity Press, 2010).

10. Two good books on this subject are H. A. Drake, *Constantine and the Bishops: The Politics of Intolerance* (Baltimore: Johns Hopkins University Press, 2002), and Elizabeth DePalma Digeser, *The Making of a Christian Empire: Lactantius and Rome* (Ithaca: Cornell University Press, 1999).

11. John West, *The Politics and Revelation and Reason* (Lawrence: University Press of Kansas, 1996), pp. 5–6.

12. This policy was called *cuius regio, eius religio*, which means something like, "whose the region, his the religion." In other words, the religion of a region would be determined by the person in charge of that region.

13. The popular defense of religious toleration is John Locke's *Letter Concerning Toleration* (Englewood Cliffs, NJ: Prentice Hall, 1950), originally published in 1689. Whatever Locke's private beliefs, his argument is explicitly Christian, and he appeals to the New Testament in support of religious tolerance. For discussion, see Forster, *The Contested Public Square*, pp. 154–65.

14. Ibid., pp. 20–21.

15. This is from *Federalist* #51, quoted in John West, *The Politics of Revelation and Reason*, p. 213.

16. There's a difference between an official church, with official responsibilities, getting involved in the nitty-gritty of politics, and individual Christians doing so. You may have responsibilities as a citizen with economic expertise that your pastor, priest, or church would not have. See Michael Gerson and Peter Wehner, *City of Man: Religion and Politics in a New Era* (Chicago: Moody Publishers, 2010), pp. 35–36.

17. See the Pew Forum's "Statistics on Religion in America Report," at: http://religions .pewforum.org/reports.

18. There are, of course, many such quotes. See the examples at the Wall Builders website at: http://www.wallbuilders.com/LIBissuesArticles.asp?id=78.

19. There were also two Catholics at the Constitutional Convention (1787), both of whom signed the Constitution. See the unbiased list of Founders and their religious affiliations here: http://www.adherents.com/gov/Founding_Fathers_Religion.html.

20. James D. Richardson, *Compilation of Messages and Papers of the Presidents, 1789–1897* (Washington, DC: US Government Printing Office, 1907), vol. 1, p. 213.

21. Though what they said publicly doesn't always square with their private beliefs.

22. It's fair to call Jefferson a deist, although he became more and more interested in the person of Jesus as he grew older.

23. This is the term that Michelle Goldberg uses in her especially paranoid book *Kingdom Coming: The Rise of Christian Nationalism* (New York: W.W. Norton & Co., 2006). While Goldberg offers some legitimate criticisms of some arguments made by some Christians, she frequently makes bizarre comparisons between American Christians and German Nazis. This is quite common in secularist literature.

24. Mohammad spread Islam by the sword, and Muslim history has followed the example of its founder. The Koran commands this over and over. In the Koran, see, for example, Suras 3:151, 8:12–13, 8:60, 9:5, 33:25–27, 59:2–4, and 59:13. And see the many quotes from the Muslim Hadith, which contains the authoritative records of Mohammad's life and work, on "Fighting for the Cause of Allah," at: http:// www.usc.edu/schools/college/crcc/engagement/resources/texts/muslim/hadith /bukhari/052.sbt.html.

25. See, for instance, Rodney Stark, *The Victory of Reason: How Christianity Led to Freedom, Capitalism, and Western Success* (New York: Random House, 2006).

26. This is from President Obama's speech at a Call to Renewal event on June 28, 2006, at: http://www.nytimes.com/2006/06/28/us/politics/2006obamaspeech.html.

27. John Adams, *The Works of John Adams, Second President of the United States*, edited by Charles Francis Adams (Boston: Little, Brown, and Co., 1854), vol. IX, p. 229. See many other quotes along these lines at: http://www.wallbuilders.com /LIBissuesArticles.asp?id=63.

28. See the many references to scientific studies on the positive role of religion in Patrick Fagan, "Why Religion Matters Even More: The Impact of Religious Practice on Social Stability," *Heritage Foundation Backgrounder*, no. 1992 (December 18, 2006), at: http://www.heritage.org/research/reports/2006/12/why-religion-matters-even -more-the-impact-of-religious-practice-on-social-stability#_ftnref4.

29. Arthur Brooks and Robin Currie, "Religion: Why Faith Is a Good Investment," in *Indivisible: Social and Economic Foundations of American Liberty*, edited by Jay W. Richards (Washington, DC: Heritage Foundation, 2009).

Chapter 5. Bearing the Sword

1. *The Collected Works of Abraham Lincoln*, edited by Roy P. Basler, vol. 2 (Piscataway, NJ: Rutgers University Press, 1953), p. 220. Quoted in James D. Gwartney, Richard L. Stroup, Dwight R. Lee, and Tawni H. Ferrarini, *Common Sense Economics* (New York: St. Martin's Press, 2010).

2. We're not saying that legitimate questions cannot be raised about the raid on bin Laden. Should bin Laden have been killed when he was unarmed? Was he subject to an assassination order? Should he have been captured instead? Did the debates over waterboarding and civilian trials for terrorists create an incentive to kill rather than capture high-value targets such as bin Laden? We don't know the answers to these questions; but in any case, they are the questions of hindsight. They can fairly be asked of those who planned and ordered the mission. Troops in the heat of battle under the shroud of darkness, however, rarely have the luxury of weighing abstract options. Given bin Laden's penchant for targeting civilians, it's hardly surprising that the troops who captured him assumed he was armed and dangerous. His death does not prove that US policy for high-value targets is assassination. Saddam Hussein, for instance, was captured by American troops, then tried and executed by Iraqi officials. And other high-value, former leaders of al Qaeda, such as Khalid Sheikh Mohammed, remain in US custody, when they could easily have been assassinated.

3. The details are complicated. The Hebrew word, *ratsach*, is used elsewhere for a legally permissible form of killing. Numbers 35:30, for instance, prescribes execution for a person convicted of murder. The word *ratsach* is used to refer to the execution. So the word doesn't not mean "murder" exclusively.

4. Quoted in Mark Tooley, "Religiously Battling for Pacifism," *The American Spectator* (December 13, 2010), at: http://spectator.org/archives/2010/12/13/religiously-battling-for-pacif.

5. As it happens, biblical scholars dispute the meaning of these Old Testament commands. While they look straightforward to modern readers—if somebody intentionally blinds you in one eye, you should blind them in one eye—ancient readers may not have interpreted the commands in this way. See, for example, Raymond Westbrook, *A History of Ancient Near Eastern Law* (Boston: Brill Academic Publishers, 2003).

6. Francis J. Beckwith, *Politics for Christians: Statecraft as Soulcraft* (Downers Grove, IL: InterVarsity Press, 2010), p. 56.

7. See the characteristic argument, for instance, in Ted Grimsrud, "Romans 13 Supports Pacifism!" *Thinking Pacifism* (May 1, 2011), at: http://thinkingpacifism.net/2011/05/01/romans-13-supports-pacifism/.

8. Remember, every biblical translation is also an interpretation. To study Scripture carefully, we must attend to the original language, the original audience, and if possible, the original context. We should also attempt to read individual texts of

Scripture in light of the books they are part of, and then in light of the whole canon rather than piecemeal. Finally, we should consult faithful teachers and interpreters throughout the ages rather than assuming our own infallibility. This "democracy of the dead," as G. K. Chesterton called it, gives us critical distance from the assumptions and prejudices of our own time and place. Otherwise, we're bound to end up making our private interpretation the ultimate authority, which Peter warned us against (2 Peter 1:20). A good source for the writings of the Church Fathers is the *Ancient Christian Commentary on Scripture* series published by InterVarsity Press.

9. For a fuller discussion of these points, see Wayne Grudem, *Politics According to the Bible* (Grand Rapids, MI: Zondervan, 2010), pp. 387–94.

10. Quoted in Mark Tooley, "Mourning the Fourth of July," *The American Spectator* (July 7, 2011), at: http://spectator.org/archives/2011/07/07/mourning-the-fourth-of-july.

11. This is from an informal Facebook discussion between Ben Witherington and Lawson Stone, which Witherington posted on his blog at *Beliefnet* (December 2, 2010), at: http://blog.beliefnet.com/bibleandculture/2010/12/recently-heard-on-facebook----a-conversation-between-lawson-stone-and-ben-witherington-on-the-bible.html.

12. For instance, he called for a September 2012 drawdown of American forces in Afghanistan, against the unanimous opposition of military leaders. It seems clear that the president's decision had nothing to do with military strategy or wisdom and everything to do with the fact that a presidential election will be held in November 2012.

13. In *The Politics of Jesus* (Grand Rapids, MI: Eerdmans, 1972), pp. 157, 12, 100. Quoted in James Davison Hunter, *To Change the World* (New York: Oxford University Press, 2010), p. 162.

14. In *Resident Aliens: Life in the Christian Colony* (Nashville: Abingdon Press, 1989), p. 30. Quoted in Hunter, *To Change the World*, p. 162.

15. See Mark Tooley, "Exceptional America?" *The American Spectator* (April 8, 2011), at: http://spectator.org/archives/2011/04/08/exceptional-america/print.

16. Perhaps the most prominent secular just war proponent at the moment is Michael Walzer.

17. Brian Orend, "War," *Stanford Encyclopedia of Philosophy* (2005), at: http://plato.stanford.edu/entries/war/.

18. We could write an entire chapter on the subject of waterboarding, for instance. The recent public debate over "torture," including the debate among Christians, left something to be desired. In 2007, the National Association of Evangelicals gathered signatures for a lengthy document denouncing "torture," but never even defined the term. The point of the document seemed to be capturing headlines rather than offering intellectually serious moral reflection on a difficult topic. Wayne Grudem deals with the subject well in *Politics According to the Bible*. He also offers a reasonable response to the question of waterboarding. See pp. 425–31.

19. This disagreement is mostly a difference of emphasis rather than of basic principles, with the exception, perhaps, of Ron Paul and some strong libertarians, who are more or less isolationist.

20. In the 2011 debate over Libya, for instance, the editors of *National Review* came out in support of a US-enforced no-fly-zone and military strikes against Muamar Qaddafi.

The next day, they published a high-profile 3,500-word critique of their editorial by Andrew McCarthy. Andrew McCarthy, "On NRO Libya Editorial, I Respectfully Dissent," *National Review Online* (March 17, 2011), at: http://www.nationalreview .com/corner/262377/nro-libya-editorial-i-respectfully-dissent-andrew-c-mccarthy.

21. See the discussion, for instance, in Niall Ferguson, *Empire: The Rise and Demise of the British World Order and the Lessons for Global Power* (New York: Basic Books, 2001), pp. 303–17.

22. Michael Novak defends this idea in his book *The Universal Hunger for Liberty* (New York: Basic Books, 2004).

23. Michael Novak argues that there is some reason for hope that Islam may undergo a "development of doctrine" in the near future. See "Religious Liberty and the Development of Doctrine in Islam," *Public Discourse* (June 27, 2011), at: http://www .thepublicdiscourse.com/2011/06/3337. See also the detailed argument by Mustafa Akyol, *Islam Without Extremes: A Muslim Case for Liberty* (New York: W.W. Norton & Co., 2011).

24. "Just Over Half Aware U.S. Spends Six Times as Much on Defense as Any Other Nation," *Rasmussen Reports* (February 7, 2011), at: http://www.rasmussenreports .com/public_content/politics/general_politics/february_2011/just_over_half _aware_u_s_spends_six_times_as_much_on_defense_as_any_other_nation.

25. For a lucid study of this, see Walter Russell Mead, *God and Gold: Britain, America, and the Making of the Modern World* (New York: Vintage, 2008).

26. Mark Steyn, "Dependence Day," *The New Criterion* (January 2011), at: http://www .newcriterion.com/articles.cfm/Dependence-Day-6753.

27. Based on data from *CIA World Fact Book* (2010) and *Stockholm International Peace Research Institute Yearbook 2011* (Oxford: Oxford University Press, 2011).

Chapter 6. How Big Is Too Big?

1. The size of government is only part of the issue. After all, the bigger a country is, the bigger its government will be. And a government surrounded on all sides by steep mountains may not need as big a military as would a country surrounded by hostile powers, or a country that is responsible for maintaining peace and order on the seas.

2. As Steven Hayward puts it in *Mere Environmentalism: A Biblical Perspective on Humans and the Environment* (Washington, DC: AEI Press, 2010), p. 60.

3. David Boaz, ed., *The Libertarian Reader: Classic and Contemporary Writings from Lao-tzu to Milton Friedman* (New York: The Free Press, 1997).

4. From Stéphane Courtois et al., *The Black Book of Communism: Crime, Terror, Repression* (Cambridge: Harvard University Press, 1999).

5. Quoted in Craig Ducat and Harold Chase, *Constitutional Interpretation* (St. Paul, MN: West Pub. Co., 1983), p. 3.

6. Jay W. Richards, ed., "Drowning in Red Tape: How the Flood of Regulations Hurts Americans," *The Economy Hits Home Series*, number VI (Washington, DC: Heritage Foundation, 2009).

7. Wayne Crews, *Ten Thousand Commandments* (Washington, DC: Competitive Enterprise Institute, 2011), available at: http://cei.org/10kc.

8. "The Government's War on Kid-Run Concession Stands," *Freedom Center of Missouri* (July 26, 2011), at: http://www.mofreedom.org/2011/07/the-government-war-on-kid-run-concession-stands/.

9. Mark Steyn, *After America* (Washington, DC: Regnery, 2011).

10. Chris Edwards, "Cutting Spending to Revive Federalism," *National Review* (February 10, 2011), at: http://www.nationalreview.com/articles/259414/cutting-spending-revive-federalism-chris-edwards.

11. These estimates seem to get worse over time. This number is from summer 2011. Dennis Cauchon, "Government's Mountain of Debt," *USA Today* (June 7, 2011), at: http://www.usatoday.com/news/washington/2011-06-06-us-debt-chart-medicare-social-security_n.htm.

12. Andrew Biggs explains the ways that Social Security is, and is not, like a Ponzi scheme in "From Ponzi to Perry: The Truth about Social Security," *The American* (September 14, 2011), at: http://www.american.com/archive/2011/september/from-ponzi-to-perry-the-truth-about-social-security.

13. These numbers are from an Office of Management and Budget estimate in early 2011. See Jeffrey Anderson, "A Deficit Without Defense," *The Weekly Standard* (March 15, 2011), at: http://www.weeklystandard.com/blogs/deficit-without-defense_554150.html.

14. Jeffrey Anderson, "Mandatory Spending to Exceed All Federal Revenues—50 Years Ahead of Schedule," *The Weekly Standard* (March 16, 2011), at: http://www.weeklystandard.com/blogs/mandatory-spending-exceed-all-federal-revenues-fiscal-year-2011_554659.html.

15. Robert Samuelson, "We've Promised More than We Can Deliver," *Newsweek* (April 11, 2011).

16. If you like the feeling of heart palpitations, you can watch US debt grow in real time, at: http://www.usdebtclock.org/.

17. In 2011, the debt equaled the total annual output of our economy. Stephen Dinan, "Debt Now Equals Total US Economy," *The Washington Times* (Feb. 14, 2011), at: http://www.washingtontimes.com/news/2011/feb/14/debt-now-equals-total-us-economy/.

18. You can see the pictures of this illustration from PageTutor.com at: http://www.pagetutor.com/trillion/index.html.

19. John Kitchen and Menzie David Chinn, "Financing U.S. Debt: Is There Enough Money in the World—And at What Cost?" *La Follette School of Public Affairs Working Paper No. 2010-015* (August 12, 2010), at: http://ssrn.com/abstract=1658543.

20. For details on the size of the deficit and debt, see William Beach and Robert Bluey, "Slay the Beast: How You Can Save Us from the Massive Debt," *Heritage Foundation Special Report* (Revised and updated, January 6, 2011), at: http://www.heritage.org/Research/Reports/2010/09/Will-Growing-Government-Debt-Undermine-the-American-Dream.

21. A classic book on the collapse of money in Germany and Austria after World War I was written in 1975, and was rereleased in 2010. Adam Fergusson, *When Money Dies: The Nightmare of Deficit Spending, Devaluation, and Hyperinflation in Weimar Germany* (New York: PublicAffairs, 2010).

22. John Maynard Keynes, *The Economic Consequences of the Peace*, pp. 235–48. Quoted in John Tamy, "Book Review: Adam Fergusson's When Money Dies," *RealClearMarkets* (May 12, 2011), at: http://www.realclearmarkets.com/articles/2011/05/12/book_review_adam_fergussons_when_money_dies_99016.html.

23. See the following Pew study on voter attitudes, "Rethinking Voter Attitudes, Fewer Want Spending to Grow, But Most Cuts Remain Unpopular," *Pew Research Center for the People and the Press* (February 10, 2011), at: http://pewresearch.org/pubs/1889/poll-federal-spending-programs-budget-cuts-raise-taxes-state-budgets.

24. One popular poll of Tea Party supporters in 2010 was done by *The New York Times* and *CBS News*. "Polling the Tea Party," *The New York Times* (April 14, 2010), at: http://www.nytimes.com/interactive/2010/04/14/us/politics/20100414-tea-party-poll-graphic.html?ref=politics. A 2011 poll by *The New York Times* and *CBS News* showed that these contradictory views are even starker among the general public. Jackie Calmes and Dalia Sussman, "Poll Finds Wariness About Cutting Entitlements," *The New York Times* (Jan. 20, 2011), at: http://www.nytimes.com/2011/01/21/us/politics/21poll.html?_r=1&nl=todaysheadlines&emc=tha24.

25. In response, I (Jay) joined with another group of religious writers and public figures to form Christians for a Sustainable Economy. (See http://www.case4america.org/.) For some reason, the media didn't give CASE the fawning attention they had given to the "Circle of Protection." We should note that although USCCB and NAE representatives participated in the campaign, that doesn't mean that every Catholic bishop, or the Catholic Church, supported the campaign. The same is true for the NAE. The fact that one NAE representative participated did not mean that the NAE officially endorsed it. Unfortunately, the legacy media tend not to make these distinctions when reporting on the campaign.

26. Though these words are widely attributed to Alexander Fraser Tytler, it's not clear who first wrote them. See Loren Collins, "The Truth About Tytler" (January 25, 2009), at: http://www.lorencollins.net/tytler.html.

27. Stephen Moore, "We've Become a Nation of Takers, Not Makers," *The Wall Street Journal* (April 1, 2001), at: http://online.wsj.com/article/SB10001424052748704050204576219073867182108.html.

Chapter 7. Choose Life

1. Tim Walker, "Martin Amis Says Euthanasia is an 'Evolutionary Inevitability," *The Telegraph* (January 17, 2011), at: http://www.telegraph.co.uk/news/newstopics/mandrake/8262770/Martin-Amis-says-euthanasia-is-an-evolutionary-inevitability.html.

2. John Calvin, *Commentaries on the Last Four Books of Moses*, translated by Charles William Bingham (Grand Rapids, MI: Eerdmans, 1950), vol. 3, pp. 41–42.

3. And yet, when the US Supreme Court overturned state restrictions on abortion in 1973 (in *Roe v. Wade*), the majority claimed that Christian history was hazy on the question of when life began. It's true that a few theologians, such as Saint Thomas Aquinas and Saint Augustine, had speculated (based on bad science) about when a fetus is formed and when the soul enters the body. But they never disagreed that

abortion was wrong, and their isolated speculations never led the Church to alter her views of when human life began.

4. See report by Randy Sly, "From New President of Episcopal Divinity School: 'Abortion is a Blessing,'" *Catholic Online* (April 2, 2009), at: http://www.catholic.org /national/national_story.php?id=32962.

5. A pessary was a device that could be inserted into the uterus to induce an abortion.

6. Abby Johnson, "The Ultrasound That Changed My Mind—Abby Johnson's Pro-Life Conversion in Her Own Words," *LifeSiteNews.com* (Jan. 10, 2011), at: http://www .lifesitenews.com/news/the-ultrasound-that-changed-my-life-abby-johnsons-pro -life-conversion-in-he. She tells the story in her book, *Unplanned* (San Francisco: Ignatius, 2011).

7. The overall opinion numbers have moved slightly in the pro-life direction since 1973. The pro-life shift is stronger among younger Americans. This is especially significant because the culture since 1973 has been saturated with "pro-choice" ideology. For analysis of polls, see Karlyn Bowman and Andrew Rugg, "Attitudes About Abortion," *AEI Public Opinion Surveys* (January 2011), at: http://www.aei.org /docLib/Abortion2011.pdf.

8. This quote is from the "comments" section below the article by David Paul Kuhn, "Some Social Conservative Leaders Feel Scapegoated," *RealClearPolitics* (May 11, 2009), at: http://www.realclearpolitics.com/articles/2009/05/11/social_conservatives_leaders _feel_scapegoated_96435.html.

9. Dan Harris, "Are Young Evangelicals Skewing More Liberal?" *ABC News* (February 10, 2008), quoted in Nancy Pearcey, *Saving Leonardo: A Call to Resist the Secular Assault on Mind, Morals, & Meaning* (Nashville: B & H Publishing, 2010), p. 23.

10. Lisa Miller, "No God—and No Abortion," *Newsweek* (November 29, 2008), at: http://www.newsweek.com/2008/11/28/no-god-and-no-abortions.html.

11. We take this phrase from Robert P. George and Patrick Lee, "Acorns and Embryos," *The New Atlantis* (Fall 2004–Winter 2005), at: http://www.thenewatlantis.com /publications/acorns-and-embryos.

12. Of course, there's a lot more that could be said here. For more details along these lines, see Robert P. George and Patrick Lee, "The Wrong of Abortion," in *Contemporary Debates in Applied Ethics* (New York: Blackwell Publishers, 2005), edited by Andrew I. Cohen and Christopher Wellman, available online at: http://www .blackwellpublishing.com/content/BPL_Images/Content_store/Sample_chapter /1405115475/Cohen_sample%20chapter_Contemporary%20debates%20in%20 applied%20ethics.pdf. We are following their argument here.

13. This is a mundane conclusion of biology. See, for instance, the sample quotes from medical and embryology textbooks at the webpage, "Life Begins at Fertilization," at: http://www.princeton.edu/~prolife/articles/embryoquotes2.html. For a brief, clever summary of the basic argument against every alternative to concluding that a human embryo is a human being, see Michael Egnor, "What *Is* a Human Embryo?" *Evolution News & Views* (January 15, 2011), at: http://www .evolutionnews.org/2011/01/tantalus_primes_nobel_prize_in042411.html#more.

14. For instance, in *Embryo: A Defense of Human Life* (New York: Doubleday, 2008), Robert George and Christopher Tollefson criticize research that destroys human

embryos, using public arguments, based on the broadly shared moral assumption that murder is wrong and straightforward distinctions based on what we know about biology. None of their arguments depends on scruples unique to one religion. We suppose that one could argue that since opposition to murder is itself religious, it ought not to be a part of secular law. But few make that argument.

15. This is from Rand's essay "Introducing Objectivism," available at the Ayn Rand Institute website: http://www.aynrand.org/site/PageServer?pagename=objectivism _intro. So why was Rand so rabidly pro-choice? Because she denied the facts of biology, comparing unborn human beings to skin cells, tonsils, and a ruptured appendix. In "The Age of Mediocrity," *The Objectivist Forum* (June 1981).

16. Paul Ryan, "The Cause of Life Can't Be Severed from the Cause of Freedom," *Indivisible: Social and Economic Foundations of American Liberty*, edited by Jay W. Richards (Washington, DC: Heritage Foundation, 2009).

17. Virtually every major city has a crisis pregnancy center that you can find over the Internet. But be careful. Organizations such as Planned Parenthood have developed well-disguised websites to capture women in desperate situations.

Chapter 8. A Man Shall Cling to His Wife

1. Elizabeth Fox-Genovese, *Marriage: The Dream That Refuses to Die* (Wilmington: ISI Books, 2008), pp. 113ff.

2. In no-fault divorce, neither party has to prove wrongdoing by the other. A husband or a wife can simply declare a desire and grounds for divorce, and get out of a marriage, whether or not the spouse agrees.

3. For an engaging discussion of the problems with Mead and Kinsey, see Benjamin Wiker, *Ten Books That Screwed Up the World: And 5 Others That Didn't Help* (Washington, DC: Regnery, 2008).

4. Maggie Gallagher, *The Abolition of Marriage: How We Destroy Lasting Love* (Washington, DC: Regnery, 1996), p. 150.

5. See Bridget Maher, *Deterring Divorce* (Washington, DC: Family Research Council, 2004). This booklet is available online at: http://downloads.frc.org/EF/EF04E17.pdf.

6. Sabrina Tavernise and Robert Gebeloff, "Once Rare in Rural America, Divorce Is Changing the Face of Its Families," *The New York Times* (March 23, 2011).

7. See this and other US marriage statistics in *When Marriage Disappears: The State of Our Unions 2010* (Charlottesville, VA: The National Marriage Project, 2010), at: http://www.eharmony.com/labs/2011/03/trends-in-marriage-cohabitation-and-divorce/.

8. For details, see Mike McManus and Harriet McManus, *Living Together: Myths, Risks, and Answers* (New York: Howard Books, 2008).

9. Whatever your views of contraception, virtually all scholars recognize the connection between a redefinition of marriage and the "culture of contraception." Glenn Stanton and Bill Maier of Focus on the Family explain it this way: "[A] major redefinition of marriage occurred with the growth of our culture of contraception. The emergence of widespread contraception, especially the emergence of the pill, helped separate sexuality and marriage from childbearing." *Marriage on Trial* (Downers Grove, IL: InterVarsity Press, 2004), pp.121–22.

10. Ibid., pp. 96, 98.

11. Ibid., p. 100.

12. Ibid., pp. 100–2.

13. George Gilder, *Men and Marriage* (Gretna, LA: Pelican Books, 1986).

14. See Carle C. Zimmerman, with James Kurth, *Family and Civilization*, 2nd abridged edition (Wilmington: ISI Books, 2008).

15. Linda Waite and Maggie Gallagher, *The Case for Marriage: Why Married People are Healthier, Happier, and Better Off Financially* (New York: Doubleday, 2000). Quoted in Glenn Stanton and Bill Maier, *Marriage on Trial*, p. 95.

16. Mark Steyn, "There's No Stopping Them Now," *Chicago Sun-Times* (July 13, 2003).

17. Sherif Girgis, Robert P. George, and Ryan Anderson, "What Is Marriage?" *Harvard Journal of Law & Public Policy* 34 (2010): p. 252.

18. In women, this includes both the sexual organs and the lactation system in breasts. The lactation system itself is complete, but it requires another human being, a baby, to fulfill its proper end. This strengthens the argument above.

19. Elizabeth Fox-Genovese, *Marriage: The Dream That Refuses to Die*, p. 21.

20. Girgis, George, and Anderson, "What Is Marriage?" p. 255.

21. "The Case for Marriage," an editorial in *National Review* (September 20, 2010).

22. "After all, if a certain emotional state…were necessary [for marriage], then it would be impossible to *commit* sincerely to marriage. For this would require promising to keep up feelings, over which you have no direct control, and you can't sincerely promise to secure what you can't control." Sherif Girgis, "Real Marriage," *National Review* (March 21, 2011).

23. Stanton and Maier, *Marriage on Trial*, p. 43.

24. Although it is now several years old, Stanley Kurtz's essay is still timely. See "Beyond Gay Marriage," *The Weekly Standard* (August 4, 2003), at: http://www.weeklystandard.com/Content/Public/Articles/000/000/002/938xpsxy.asp?page=1.

25. Maggie Gallagher and Joshua K. Baker, "Demand for Same-Sex Marriage: Evidence from the United States, Canada, and Europe," *Institute for Marriage and Public Policy Brief* 3, no. 1 (April 26, 2006), at: http://www.marriagedebate.com/pdf/imapp.demandforssm.pdf.

26. Ibid., p. 66.

27. See discussion of this and other examples in Girgis, George, and Ryan, "What Is Marriage?" pp. 263–65.

28. Stanton and Maier, *Marriage on Trial*, p. 42.

29. Peter Vere, "Canada Orders Pastor to Renounce His Faith," *Catholic Exchange* (June 9, 2008), at: http://catholicexchange.com/2008/06/09/112825/.

30. Though it's unlikely now that the Fairness Doctrine will be reinstated in its previous form, since the FCC Chairman erased it from the federal registry of regulations in August 2011. Speech codes, however, are alive and well.

31. Patrick F. Fagan and Grace Smith, "The Transatlantic Divide on Marriage: Dutch Data and the U.S. Debate on Same-Sex Unions," Heritage Foundation *WebMemo* #477 (September 29, 2004), at: http://www.heritage.org/research/reports/2004/09/the-transatlantic-divide-on-marriagenbsp-dutch-data-and-the-us-debate-on-same-sex-unions.

32. Michelangelo Signorile, "I DO, I DO, I DO, I DO, I DO," *OUT* (May 1996): pp. 30, 32 (emphases in original), quoted in Stanton and Maier, *Marriage on Trial*, p. 35.

33. For an argument along these lines, see David Boaz, "Privatize Marriage: A Simple Solution to the Gay-Marriage Debate," *Slate* (April 25, 1997), at: http://slate.com /id/2440.

34. John Cloud, "Will Same Sex Marriage Be Legal?" *Time* (February 21, 2000), at: http://www.time.com/time/magazine/article/0,9171,996172,00.html.

35. As Elizabeth Fox-Genovese wrote, "In the premodern world of clans and tribes, one's people carried even greater significance, for family grounded and defined what today is known as the individual's 'identity.' The self was understood as the articulation or expression of the group, which was viewed as prior to it, not as an 'autonomous' being that could assume and discard commitments at will." In *Marriage: The Dream That Refuses to Die*, p. 18.

36. "Unmade in New York," *National Review* (June 29, 2011), at: http://www .nationalreview.com/articles/270754/unmade-new-york-editors.

37. "Obama: DOMA Unconstitutional: DOJ Should Stop Defending in Court," *AP/The Huffington Post* (February 23, 2011), at: http://www.huffingtonpost.com/2011/02/23 /obama-doma-unconstitutional_n_827134.html.

38. See "Obama and Marriage" at: http://www.cwfpac.com/files/Obama%20II%20 marriage.pdf.

39. See the overview "Fewer Are Angry at Government, But Discontent Remains High" of the *Pew Research Center* (March 3, 2011), at: http://people-press.org/2011/03/03 /fewer-are-angry-at-government-but-discontent-remains-high/.

40. For more practical advice on how to strengthen marriage in our culture, see Maggie Gallagher, "Defend Marriage: Mom and Dads Matter," *The Public Discourse* (August 23, 2011), at: http://www.thepublicdiscourse.com/2011/08/3761.

41. Mike McManus argues that we could cut the divorce rate in half just by replacing no-fault divorce laws with "mutual consent" laws for marriages with young children. See Mike McManus, *How to Cut America's Divorce Rate in Half* (Potomac, MD: Marriage Savers, 2008).

42. See references in Glenn Stanton, "The Christian Divorce Rate Myth (What You've Heard Is Wrong)," *Baptist Press* (February 15, 2011), at: http://www.bpnews.net /BPnews.asp?ID=34656.

43. Mercedes Arzú Wilson, "Divorce Rate Comparisons Between Couples Using Natural Family Planning & Artificial Birth Control," *Physicians for Life* (March 1–4, 2001), at: http://www.physiciansforlife.org/content/view/193/36/. The statistical connection between Natural Family Planning and low divorce rates does not, by itself, reveal cause and effect. Perhaps couples who practice NFP tend to be much more religiously committed. Perhaps the complexities of the method bring couples closer together. Or perhaps it's a special blessing from God. Who knows? The truth is, we don't know exactly why the two are correlated.

Chapter 9. It Takes a Family

1. Letty Cottin Pogrebin is a feminist author and founding editor of *Ms.* magazine, which is not especially pro-family. Nevertheless, this is a beautiful explanation of the unique importance of the family.

2. Glenn Stanton and Bill Maier, *Marriage on Trial* (Downers Grove, IL: InterVarsity Press, 2004), p. 103.
3. Ibid, pp. 104–5.
4. David Ellwood, *Poor Support: Poverty in the American Family* (New York: Basic Books, 1988), p. 46, quoted in Stanton and Maier, p. 106.
5. "Marriage: America's No. 1 Weapon Against Childhood Poverty," *A Heritage Foundation Book of Charts* (Washington, DC: The Heritage Foundation, 2010). Related statistics: Some 71 percent of poor families in the United States are not married.
6. Ibid., pp. 108–9.
7. Ken Blackwell and Ken Klukowski, "Blacks Don't Need Same-Sex Marriage," *The Daily Caller* (June 29, 2011), at: http://dailycaller.com/2011/06/29/black-community-doesnt-need-same-sex-marriage/. Matthews claims to be Catholic, but his comments directly contradict the teaching of the Catholic Church.
8. Exceptions would be children adopted as newborns or borne by surrogate mothers.
9. From an interview with Kathryn Lopez, "30 Rock Knows Best," *National Review* (June 18, 2011), at: http://www.nationalreview.com/articles/269942/i30-rocki-knows-best-interview.
10. Ibid., p. 116. In this paragraph, we are summarizing details from ibid., pp. 113–16.
11. Sara McLanahan and Gary Sandefur, *Growing Up with a Single Parent: What Hurts, What Helps* (Cambridge: Harvard University Press, 1994), p. 38. McLanahan and Sandefur are sociologists.
12. "The Case for Marriage," an editorial in *National Review* (September 20, 2010).
13. See David Popenoe, *Disturbing the Nest: Family Change and Decline in Modern Societies* (Piscataway, NJ: Aldine Transactions, 1988), and Alan Wolfe, *Whose Keeper? Social Science and Moral Obligation* (Berkeley: University of California Press, 1991).
14. Mike Huckabee, *A Simple Government* (New York: Sentinel HC, 2011).
15. Of course, the rules of family life are different from the rules of politics and economics. Unlike a market, where we buy and sell our goods and services for a price, parents freely provide for the needs of their children. Good parents will often sacrifice their own desires for the needs of their children. While children are costly, good parents don't treat their children as liabilities. Parents often have to coerce their children, but they rarely have to resort to guns, tanks, and prison to get their children to behave.
16. Both quotes are from Patrick F. Fagan, "The Family GDP: How Marriage and Fertility Drive the Economy," *The Ruth Institute* (October 5, 2010), at: http://www.ruthblog.org/2010/10/05/the-family-gdp-how-marriage-and-fertility-drive-the-economy/.
17. Ibid.
18. Quoted in ibid.
19. Of course, there's more to the story. This incident illustrates the profound impact love within the community of faith can have on those who face serious challenges in life. And ultimately, it was only through faith and a relationship with Christ that I was able to overcome the damaging effect of these experiences.
20. See Michael Miller, "The Victory of Socialism?" *Legatus Magazine* (December 1, 2009), at: http://www.legatusmagazine.org/?p=1826.

21. Jennifer Roback Morse, "The Limited-Government Case for Marriage," *Indivisible: Social and Economic Foundations of Liberty*, edited by Jay W. Richards (Washington, DC: The Heritage Foundation, 2009).

22. "Marriage: America's No. 1 Weapon Against Childhood Poverty," *A Heritage Foundation Book of Charts.*

23. Ibid. This Heritage Foundation study lists seven commonsense public policy changes that could help reverse these problems:

    1. Reduce antimarriage penalties in welfare programs.
    2. Create public education campaigns in low-income communities on the benefits of marriage.
    3. Require welfare offices to provide factual information on the value of marriage in reducing poverty and welfare dependence.
    4. Explain the benefits of marriage in middle and high schools with a high proportion of at-risk youth.
    5. Require federally funded birth control clinics to provide information on the benefits of marriage and the skills needed to develop stable families to interested low-income clients.
    6. Require federally funded birth control clinics to offer voluntary referrals to life planning and marriage skills education to all interested low-income clients.
    7. Make voluntary marriage education widely available to interested couples in low-income communities.

24. See the references in John R. Lott, Jr., *Freedomnomics: Why the Free Market Works and Other Half-Baked Theories Don't* (Washington, DC: Regnery Publishing, 2007), pp. 164–65.

25. For more detailed statistics on family trends, see Family Facts at: http://www.familyfacts.org.

26. Jay W. Richards, *Poverty in the United States, The Economy Hits Home Series* (Washington, DC: The Heritage Foundation, 2009).

27. Jonathan V. Last, "America's One-Child Policy," *The Weekly Standard* 16, no. 2 (September 27, 2010).

28. In *Everything I Want to Do Is Illegal: War Stories from the Local Food Front* (Swoop, VA: Polyface Press, 2007), Joel Salatin points out that the complex web of child labor laws creates byzantine barriers to modest, reasonable child labor. That means that kids are more expensive, since they're less likely to provide an income stream for the family, not to mention more likely to get into mischief. Again, this is an example of how even reasonable laws that few people oppose can have perverse unintended consequences.

29. Ibid.

30. Patrick F. Fagan, PhD, and Scott Talkington, "Ever Had an Unwed Pregnancy," *Marriage, Religion, and the Common Good 101, Mapping America* (Washington, DC: Marriage and Religion Research Institute, 2011), at: http://www.frc.org/mappingamerica/mapping-america-101-likely-to-have-an-unwed-pregnancy.

31. In studies, religious intensity is measured by the stated opinions of people polled, and by the frequency of their attendance in worship. See, for example, Tomas Frejka

and Charles F. Westoff, "Religion, Religiousness and Fertility in the U.S. and Europe," working paper for the Max Planck Institute for Demographic Research (May 2006), available at: http://www.d.umn.edu/~okuhlke/Fall%20 2006%20Classes/GEOG%203762%20Europe/Readings/Week%2013%20-%20 Demography/EUdemogr1.pdf.

32. Kathryn Jean Lopez, "Ground Zero for Human Rights," *National Review Online* (May 9, 2011), at: http://www.nationalreview.com/articles/266642/ground-zero -human-rights-kathryn-jean-lopez.

33. For a scholarly look at this trend, see Eric Kaufmann, *Shall the Religious Inherit the Earth?* (London: Profile Books, 2011).

34. Jonathan Leake, "Atheists a Dying Breed as Nature 'Favours Faithful,'" *The Sunday Times* (of London) (January 11, 2011).

Chapter 10. Train Up a Child in the Way He Should Go

1. "Most Twentysomethings Put Christianity on the Shelf Following Spiritually Active Teen Years," *Barna Group* (September 11, 2006).

2. R. V. Young, "Liberal Learning Confronts the Composition Despots," *The Intercollegiate Review* (Spring 2011), p. 4.

3. For a detailed discussion, see Andrew J. Coulson, *Market Education: The Unknown History* (Piscataway, NJ: Transaction Publishers, 1999). For a detailed outline of the history of American education, go to: http://www.cblpi.org/ftp/School%20Choice /EdHistory.pdf.

4. Dewey was contemptuous of the idea that our concepts corresponded to a reality outside us. Instead, he tried to define "truth" in terms of what works. Any clear-thinking college freshman can see the problem with Dewey's argument: he assumed that his theory of truth didn't just work; it corresponded with reality in just the way he claimed was impossible or nonsensical. So he treated his own theory as the one exception to his theory. This is not an especially promising start for a philosophy. But the little problem of logical incoherence didn't seem to hinder its influence among educational theorists less clear-thinking than our hypothetical college freshman.

5. John R. Lott, Jr., *Freedomnomics* (Washington, DC: Regnery, 2007), p. 191.

6. Richard Land, *The Divided States of America* (Nashville: Thomas Nelson, 2011), pp. 54–55.

7. Lott, *Freedomnomics*, pp. 190–91. See the references on these pages for Lott's academic publications on American education.

8. For a recent example, see Kevin Ryan, "Another Coffin Nail for US Public Education," *Mercatornet* (July 11, 2011), at: http://www.mercatornet.com/articles/view /another_coffin_nail_for_us_public_education/.

9. Amy Chua, "Why Chinese Moms Are Superior," *The Wall Street Journal* (January 8, 2011).

10. Amy Chua, "Tiger Mom: Here's How to Reshape U.S. Education," *USA Today* (May 13, 2011); and Amy Chua, *Battle Hymn of the Tiger Mother* (New York: Penguin Press HC, 2011).

11. Ron Haskin, "Getting Ahead in America," *National Affairs* 1 (Fall 2009), at: http://www.nationalaffairs.com/publications/detail/getting-ahead-in-america. Quoted in Pete Wehner, "Rescuing the American Dream," *Spotlight on Poverty & Opportunity* (August 22, 2011), at: http://www.spotlightonpoverty.org/ExclusiveCommentary.aspx?id=3690acc9-1246-48d8-a1fe-cd83e8d06c7c.

12. For some horror stories, see the Free Sweden website at: http://freesweden.net/religion_index.html.

13. *Pierce v. Society of Sisters*, 1925.

14. Read about the film at: http://www.waitingforsuperman.com/action/.

15. A recent scandal involves the Atlanta Public Schools, in which teachers, principals, and superintendents conspired for a decade to falsify scores on standardized tests used to evaluate the schools. A private business that was exposed for such massive fraud would collapse almost immediately and the ringleader would go to prison. See Heather Vogell, "Investigation into APS cheating finds unethical behavior across every level," *The Atlanta Journal Constitution* (July 6, 2011), at: http://www.ajc.com/news/investigation-into-aps-cheating-1001375.html.

16. Education scholar James Tooley has done groundbreaking research on how private schools and entrepreneurs are successfully educating the poor in developing countries, far better than government schools. See James Tooley and Pauline Dixon, *Private Education Is Good for the Poor* (Washington, DC: Cato Institute Press, 2005), at: http://www.cato.org/pubs/wtpapers/tooley.pdf. See also James Tooley, *The Beautiful Tree: A Personal Journey into How the World's Poorest People Are Educating Themselves* (Washington, DC: Cato Institute Press, 2009).

17. The tragedy is that many hardworking and conscientious teachers, including Christian teachers, in the public school system, who know better than anyone the problems with the system and will tell you all about it in private, nevertheless get their dues co-opted by these unions, which are used to support the very status quo that so many of these public school teachers long to reform.

18. Both of these statements are from the interview of Alter in *Waiting for "Superman"* (Electric Kinney Films, 2010).

19. US Department of Education, National Center for Education Statistics, *Digest of Education Statistics, 2010* (NCES 2011-015), at: http://nces.ed.gov/fastfacts/display.asp?id=66.

20. *Waiting for "Superman"* (2010).

21. Andrew J. Coulson, "The Real Cost of Public Schools," *The Washington Post* (April 6, 2008), at: http://www.washingtonpost.com/wp-dyn/content/article/2008/04/04/AR2008040402921.html.

22. For instance, KIPP charter schools around the country have raised scores for low-income students—and these are still public schools. For the results of independent studies, see the documents at the KIPP website: http://www.kipp.org/about-kipp/results/independent-reports.

23. Frederick M. Hess, Olivia Meeks, and Bruno V. Manno, "From School Choice to Educational Choice," AEI *Education Outlook* 3 (April 2011). This is a summary of their book *Customized Schooling: Beyond Whole-School Reform* (Cambridge: Harvard Education Press, 2011).

24. See the tally in Matthew Ladner, "Greg Goes Heismann in 2011 Blowout," *Jay P. Greene's Blog* (July 1, 2001), at: http://jaypgreene.com/2011/07/01/greg-goes-heisman-in-2011-reform-blowout/.

25. "U.S. tops the world in school spending but not test scores," *USA Today* (September 16, 2003), at: http://www.usatoday.com/news/education/2003-09-16-education-comparison_x.htm.

26. Jessica Shepherd, "World Education Ranking: Which Country Does Best at Reading, Maths, and Science?" *The Guardian* (UK) (December 7, 2010), at: http://www.guardian.co.uk/news/datablog/2010/dec/07/world-education-rankings-maths-science-reading.

27. The exact ranking varies from year to year, of course, but here is a representative study from 2006: Maria Glod, "U.S. Teens Trail Peers Around the World on Math-Science Test," *The Washington Post* (December 5, 2007), at: http://www.washingtonpost.com/wp-dyn/content/article/2007/12/04/AR2007120400730.html.

28. For poll information and the latest summary and explanations of school choice in America, see *The ABC's of School Choice*, produced annually by The Foundation for Educational Choice. The 2011 edition is available online, at: http://www.edchoice.org/CMSModules/EdChoice/FileLibrary/625/The-ABCs-of-School-Choice---2011-Edition.pdf.

29. One popular argument is that vouchers "take money away from public schools." This is the stock argument of monopolists, who treat the money of others as if it belongs to them. In truth, vouchers would create competition both for and among public schools, which will improve all schools and bring costs down. If a student doesn't attend a school, that school saves the costs of educating that child. If no parents freely choose to send their children to a school, then the school will close—*as it should*. See Katrina Trinko, "Why School Vouchers Are Worth a Shot," *USA Today* (April 18, 2011), at: http://www.usatoday.com/news/opinion/forum/2011-04-18-school-vouchers-worth-a-shot.htm. See also Jay P. Greene, *Why America Needs School Choice*, Encounter Broadside No. 22 (New York: Encounter Broadside, 2011).

30. For instance, you can watch "Critical Reasoning for Beginners" at iTunes U, taught by leading Oxford instructors.

31. Joshua W. Anderson, "How to Receive a Theological Education through iTunes U," *Sententia* (August 17, 2011), at: http://networkedblogs.com/lNstl.

32. See the course description and a sample video online, at: http://www.ai-class.com/.

33. Quoted in Khan's TED lecture, available online at the Khan Academy website, at: http://www.khanacademy.org/.

34. See the glowing article by Mike Lee, "Salman Khan, Founder of the Khan Academy, Educates the Masses," *8 Asians* (May 24, 2011), at: http://www.8asians.com/2011/05/24/salman-khan-educator-and-founder-of-the-khan-academy/.

35. Our university system is much better than our primary and secondary public school system, in part because of competition. It still has serious problems, though. Federal grant and student loan programs were meant to help poor students get a college education. They've had the effect of shooting college costs into the stratosphere. Since 1985, college costs have gone up four times faster than the rate of inflation. See Gordon H. Wadsworth, "Sky Rocketing College Costs," *InflationData.com*

(October 15, 2010), at: http://www.inflationdata.com/inflation/Inflation_Articles /Education_Inflation.asp. In 2011, total student loan debt topped a trillion dollars. Tamar Lewin, "Burden of Loans on College Graduates Grows," *The New York Times* (April 11, 2011), at: http://www.nytimes.com/2011/04/12/education/12college.html.

The same technological innovations that are going to force change in elementary and secondary education will force change on higher education as well. The main value of much higher education is not its unique ability to educate and dispense knowledge. It is *social connections and credentialing.* When alternative forms of credentialing become available, we expect to see the education bubble pop. The economics just don't make sense.

36. A popular study showing the political imbalance of American college and university faculties is Stanley Rothman, S. Robert Lichter, Neil Nevitte, "Politics and Professional Advancement Among College Faculty," *The Forum* 3, no. 1 (2005), at: http:// www.bepress.com/forum/vol3/iss1/art2.

37. Christian philosopher Alvin Plantinga mentions these two ideas under the names of "creative anti-realism" and "naturalism" in his famous article, "On Christian Scholarship." Read it online at: http://www.veritas-ucsb.org/library/plantinga/ocs.html. See also his "Advice to Christian Philosophers," *Faith and Philosophy: Journal of the Society of Christian Philosophers* 1 (October 1984), at: http://www.leaderu.com /truth/1truth10.html.

38. Fortunately, scholars do tip their hand in public once in a while. In 1997, the Harvard evolutionary biologist Richard Lewontin reviewed a book by Carl Sagan in *The New York Review of Books*. He laid out the materialist credo for all to see:

> Our willingness to accept scientific claims that are against common sense is the key to an understanding of the real struggle between science and the supernatural. We take the side of science *in spite* of the patent absurdity of some of its constructs, *in spite* of its failure to fulfill many of its extravagant promises of health and life, *in spite* of the tolerance of the scientific community for unsubstantiated just-so stories, because we have a prior commitment, a commitment to materialism. It is not that the methods and institutions of science somehow compel us to accept a material explanation of the phenomenal world, but, on the contrary, that we are forced by our *a priori* adherence to material causes to create an apparatus of investigation and a set of concepts that produce material explanations, no matter how counter-intuitive, no matter how mystifying to the uninitiated. Moreover, that materialism is absolute, for we cannot allow a Divine Foot in the door. [Richard Lewontin, "Billions and Billions of Demons," review of Sagan's *The Demon-Haunted World*, in *New York Review of Books* (Jan. 9, 1997).]

We should be grateful for Lewontin's candor; but most students will experience these ideas only indirectly, in a million little ways.

39. Alana Semuel, "Television Viewing at All-Time High," *The Los Angeles Times* (February 24, 2009), at: http://articles.latimes.com/2009/feb/24/business/fi-tvwatching24.

40. J. Budziszewski, *How to Stay Christian in College* (Colorado Springs: NavPress, 2004).

41. From *Focus on the Family's TrueU program*. See the trailer at: http://www.thetruth project.org/about/culturefocus/A000000282.cfm. This is an introductory DVD of the larger *TrueU* DVD series, featuring philosopher Stephen Meyer, which we highly recommend as well. Check it out at: https://www.mytruthproject.org/.

42. Some of the apologists and apologetics organizations we know and are familiar with include (in no particular order): Stand to Reason (http://www.str.org), William Lane Craig and Reasonable Faith (http://www.reasonablefaith.org/), John Lennox (http:// johnlennox.org/), Peter Kreeft (http://www.peterkreeft.com/), Lee Strobel (http:// www.leestrobel.com/), Ravi Zacharias International Ministries (http://www.rzim .org/), C. S. Lewis Society (http://www.apologetics.org/), New Advent (http://www .newadvent.org/), Catholic Answers (http://www.catholic.com/), Christian Apologetics Alliance (http://apologeticalliance.blogspot.com/), and Reasons to Believe (http://www.reasons.org/). Biola University (http://www.biola.edu/) and Summit Ministries (http://www.summit.org/) have apologetic programs and seminars. For older teenagers, we highly recommend *Salvo* magazine (http://www.salvomag.com/).

43. Most of the founders of modern science were Christians of one sort or another, and science itself was fed on the Judeo-Christian conviction that the universe is created by a good and rational Creator. See Guillermo Gonzalez and Jay W. Richards, *The Privileged Planet: How Our Place in the Universe Is Designed for Discovery* (Washington, DC: Regnery, 2004), chapter 11. See also Rodney Stark, *For the Glory of God: How Monotheism Led to Reformations, Science, Witch-Hunts, and the End of Slavery* (Princeton: Princeton University Press, 2003).

44. In the twentieth century, Darwin's "random variation" came to be identified with random genetic mutations. This is called Neo-Darwinism.

45. If you're into hard science, check out the various articles describing rigorous tests of the Darwinian mechanism at *BIO-Complexity*, at: http://bio-complexity.org/ojs /index.php/main.

46. This book, which can be used in any public school that wants to teach this issue fairly and fully, presents the best scientific evidence for and against the key parts of Darwin's theory. If your kids study it carefully, they'll understand Darwinism better than most of their peers.

    Incidentally, some states now have "academic freedom" laws that protect teachers and school districts who teach the full range of scientific evidence, especially on controversial issues such as Darwinian evolution, climate change, and cloning. For information on how to develop teaching policies appropriate for public schools, see "Key Resources for Parents and School Board Members," *Discovery Institute* (August 21, 2007), at: http://www.discovery.org/a/2112.

47. For a readable survey of these and a few other authors writing about intelligent design, see Lee Strobel, *The Case for a Creator* (Grand Rapids, MI: Zondervan, 2004). For younger kids, try Lee Strobel, Rob Suggs, and Robert Elmer, *Case for a Creator for Kids* (Grand Rapids, MI: Zondervan, 2010). Also see the terrific science documentaries on intelligent design available from Illustra Media, at: http://illustramedia.com/. On the debate over "theistic evolution," see Jay W. Richards, ed., *God and Evolution: Protestants, Catholics and Jews Explore Darwin's Challenge to Faith* (Seattle: Discovery Institute, 2010). For many more resources on this subject, check out the Center for

Science & Culture at Discovery Institute at: http://www.discovery.org/csc/. See also Faith and Evolution at: http://www.faithandevolution.org/.

48. Read about this curriculum at: http://www.economicsinabox.com/. Even if you don't do the whole course, many of the readings and other materials are worthwhile.

49. J. Budziszewski points out that a lot of kids fall into college-life hedonism and then they grab for the ideology that justifies it. So helping them gradually develop their own moral self-discipline by gradually cutting some apron strings rather than going from no freedom to total freedom overnight is a good idea, along with warning them about the tendency to fall into sin and then to be tempted to justify it by embracing a worldview that justifies it. This is why, again, an inoculation must be so much more than just rigorous apologetics.

Chapter 11. Culture Matters

1. James Q. Wilson, *American Politics: Then and Now* (Washington, DC: AEI Press, 2010), quoted in Robert Samuelson, "We've Promised More than We Can Deliver," *Newsweek* (April 11, 2011).

2. A classic book on this subject is Peter L. Berger and Richard John Neuhaus, *To Empower People: The Role of Mediating Structures in Public Policy* (Washington, DC: AEI Press, 1977).

3. The phrase was originally the title of Richard Weaver's constantly-referenced-but-rarely-read book, written in 1948. It was also one of the "absolutes" in my book (James) *The Absolutes* (Wheaton, IL: Tyndale House, 2003).

4. These quotes are from James Davison Hunter, *To Change the World: The Irony, Tragedy, & Possibility of Christianity in the Late Modern World* (New York: Oxford University Press, 2010), pp. 10–11.

5. Ibid., pp. 16–17. Here's how Hunter summarizes this popular view: "If you have the courage and hold to the right values and if you think Christianly with an adequate Christian worldview, you too can change the world."

6. Ibid., p. 45.

7. For some vivid examples, see the documentary *Expelled* (Premise Media Films, 2008).

8. Under established legal standards, Walker should have recused himself from the case, since any reasonable person would conclude that he could not be impartial. See Ed Whelan, "Disclosure Delayed Is Justice Denied," *National Review* (April 19, 2011), at: http://www.nationalreview.com/articles/265066/disclosure-delayed-justice-denied-ed-whelan.

9. Hunter, *To Change the World*, p. 41. Emphasis is in the original.

10. Ibid.

11. The cube is called La Grande Arche de la Défense. It serves as a metaphor for Europe's descent into secularism in George Weigel's book *The Cube and the Cathedral* (New York: Basic Books, 2005).

12. Nancy Pearcey gives a detailed analysis of this cultural change in *Saving Leonardo: A Call to Resist the Secular Assault on Mind, Morals, & Meaning* (Nashville: B & H Publishing Group, 2010).

13. See Hunter's discussion along these lines in *To Change the World*, pp. 86–88.

14. See discussion in ibid., p. 281.

15. Ibid., p. 47.

16. Ibid, pp. 99–100.

17. Ibid., p. 291. Emphasis in the original.

18. See "Faith on the Hill: The Religious Composition of the 112th Congress," *Pew Research Center* (January 5, 2011), at: http://pewresearch.org/pubs/1846/religious -composition-112th-congress. According to the survey of the 112th Congress, 56.8 percent are Protestant of various denominations, 29.2 percent are Catholic, 7.3 percent Jewish, 0.9 percent Orthodox, and 2.8 percent Mormon. In other words, the *vast* majority identify with the Judeo-Christian religious tradition.

19. A media double standard makes this hard to do. Liberal candidates can count on a free pass from the media when they talk about God. Conservatives will receive scrutiny. President George W. Bush was often criticized for speaking openly about his Christian faith. Christian leftist Jim Wallis asserted in 2005 that "President Bush uses religious language more than any president in history." Professor Paul Kengor went to the trouble of comparing the religious references and photo ops of President Bush and President Clinton. What did he find? Wallis was wrong. President Clinton made references to Christ more often than President Bush during every year of his presidency. Clinton's God talk *doubled* during election years. "During the 2000 election campaign," President Clinton, Hillary Clinton, and Vice President Gore "made more church appearances in one week than George W. Bush made during his entire first term as President." We don't recall Wallis or the old media complaining about the Clintons and Gore church-hopping. See Richard Land, *The Divided States of America* (Nashville: Thomas Nelson, 2011), p. 82. Land is discussing research from Paul Kengor, *God and George W. Bush: A Spiritual Life* (New York: HarperCollins, 2004). The Jim Wallis quote is from *God's Politics: Why the Right Gets It Wrong and the Left Doesn't Get it* (San Francisco: HarperSanFrancisco, 2005).

20. These Democratic activists seem to understand the American electorate better than the Republican "strategists" who mistakenly think that having too many Christians in the party is a liability.

21. Jay W. Richards, "Why Is Jim Wallis Denying that He Receives Grants from Deep-pocket Leftists like Soros?" *National Review* (August 17, 2010), at: http://www .nationalreview.com/corner/244011/why-jim-wallis-denying-he-receives-grants -deep-pocketed-leftists-george-soros-jay-w-ri; Marvin Olasky, "Jim Wallis vs. the Truth, *World* (August 18, 2010), at: http://www.worldmag.com/webextra/17052. Eric Lemasters, "Soros Money to Fund NCC Lobbying Efforts," *Institute on Religion & Democracy* (May 24, 2011), at: http://www.theird.org/page.aspx?pid=1904.

22. Paul Krugman, "The Unwisdom of Elites," *The New York Times* (May 8, 2011), at: http:// www.nytimes.com/2011/05/09/opinion/09krugman.html?_r=3&ref=opinion.

23. H. Richard Niebuhr, *Christ and Culture* (New York: Harper and Row, 1951).

24. James Davison Hunter refers to Christians in modern America as "exiles in a land of exile," but that's an overstatement. Christianity is far more a part of our culture than Christianity was to first-century Rome, or Judaism was to ancient Babylon. Despite this overstatement, Hunter has many good things to say about how we ought to conduct ourselves as "exiles." He's right to say that "the people of God are to be committed to the welfare of the cities in which they reside in exile, even when the city is indifferent, hostile, or ungrateful." *To Change the World*, p. 278.

25. We often think of the story of Sodom and Gomorrah as an example of God's vengeance, but even here, Scripture reveals God's desire to forgive. The cities are famous
because we know the end of the story—God destroyed them for their rampant sin.
But we often forget the early part of the story: Abraham interceded on behalf of
his cousin, Lot, who was living in Sodom, and God agreed to spare the city for the
sake of just ten righteous people. (Apparently there weren't even ten, because God
sent angels in to rescue Lot and his family, just in the nick of time.) Imagine that.
In response to Abraham's fervent prayer of intercession and the presence of just a
few righteous people, God was willing to withhold his judgment on the whole sorry
bunch.

Chapter 12. Am I My Brother's Keeper?

1. Italian Jesuit Luigi Taparelli coined the term around 1840. For an analysis of Taparelli, see Thomas C. Behr, "Luigi Taparelli D'Azeglio, S.J. (1793–1862) and the Development of Scholastic Natural-Law Thought As a Science of Society and Politics,"
Journal of Markets & Morality 6, no. 1 (Spring 2003). For an accessible critique of
social justice as the term is now used, see Michael Debow, "Social Justice: Reasons
for Skepticism," *Areopagus Journal* (Summer 2010).
2. John Leo, "Code Words," *National Review* (March 17, 2010), at: http://www
.nationalreview.com/articles/229335/code-words/john-leo.
3. Jim Wallis, "In Spite of Glenn Beck's New Threats, My Invitation to Dialogue
Stands," *The Huffington Post* (March 15, 2010), at: http://www.huffingtonpost.com
/jim-wallis/in-spite-of-glenn-becks-n_b_499845.html.
4. For detailed documentation, see Amity Shlaes, *The Forgotten Man: A New History of
the Great Depression* (New York: HarperCollins, 2007).
5. Michael Tanner, "Replacing Welfare," *Cato Policy Report* (November/December
1996), at: http://www.cato.org/pubs/policy_report/cpr-18n6-1.html.
6. See "Welfare Reform: The Next Steps," *The Heritage Foundation* (March 17, 2011), at:
http://www.heritage.org/Research/Factsheets/2011/03/Welfare-Reform-The-Next
-Steps.
7. See Jay Richards, "The Economy Hits Home: Poverty," *Heritage Foundation Reports*
(Washington, DC: The Heritage Foundation, 2010), at: http://www.heritage.org
/Research/Reports/2010/06/The-Economy-Hits-Home-Poverty. See also Jay W.
Richards, *Money, Greed, and God: Why Capitalism Is the Solution and Not the Problem* (San Francisco: HarperOne, 2009), pp. 48–49. The statistics are drawn from
Charles Murray, *Losing Ground: American Social Policy 1950–1980*, 10th anniversary
edition (New York: Basic Books, 1994); D. Eric Schansberg, *Poor Policy: How Government Harms the Poor* (New York: Westview, 1996); Michael Tanner, *The Poverty
of Welfare: Helping Others in Civil Society* (Washington, DC: Cato Institute, 2003);
and George A. Akerlof and Janet L. Yellen, "An Analysis of Out-of-Wedlock Births in
the United States," Brookings Institution *Policy Brief* No. 5 (August 1996), at: http://
www.brookings.edu/papers/1996/08childrenfamilies_akerlof.aspx.
8. See discussion and references by economist Mark Perry, "U.S. Poverty Rate: 1959 to
2009," *Carpe Diem* (September 20, 2010), at: http://mjperry.blogspot.com/2010/09
/us-poverty-rate-1959-to-2009.html. Of course, a problem with the poverty rate in

the United States is that it refers to relative rather than absolute poverty. Today's "poor" are much better off than those classified as poor fifty years ago, though this has much more to do with developments in technology than government welfare programs. Unfortunately, this is almost impossible to discern because of how poverty statistics are kept by the US Census Bureau. We discuss this in chapter fourteen.

9. See discussion of the Millennium Development Goals at: http://www.un.org /millenniumgoals/. Many of these goals are desirable, though, in the last several years, the list has gotten diluted with more ill-defined, left-wing causes, such as "environmental sustainability."

10. See the page at: http://www.one.org/us/actnow/.

11. William Easterly, *The White Man's Burden: Why the West's Efforts to Aid the Rest Have Done So Much Ill and So Little Good* (New York: Penguin Books, 2006), pp. 147–49.

12. The World Bank study and quote are referenced in Dambisa Moyo, *Dead Aid: Why Aid Is Not Working and How There Is a Better Way for Africa* (New York: Farrar, Straus and Giroux, 2009), p. 39.

13. See, for instance, ibid., pp. 3–5.

14. See Raghuram G. Rajan and Arvind Subramanian, "Aid and Growth: What Does the Cross-Country Evidence Really Show?" *The Review of Economics and Statistics* 90, no. 4 (November 2008). Abstract available at: http://www.mitpressjournals.org /doi/abs/10.1162/rest.90.4.643.

15. Dambisa Moyo, *Dead Aid*, pp. 143, 144.

16. Ibid., p. xix.

17. Not surprisingly, the ONE Campaign has a webpage, "*Dead Aid* Is Dead Wrong," dedicated to critiques of Moyo's book *Dead Aid*. One of the things they highlight is the increase in medications as a result of aid. See the articles at: http://www.one .org/c/us/hottopic/910/. Of course, Moyo doesn't argue that nothing anyone has done has ever helped any African. She is criticizing the long-term damage done by government-to-government and "multilateral" aid from the World Bank and the International Monetary Fund.

18. Easterly, *The White Man's Burden*, pp. 13–14.

19. Deborah A. Small, George Loewenstein, and Paul Slovic, "Sympathy and Callousness: The Impact of Deliberative Thought on Donations to Identifiable and Statistical Victims," *Organizational Behavior and Human Decision Processes* 102, no. 2 (March 2007), pp. 143–54.

20. This quote is from the summary of the paper, "To Increase Charitable Giving, Appeal to the Heart, Not the Head," at the Center for Social Innovation at the Stanford Graduate School of Business, at: http://csi.gsb.stanford.edu/increase-charitable -donations-appeal-heart.

21. From *Quadragesimo Anno*. Pope John Paul II defended it much more recently (in *Centesimus Annus*, 48):

> [T]he principle of subsidiarity must be respected: a community of a higher order should not interfere in the internal life of a community of a lower order, depriving the latter of its functions, but rather should support it in case of

need and help to coordinate its activity with the activities of the rest of society, always with a view to the common good.

22. You can read about VisionTrust at: http://www.visiontrust.org/.

Chapter 13. A Place to Call Our Own

1. Ronald J. Sider, *Rich Christians in an Age of Hunger* (Nashville: W Publishing Group, 1997), p. 78.

2. Communal living does exist, but the only successful examples are outside the political realm. Families, for example, live communally. Parents don't charge their young children for room and board. But neither are they democratic. Someone ultimately calls the shots—preferably, the parents. Many monasteries and religious orders also live communally. These are small, disciplined, and voluntary groups. Many of them survive for centuries—and in fact, some early monasteries, which combined productivity and thrift, helped give rise to capitalism in medieval Europe. See Rodney Stark, *The Victory of Reason: How Christianity Led to Freedom, Capitalism, and Western Success* (New York: Random House, 2005).

   There have been other voluntary, nonmonastic groups that have tried to live communally. The Amish and the Jesus People live in semicommunal groups today. And there were lots of examples of Christian communes in the eighteenth and nineteenth centuries. The ones that survived very long were small, voluntary, and intensely disciplined. For a history of socialism that discusses some of these experiments, see Joshua Muravchik, *Heaven on Earth: The Rise and Fall of Socialism* (San Francisco: Encounter Books, 2003).

3. Quoted in Matthew Spalding, *We Still Hold These Truths* (Wilmington: ISI Books, 2009), p. 70.

4. Richard Pipes, *Communism: A History* (New York: Modern Library Chronicles, 2003), p. 45.

5. Lenin thought of manufacturing, transportation, the generation of energy, and the like as the "commanding heights" of the economy, so he was able to sell the idea of partial privatization of agricultural land to his party, the Bolsheviks. See Arnold Kling and Nick Shultz, "The New Commanding Heights," *National Affairs* 8 (Summer 2011), at: http://nationalaffairs.com/publications/detail/the-new-commanding-heights.

6. James D. Gwartney, Richard L. Stroup, Dwight R. Lee, and Tawni H. Ferrarini, *Common Sense Economics* (New York: St. Martin's Press, 2010), p. 48.

7. This information and much more are described in scholarly detail in Jean-Louis Margolin, "China: A Long March into Night," in *The Black Book of Communism*, edited by Stéphane Courtois et al. (Cambridge: Harvard University Press, 1999), pp. 463–46.

8. See it online, at: http://www.vatican.va/holy_father/leo_xiii/encyclicals/documents/hf_l-xiii_enc_15051891_rerum-novarum_en.html.

9. From *The Politics*.

10. Quoted in Spalding, *We Still Hold These Truths*, p. 80.

11. Hernando de Soto, *The Mystery of Capital: Why Capitalism Triumphs in the West and Fails Everywhere Else* (New York: Basic Books, 2000).

12. Ibid., p. 19.

13. Ibid., pp. 21, 26–27.

14. Ibid., p. 40. De Soto estimates that as much as 70 percent of the credit received for new businesses "comes from using formal titles as collateral for mortgages," p. 84.

15. Ibid., pp. 35, 36.

16. Hernando de Soto, "Why Capitalism Works in the West but Fails Elsewhere," *International Herald Tribune* (January 5, 2001).

17. The "cloud" refers to various resources, applications, and services available on the Internet rather than on your computer. It's the Internet as it is now developing, which has gone far beyond a network of computers, servers, search engines, routers, and websites.

18. For more on the importance of private property, see Tom Bethell, *The Noblest Triumph* (New York: St. Martin's Press, 1998).

19. Rafael Di Tella, Sebastian Galiani, and Ernesto Schargrodsky, "Property Rights and Beliefs: Evidence of the Allocation of Land Titles to Squatters," *Quarterly Journal of Economics* (February 2007). See also the review article by Julia Hanna, "How Property Ownership Changes Your World View," *Harvard Business School: Working Knowledge* (May 28, 2007).

20. Fed policy wasn't the only cause, but it contributed to the problem. See John B. Taylor, "How Government Created the Financial Crisis," *The Wall Street Journal* (February 9, 2009), at: http://online.wsj.com/article/SB123414310280561945.html.

21. "Too big to fail" refers to the idea that some institutions are so integral to the national or international financial system that they cannot be allowed to go bankrupt. The problem with the policy, obviously, is that any company that suspects it is too big to fail will also suspect that if it gets into financial trouble, the government will bail it out. So the policy actually *encourages* risky behavior, since a company will enjoy the benefits of good decisions, but won't directly suffer the consequences of bad decisions. Nicole Gelinas describes this aspect of the crisis in *After the Fall: Saving Capitalism from Wall Street and Washington* (New York: Encounter Books, 2009). For a short article by Gelinas summarizing the details, see Nicole Gelinas, " 'Too Big to Fail' Must Die," *City Journal* 9, no. 3 (Summer 2009), at: http://www.city-journal.org/2009/19_3_financial-institutions.html.

22. For the longer historical perspective, see Alyssa Katz, *Our Lot: How Real Estate Came to Own Us* (New York: Bloomsbury USA, 2010).

23. Peter J. Wallison, "The True Story of the Financial Crisis," *The American Spectator* (May 2011), at: http://spectator.org/archives/2011/05/13/the-true-story-of-the-financia. Wallison is a keen interpreter of the financial crisis, and this article is probably the best short summary of the role of subprime mortgages in the crisis. For an excellent longer treatment, see Thomas Sowell, *The Housing Boom and Bust*, revised edition (New York: Basic Books, 2010).

24. Fannie Mae, chartered in 1968, is short for the Federal National Mortgage Association. Freddie Mac, chartered by Congress in 1970, is short for the Federal Home Loan Mortgage Association.

25. Gwartney et al., p. 64.

26. Ibid., p. 63.

27. Wallison, "The True Story of the Financial Crisis."

28. Christopher Papagianis and Reihan Salam, "We Can't Afford This House," *National Review* (August 2, 2010), at: http://www.nationalreview.com/articles/243497/we-cant-afford-house-christopher-papagianis?page=1.

29. With the obvious exception of the investment bank Lehman Brothers, which had to declare bankruptcy.

30. Of course, some people have down payments because of financial gifts or inherited wealth. But banks treat this money differently than down payments from earned savings, since it reflects less on a homebuyer's financial habits.

31. The benefits of home ownership seem to apply only when a person has equity in the home. The more equity they have in a home, the less likely they are to default on the rest of their mortgage.

32. Edmund Conway, "'Ninja' Loans Explode on Sub-prime Frontline," *The Telegraph* (March 3, 2008), at: http://www.telegraph.co.uk/finance/economics/2785403/Ninja-loans-explode-on-sub-prime-frontline.html.

33. By 2006, a fourth of all subprime loans were "negative amortization loans." Obviously the benefits of home ownership are almost entirely eliminated with this type of loan. Papagianis and Salam, "We Can't Afford This House."

34. There were a few good things in the reform package, such as requiring government-sponsored enterprises to keep more capital in reserves. Unfortunately, the reform doesn't solve the big problem—political manipulation of the mortgage market. See Kevin Williamson, "Fannie Times Five," *National Review* (May 13, 2011), at: http://www.nationalreview.com/exchequer/267124/fannie-times-five.

Chapter 14. Free to Win-Win

1. It's not quite clear what Wallis means by this term, but he uses it a lot. See, for instance, Jim Wallis, "Elizabeth and Goliath," *Sojourners* (February 11, 2010), at: http://blog.sojo.net/2010/02/11/elizabeth-warren-and-goliath/.

2. J. D. Foster and Jennifer Marshall, *Freedom Economics and Human Dignity* (Washington, DC: Heritage Foundation, 2010), p. 4. This is an excellent booklet that everyone should read.

3. Ibid.

4. The word was actually popularized by its critics. Karl Marx, the founder of modern communism, picked it up to describe the system that he thought would eventually self-destruct and give rise to socialism. But Marx's definition didn't stick. Most people use the term "capitalism" to refer to an economy that has private property and free markets. We agree with the definition given by sociologist Rodney Stark:

> Capitalism is an economic system wherein privately owned, relatively well organized, and stable firms pursue complex commercial activities within a relatively free (unregulated) market, taking a systematic, long-term approach to investing and reinvesting wealth (directly or indirectly) in productive activities involving a hired workforce, and guided by anticipated and actual returns.

> Rodney Stark, *The Victory of Reason: How Christianity Led to Freedom, Capitalism, and Western Success* (New York: Random House, 2005), p. 56.

5. Thanks to Jonathan Witt for this felicitous construction.

6. At: http://www.teachtci.com/. Thanks to Lance Anderson for alerting us to this lesson.

7. This is from Activity 1.3 in the lesson on "The Rise and Fall of the Soviet Union."

8. Smith leads with this idea of valuing things in terms of labor or cost of production in *An Inquiry into the Nature and Causes of the Wealth of Nations*, edited by Edwin Cannan (New York: Modern Library, 1994), p. lix. Nevertheless, the idea was more central to Marx's thought than to Smith's.

9. These issues are explored in more depth in Jay W. Richards, *Money, Greed, and God* (San Francisco: HarperOne, 2009), pp. 60–72.

10. Adam Smith, *An Inquiry into the Nature and Causes of the Wealth of Nations*, edited by Edwin Cannan (New York: Modern Library, 1994), p. 485.

11. A mature form of Hayek's argument is in *The Fatal Conceit: The Errors of Socialism* (Chicago: University of Chicago Press, 1989).

12. This story is told in James D. Gwartney, Richard L. Stroup, Dwight R. Lee, and Tawni H. Ferrarini, *Common Sense Economics* (New York: St. Martin's Press, revised and updated 2010), p. 8.

Chapter 15. Going Global

1. Leonard E. Read, *I, Pencil: My Family Tree as Told to Leonard E. Read* (Irvington-on-Hudson, NY: The Foundation for Economic Education, 1958), at: http://www.econlib.org/library/Essays/rdPncl1.html.

2. Compiled from the information on the iPad (available July 2011) at: http://www.apple.com/ipad/specs/.

3. See "How Aluminum Works," *howstuffworks*, at: http://science.howstuffworks.com/aluminum2.htm.

4. Of course, we may have noneconomic reasons for not trading with some country. Consider the oil market. All things considered, we might decide that we'd rather pay a premium for oil that we get domestically or more expensively from an ally rather than trading with a hostile country that would give us a better price. This would be a security decision rather than an economic one. Moreover, the actual oil market is distorted by OPEC, a cartel that artificially sets the supply of oil, and by the fact that we artificially restrict access to promising domestic sources of oil. But even if OPEC dissolved and we started exploiting these other domestic sources of oil, we would probably still be better off (economically) by importing some oil.

5. See the animated graphs on worldwide economic growth at Gapminder, at: http://www.gapminder.org/world/.

6. Unfortunately, in 2011, the United States dropped from fourth to ninth on the Index, behind both Denmark and Switzerland on the Index of Economic Freedom. See the latest ranking of countries on the *Index of Economic Freedom*, at: http://www.heritage.org/Index/. See also the *Economic Freedom of the World* index. This index is compiled on the basis of forty-two distinct pieces of data. At: http://www.freetheworld.com/release.html.

7. See the Iowa State University Study by Mark Draenstott, "Do Farm Payments Promote Rural Economic Growth?" *AgDM newsletter* (May 2005), at: http://www.extension.iastate.edu/agdm/articles/others/DraMay05.htm.

8. Dambisa Moyo, *Dead Aid* (New York: Farrar, Straus, and Giroux, 2010), p. 115.

9. Ibid.

10. Ibid., pp. 117–18.

11. One of the best resources on these issues is *PovertyCure*. Read about the effects of subsidies on the poor in the developing world, at: http://www.povertycure.org/.

Chapter 16. Crossing the Border

1. Edward Glaeser, "Boeing's Uniquely American Right to Take Flight," *Bloomberg* (July 18, 2011), at: http://www.bloomberg.com/news/2011-07-19/boeing-s-uniquely-american-right-to-take-flight-edward-glaeser.html.

2. See "US Bishops Announce Push for Immigration Reform in 2010," *US Conference of Catholic Bishops*, at: http://www.usccb.org/comm/archives/2010/10-003.html.

3. The NAE statement is quite vague, and does not clearly distinguish its proposal from blanket amnesty. See "Immigration Reform," *National Association of Evangelicals*, at: http://www.nae.net/government-relations/policy-resolutions/354-immigration-2009.

4. From comment at the bottom of Mark Krikorian, "Creating Facts on the Ground," *National Review* (May 26, 2011), at: http://www.nationalreview.com/corner/268200/creating-facts-ground-mark-krikorian.

5. Richard Land, "Baptists Back Path for Immigrants," *The Ethic & Religious Liberty Commission of the Southern Baptist Commission* (July 1, 2011), at: http://erlc.com/article/baptists-back-path-for-immigrants/.

6. The best proposal we've seen is the Southern Baptist Convention resolution approved in 2006. "On the Crisis of Illegal Immigration," *Southern Baptist Convention* (June 2006), at: http://www.sbc.net/resolutions/amResolution.asp?ID=1157.

7. Bruce Bawer, "Inside the Mind of the Oslo Murderer," *The Wall Street Journal* (July 25, 2011). Bawer is the author of *Surrender: Appeasing Islam, Sacrificing Freedom* (New York: Doubleday, 2009).

8. Bill Platschke, "Again, It's Red, White, and Boo," *The Los Angeles Times* (June 26, 2011), at: http://articles.latimes.com/2011/jun/26/sports/la-sp-0626-plaschke-gold-cup-20110626.

9. At: http://www.vdare.com/misc/archive00/friedman.htm. User login is required to access this.

10. Richard Land, "Immigration Reform and Southern Baptists," *The Ethic & Religious Liberty Commission of the Southern Baptist Commission* (April 3, 2007), at: http://erlc.com/article/statement-by-richard-land-on-truly-comprehensive-immigration-reform/.

11. This is one line from a poem by Emma Lazarus called "New Colossus." The entire poem applies to the Statue of Liberty and what she symbolizes:

Not like the brazen giant of Greek fame,
With conquering limbs astride from land to land;
Here at our sea-washed, sunset gates shall stand
A mighty woman with a torch, whose flame
Is the imprisoned lightning, and her name
Mother of Exiles. From her beacon-hand
Glows world-wide welcome; her mild eyes command

The air-bridged harbor that twin cities frame.
"Keep, ancient lands, your storied pomp!" cries she
With silent lips. "Give me your tired, your poor, your huddled masses yearning to
    breathe free,
The wretched refuse of your teeming shore.
Send these, the homeless, tempest-tossed to me,
I lift my lamp beside the golden door!"

Chapter 17. All Men Are Created Equal

1. "Survey: Plurality of Americans Believe Capitalism at Odds with Christian Values,"
   Public Religion Research Institute/RNS (2011), at: http://www.publicreligion.org
   /research/?id=554.
2. Jim Wallis, "God Hates Inequality," *The Huffington Post* (February 1, 2007), at:
   http://www.huffingtonpost.com/jim-wallis/god-hates-inequality_b_40170.html.
3. Arthur C. Brooks, "Obama Says It's Only 'Fair' to Raise Taxes on the Rich. He's
   Wrong," *The Washington Post* (April 22, 2011).
4. Marx tried to get around these problems by defining economic value in terms of
   "socially necessary labor." But that just moves the problem back a step. What is
   socially necessary? If we say labor is socially necessary if it produces some good or
   service that someone values, then the labor theory collapses into the "subjective
   theory" of economic value. So Marx's qualification of his labor theory of value, if
   followed consistently, guts the theory.
5. Jim Wallis, "God Hates Inequality," *The Huffington Post* (February 1, 2007), at:
   http://www.huffingtonpost.com/jim-wallis/god-hates-inequality_b_40170.html.
6. You can read the whole interchange at Jake Tapper, "'Spread the Wealth'?" *ABC
   News Political Punch* (October 14, 2008), at: http://blogs.abcnews.com/political-
   punch/2008/10/spread-the-weal.html.
7. Henry Hazlitt, *Economics in One Lesson* (New York: Three Rivers Press, 1979), p. 136.
8. Samuel Hearne, "Minimum Wage Law Backfires in American Samoa," *Acton Institute
   Commentary* (June 6, 2011), at: http://www.acton.org/pub/commentary/2011/07/06
   /minimum-wage-law-backfires-american-samoa.
9. This is the data for 2008, updated in October 2010. From Gerald Prante and Mark
   Robyn, "Summary of Latest Federal Individual Income Tax Data," *Tax Foundation*
   (October 2010), at: http://www.taxfoundation.org/news/show/250.html#Data.
10. "Survey: Plurality of Americans Believe Capitalism at Odds with Christian Values,"
    Public Religion Research Institute/RNS (2011), at: http://www.publicreligion.org
    /research/?id=554.
11. See information at: http://www.fairtax.org/. As with any tax, there are clear limits
    on how high consumption taxes can go. If they get too high, people will have a strong
    incentive to trade in an underground economy, away from government monitoring.
    When that happens, government revenues could actually go down even though the
    tax rate has gone up.
12. We should add that we would support a consumption tax only as a replacement for
    an income tax, and that would probably require a constitutional amendment. So

the flat tax is more politically feasible than a fair tax, even though we find the flat income tax less attractive.

13. This is from an interview with Governor Mike Huckabee on Fox News in August 2011.

14. Ron Sider, *Rich Christians in an Age of Hunger* (Nashville: W Publishing Group, 1997), p. 144.

15. Bishop Thomas Gumbleton, in the documentary *The Call of the Entrepreneur* (Acton Media, 2007).

16. When Jay and I first talked on the phone, he said: "Oh yes. My wife and I actually have some pictures from your ministry on our refrigerator. We use them to try to remind our daughters of how much they have to be thankful for."

17. For years, we heard the standard of a dollar a day per person. The World Bank bumped that to $1.25 in 2005. See Martin Ravallion, Shaohua Chen & Prem Sangraula, "Dollar a Day," *The World Bank Economic Review* 23, no. 2 (2009), pp. 163–84. These monetary definitions make it easier to make statistical comparisons, but they seem a bit arbitrary. Poverty surely has more to do with material needs than with income.

18. "Poverty Pulse: Wave IV," *Catholic Campaign for Human Development* (January 2004), at: http://www.usccb.org/cchd/PP4FINAL.PDF.

19. See "How the Census Bureau Measures Poverty," *U.S. Census Bureau*, at: http://www.census.gov/hhes/www/poverty/methods/measure.html.

20. Robert Rector and Rachel Sheffield, "Air Conditioning, Cable TV, and an Xbox: What Is Poverty in the United States Today?" *Heritage Foundation Backgrounders* 2575 (July 18, 2011), at: http://report.heritage.org/bg2575.

21. Ibid., p. 8.

22. Ibid., p. 10.

23. Kevin Drum, "A Simple Look at Income Inequality," *Mother Jones* (September 18, 2010), at http://motherjones.com/kevin-drum/2010/09/simple-look-income-inequality.

24. See household income data at the US Census Bureau, at: http://www.census.gov/hhes/www/income/data/historical/household/index.html.

25. Age is one of the main factors that determine one's income and location on the distribution of national incomes. See Santiago Budria Rodriguez, Javier Diaz-Gimenez, Vincenzo Quadirni, and Jose-Victor Rios Rull, "Updated Facts on the U.S. Distributions of Earnings, Income, and Wealth," *Federal Reserve Bank of Minneapolis, Quarterly Review* 25, no. 3 (2002), p. 3.

26. Annette Clauson, "Despite Higher Food Prices, Percent of U.S. Income Spent on Food Remains Constant," *Amber Waves* (Sept. 2008), at: http://www.ers.usda.gov/AmberWaves/September08/Findings/PercentofIncome.htm.

27. "Percent of Income Spent on Food in the U.S.," *Farm & Food Facts* (2006), at: http://www.ilfb2.org/fff06/51.pdf.

Chapter 18. Be Fruitful

1. The generic word "man" in Hebrew is *adam*, which is related to the word "ground," *adamah*.

2. Hernando de Soto, *The Mystery of Capital; Why Capitalism Triumphs in the West and Fails Everywhere Else* (New York: Basic Books, 2000), p. 40.

3. Michael Novak, *The Spirit of Democratic Capitalism*, revised edition (Lanham, MD: Madison Books, 2000).

4. Richard L. Stroup, *Eco-nomics: What Everyone Should Know About Economics and the Environment* (Washington, DC: Cato Institute Press), p. 10.

5. See Ray Kurzweil, *The Age of Spiritual Machines* (New York: Penguin, 2000). For discussion and criticism of some of Kurzweil's ideas, see Jay Richards and George Gilder, editors, *Are We Spiritual Machines?* (Seattle: Discovery Institute Press, 2002).

6. Evelyn Rusli, "Google's Big Bet on the Mobile Future," *The New York Times* (August 15, 2011), at: http://dealbook.nytimes.com/2011/08/15/googles-big-bet-on-the-mobile-future/?nl=todaysheadlines&emc=tha2.

7. http://www.kurzweilai.net/index.html?flash=1.

8. It's misleading to call such trends laws since they refer to human innovation, not some physical law like gravity. Bad economic policy, for instance, could stop the growth.

9. Nick Shultz, "Steve Jobs: America's Greatest Failure," *National Review Online* (August 25, 2011), at: http://www.nationalreview.com/articles/275528/steve-jobs-america-s-greatest-failure-nick-schulz#.

10. George Gilder, *Wealth & Poverty* (San Francisco: ICS Press, 1993), p. 30.

11. Ibid., pp. 20–24.

12. For more on the question of greed and the free economy, see Jay W. Richards, *Money, Greed, and God: Why Capitalism Is the Solution and Not the Problem* (San Francisco: HarperOne, 2009), chapter 5.

13. Grand Rapids, MI: Acton Media, 2007. Check out the website at: http://www.calloftheentrepreneur.com/.

14. *Wealth & Poverty*, p. 37.

15. Robert A. Sirico, *The Entrepreneurial Vocation* (Grand Rapids, MI: Acton Institute, 2001).

16. These phrases are from the title and subtitle of the book by Dan Senor and Saul Singer, *Start-Up Nation: The Story of Israel's Economic Miracle* (New York: Twelve, 2011).

17. George Gilder, *The Israel Test* (Minneapolis: Richard Vigilante Books, 2009), p. 105.

18. Ibid., p. 101.

19. Ibid., p. 106.

20. Ibid., pp. 106–7.

21. Ibid., p. 113.

Chapter 19. Have Dominion

1. Lynn Townsend White, Jr., "The Historical Roots of Our Ecologic Crisis," *Science* 155, no. 3767 (March 10, 1967): pp. 1203–7.

2. Václav Klaus, the president of the Czech Republic, has been making this argument for several years. He obviously has personal experience with antifreedom ideologies. See his book *Blue Planet in Green Shackles* (Washington, DC: CEI, 2008).

3. For instance, the Evangelical Climate Initiative, which garnered national headlines in 2006, received $475,000 from the Hewlett Foundation. In the first two months of

that year, the Hewlett Foundation gave grants totaling $13.7 million for population control efforts, most of which went to abortion-related causes. At the same time, they allocated $12.1 million for environmental work, $8 million of which went to global warming and energy-related efforts, and of this, nearly a half million went to the ECI, funneled through the National Religious Partnership for the Environment. For more information, see the report, "From Climate Control to Population Control: Troubling Background on the 'Evangelical Climate Initiative,'" at the website of the Institute on Religion & Democracy: http://www.theird.org/Document .Doc?id=67.

4. See their webpage: http://www.nrpe.org/issues/air_intro01.htm. The NRPE is an ecumenical partnership of evangelical, mainline Protestant, Catholic, and Jewish groups.

5. Quote by Mary Robinson, quoted in Mark Hertsgaard, "A Planetary Movement," *The Nation* (January 4, 2010), at: http://www.thenation.com/article/planetary-movement.

6. Andrew Bolt, "Putting Our Economy in the Hands of Chavez Fans," *The Herald Sun* (December 17, 2009), at: http://blogs.news.com.au/heraldsun/andrewbolt/index .php/heraldsun/comments/putting_our_economy_in_the_hands_of_chavez_fans.

7. We're exaggerating, but only slightly. To see the phenomena that have been attributed to "global warming" or "climate change," see "A complete List of Things Caused by Global Warming," at: http://www.numberwatch.co.uk/warmlist.htm. There are about 862 items on the list so far.

8. Hundreds of articles about the scandal are consolidated at: http://www.climategate .com/.

9. Of course, a cold snap in Copenhagen and Washington, DC, doesn't prove anything about the larger issue of climate change. But coinciding as it did with the Copenhagen meeting, even the mainstream media had a hard time not mentioning the irony.

10. See, for instance, Frank Newport, "Americans' Global Warming Concerns Continue to Drop," *Gallup* (March 11, 2010), at: http://www.gallup.com/poll/126560 /Americans-Global-Warming-Concerns-Continue-Drop.aspx.

11. Here's basically what happens. Earth intercepts some of the sun's radiation. Some is reflected back into space, but some is absorbed by the surface and the atmosphere. They heat up and then emit the energy as longer wavelength *infrared* radiation. This outgoing infrared radiation gets partially trapped in the atmosphere by greenhouse gases, where it can further heat the surface and atmosphere. This helps create an energy balance so that the atmosphere is warmer than it would be without these gases, which is a good thing. If we removed them, the earth would become a barren, frigid wasteland.

12. See, for example, Roy W. Spencer and William D. Braswell, "On the Misdiagnosis of Climate Feedbacks from Variations in the Earth's Radiant Energy Balance," *Remote Sensing* (July 25, 2011), at: http://www.drroyspencer.com/wp-content/uploads /Spencer_Misdiagnos_11.pdf. See also Roy Spencer, *The Great Global Warming Blunder: How Mother Nature Fooled the World's Top Climate Scientists* (New York: Encounter Books, 2010).

13. In *An Inconvenient Truth*, Al Gore grossly misrepresented this. He shifted the placement of the records on his display to make it look like warming took place after carbon dioxide increased.

14. Canadian mathematician and mining consultant Stephen McIntyre was one of the key figures in debunking the hockey stick. His website is Climate Audit, at: http://climateaudit.org/.

15. See Guillermo Gonzalez and Jay W. Richards, *The Privileged Planet* (Washington, DC: Regnery Publishing, 2004), pp. 21–43.

16. Major research published by scientists at CERN (the European Organization for Nuclear Research) in 2011 suggests that the sun may affect our climate not just in the obvious ways, but also with its magnetic activity. If correct, the results could confirm that the sun's magnetic field blocks cosmic rays, which stimulate the production of cloud condensation nuclei and thus clouds. Unfortunately, such research contradicts the official mainstream media line on climate change, so it tends not to be reported, or to be downplayed. See the discussion by Lawrence Solomon, "Science Getting Settled," *The Financial Post* (August 26, 2011), at: http://opinion.financialpost.com/2011/08/26/lawrence-solomon-science-now-settled/.

17. For a report of this, see Kate Ravilious, "Mars Melt Hints at Solar, Not Human, Cause for Warming, Scientist Says," *National Geographic News* (February 28, 2007). Ironically, this story does report the facts but tries to dismiss their obvious meaning.

18. For a detailed study of global climate variations in geologic history, and the possible causes, see Dennis Avery and Fred Singer, *Unstoppable Global Warming: Every 1,500 Years* (Lanham, MD: Rowman & Littlefield, 2007).

19. Bjørn Lomborg, *Cool It* (New York: Knopf, 2007).

20. Ibid., pp. 40–43.

21. To read about this, go to: http://www.co2science.org/.

22. The Copenhagen Consensus did a cost-benefit analysis to determine how best to spend $50 billion in humanitarian aid. Their top picks were projects to prevent HIV/AIDS, iron deficiency in women and children, and malaria. The Kyoto Protocol ranked sixteenth out of seventeen ways to spend the money. Moreover, the scholars assumed that human contributions of carbon dioxide are largely responsible for global warming. See discussion at http://www.copenhagenconsensus.com. See also the compilation *Global Crises, Global Solution*, edited by Bjørn Lomborg (Cambridge: Cambridge University Press, 2004).

23. His recent book is full of environmental advice based on sound science and economics. See Patrick Moore, *Confessions of a Greenpeace Dropout: The Making of a Sensible Environmentalist* (Vancouver: Beatty Street Publishing, 2010).

24. Patrick Moore, "Confessions of a Greenpeace Co-founder," *The Vancouver Sun* (January 7, 2011).

25. Quoted in CFACT's *Special Report from Washington* 5, no. 2 (January 2011).

26. When the political winds are favorable, the left openly seeks restrictions. That's why we were hearing a lot about a cap-and-trade law to regulate carbon dioxide (and shut down coal plants) around 2007. President Obama pushed this economy-squashing legislation when he became president. But since the United States had entered a recession and the public grew more skeptical of the dangers of climate change, not even a Democrat-controlled Congress could pass cap-and-trade. So what happened? It looks like the EPA, under President Obama, will impose the restrictions anyway,

even though Congress passed no law authorizing the EPA regulations. This is outrageous. Commenting on such end-runs around Congress, Charles Krauthammer argued, "Under our constitutional system, the executive executes the laws that the Congress has passed. It should not be executing laws that Congress has rejected." In an interview with Bill O'Reilly on Fox News (August 30, 2011).

27. Crichton's lecture, which he delivered on January 11, 2003, at Cal Tech, was called "Aliens Cause Global Warming." See it reprinted online, at: http://wattsupwith that.com/2010/07/09/aliens-cause-global-warming-a-caltech-lecture-by-michael -crichton/.

28. See Bjørn Lomborg, *The Skeptical Environmentalist*, pp. 3–33.

29. See Steven F. Hayward, *Index of Leading Environmental Indicators*, 14th edition (San Francisco: Pacific Research Institute and Washington, DC: American Enterprise Institute, 2009), at: http://www.pacificresearch.org/docLib/20090414_Env _Index_09.pdf.

30. See Lomborg, *The Skeptical Environmentalist*, p. 33. For more recent information, see Indur M. Goklany, "Have Increases in Population, Affluence and Technology Worsened Human and Environmental Well-Being?" *Electronic Journal of Sustainable Development* 1, no. 3 (2009), at: http://www.ejsd.org/public/journal_article/11.

31. In fact, life expectancy has gone up (around the world) in the last fifty years, even in the poorest countries. The exceptions are countries with widespread war and extremely corrupt and despotic governments. For more statistics and charts, see Simon, *Ultimate Resource 2*, pp. 223–73. See also the worldwide demographic data at http://www.gapminder.com.

32. Even the UN has admitted this. Its 2007 document "State of the Future," which the media doomed to obscurity, began, "People around the world are becoming healthier, wealthier, better educated, more peaceful, more connected, and they are living longer…" Jerome C. Glenn and Theodore J. Gordon, *2007 State of the Future* (New York: UN, 2007). The document even goes so far as to admit that these improvements are the fruit of free trade and technology. Of course, the documents include the characteristic fixations of the UN. The introductory sentence continues, "but at the same time the world is more corrupt, congested, warmer, and increasingly dangerous. Although the digital divide is beginning to close, income gaps are still expanding around the world and unemployment continues to grow." See the executive summary at: http:// www.millennium-project.org/millennium/sof2007-exec-summ.pdf.

33. There is, of course, a lot of debate about the details, but the EKC seems to be holding up well for a number of significant pollutants such as sulfur dioxide. See Steven F. Hayward, "The China Syndrome and the Environmental Kuznets Curve," *AEI Outlook* (December 2005), at: http://www.aei.org/outlook/23617. See also Indur M. Goklany, *The Improving State of the World: Why We're Living Longer, Healthier, More Comfortable Lives on a Clean Planet* (Washington, DC: Cato Institute, 2007).

34. One Christian organization that we find helpful is the Cornwall Alliance for the Stewardship of Creation at: http://www.cornwallalliance.org/.

35. Two organizations that specialize in finding market solutions to environmental problems are FREE (Foundation for Research on Economics & the Environment),

at: http://www.free-eco.org/, and PERC (the Property and Environment Research Center), at: http://www.perc.org/.

Chapter 20. Till It and Keep It

1. Tracy McVeigh, "Beckhams a 'Bad Example' for Families," *The Observer* (July 17, 2011), at: http://www.guardian.co.uk/lifeandstyle/2011/jul/17/population-control-beckham-family.

2. See discussion in Jay W. Richards, *Money, Greed, and God: Why Capitalism Is the Solution and Not the Problem* (San Francisco: HarperOne, 2009), p. 204.

3. David Graber, "Mother Nature as a Hothouse Flower," *Los Angeles Times* (October 22, 1989), BR1; quoted in Steven F. Hayward, *Mere Environmentalism* (Washington, DC: AEI Press, 2010), p. 18. This is a very nice, brief volume describing the biblical perspective on humans and the natural world.

4. Stephen Moore, "Clear-Eyed Optimists," *The Wall Street Journal* (Oct. 5, 2007): p. w-11.

5. Paul Ehrlich, *The Population Bomb* (New York: Ballantine Books, 1968), p. xi.

6. Thomas Friedman, "The Earth Is Full," *The New York Times* (June 8, 2011), at: http://www.nytimes.com/2011/06/08/opinion/08friedman.html.

7. If you've seen the online lecture called "The Crash Course" by Chris Martenson, or read his book of the same name, you know that he talks a lot about exponential curves. One of those curves is the exponential growth in human population. Over and over, he shows a chart in which human population moves along a horizontal trajectory, staying more or less level for most of human history, and then suddenly, starting with the industrial revolution, the population spikes, and the line curves upward until it goes almost straight up. The curve looks this way on the chart because he uses a numerical rather than a logarithmic scale (powers of 10). The increase would look like a small line moving up and to the right on a logarithmic scale, and so wouldn't have the same psychological effect. See the online presentation at: http://www.chrismartenson.com/crashcourse. His book follows the argument of his presentation. Chris Martenson, *The Crash Course: The Unsustainable Future of Our Economy, Energy, and Environment* (New York: Wiley, 2011). The Crash Course includes lots of important insights, especially about the fiscal dangers on the horizon. But unexamined Malthusian assumptions sully Martenson's analysis throughout.

8. We're not saying that this is a good or bad thing. We're just reporting what the demographic facts are at the moment. It's always possible that people in some cultures will suddenly start having lots of babies in 2045. But there is no trend suggesting that right now, and the move toward lower fertility rates at high levels of industrialization holds, to some degree, in every single culture. See *World Population to 2300*, by the UN's Department of Economic & Social Affairs (New York: United Nations, 2004), at: http://www.un.org/esa/population/publications/longrange2/WorldPop 2300final.pdf.

9. *The Green Bible* (San Francisco: HarperOne, 2008). The Green Bible is based on the NRSV translation.

10. Rusty Pritchard encourages Christian environmentalists to purge notions about overpopulation from their thinking in "The Myth of Overpopulation,"

Flourish (January 31, 2011), at: http://flourishonline.org/2011/01/the-myth-of
-overpopulation/. This is a good piece, though Pritchard seems to downplay the
prevalence of population control thinking in the contemporary environmental
movement, attributing it largely to the family planning movement. But these movements still keep close company. Far more work needs to be done to separate environmentalism from outdated ideas about overpopulation.

11. There is a book that argues otherwise: Peter Huber and Mark P. Mills, *The Bottom-
less Well: The Twilight of Fuel, the Virtue of Waste, and Why We Will Never Run Out of
Energy* (New York: Basic Books, 2006). Their contrarian arguments are worth considering; but some of their conclusions seem to verge on techno-utopianism, which
is the opposite extreme from Malthusianism.

12. Thomas Sowell, *Basic Economics* (New York: Basic Books, 2004), p. 205.

13. Ibid., p. 207.

14. For examples of historical prices of resources, see Julian Simon, *The Ultimate
Resource 2* (Princeton: Princeton University Press, 1996), pp. 23–52. Simon discusses his famous bet with Ehrlich on pp. 32–33. See also Bjørn Lomborg, *The
Skeptical Environmentalist: Measuring the Real State of the World* (Cambridge: Cambridge University Press, 2001), pp. 118–48.

15. Gregg Easterbrook, "The Man Who Defused the 'Population Bomb,'" *The Wall
Street Journal* (September 16, 2009), at: http://online.wsj.com/article/SB1000142405
2970203917304574411382676924044.html.

16. "PM Pays Tribute to Father of Green Revolution," *Rediff News* (September 14, 2009),
at: http://news.rediff.com/report/2009/sep/14/pm-pays-tribute-to-father-of-green
-revolution-borlaug.htm.

17. Sheik Yamani, Saudi Arabian oil minister and founder of OPEC. Quoted in Lomborg, *The Skeptical Environmentalist*, p. 120. This quote has been attributed to different people.

18. From the NRPE page on "Environmental Justice," at: http://www.nrpe.org/issues
/justice_intro01.htm.

19. See a diagram of the technology at: http://www.consumerenergycenter.org/home
/heating_cooling/geothermal.html.

20. Two recent documentary films illustrate this point: *The Call of the Entrepreneur*
(Acton Media, 2007) and *The Ultimate Resource* (Free to Choose Media, 2007).

21. *Centesimus Annus* (1991), paragraph 32, at: http://www.vatican.va/holy_father
/john_paul_ii/encyclicals/documents/hf_jp-ii_enc_01051991_centesimus
-annus_en.html.

Conclusion. Living Within the Truth

1. "Republicans Should Blow Up Party, Not Marriages," *Bloomberg* (June 30, 2009), at:
http://www.bloomberg.com/apps/news?pid=20601039&sid=aEdjk7naC.zY.

2. David Paul Kuhn, "Some Social Conservative Leaders Feel Scapegoated," *RealClear-
Politics* (May 11, 2009), at: http://www.realclearpolitics.com/articles/2009/05/11
/social_conservatives_leaders_feel_scapegoated_96435.html.

3. For instance, some of the principles we describe here are quite similar to the principles of economic personalism that have been developed by scholars in recent

years who seek to bring together insights from market economics with the endur-
ing truths of the Judeo-Christian tradition. See a brief summary of these principles at the Acton Institute website, at: http://www.acton.org/about/acton-institute
-core-principles. And in his terrific book *We Still Hold These Truths* (Wilmington:
ISI Books, 2009), Matthew Spalding discusses "ten core principles that define our
national creed and common purpose: *liberty* is the grand, overarching theme of
our nation's history; *equality, natural rights,* and the *consent of the governed* are the
foundational principles that set the compass for our politics; *religious liberty* and
private property follow from these, shaping the parameters of our nation's day-to-
day life; the *rule of law* and a *constitutionalism* of limited government define the
architecture that undergirds our liberty; all of these principles culminate in *self-
government,* in the political sense of republican governance and the moral sense of
governing ourselves; and lastly, *independence* encompasses the meaning of America's principles in the world," pp. 4–5. We have tried to describe the principles in a
way that embeds all these "American" principles in broader theological and philosophical truths.

4. Also, we should remember that politicians may arrive at different policy positions,
   even when guided by true principles, since many things come down to prudential
   judgments. Should a country spend 5% or 5.1% of its budget on national defense?
   An income or a sales tax? Lifetime Supreme Court justices or term limits? A minimum drinking age? First principles can't answer such questions.
5. See the text of the Pope's inaugural address at: http://www.boston-catholic
   -journal.com/inaugural_address_of_Pope_Benedict_XVI.htm.
6. Quoted in Spalding, *We Still Hold These Truths,* p. 200.
7. Quoted in ibid., p. 203.
8. Ibid., p. 207.
9. We're talking about the basic drift of these ideologies. This doesn't mean that every
   person who calls himself a progressive denies God and objective morality.
10. Excerpted from a longer quote reprinted as the Meditation of the Day for August 9,
    in *Magnificat* (August 2011).